Eastern Africa Series

ETHIOPIAN
WARRIORHOOD

Ethiopian Warriorhood

Defence, Land and Society
1800–1941

TSEHAI BERHANE-SELASSIE

James Currey
is an imprint of
Boydell & Brewer Ltd
PO Box 9, Woodbridge
Suffolk IP12 3DF (GB)
www.jamescurrey.com
and of
Boydell & Brewer Inc.
668 Mt Hope Avenue, Rochester,
NY 14620-2731 (US)
www.boydellandbrewer.com

© Tsehai Berhane-Selassie 2018
First published 2018
Paperback edition 2022

The right of Tsehai Berhane-Selassie to be identified as the author of this work has been asserted in accordance with sections 77 and 78 of the Copyright, Designs and Patents Act 1988

All Rights Reserved. Except as permitted under current legislation no part of this work may be photocopied, stored in a retrieval system, published, performed in public, adapted, broadcast, transmitted, recorded or reproduced in any form or by any means, without the prior permission of the copyright owner

The publisher has no responsibility for the continued existence or accuracy of URLs for external or third-party internet websites referred to in this book, and does not guarantee that any content on such websites is, or will remain, accurate or appropriate

British Library Cataloguing in Publication Data
A catalogue record for this book is available from the British Library

ISBN 978-1-84701-191-6 (James Currey hardback)
ISBN 978-1-84701-336-1 (James Currey paperback)

Typeset in 10 on 12pt Cordale with Gill Sans MT display
by Avocet Typeset, Somerton, Somerset TA11 6RT

Dedication

To the memory of my parents, *Weyzero* Workaferahu Haile and *Balambaras* Berhane-Selassie Yigeremu

Contents

List of Illustrations	viii
Note on Transliteration	ix
Glossary of Mainly Political and Military Terms	x
List of Regiments	xv
Acknowledgements	xvii
Preface	xix
Introduction	1
1. Traditions of hierarchical warriorhood	8
2. The historical context of emergent warriors	27
3. Military lands and power politics	59
4. Ecological roots of local leadership	107
5. Social localities of emergent warriors	119
6. Military training in sports, horsemanship and hunting	145
7. Political authority and military power	175
8. Zeraf: symbols and rituals of power and rebellion	196
9. First Italian invasion, 1896	222
10. Guerrilla warfare, 1935–1941	240
Conclusion	286
Bibliography	292
Index	300

List of Illustrations

MAPS

1 Some of the place names referred to in the text	26
2 Some rivers and peaks of Ethiopia	106
3 Some defensive movements and retreats in the early phase of the 1935–41 invasion	242

PHOTOGRAPHS

1 Queen of Kings Zewditu	102
2 Outside the governor's residence, Jijiga, c.1901	121
3 Two *chewa* warriors on mules	176
4 *Ras* Mekonnen and retinue in *chewa* military wear	185
5 Return from combat	197
6 *Ras* Mengesha's arrival at Menelik's palace, Addis Ababa, 1894	204
7 Menelik II in coronation garb	227
8 Ethiopian ambassadors at the Elysée, Paris, 1898	237
9 Haile Selassie in modern military uniform just before the second Italian invasion	241
10 Mobilization in 1935	244
11 Heading to the northern front of the Italian invasion, 1935	244
12 Part of the modern Imperial Guard army	249
13 *Dejazmach* Balcha Safo	259

FIGURES

1 Plan of a hamlet	122
2 A *chewa* army on the attack	181

TABLES

1 Nineteenth-century horse names	157
2 Military regalia for *dejazmach*	185

Note on Transliteration

In transliterating Amharic words, the consonants appear as:
ሀ H; ለ L መ M; ሰ S; ረ R; ሸ Sh; ቀ Q; በ B; ተ T; ቸ Ch; ነ N; ኘ Gn; አ A; ከ K; ወ W; ኀ Z; ደ D; ጀ J; የ Y; ፐ P; ጸ Ts; ጠ Tt; ጨ CH; ፈ F; ፒ P

Vowels for the consonant germinations, e, u, i, a, ie, [i] o are used as in the following examples:

በ be
ቡ bu
ቢ bi
ባ ba
ቤ bie
ብ b
ቦ bo

Glossary of Mainly Political and Military Terms

Abba	'father', used as title in association with 'horse-name'
Abe Lahm	military cattle minder corps
abegaz	military governor
abeto	high title in historical Shewa
abun	bishop heading the Ethiopia Orthodox Church; *Abune* before a person's name
adarash	reception hall
adbar	something or someone of central focus
addo wesheba	hunting song
aden	hunting
agafari	master of ceremonies
ageree	people of the country
ajeb	retinue
akandura	darts
aleqa, chefra	commanders, subordinates
amba-gora	in the context of the present book, *amba-gora* means 'mountaintop and valley'
amba-gennen	(of a leader) lacking in social backing; now meaning 'usurper'
arbegna	patriotic lover of country
ashker	follower
aste	tree heather sticks for starting fire; also divination with fire
atint ena gultmit	ancestral bones
atsme rest	ancestral communal land
awaj	edict; decree
azazh	head of personal and household troops
azmari	a songster, songstress and/or musician; nowadays a singer
ba'ed	literally outsiders, meaning non-related
baher negash	governor of sea coast areas
balabat	lowest political officer of local origin
balager	rural person; compatriot. Can be singular or plural
balambaras	lowest military title (literally 'mountaintop commander')

balderas	cavalry; officer in charge of cavalry
baldereba	official appointed to mind a supplicant's case
bale meret	landowner
balemiwal	favourite officer; favoured official
balenegarit dejazmach	high-level third in command with a number of drums
banda	group (in Italian); mercenary; derisively 'deserter' (in Amharic)
Barud Bet	gunpowder maker corps
Bejirond	treasurer; also used as title
beles	luck
bitweded	favourite of the king – first step to becoming a *ras-bitweded*
Boyna-Tigre	local appellation for cultivators or farmers among the Wolayta
budin; *b.-abat*, *b.-ambel*	group; g.-father, g.-leader
cheqa	boundary marker between plots, such as a tree, stream or trench
chelot	court
chewa, tsewa	army, made up of those who self-train
debo or *jigi*	farming cooperatively
dejazmach	third in command
dembegna	authorized corps of soldiers to restrain *chewa* influence and power
denn	forest
dejazmach; *yewech d.*; *balenegarit d.*	third-level titleholder; *dejezmach* appointed in remote provinces; 'drum-beating' *dejazmach*
dina	external enemy with whom blood money cannot be exchanged; alien external to or outside the northeast Africa region
elfign	high-level reception area; inner room
elfign-adarash	reception area leading to higher-level reception room
elfign-askelkay	household marshal, receptionist
emir	Arabic for prince; also used as a title by Muslims in Ethiopia
enderase	personal representative
enjera	flat, pancake-like bread (75–100 cm in diameter) made from *teff*, the endemic and ancient grain of Ethiopia
fanno	hunters; leaderless bands
fitawrari	title of commander of advance soldiers; also contingent that initiates attacks; '*fit*' being 'face' or 'advance', the title is associated with the word *werari* or 'invader'
fukera	warrior's emotional promise of threat, support, or political intention; an essential aspect of *zeraf*
gada	system of organizing society according to age-sets

gasha jagre	shield bearers for individuals (not a contingent)
gebbar	'tribute payer' (tax in labour or in kind, and later in cash)
gedam	king's battlefield position at the centre of army; monastery
geday	'kill'; killer
Gendebel; Weregenu	troops from lands allocated for army livestock
genna	game similar to hockey; Christmas
gerazmach	commander of left wing; also title
gib	target, goal
gibbi	compound; palace
gibir	tax; formal military banquet
gilbiya	galloping
gite	game of javelin or spear throwing
gobez	brave; 'young'
gondere	of Gonder; contingent by that name (*Gondere*)
guks	game similar to polo
gult	land in lieu of administrative salary
gult-geza	monarch's appointee who administers non-heritable lands for raising revenue for the state as well as for his or her personal maintenance
guma	blood money
hager	'the country', Ethiopian territory (also pronounced *ager*)
hudad	expansive farmland; government land to be farmed communally
ilka	highest achievement for a hunter
jegna	brave
jiraf	whipping games
kao	king of Wolayta
kegnazmach	commander of right wing; also title
ketema	garrison town
kuter tor	numbered troops
leta	unbridled horse
ligaba	mayor
lij	junior prince; uncrowned 'king of kings' in *Lij* Iyasu's case
liqe mekuas	monarch's impersonator
madbet	land reserved as sovereign's personal resource; also kitchen
madef	mountain gun
maderya	lands granted to military leaders in lieu of personal salary; lands whose occupants are called up for military service
mahiber	social association
mar agar	land that pays honey as tribute
marta	trophy from first hunt

medeb	seat or bed made of compacted earth
meder; meret	land; earth; soil
megazha	big, strong pack horse
meketel	deputy
mekonnen (pl. *mekwanent*)	government or military official; noble (currently limited to military officers)
mengest	government
mer'ed azmach	rearguard commander; historically, title for the ruler of Shewa
mera mewetat	achieve first kill
Meskel	Feast of the Finding of the True Cross
mesfin (pl. *mesafint*)	prince (princes)
metin	food rations
milikit	signal
mireet	billet; also allot (literally 'guidance')
moga	forest boundary marker
moti	supreme ruler or king among the Sidama and Oromo
neftegna	gunmen
negarit; n. mechan	drum (lit. 'teller') of authority; metaphor for declaring or marching to war
negus	king
neguse negest	'king of kings'
qelad	measured land
qeleb	rations
qesqash	mobilizer, galvanizer
qitet	mobilization decree
qot	bunk; alcove
ras	title below king, literally 'head'
ras-bitweded	favourite *ras*; councillor
rest	inalienable right to ancestral lands
reste-gult	land allocated both for raising state revenue and for the personal maintenance of the person administering it
sefer	camp
seleba	trophy
senbete	weekend feasting by a congregation
serawit	army
seyfe jagre	bearer of swords and other significant weapons belonging to the 'master'
Seyfe Jagre	name of sword bearer contingent under top title-holders (*neguse negest, negus, ras, dejazmach*)
seyfe jagre aleqa	title of officer responsible for the personnel and personal weapons of the 'master'
shifta	rebel
shilela, qererto	war songs of challenge
shumament	civilian and military appointees
sultan	supreme rulers of Afar and of Jimma

Tabot	according to *chewa* beliefs the actual Ark of the Covenant is in Axum; also replicas of this
tato	king of Keffa
telat	enemy
teleq sew	important person
teseri serawit	soldiery brought to live as part of a local community; broadly, but not exactly, billeted soldiery
weddo-geb	volunteers
wagshum	title given to governors in Wag and Lasta
wegen	insiders, friends
wenfel	processing cotton cooperatively for cloth making
werari	advance invader
Werwari	name of a military corps, literally 'thrower'
wet	sauce
wetader	soldiers
weyzero	word derived from the Turkish 'vizier', once used for important women officials, now reserved as title for a married woman
wof	battlefield scouts (literally 'bird')
ye bet lij	personal retainer; child of the house; contingent
yeferes mekomiya	military lands for rearing horses; horse-halting places for travelling officer
yegobez aleqa	locally elected military leader
zebegna	guard
zega	landless farmers
zemecha	campaign; expedition
Zemene Mesafint	Era of Princes, referring to the years 1769–1855
zeraf	assertive declamations, also poems with accentuations of militaristic candour

List of Regiments

Abe Lahm
Afro-Aygeba
Amhara
Aqetzer
Balderas
Barud Bet
Be Adal Mebreq (Zera Yaqob, 1434–68)
Bedel Tsehai
Dakwen
Damawa
Damot Hadar
Falha
Gane-Geb
Gendebel (Amharic) or *Weregenu* (Oromo); also known as *Abe lahm* (Ge'ez) or *Abe lam* (Amharic)
Giyorgis Haile
Gondere
Halen
Hamelmal
Hara
Harab Gonda
Ilmegwazit Boran
Jan Amora
Jan Qantaffa
Kokeb
Laken
Legewon
Maggaro
Mattin
Milmil
Qeste Nihib
Qurban
Sabarat Sena

Senan
Serwe Dakwen
Serwe Hara
Serwe Muhazat
Seyfe Jagre
Tekula
Wenbedie
Werwari
Wiha Senqu
Ye bet Lij
Yehabeta

Acknowledgements

Over the years since I started to work on this book, colleagues, friends and family have encouraged my research and thinking about it. Many have shared their experiences, knowledge and valuable time, giving me suggestions, interviews and access to their documents on Ethiopia. I wish to mention those who answered my questions and queries without tiring of them. Special gratitude goes to *Dejazmach* Demess Welde Amanuel for the documents of the Patriotic Association that he gave me and were later deposited at the Institute of Ethiopian Studies (IES), Addis Ababa University. I thank the librarians at the IES and the Library of Congress, USA, for their unreserved cooperation. I have used here notes that *Dejazmach* Bezuwork Gabre wrote specifically for me on the history of the resistance and the exiles that he knew about during that time. Likewise invaluable have been my father's autobiography and his various letters answering my questions and my mother's constant reminders and information. Others who granted me interviews are too many to mention here, but are fully quoted and acknowledged as necessary in this volume, and most will be used in my forthcoming book on 1935–41.

I am particularly grateful to Professor Wendy James who raised questions about the background to the Ethiopian resistance to the Italian invasion of 1935–41 and very kindly discussed several drafts of this work. I also wish to thank Professor Shumet Sishagne who made valuable suggestions on one of the early drafts, Anthony Mockler and Professor Peter Garretson for their very helpful comments, and Jaqueline Mitchell and Lynn Taylor, the other staff members of James Currey of Boydell and Brewer, and the copy-editor, Belinda Cunnison, for their advice and patience. I am equally grateful to those who very kindly allowed me the use of pictures out of their published books. Special thanks in this regard to Professor John Farago and to the family of the late Professor Richard Pankhurst and his co-author, Denis Gérard.

An expression of special gratitude is long overdue to my family. My late parents, *Balambaras* Berhane-Selassie Yigeremu and *Weyzero* Workaferahu Haile, never tired of educating me and answering my questions, freely sharing their knowledge, and guiding me on where and what to explore. Discussions with my sister, Dr Simenish Berhane-Selassie, have been very helpful. My dear husband, Peter Witham Esmonde, undertook the task of tirelessly reading and language editing drafts. With a special place in the actual toil of bringing the work to fruition, he has my deep thanks. All these contributions have made the book what it is, but responsibility for any shortcomings is entirely mine.

Preface

Members of the ancient warrior category known as *chewa* (ጨዋ) bore personal responsibility for defending land and society in Ethiopia. Private soldiers, titled officers and monarchs considered it manly to engage in martial arts to assert the communal ownership of lands and rights of access to them. Their widespread practices and principles came from a socio-political background that promoted both defending and defining local lands and country.[1] Except for monks, priests, merchants and judges, most rural men trained themselves as warriors. In exploring that culture of warriorhood, the present book relies on Amharic, the working language of Ethiopia and its state, orally since the thirteenth century and in written form since the sixteenth century. The *chewa* soldiers expressed their skills and achievements through recitals known in Amharic as *zeraf* (ዘራፍ), 'assertive declamations', the format of which was common among warriors in most Ethiopian linguistic groups. Expressing significant militaristic perspectives, *zeraf* reflected also the historical identity and resilience of the state structure, which had survived for millennia. The *chewa* characteristically held their recitals while consuming honey mead (*tej* ጠጅ) and meat, both of which were endowed with meaning. *Tej* was reserved for the most accomplished, high-ranking officials, and specifically named cuts of meat were presented as rewards to hunters and warriors, as gifts on special occasions, or as food for guests of different ranks. Through the *zeraf* sessions, which were more important than the food and drink that accompanied them, the warriors promised loyalty to immediate masters, proclaimed services rendered, drew up images of pride and glory in their own or other warriors' past, and publicly stated their personal policies concerning the use of power. They also engaged in declaiming messages of defiance, or haranguing, berating and warning the enemy.

[1] I carried out the original study of this defence system in 1976–80. The system persisted for a millennium, possibly much longer, and continued into the twentieth century. I have been working on this book over the last eight years, in order to provide the necessary background for an understanding of the Ethiopian resistance to the Italian invasion of 1935–41. I completed a draft manuscript on the latter in 1972, and I am now revising it for publication.

This book attempts to explore *chewa* military traditions, histories and views on state politics and society using documented records and oral traditions. For the purpose of presenting perspectives that the warriors would recognize as their own, it explores their military traditions, their social roots and the history of the society that constantly generated these trained fighters. The work highlights the political association of the *chewa* with the long history of the state, and, with particular emphasis on the nineteenth and early twentieth centuries, it hopes to complement other studies on Ethiopian society and state in transit to modernity.

Any work on Ethiopian warriors is relevant to many academic studies of the intense conflicts that characterize pre-industrial societies. In the case of Ethiopia, ideological and ethno-nationalist perspectives on the relations of conflict have recently generated certain typologies of the monarchic state. The ethno-nationalist perspective gives due emphasis to the historical *chewa* warriors' identities, and while this study recognizes that need, it refrains from engaging in a throw-back exploration of genealogies of the historical warriors. Such an exercise would falsify the preferred identity of the *chewa* as Ethiopians,[2] and would play down the dynamisms of land policies, socio-political structures and politico-military history that helped Ethiopia resist invasions such as those of Italy in 1896 and 1935–41. It would also fail to acknowledge the specific features of Ethiopian defence that brought forward women and other categories of warriors.

Research on the relationship between the state and ethno-nationalist groups, some of which have been considered 'core' and others 'peripheral', has been supplemented by particular analyses of economic and social categories in the so-called feudal state, its expansion and its military structure. The current book shows that despite its continuity, the monarchical state has not been unchallenged in Ethiopian history. In addition, a significant amount of campaign literature has produced a number of battle sites, villains and heroes, and victims and victimizers. Though all these are relevant to historical conflicts, the following pages specifically illustrate that the monarchy in question was not feudal. Despite a vague resemblance to feudalism in the structure of military titles and the absolutist rule of Emperor Haile Selassie I (r.1930–75), the present book shows that neither titles nor positions were inherited. The warriors known as *chewa* gained these by fulfilling what society expected of them. Even today, individuals hold on to their shared mannerisms and ancestral pride

---

[2] Of course, both blame and praise have been showered on the supposed domination of so-called Amhara and Tigre ethno-national groups. A volume that focused on the ethno-nationalism of all the *chewa*, denying their expressed preferred identity as Ethiopians, would have to retrace the ethnic roots of their parentage ambilineally. Rehashing the wartime claims made by the country's historic enemies could highlight the dynamics of those who were supposed to be or who claimed to be excluded, rather than the external enemies themselves. This would be a book in its own right.

in the Ethiopian sense of defence and identity, irrespective of their ancestral ethnic origins.

Of significance in the study here are the reasons for the frequent wars associated with supporting or rejecting the monarchs and their representatives. At the centre of this process was a struggle for inclusion by a generalized politico-military structure that the *chewa* identified in their socio-political history. Whether in support or in rebellion, they also had to struggle to keep out the external enemy, a dangerous category requiring exclusion. Inclusion and exclusion being different sides of the same coin of defence, the warriors engaged in it, claiming it as critical in defining society and country as Ethiopia.

PERSONAL INTEREST

The generation of Ethiopians like me, who grew up in the 1950s and 1960s, accessed information on the *chewa* from various sources. Public holidays were accompanied by pertinent radio (and later television) talks and songs, and from my early years stories and images of public parades were brought back to us girls by my brothers and others. I was immersed in tales about the resistance, and for a reason. Our household life was very constricted and somehow harassed by officialdom because my father had refused to apologize following a trumped-up case in Sidamo Province in 1949 in which he and sixty-five others were falsely charged. He was imprisoned in the province for two years, and Emperor Haile Selassie placed him under house arrest in Addis Ababa after he appealed. The charge was eventually dropped in 1973, and the monarch 'pardoned' him when preparing, seemingly in the *chewa* tradition, to face a looming crisis: the 1974 revolution.

During the many years that the restrictions lasted, my father had to sign at the security office twice weekly, appear in the emperor's court practically every day, not leave the capital at all, not seek any government employment, never engage in either trade or farming, and suffer the visits of a palace lackey. Society shunned us, fearing guilt by association. Almost the only visitors we had while I was growing up were close relatives, farmers (former camp followers) from various lands in Sidamo and Shewa, and former guerrilla warrior colleagues of my parents. In his autobiography (which I annotated and published in Amharic in 2004, a year after his death) my father pays a compliment to my mother, calling her the shield who buffered him from the troubles of those days. In the midst of this constricted life, the autobiography reveals that the emperor gave him the title *kegnazmach*, which my father chose not to use. Everybody I came across noted my father's *chewa* manners, especially his restraint over responding to the petty harassment from the man from the palace who, with thinly disguised excuses, checked on the household every public holiday, often intrusively. Our visitors' admiration for my father's tenacity in holding to his principles and beliefs, and for his spirit of humility, helped us appreciate the *chewa*, not just in its present-day meaning of a well-mannered and disciplined person but also as a member of the category of past warriors who stood by their ideals in war and in peace. Among other things, the visitors imparted such an important sense of pride in their national rather than ethnic identities that I did not bother about my ethnic composition until peer pressure in my final undergraduate year in 1969 forced me to ask about it.

As we played childhood games such as *gebetta* (a board game with pebbles), we got to hear of older versions of them. We received full explanations of the military significance of children's sing-songs and horseplay on such public holidays as *Buhe* (Feast of the Transfiguration) and New Year as we watched other children engage in them. Though we could have joined in, my parents were determined that, rather than wandering around the neighbourhood, we maintained their *chewa* manners despite the low economic condition the restrictions subjected them to.

We also asked and learned about games associated with *Meskel* (Feast of the Cross) and *Gena* (Christmas). In hearing about horse racing during Christmas celebrations we were introduced to its past military importance. Horsemanship also raised the subject of hunting associated with military activities. Radio broadcasts of seasonal music in fasting seasons or on national anniversaries were responded to by family members and visitors with additional or alternative poems if we asked for them – which we usually did. Different musical instruments such as the *begena* (a ten-stringed lyre) and *kerar* (a six- or five-stringed lyre) evoked associated stories. Any display of artistic talent by us brought up memories in old family members. For example, a great aunt painted, including real-life portraits, but painting was considered so eccentric for a woman that she had to be hidden in the backyard of her brother's house! The various traditions – the dominant themes of conversations among our visitors – impressed and influenced me perhaps more deeply than most growing up in those years. Other children had these experiences in similar families, but our interests in historical lives and games, though unusually intense, did not exclude hobbies that attracted our contemporaries.

Some of my favourite visitors to our house were camp followers of the *chewa* army of the past. These older men and women had direct personal experience of the particular past that we were being told about, and had such phenomenal attachment to my parents that my siblings and I added terms of respect to their names as though they were our blood relatives. By the time we knew them, they were all farmers coming both to visit and to deliver produce from my father's various lands. One of them, formerly an *azazh* (head of personal and household troops), told me about his role. Another man spoke of how *chewa* 'masters' arranged marriages for their former slaves, settling them on their lands. A former cook of my paternal grandparents actually left her home two hundred kilometres away, late in her life, to spend a year with me when I left home for the first time to do my 'national service' as a third-year undergraduate. She continued to be a source of valuable information afterwards. Most other participants in the resistance to the colonial onslaught told us tales of a similar nature, expressing their values and expectations. They reflected pride in the *chewa* army that fought in unison to die or survive in 1896, and recalled the joy, pride or shame of those who responded in various ways to the invasion of 1935–41.

My articulation of the subject of Ethiopian warriorhood took shape only while I was employed as a researcher at the Institute of Ethiopian Studies (IES) following my first degree (in history) from Haile Selassie I University (later renamed Addis Ababa University). My personal interest, and encouragement from Professor Richard Pankhurst, then IES Director, made me undertake serious research on the old Ethiopian warriors. I collected 'oral history' on local political settings in Jimma, Welayta, Sidamo, Borena and other places in the south. Chaperoned as I sometimes was by someone my father assigned to accompany me, I lacked anonymity in parts of the south, while in Gojam and elsewhere scepticism was widespread about a young woman going around collecting information. Despite the resultant screening of information, the wealth of oral history that informants shared with me on the military and its *zeraf* certainly conveyed its spirit.

The research findings made me rethink the academic 'neutrality' of the scholarship I had imbibed as an undergraduate. The classroom history and political analysis was incongruent with the information I grew up with and collected while working at the IES, and with the oral history and other resources provided by former guerrilla fighters in Gojam, Shewa and elsewhere. Such discrepancies led me to read social anthropology at graduate level at the University of Oxford, with encouragement from Professor Wendy James, and explore Ethiopian military and political history in terms of the sociology of war. This confirmed what I had learned of the *chewa* both at home and during my oral history research, and it led me to supplement the oral information I collected with documentary sources. It is the sociological angle that has resulted in the current book.

My family, insignificant in the overall picture of the *chewa*, first gave me the knowledge and confidence that these warriors were a topic worth learning more about. My father's autobiography inspired my interest further, with its narratives of his *chewa* upbringing and his 'modern' army training as one of 260 recruits in Sidamo. The strongly militaristic household of his parents, *Fitawrari* Yigeremu Gebre Tsadik and *Weyzero* Mafegnash Work Borja, was deeply rooted in *chewa* tradition. My late mother recollected that her mother-in-law was a fourth-generation descendant of Dalqa, a female *balabat* of Menz. Someone else[3] reputedly traced this lineage to Abiye of Shewa and Askale of Gonder, and ultimately to Yekuno Amlak (r.1270–85), restorer of the so-called Solomonic

[3] *Ato* Mekonnen Yigletu, a relative from Menz, who provided us with oral information; he used to encourage us children to write down genealogy, though our jottings have not survived.

dynasty. A soldiers' *zeraf* couplet, the only other extant information on Dalqa, clearly suggests that she was a forceful woman:

> ዳልቃ ለፈረስ አተር አፍስሳ
> ልትፈጀን እስዋ እምሳ እምሳ!
> Dalqa poured out peas for horses,
> Intending to finish us, stirring and stirring!⁴

My paternal grandfather, *Fitawrari* Yigeremu, was a son of *Kegnazmach* Gebre Tsadik Merfo, the last *balabat* of the Eza, whom *Ras* Gobena removed with many others from their homes in Gurage country. The son of this *ras*, Wodajo Gobena, organized them as a *chewa* corps of *Barud Bet* (literally, gunpowder makers), and these were settled in Sidamo around 1891, and later in Bale and Harar. *Kegnazmach* Gebre Tsadik and his men served first under *Dajach* Beshah Aboye and later under *Ras* Lulseged. During the turbulent years following the death of Menelik in 1913, *Fitawrari* Yigeremu continued to serve within the *Barud Bet*, and after the Battle of Segele (1916) he followed *Dejazmach* Balcha Safo to Bale, then went to Harar and finally back to Sidamo.

My father was born in 1913 at Aberra, a mountaintop *ketema* (garrison town) founded by *Dejazmach* Beshah Aboye. Among his childhood memories were hunting birds, helping organize beehives around the house, and being presented to *Dejazmach* Balcha 'to learn court manners' while serving as a page for this 'big man'. He followed his father every day back and forth to Balcha's court, and, successfully supplicating his father to be allowed to go hunting, enjoyed the glories of warriorhood by killing a buffalo. He recalled following his father in the *ajeb* (retinue) of *Dejazmach* Balcha when the latter reluctantly went to pay homage to Empress Zewditu in Addis Ababa and was detained in Holeta. Father and son returned with *Ras* Biru,⁵ a salaried administrator of the 'modern' sector who made very little use of the *Barud Bet*, reflecting a process of change that had serious consequences during the 1935–41 resistance, as will be seen later in this book.

Ras Desta, who succeeded *Ras* Biru, recruited the sons of the *chewa*, including my father, and trained them as members of the 'modern army'. In 1935, the *ras* commanded the forces from Arsi, Bale and Sidamo against Italian advances through Dolo. This is featured in this book as an example of one of the last *chewa* engagements. *Ras* Desta

---

⁴ This couplet has come down in family oral history, repeated latterly by my late mother, who heard it from her mother-in-law.
⁵ I made enquiries about the oft-repeated story that *Dejazmach* Balcha was abandoned by members of the regiment that had followed him, while having an audience with *Ras* Tafari and Empress Zewditu. The response, including from my father and others who knew about the event, attributed the story to two factors. The first was that the *dejazmach* was so popular in Sidamo that those who resented his imprisonment blamed his demise on his retinue. Secondly, this large retinue did not comprise only his household servants. As it was essentially the *Barud Bet* (which features later in this book), and as Balcha had never indicated any intention of threatening those in the palace, the retinue that had come with him were obliged to obey the central government and return to its base.

brought to Dolo the small, trained 'modern' force, and around seven thousand *chewa* warriors under the thirty-seven *fitawrari* of the *Barud Bet*, the latter commanded by *Fitawrari* Yigeremu. After a brave stand against Italian poison gas and bombing that killed many of the men, *Ras* Desta rewarded the survivors with titles, including *balambaras* given to younger ones such as my father. Retreating northwards, the forces under the *ras* continued to resist until early 1937. After these forces were defeated, my father and others like him fought protracted guerrilla campaigns until the conclusion of the Ethiopian war in 1941.

When peace came, my father turned to farming, like most fighters then, but when the government recruited him and a few others from similar backgrounds into its service, they accepted their positions as a matter of course. After some years as a district governor in Sidamo, my father clashed with the provincial governor, *Ras* Adefresew Yinadu, over the latter's expectation that district governors would raise free labour for public works despite a national edict against such a practice. The *ras*'s reprisal came in 1948 when thieves from the Rift Valley killed a local *balabat* near our house in the jurisdiction of my father's district. My father and his assistants gave chase but could not catch the thieves before they disappeared into someone else's jurisdiction. The police caught the killers later, but the courts released them, incarcerating my father instead. The allegations against him included training his horses to parade, which was no more than a *chewa* practice, and having a distant cousin as his guest whose ex-husband, unbeknown to the family, was causing a disturbance in Gemu Gofa, another province.

As with the prolonged restrictions under Haile Selassie, alternative views are possible concerning my father. One explanation might be the tension between the resistance fighters who had remained inside the country during 1935–41 and the exiles who returned in 1941. In that context, the prejudice of the returnees against the patriots, most blatant in the capital, may have been the more subtle cause of my father's demise. His disapproval of giving and receiving bribes could be another explanation; some of my informants recollected that he rejected suggestions by a number of friends and relatives to give gifts to the governor to mollify him. His autobiography offers little more than the will of God as an explanation, and does not record any irksome experiences other than those associated with the restrictions imposed on him during 1948–73. It ends with an account of his efforts in 1973–75 to farm and to start a school among the Guji on his land in the forest of Megada. Political cadres harassed him from 1974 as a 'reactionary', or a 'feudal landowner' – a misconception, as this book will show. I remember him as a more pragmatic person regarding Ethiopia and its political processes. Examples include his verbal evaluation of state political transitions, his condemnation of the killing of government officials in 1960, of over sixty more killings in 1974, and of the alleged killing of Haile Selassie in 1975, and his serious concern about the use of ethnicity as a nexus of state politics from 1991 onwards.

His reticence in light of his incarceration, house arrest and harassments did not signal passivity, but a *chewa* principle: Where political decisions closed the options for leadership, *chewa* warriors tolerated and stood above personal discomfort until opportune moments presented practical options. That is, when opportunities to contribute to the Ethiopian military and political processes were closed, talk and excuses were idle – they were not viable alternatives. A similar *chewa* reaction was that of *Dejazmach* Balcha, who remained quietly under house arrest for a decade until the invasion of 1935–41, and then made use of every opening for action so as to resist the Italians. His actions contrasted with those of some other government officials who, lacking the intensive experience of *chewa* training, submitted to the invaders. The *chewa* warriors' strategy of seizing the timely opening up of political space for self-assertion was also used by the guerrilla fighters against the Italian invasion. Unaware of this broad source of nationalism, the invaders blamed and slaughtered the 'modern', educated youth.

Introduction

Studies on Ethiopian history have tended to overemphasize the prominent state structure and the place of the monarchs in defence, administration, and legislative and judicial systems. There is much more to the state and society, however, than the leaders, who may have seemed to be feudal warmongers, and their governments, which may have appeared inefficient. Closer scrutiny suggests that such images have been misleading. I contend that European travellers, journalists, military historians and other writers responsible for representing the defence system, the subject of this work, have glossed over the *chewa* troops' sense of responsibility. Sometimes referring to them as 'a horde' or as *neftegna* (literally 'gunmen') – a supposedly pointless group of killers and tools of oppression,[1] these writers have played down the *chewa* contribution, even to Ethiopia's struggles against Italian invasions in 1896 and 1935–41. The compulsion felt by many authors to reflect international support for the second Italian invasion has led them to single out 1935–36 as evidence supporting Mussolini's claim to have *occupied* Ethiopia, irrespective of the efforts of the Ethiopian guerrilla warriors who started fighting as soon as the emperor departed ('fled' according to some), and continued to restrict the Italians to the main roads and to some cities, towns and forts.[2] Such an approach

---

[1] Scholars have characterized the *chewa* genre of warriors as 'militia' or 'citizen soldiery'. Others have called them feudal or provincial 'levies', for instance John Markakis, *Ethiopia: Anatomy of a Traditional Polity* (Oxford Studies in African Affairs), Oxford: Clarendon Press, 1974, p. 40.

[2] Both *chewa* and 'modern' perceptions regarding the battles of 1935–41 are available in first-hand Amharic accounts, notably ኃይለ ሥላሴ ሕይወቴና የኢትዮጵያ ኣርምጃ (Haile Selassie, *My Life and the Progress of Ethiopia*, 1929 EC); ከበደ ተሰማ (ደጃዝማች) የታሪክ ማስታወሻ፡ አዲስ አበባ፡ አርቲስቲክ ማተሚያ ቤት፡ ኢትዮጵያ 1962:: (Kebede Tessema (*Dejazmach*), *History Notes*, Addis Ababa: Artistic Printing Press, 1962 EC); ገሪማ ታፈረ፡ ጎንደሬ በጋሻው፡ አዲስ አበባ፡ 1949 (Gerima Tafere, *The Gondere with his Shield*, Addis Ababa, 1949 EC); ታደሰ ዘወልዴ፡ ያባለሸ ዘመን (Tadesse Zewelde, *Era of Discord*, n.d.); ሐዲስ አለማየሁ ትዝታ (Haddis Alemayehu, *Memories*, n.d., Institute of Ethiopian Studies, Addis Ababa University: Digital Collection of Ethiopian Manuscripts, No. 286_IES03387). Several commendable conventional histories have appeared in various languages in recent decades, some of which are referred to here. Among

ignores the prominent *chewa* term *yetelat werera zemen*, 'era of enemy invasion', describing the years 1935–41. No mere choice of words, this expressed a deep sense of the warriors' responsibility for defining and defending Ethiopia's territorial integrity, administrative structure and sovereignty. Colonialism was inconceivable to the socially rooted rural warriors, who thought of themselves and their activities as serving their country and society.

This book explores the historical and social roots of such local views, but first a few words are needed to highlight the international context of twentieth-century Ethiopia. The claim that colonial rule in Ethiopia was a *fait accompli*, give or take a few localized groups of troublemakers, presented Ethiopia as a victim and enhanced Italy's self-perception as a victor which won battles in short order. Underestimating Ethiopian guerrilla activities covered up Fascist atrocities, notably the use of aerial bombing, mustard gas, intimidation and planned annihilation of the population. Of course it also reflected British and French political and strategic interests, not least in containing Germany's growing military power, and their fear that Italy might side with it. It highlighted their manipulation of the fickle League of Nations on its road to collapse. Their deliberate policy of reticence and obfuscation regarding Ethiopia's guerrilla warfare benefited Mussolini.[3]

Foreign views on the period were also partly fed by European pride in their military traditions and their historical views on Ethiopia as a distant and isolated Christian kingdom, lagging behind what they associated proudly with Europe. Such obscurantism was consistent with an often-repeated, rather flippant statement made by the historian Edward Gibbon: 'Encompassed on all sides by the enemies of their religion, the Æthiopians slept near a thousand years, forgetful of the world, by whom they were forgotten.'[4] Besides, industrial revolution and improvements in military hardware – weaponry and means of transport – had just enabled nineteenth-century European military structure to move away from privately owned soldiery. The countries of Europe had become nations with troops who had gone through formal military schools and were provided with supplies and resources that they no longer had to find personally. When contemporary European scholars and travellers took notice of Ethiopia, therefore, they were coming from countries whose political changes had seen the rise of the nation state with national fighting forces. Confident of their conti-

(contd) specific studies: Alberto Sbacchi, *Legacy of Bitterness: Ethiopia and Fascist Italy, 1935–1941*, Lawrenceville, NJ and Asmara: Red Sea Press; Anthony Mockler, *Haile Selassie's War*, London: Grafton, 1987. Similarly deserving attention are the summary accounts in Bahru Zewde, *A History of Modern Ethiopia, 1855–1991* (2nd edn), Oxford: James Currey, 2001, and Harold G. Marcus, *Haile Selassie I: The Formative Years, 1892–1936*, Lawrenceville, NJ: Red Sea Press, 1995.

[3] George W. Baer, *The Coming of the Italian-Ethiopian War*, Cambridge, MA: Harvard University Press, 1967, for example pp. 62–95, 374–5.

[4] Edward Gibbon, *The History of the Decline and Fall of the Roman Empire*, Vol. 4, Chapter XLVII, 'Ecclesiastical Discord', Part VI, 1782, revised 1845.

nent's world leadership, its 'modernity' and its state institutions, they had little appreciation of the viability of other systems. Among the newest nation states was the previously fragmented Italy, which was constituted as a nation in 1857, and with then characteristically racist attitudes and remarks began to invade Ethiopia in the 1890s. It came as a shock to them when the *chewa* worked with the Ethiopian state in 1896 to win victory against Italy, proving their cherished capacity as guards, indeed guardians, of the country and its people against external invasion. That victory spread pride among those whom Europe was trying to dominate around the world, and obliged observers to reassess Ethiopian fighting and political acumen.

Of course, internal causes also allowed the underplaying of *chewa* traditions. Nineteenth-century Ethiopian monarchs' attempts to reinforce Ethiopian unity and self-confidence, exerting pressure over disparate and rival local powerholders, and deliberately changing *chewa* militaristic ideals and practices, gave rise to the view of some classical anthropologists that Ethiopia was a museum of peoples that despots held together by force. This line of interpretation has become the basis for some current political activists' claims that Ethiopia is a new country that monarchs put together only in the nineteenth century. Some scholarly trends in that tradition see internal Ethiopian conflicts only as linguistic, religious, political, ethnic and/or other differences, and generally conclude that each of such groupings was more or less passively subjugated by the *chewa* – which, as we will see, was not the case. Also precluding an understanding of the *chewa* warriors are associated claims that refer to the army as feudal, especially in association with the necessary changes made in state structure towards 'modernity', notably through post-1896 internal politics and administration. These trends have failed to highlight the widespread emergent historically and socially rooted fighters, and have resulted in a deterministic history focused on the rise and fall of monarchs who incorporated autonomous regions. These views on the country and its political system differ widely from *chewa* traditions.

In this context, it is worth pointing out that the centralizing Ethiopian monarchs saw each individual *chewa* warrior as a potential competitor for their thrones. From the mid-nineteenth century, they tried to suppress the emergence of local leaders, and despite rural battles to restrain this trend, the monarchs worked on marginalizing the autonomy of individuals and regions throughout Ethiopia. The monarchs brought under their control land, the critical economic base for the political and military structures. In particular, measuring and redistributing land in the late nineteenth century ultimately made land tenure redundant as a lever that society had long used *vis-à-vis* the state. Of course, the modernizing monarchs aimed to train and equip a salaried army that was answerable to them alone, if not to the state. This meant that land became less and less an economic base for the military, and that *chewa* warriors lost their central importance to the state. This in turn meant that their close link to the population at the grassroots and to its lands was no longer a route to participation in local and state politics. The details of the reforms included, either by design or accident, changing the rules governing land, labour and other resources, including stopping individuals from training themselves as warriors. As we will see, this took away decision-making power from local *chewa* 'masters' and individuals. With the monarchs also dominating access to weapons, traditional training in horsemanship and other martial skills for influencing local politics were no longer the norms. In brief, the land policies of the late nineteenth century led to the demise of a two-way relationship between the state and the population through the dynamics of warriorhood. These processes will be explained in this book, not in order to challenge 'modernity' but to elucidate the historical dynamics of Ethiopian defence that involved people at the grassroots.

The process of marginalizing the *chewa* was at the core of the policies of Emperor Tewodros II (r.1855–68), but it matured in the days of Emperor Menelik II (r.1889–1913), and laid the ground for the 'modernity' that Menelik bravely and wisely introduced. Inadvertently, however, it failed both to bring with it the *chewa* spirit of two-way communication between state and population and to uphold the impersonal working principles that a 'modern' civil service was supposedly meant to apply. The gradual centralization of power in the hands of 'modern' state monarchs eclipsed the status and crucial role of the *chewa*. For the salaried officials of the 'modern' structure, land was a peripheral channel for their administrative services. The development of banks, ministries and other 'modern' state facilities, and resources with which the state could employ salaried administrators, effectively marginalized the long-standing role of rural people in local political matters. While the 'modern' state took over from the *chewa*, it failed to adopt their idealized spirit of participation in political decision-making by ordinary local people. This is to point out that by removing the organized networks and strategies of mutual relationship between state and rural society, central control of land paved the way for despotism. The process helped to depict and promote images of a history of either oppressive rival, feudal, unruly and wild warlords, or of benevolent monarchs whose desire for unity was self-serving – an image that was not countered by the growing power of the monarchs or ultimately by the creation of exclusive rules of succession in the 1931 constitution.

The constant emergence of the *chewa* out of its roots in rural communities meant that there were self-trained specialists in the art of leadership and in defending not only local people and lands but also a wider political space: the country, *hager*, and its people. Unlike those in post-industrial societies, these fighters had no establishments to organize, train or maintain them as an army, but they confidently ascended the military hierarchy and assumed wider political roles. With studied *zeraf* wordings recalling honoured traditions and precedence, the warriors convinced their local communities to trust them to defend their ancestral lands and their interests within the political structure of the *neguse negest* ('king of kings'). Key to this was the long view of history that *chewa* warriors, the communities that supported them and the state they served believed in. That history, and the forays into state politics made by the self-trained individuals from the grassroots, justified their presence as the defence force of pre-'modern' Ethiopia. Despite the periodic clashes they generated, the *chewa* enabled the above two-way dialogue between the monarchs and the rural population. Many scholars have been evaluating this history recently,[5] and this book presents it from the viewpoint of the warriors.[6]

Chapter 1 gives a brief outline of the history and principles of the *chewa*, followed by a discussion of their lifestyle and everyday activities. Showing the different categories of *chewa* warriors that recognized and participated in the military and administration of the Ethiopian state, it also draws out their key ways of thought, and how power and authority over communal lands were inculcated in would-be soldiers. The chapter argues that *chewa* warriors derived their authority from the grassroots that supported them. With a brief reference to the pre-Axumite origin of *negus*, 'king', and *neguse negest*, 'king of kings', it also shows the emergence of prescribed authority in a book, the *Kebre Negest (Glory of Kings)*. As the source of power from which the 'kings of kings' derived their authority, *Glory of Kings* counterpoised the monarchs to the grassroots source of authority underpinning the *chewa* warriors. However, both the warriors and the monarchs accepted a long view of history that prepared them to die in defence of communal lands and a territorial Ethiopia that they protected from enemies external to the northeast African region. The chapter discusses the challenge to this tradition by the appropriation of communal lands for private use during the so-called *Zemene Mesafint*, Era of Princes (1789–1855), which led to the rise of powerful, autonomous local rulers. That era was brought to an end by Tewodros II and his successors through the coordination of joint *chewa* resistance to the Italian invasions of 1896 and 1935–41.

Chapter 2 touches on the ancient history of external hostility that lost the 'kings of kings' their rule and urban-based commerce, and forced them into a peripatetic existence. The place of *chewa* warriorhood in that system shows the cumulative formation of the country's boundaries and the warriors' sensitivity to its friends and foes – elements that are still embedded in Ethiopian thinking. Though the monarchs' rule through *chewa* settlements over far-flung regions collapsed due to the internal rise of *Imam* Ahmad ibn Ghazi and then the rapid pace of Oromo migration, resistance to external enemies persisted, finally

---

[5] See for instance, Richard J. Reid, *Frontiers of Violence in North-East Africa: Genealogies of Conflict since 1800*, Oxford: Oxford University Press, 2011, pp. 14–20.

[6] Yirga Gelaw Weldeyes has made a similar observation in his study of the challenge that modern education presents to indigenous Ethiopian culture, specifically to the literary educational tradition. See his *Native Colonialism: Education and the Economy of Violence against Tradition in Ethiopia*, Trenton, New Jersey: Red Sea Press, 2017, p. 13.

changing the definition of external enemy from Turks and Egyptians to Europeans, Italians in particular.

Chapter 3 discusses the contradictory claims to access of communal lands by the *chewa* and the monarchs. The monarchs used *gult* and *maderya*, respectively administrative and military service lands, but their overall claims beyond these were often challenged by the warriors. In the process, local communities generated warriors, whom they sometimes chose as local leaders. How the monarchs controlled such warriors over several decades is illustrated using three examples of warfare.

Using the perspective that allows the emergence of warriors and elected local leaders (*yegobez aleqa*), Chapter 4 addresses the deeper meaning of land as constituting 'country' (*hager*). Self-training and education in military and political leadership rules familiarized warriors with the physical environment, emboldening them to offer their services to officials in nearby garrison towns (*ketema*) in defence of lands beyond their localities.

Chapter 5 explains the ideals of hierarchy and honour that warriors imbibed by being encouraged from their childhood to imitate significant patrons and military leaders. The purpose of combining material wealth with attracting as many dependants as possible symbolically transformed men into qualified warriors and women into indispensable signifiers of warriorhood. This underlined an aspect of gender modification in which women invariably stood as replacements on battlefields for absent men or male minors.

Men's specific training as warriors and progression up the politico-military hierarchy is discussed in Chapter 6. Among various degrees of warriors' qualifications in sports that trained them in physical prowess, speed and witticisms were hunting, horsemanship and weapons handling, which brought military rewards. Local communities, individual patrons and politico-military 'masters' encouraged and awarded qualified warriors with titles, land, silk shirts, and swords and other weapons.

Chapter 7 describes how rigid martial training was adapted to patrimonial politics that allowed the operation and easing of power relations. Discussing the refined politics of warriorhood at this level includes describing the task of officers known as *baldereba* who mediated relationships between patrons and clients, and the *agafari* who ensured that visitors, guests or junior warriors received due attention. The problem of supplies acquisition, however, was not adequately accommodated by these or other structures of *chewa* politico-military relationships.

The symbolisms of warriorhood elaborated in Chapter 8 are about the relationship of individual warriors and 'masters' with each other, with the country people and with those they considered their enemies. The festivities known as *gibir* (a formal military banquet), here seen as the redistribution of resources that the *chewa* collected as tax (also called *gibir*), were occasions for the commanders hosting the feasts to deliver their political messages, and for prominent recognition of the symbols that hunters and warriors delivered. The festivities celebrated those warriors who engaged in declamations known as *zeraf* and in showing off trophies they collected both from big game and from their enemies. The discussion intends to show that items from the festivities as a whole – trophies, titles, weapons, lands, *tej*, cuts of meat and other rewards – constituted the symbolisms of warriorhood.

Chapter 9 refers to the two Italian invasions. One ended with the Battle of Adewa (1896), the other lasted five years throughout the country (1935–41). The chapter draws attention to differences and similarities in the two periods in the international political and military environment and in *chewa* traditions. It also draws attention to the changes that the monarchs made in land matters after the Battle of Adewa, and the failure to encourage two-way communication between the state and ordinary rural people. The monarchy brought 'modernity' and centralized administration, but it did not institute the spirit of civil service or other means of preventing autocracy. At the time of both invasions, Europeans blocked the Ethiopian leaders' attempts to buy weapons. Nonetheless, despite the internal changes, the *chewa* re-emerged and fought during the second invasion, changing their style of warfare. The spirited population, armed with antiquated weapons and its own methods of warfare, managed to withstand aerial bombing, which included extensive use of poison gas against troops and non-fighters alike.

Chapter 10 discusses the emergence of alternative and popular leadership that used *chewa* warrior traditions to conduct the resistance during 1935–41. Examples cited include the temporary government that *Ras* Imru set up and the front that *Ras* Desta led in the south. As guerrilla activities intensified after the summer rains of 1936, warriors crowned a king in Bulga; acclaimed *Balambaras* Abebe Aregay as *ras* and Belay Zeleke as 'emperor by his might', and promoted other leaders in Begemder, Keffa, Tigre, Lasta and elsewhere. Thus, in the absence of a recognized central authority, the fighters temporarily brought back the many strands of *chewa* traditions, including the sense of hierarchy, information circulation and the cherishing of bravery and popularity. Though their various groups had differences, they also decided to cooperate with Emperor Haile Selassie when he returned in 1941.

The Conclusion notes the influences of these various historical experiences on the *chewa* traditions. It highlights two notions critical to the traditional system of defence that are relevant to 'modern' relational strategies. These are the spirit of individual responsibility for people, land and country, and the principle of two-way dialogue between the state and the population. Without advocating the return of an archaic and obsolete system, the conclusion also shows that these two *chewa* concepts have been fading away in post-war Ethiopia, and highlights the need for their re-emergence.

1
Traditions of Hierarchical Warriorhood

The self-trained *chewa* started out as qualified and socially supported individual warriors. They received social support for their alert and disciplined preparedness and political acumen, essentially to defend local society and to assert the right to control access to and distribution of communal lands. They supported the state, but also frequently clashed with the monarchs who claimed ownership of all land. By the end of the nineteenth century, the 'kings of kings' brought them together to form a national government army under one monarch, but even then foreigners saw them as only a melange of warriors who fought *en masse*. However, at least one such eyewitness, who used the European term for the country,[1] was a little more perceptive: he wrote of the army as 'the Abyssinian people with its distinctive characteristics – independence and a critical attitude to everything'.[2]

The word *chewa* (in Amharic) or *tsewa* (in Ge'ez), has been defined as 'captives' or 'prisoners', and, elaborating this further, as one 'who has left his country, a refugee, and one who lives by roving or wandering about'.[3] A historian has asserted that the earliest soldiers were war captives.[4] By the early nineteenth century the meaning of *chewa* had altered radically. Far from being 'captive' to a king, the word designated an urbane and sophisticated population of soldiers milling around the courts of the powerful. Engrossed from childhood in the art of warriorhood and politics, and receiving encouragement to explore the ecological features away from their rural roots, the *chewa* cultivated qualifications of assertiveness in ways that transcended social, familial, political and other groupings. They learned their direction in

---

[1] On Abyssinia as a foreign name for Ethiopia and the ethnic identities related with it, see Tsehai Berhane-Selassie, 'Where or what is "Abyssinia" – An investigation', 15 August 2016.
[2] Alexander Bulatovich, *Ethiopia through Russian Eyes: Country in Transition, 1896–1898* (trans. and ed. Richard Seltzer), Lawrenceville, NJ; Asmara: Red Sea Press, 2000, p. 101.
[3] ኪዳነ ወልድ ክፍሌ መጽሐፈ ሰዋስው ወግስ ወመዝገበ ቃላት ሐዲስ፡ ዲሬዳዋ አርቲስቲክ ማተሚያ ቤት:: 1948 (Kidane Weld Kifle (*Aleqa*), *Book of Grammar, Verbs and Dictionary of New Words*, Dire Dawa: Artistic Matämiya Bet, 1948 EC).
[4] Merid W. Aregay, 'Military Elites in Medieval Ethiopia', *Journal of Ethiopian Studies*, Vol. 30, No. 1 (June 1997, pp. 31–7), p. 34.

life while growing up, characteristically recognizing their duty to their local communities. Their basic organization revolved around a local leader recognized as *yegobez aleqa*, 'leader of the brave', who rallied those who had political and military ambitions to engage in accepting or rejecting the agents of the state. Their lifestyles and practices made them accountable to rural society, and their traditions significantly influenced Ethiopian state political processes.

THE MAIN *CHEWA* WARRIOR CATEGORY

While personal expressions of their beliefs, commitments, organizational principles and operational strategies brought them to work with the grassroots, these ordinary soldiers who defined and defended local lands and the Ethiopian territory were not 'volunteer' soldiers. They were generated, supported and commended by their communities. Three categories of soldiers who lived away from their homes were perceived in the same way. These were the *fanno* (hunters), who engaged in procuring marketable forest products (mainly game), the *shifta* (rebels), fighting for their own personal reasons, and the *mekwanent*[5] (officers, governors) in state service. An important function required of local leaders was to sustain peaceful coexistence among these categories of fighters, who, for reasons that will be discussed in this work, were known collectively as *chewa*.

The warriors joined as individuals in the service of the state in its historically varied political contexts, from its early times to the era of the 'wandering capitals', and continuing onwards through the eighteenth and nineteenth centuries. Their self-training, as we will show later, made them aware of the historical settlements of other warriors in the wider northeast African region, and committed them to the defence of those lands. *Chewa* belief combined the historical continuity of both the national identity of these lands and the rights of local people to them. *Chewa* participation in serving the state helped strong monarchs define people and lands as Ethiopia, guarding them against invaders by organizing the *chewa* into named corps. Together, the monarchs and the *chewa* constituted the formal defence force.

However, though their sense of warriorhood encouraged them to die for the territory under the state, farmers' views were more localized. They asserted their rights to communal lands for organizing their local communities' access to plots within the *rest* (inalienable land rights). Emerging locally, and with deep attachment to their lands, individual warriors engaged in armed contestations between rural society and the state. These did not always endear them to the *neguse negest*. Compared to these *balager*, the officials' relationship to land was different. Government views of the history of land were expansive and relatively large scale. Besides, as will be illustrated in the three battles

---

[5] Kidane Weld Kifle, *Book of Grammar*, 1948 EC.

discussed later, land had military purposes such as raising and maintaining fighting forces. The soldiers that the state billeted necessarily had limited identification with or use of the plots they received for their military service. Even where they could use state administrative privileges to privatize such military lands, residual, official time-limited access worked against identifying with them, and encouraged these soldiers to follow their leaders anywhere they could access other land grants.

The *chewa* conviction of having inherited a historically deeply rooted commitment to defence was derived in part from growing up experiencing and taking personal responsibility for controlling and defending the country's mountains, escarpments and associated lowlands, forests, rivers and any other land features such as the Red Sea coast, that they believed to be Ethiopian. This geopolitical consciousness, so to speak, meant actively qualifying themselves, and developing a reputation for experience with these features, and for being awarded with coveted titles and political positions by local leaders and monarchs for defending them responsibly. Such recognition opened avenues of communication between the state and local society. It gained the warrior leaders positions as revenue collectors, justice administrators and military servicemen.

A serious indicator of commitment was the deliberate display of personal military defence engagements during *chewa* ceremonial occasions. Articulating the pride they took in their warriorhood, warriors invariably pronounced their commitment to communal and national boundaries, and made promises of loyalty to their preferred high military titleholders. Personal recitals of militaristic exploits and other histories were supported by witnesses and references to historical precedents. These were the *zeraf* (which foreigners have wrongly described as boasting), examples of which are cited in this book. Young adults, in particular, took inspiration from the recitals. As fighters formed or joined embryonic military groups, often immediately following the sessions, the whole exercise contributed to the continuous emergence of warriors.

The recitals also opened up political space to members of local society. In spite of claims of their passivity, ordinary people actively used the sessions to express their ideas, and their support for or rejection of what others said. They recited *zeraf* poems, voicing opinions on local justice, for instance against burdensome taxation, unfair administrative demands or military intentions. Bold announcements to officials included threatening written messages, an example of which was a letter in 1780 to a high court official, *Ras-Bitweded* Ali the Great, asking him to ease off his demands:

> The people of Begemidir's tribute to our sovereign has consisted of giving our breast to the blades of the spears, and our feet to the sands of the earth. We cannot tolerate any more the type of extortion which the Emperor has been conniving to impose on us. If you wish, you can remain and enjoy your office as our representative, subject to our counsel. If you, on the other hand,

prefer to remain loyal to the Emperor, we are determined to settle the matter by force.[6]

Zeraf assertions in the presence of a vibrant socio-political base both solicited and affirmed local capacity to protect land tenure, especially the inalienable land right known in Amharic as *rest*.[7] Indeed land was the major matter of contestation between constantly emergent local warriors and 'masters', including those in higher positions. They expressed pride in representing locally a heritage of powerful military competence. Individual warriors clamoured to gain or give hierarchical symbols of leadership and power such as titles, regalia and weapons, thereby increasing their prestige and capacity to choose formally to support or challenge the 'kings of kings'. Besides, these warriors and the monarchs all had the same militaristic upbringing. Indeed, as we will see, even those vying with each other for the crown were not above addressing warriors at the grassroots directly in order to gain supporters against opponents, sometimes taking the risk of asserting their local rights over rural lands.

Rituals that rendered the persons of warriors symbolically identical with land, and, by extension, country and people, inculcated in warriors the practice of supporting or challenging forces with opposing political beliefs. As we will see, the base for the ritual was hunting, a sport that exposed boys to difficult landscape features, and familiarized them with the people living there. Experiencing hardship meant surviving the difficulties of topography and ecology, and in doing so, developing a people-focused confidence. Learning histories of 'old' settlements and relating to them meant entering a shared commitment to defining Ethiopia's boundaries and resisting enemy invasion. Attaining symbols of

[6] Translated and quoted from Tekle Tsadiq Mekuria, *A History of Ethiopia* (in Amharic, Addis Ababa, 1957), p. 207 by Zawde Gabre-Sellassie in his *Yohannes IV of Ethiopia: A Political Biography*, Oxford: Clarendon Press, 1975, p. 4, fn. 2: Oxford Studies in African Affairs. According to this source, Tekle Tsadiq's quotation was itself from the *Chronicle of Emperors* written by order of *Dejazmach* Eshete Hailu.

[7] Of studies on land and access to it in Ethiopian political history, particularly pertinent to the theme of this book have been those on the provision of land grants called *gult*. An original and extensive study is Donald Crummey, *Land and Society in the Christian Kingdom of Ethiopia: From the Thirteenth to the Twentieth Century*, Oxford: James Currey, 2000. A similar study, adding a finer point about the effects of *gult* provision on society, is Habtamu Mengistie Tegegne, *Land Tenure and Agrarian Structure in Ethiopia, 1636–1900*, PhD dissertation, University of Illinois at Urbana-Champaign, 2011. On land reforms carried out by Menelik II see Guèbrè Sellassié (*Tsehafi Tezaz*), *Chronique du Règne de Ménélik II Roi des Rois d'Éthiopie*, (trans. Tèsfa Sellassié), Paris: Librairie Orientale et Américaine, Vol. I, 1930, Vol. II, 1932. On the same topic see ማህተመ ሥላሴ ወልደ መስቀል (ባለምባራስ)፡ ዝክረ ነገር፡ አዲስ አበባ፡ 1962 (Mahteme Selassie Welde Meskel (*Blaten Geta*), *Memories of Significance*, Addis Ababa, 1962 EC), pp. 105–28. Richard Pankhurst, *The Economic History of Ethiopia, 1800–1935*. Haile Selassie I University Press, 1968, p. 147, underlines the significance of *rest* and *gult* in the nineteenth century by drawing attention to various rulers' threats of confiscation of such property in cases of treason or disloyalty.

political power and authority, including those of the monarchs, meant regaining areas that had been 'lost', and then defending them.

Critical to the adult lifestyle were processes that successful warriors, beyond hunting, were expected to engage in locally. These included making their personal hamlets the hubs of local defence, accommodating at least their 'children' – namely their pages, shield bearers, gun bearers, and domestic and personal service providers. To improve their chances of leadership they sponsored socially supported *ashker*, i.e. political and military followers. (Nowadays the word *ashker* means 'servant' – someone in domestic employment.) They increased their military force of 'children' by recruiting loyal *ashker* and retainers, whose entitlement to promotion would be determined after battles. Needless to say, such 'master' warriors with large retinues had credibility as strong leaders. The collection of booty in their names increased their fame, while the act of giving rewards to the brave, who threw down *geday* (the 'kill', as booty was called) before them, attracted even more. Benevolently rewarding outstanding followers, protégés, favourite slaves or waged employees with titles, land grants and weapons proved their capacity as viable political 'masters' of wider influence.

It was important for a local leader's status to shape opinion on the basis of vigilant gathering and dissemination of information about inheritance, and news on justice in land rights and other local political concerns. It was also very important that local 'masters' showed themselves alert to alarms raised by shepherds, farmers or anybody out in the fields, for instance at any sudden appearance of *dina* ('an enemy with whom blood money could not be exchanged').[8] Leaders were expected to respond appropriately. As their authority overlapped with that of state politico-military power, they might even call on their *wegen* ('allies' in the sense of insiders, friends) and, depending on the significance of the hostility spotted, go to battle to avert the threat.

Periods of such disturbance were propitious for youth aspiring to be political leaders and seeking social recognition for their bravery. They would hasten to experience warfare and clamour to be in the service of well-respected 'masters', who would designate proxy officials to follow up the efforts of the volunteers. Such leaders kept their promise to reward land and booty to the successful or punish insubordination. Successful fighters who benefited from the experience were encouraged by the 'master' to join higher authorities, if they wished, by joining 'masters' residing in *ketema* (garrison towns).

This interdependence between the constantly emerging grassroots warriors and state level 'masters' ensured politico-military access that designated some lands exclusively for military service. Besides, the ongoing evaluation that promoted former retainers to ranks in the military hierarchy made their 'masters' members of the category of

---

[8] Kidane Weld Kifle defines the word as deriving from Diana, the name of the Biblical girl whose brothers punished the people of Sekem for violating her, and as describing any warrior who takes up arms without official sanction. See his *Book of Grammar*, 1948 EC.

mekwanent (nobles), warrior-administrators in full-time state service, as we will see later.

OTHER CATEGORIES OF *CHEWA* WARRIORS

Protests against injustice that state agents perpetrated in local communities, or other disagreements between warriors, led frequently to armed conflict. Potential leaders of such protests would abandon normal life and retreat to lands considered marginal, situated either by communal borders or near to other ecological features that could hide them. Known as *shifta*, such rebels stayed where they could easily receive supplies and information from their supporters in the community. Frequent success in these incidents inculcated in ordinary people the importance of defining spatial and geopolitical power, and the confidence to initiate defence activities. In practice, involving *shifta* and leaders of neighbouring communities before informing the local state authorities of any hostilities was considered normal. In that sense, rural loyalties ultimately determined the strength or weakness of the monarchs and, indirectly, the size and nature of the state.

Shifta were individuals who either ran away from the law or espoused the interests of local people, jeopardizing their personal standing with the local authorities, and even with the faraway *neguse negest*.[9] Unlike ordinary bandits who engaged in theft or murder, like hunters they forged fictive and other relationships with local people. They sheltered the aggrieved – often eventually gaining them amnesty, social acceptance and reconciliation – and fugitives from the law, including those who had committed theft and other disruptions that incurred social disapproval. More importantly they enabled these and others to become capable warriors with a cause and with the freedom to respond autonomously to mobilization. The category of communal or other frontiers from which rebels challenged the authorities' local power and control was later claimed by the monarchs to define the size and nature of the Ethiopian state.

The other category of *chewa* warrior was *fanno*, meaning in everyday language 'someone who travels of their own volition' or a 'band of leaderless soldiers' who were not accountable to anybody. Unlike *shifta*, these hunters survived by their engagement in hunting big game profession-

[9] Fernyhough categorizes *shifta* into 'aristocratic' and 'other', but this seems to reflect the status some of them achieved later in life. See Timothy Fernyhough, 'Interpreting Ethiopian Banditry: A Revisionist View', in Katsuyoshi Fukui, Eisei Kurimoto and Masayoshi Shigeta (eds), *Ethiopia in Broader Perspective: Papers of the XIIIth International Conference of Ethiopian Studies, Vol I–III* (Kyoto: Shokado Booksellers, 1997. Vol. I, pp. 57–81. See also Richard Caulk, 'Bad Men of the Borders: Shum and Shefta in Northern Ethiopia in the Nineteenth Century', *International Journal of African Historical Studies*. Vol. 17, No. 2, 1984, pp. 201–27, and Irma Taddia, 'Land Politics in the Ethiopian-Eritrean Border Area between Emperor Yohannes IV and Menelik II', *Aethiopica: International Journal of Ethiopian Studies*, Vol. 12, 2009, pp. 58–82.

ally. They attracted young men who sought to pass through the necessary rituals of the would-be warrior, and they imparted to them a sense of self that was symbolically imbued with personal and communal history in the local context of the hunting grounds. Informally, the *fanno* forged fictive and other informal relationships with local people.

Consequently, *fanno* military activity in border areas attracted *shifta* from nearby home communities. In the Sudan–Ethiopia borderlands, they accompanied their hunting with trade in ivory and other forest products and with raiding the local population for slaves and cattle. In the 1920s, such hostile *fanno* activity along the Kenya–Ethiopia border was clandestinely approved by local governors. Conveniently, officials took the presence of *fanno* in an area as proof of the existence of territory that they could legitimately claim as theirs.[10] As their achievements in warfare enhanced their status and influence among border communities, *fanno* contributed to defining territories in terms of people-focused belongingness.

In effect, the marginal warriors prepared the ground for extracting resources, especially on behalf of the nineteenth-century state. Increasing numbers joining the *fanno*, and even the *shifta*, gave certain borderlands the potential to become viable state territories. Contrary to assertions that the rural population lacked a 'pan-Ethiopian' patriotism,[11] their presence perhaps also spread a shared national spirit. As recognized warriors, the *fanno* provided most communities with niches for rebels, aspiring politicians and adventurous soldiers. Ever ready to act at a moment's notice, an individual *fanno* presented himself as a retainer to a specific 'master' in times of military operations. In that sense, both the *fanno* (hunter) and the *shifta* (rebel) were *chewa* in the making, though located in the immediate borderland. They were also precursors in the construction of *chewa* borderlands by operating in the outer perimeters of their communities or beyond. Occasionally, the areas they reached were those in which the *neguse negest* also campaigned to settle their *chewa* contingents, as we will see.

On the outer fringes of the *chewa* military structure – literally, physically and figuratively – *fanno* seem to have been the nearest the country came to having border area patrols. It should be noted that by disseminating and exchanging information, including borderland intelligence, *fanno* played a key role in the overall nineteenth-century Ethiopian politico-military system, and were often in collusion with powerful *chewa* leaders who recognized their role. Of course, any support and recognition they received were clandestine. They were even disclaimed, until borderland *chewa* officers felt confident enough openly to take over their initiatives and skirmishing. In that sense, they were the unrecognized and informal advance guard of borderland operations. When it was convenient to accept what they had achieved,

---

[10] For an instance of *fanno* and official representations of borders to foreigners, see Arnold Weinholt Hodson, *Seven Years in Southern Abyssinia* (Ed. C. Leonard Leese), London: T. Fisher Unwin, 1927, pp. 170–7.
[11] Bulatovich, *Ethiopia through Russian Eyes*, 2000, p. 111.

they were recognized as the formally deployed advance guard and, if they wished to abandon hunting, as administrators.

During conflicts over local lands and in major confrontations in border areas, mobilization for campaigns promised amnesty to *fanno* or *shifta* hiding in the wilderness, and rewards to other warriors. These categories responded by proclaiming loyalty in *zeraf* sessions, sometimes identifying the names of 'masters' with superior claims to conducting the issues at hand. Certainly, borders were often springboards for capable warriors to become *mekwanent* (nobles), *mesafint* (princes) and *negest* (kings) – officials with high military and state titles. Aspiring, successful *chewa* leaders could pull together a substantial number of retainers, and might even campaign to take the throne of *neguse negest*. Some retainers might advise against the latter in favour of underlining the leaders' family right of succession to the position. Powerful patrons could reward their young participants with special places at their military banquets and *zeraf* sessions, and older warriors with capes of honour, swords and higher political positions. Such evaluative interdependence ensured continued social validation for success.

The frequency of *shifta*-generating rebellions aimed at asserting the right to organize access to communal lands had two processes. First, socially influential warriors challenging established authority and made their grievances and intentions publicly known through *zeraf* – expressed through gesticulations, use of weapons, defiant statements expressing political and military intentions – which helped them identify with local society supporting their views and opinions. Secondly, the words of their *zeraf* were transmitted from one military camp to another, thus also ensuring their political influence reached the wider society. Such broadcasting of warriors' intentions could sway regional political support, notably from young would-be warriors challenging the authorities in their own local communities. Depending on the cause they espoused, warriors could take their fighting forces to the borderlands, far from the influence or jurisdiction of the more powerful. As these individual rebels formed loose networks of active soldiers, the most powerful 'masters' courted them to enrol them in their service. If leaders of strong local centres of military power articulated their purpose as upholding the ideals of country and people, they could attract a large number of warriors whose localities would be key to the re-emergence of new sets of *chewa*. Thus, well-articulated messages and *shifta* organizational capacity could either weaken or strengthen the authority of the *neguse negest* and his local agents. In short, bravery attracted powerful sponsors for the better defence of Ethiopian territory, though the practice posed an overt challenge to the monarchs' authority.

Thus, politico-military duties were not exclusive to the monarchs or their representatives. The rivalry between the warriors and the monarchs over the right to control communal lands was in part the claim of the 'kings of kings' to ownership of all land. Their claim arose from resorting to the legitimacy given them by a prescribed source of authority, the *Kebre Negest*, of which we shall see more soon. Scholars have rightly identified the claim as theoretical, partly because *chewa* principles could not allow them such a claim to ownership of local lands. According to this principle, doing so would limit their belongingness only to single communities. They could only designate certain areas as *gult*, lands awarded as payment in lieu of salary to their administrative and military officers. Besides, by asserting themselves over lands in their communal territories, *chewa* warriors could aspire to achieve the highest political office, that of *neguse negest* or 'king of kings'. If land-focused challenges drove them to assert their right to giving *gult* rewards, monarchs who acquired that office by birthright had to reassert it militarily. The office of monarch was often attained by succeeding as a *chewa* warrior – through the *chewa* process rather than by birthright. Along with control of communal lands, therefore, this conflict of interest over the highest political position caused the frequent battles that have characterized Ethiopian history.

The monarchs' arms acquisition, mainly in the post-1855 period, won for them the primacy of their preferred prescriptive source of legitimacy. This is to say, the monarchs had practised warriorhood during their upbringing like other *chewa*, but in the 'modern' state, they found it convenient to remove the largely voluntary defence force and replace it with salaried soldiers and appointed leaders. Purposefully applying their principles to guard the frontiers in the service of a *negus* or of the *neguse negest*, some warriors exercised the option of openly rejecting or supporting the *neguse negest* and his agents. Their preference for being loyal to either the local conditions or the monarch accentuated their relationships (whether of conflict or coexistence) with people in the border areas. This resulted in too many strong warriors assuming authority and exercising power as their personal right while lacking the awareness needed for special policies along border areas. Tewodros II learned this from his early experience of external attack in his home area of Qwara. As a *neguse negest*, therefore, he deliberately set in motion a process that funnelled all the energy and capacity of protesters to strengthening and securing a strongly supported government. Partly under the influence of World War I, protagonists fought (at the Battle of Segele in 1916) over how to maintain a powerful government under a central monarch, as will be discussed later.

To apply land tenure and other resources across the population in the expansive spatial and ecological zones, the *chewa* warriors saw themselves as agents for organizing society and the individuals in it. In the far outer limits, where they were viewed as strangers, they referred to the superstructure of the state as the claimant of lands and people. They even evoked the monarchs' official claim to own all the land in Ethiopia. In deploying troops, as in actual battles, *fanno* groups that survived to the 1920s were not only useful but significant, for their presence indicated the local community's support. In the nineteenth century, they were famed for frequent small, informal offensives and harassment of the borderlands until the British colonial crackdown affected their roles. Many were subsequently incorporated as soldiers until the turn of the twentieth century. After Menelik changed the system of collecting tribute and achieved direct control, *chewa* leaders and their informal contacts such as the *fanno* lost the capacity to define what constituted 'borderlands'. The monarchs then negotiated with foreign colonial powers.

SOCIAL RIVALRY BETWEEN WARRIORS AND MONARCHS

The warriors' terms for asserting a unitary state of people and lands were antithetical to the prescriptive authority of the monarchs, and defining the 'insider–outsider' relationship described idiomatically the status of those in political power. Thus, in terms of controlling local land, the *neguse negest* were local 'outsiders' whose legitimacy derived only from the descent principle prescribed in the *Kebre Negest*. This associated them with an external ancestry of Israelite origins. Accordingly, although this biblical reference lessened their 'otherness', their exclusive putative access to the throne distanced them. Politically, socially and legally they were different from all 'others' in the community who actually owned and worked the land. In the medieval era of the 'wandering capitals', the monarchs roamed over all the lands to exact tribute and run their administration. The dominant warriors, whom the monarchs settled in far-off places, stressed their forebears' ancient communication with the locals. Of course, the power of these monarchs was different from that of the despised 'insiders' by virtue of its potency for exercising secular authority and political rights. Somewhat similarly, ruling families in some communities claimed to be both foreign and politically senior. Examples were the dynasty in Welayta that was said to be of Tigre origin, like most of the community; the *Boyna-Tigre*, as the farmers were called; and the despised category, *Chinesha*, which consisted of potters, blacksmiths and other manual workers. Some other communities in the region, who had similar claims connecting their rulers mostly to the Amhara and the Tigre, distanced the local population from power by recruiting mercenaries from neighbouring communities as their warriors and guards. In terms of the idiom of power relations among communities within the region, even mutually hostile neighbours lived in the same highlands and lowlands, the landscape features that the *chewa* used to define 'country'. Their relationships endured over long periods of history, as indicated in their myths and oral traditions. Whether the rulers actually came from the communities they claimed to hail from was immaterial, but claims of their historical origins placed powerholders at a safe distance, far removed from potential rivals locally or in the immediate neighbouring communities. In a sense, they resembled the so-called submerged and despised groups, but lacked their spiritual authority, whose inexplicable powers could not be challenged. As symbolic 'local outsiders' who were feared and distanced, the monarchs were placed in the same implicitly liminal position as traders and crafts producers. Nonetheless, as reflected in descriptions of both the powerful and the marginalized in relation to local communities, their 'otherness' was ambiguously downplayed.

Though socially supported local warriors collected tribute for the state, rivalling them over land were the monarchs whose prescriptive political legitimation gave them a symbolic value dating back millennia; their appointees from elsewhere referred to this. The rivalry was resolved by four nineteenth-century 'kings of kings', Tewodros II (r.1855–68), Tekle Giyorgis II (r.1868–71), Yohannes IV (r.1872–89) and Menelik II (r.1889–1913). Weapons acquisition by these monarchs played a large part in strengthening the regional tribute collectors, administrators and other 'masters' loyal to the state. Curbing the emergent warriors' assertion of rural authority over land required blocking the warriors' practices and processes of acquiring military skills, social rootedness and networking capacities. The upshot was that local communities became deprived of their main leverage with the state – land. The ban on hunting in the 1920s, for instance, undermined a vital element of self-training – the sense of symbolic transition from boyhood to responsible adulthood, and the chance of knowing the landscape traditionally touted as features of defence. With the old ideals eroded by the curbing of warriors' practices, the new conditions created a unidirectional flow of power in favour of the state.

The state was further strengthened when it increased its power through centralized administration. The monarchs had first encouraged the fighters to join their agents in the garrison towns to acquire higher status. The socially supported local leaders left their hamlets, the hubs of networking and support, and abandoned the idea of vying for the position of *neguse negest* ('king of kings'). Easily co-opted, upcoming retainers and freshly emerging local warriors found employment as guards and other functionaries in the urban centres. This left the monarchs as sole providers of military and political titles and paraphernalia. Of course, similar self-oriented and justice-asserting categories of warriors also emerged as rebels among the non-farming communities. The *chewa* differed from these by underlining a political link with the state of Ethiopia and its networks of communal lands and people that it claimed should hold together as Ethiopia.

Of course, some emergent warriors also supported the monarchs, realizing the changes in international politics, especially European colonialism. After Menelik II finally led the warriors against the first Italian invasion of 1896, his central control of land and other aspects of local administration continued to marginalize and undermine the warriorhood traditions. However, these *chewa* traditions resurfaced during the 1935–41 period thanks to the historical memories of the older generation of self-trained individuals. Some had brought up their young in the old *chewa* tradition during the 1920s, and though they were marginalized from politics, their positive response to mobilization in October 1935 helped to convince many people to rise to defend the country from external invasion. By the summer of 1936, they were criticizing the emperor's preference for diplomacy and his deference to the League of Nations. The state and its agents identified politically as Ethiopian, and consequently the informally emerging warriors of the

1930s identified with them. Their encouragement of the youth was partly responsible for the guerrilla warfare that the resistance fighters sustained until victory in 1941.

In that sense, the *chewa* constituted a state institution that, in comparison for instance with the judiciary,[12] was alone in employing the tradition of involving people from the grassroots. The degree of inherited pride that warriorhood generated seems to have been little affected down subsequent decades. In fact, *chewa* versions of history and ideals of personal responsibility for the public, and, depending on circumstances, for the monarchy and the state, permeated expressions of Ethiopian identity up to the early 1970s. This pride in the past was little affected even in the generations who were exposed to new, state-driven, ideological rhetoric and political acculturation – notably 'modernity', the adoption of socialism in the 1970s and ethno-federalism of state and society since 1991 – all of which remained impracticable.

FRIENDS AND FOES

Redefining people-based borders of the country with an eye on European colonial encroachments meant recognizing that Ethiopian territories began where British, French or Italian land-based control ended. This had implications for defining the borders both inclusively and exclusively. The way the Ethiopian state made decisions on the borders from afar vexed the warriors including the *fanno* and *shifta* who were still engaged in assertive activities of their own volition. However, at least in the south, west and east, the presence of colonialists on the doorstep of the regained 'lost territories' modified border politics and 'borderlands' as defined by the state. That is, though fully aware of the borders that Europeans were creating, the state had little option but to comply, while managing to accommodate the *fanno* sensitively.

The ever-emerging, self-confident warriors' notion of combining land and people to define Ethiopia differed from the European sense of territory. When faced by European colonial ventures along the borderlands in the nineteenth century, they joined the monarchs in asserting the sovereignty of the country. Needless to say, their power to decide independently on the matter lasted only until the third decade of the twentieth century. In the eyes of the *chewa*, the monarch's formal soldiery was an odd creation, ambiguous in being more akin to a private army than to what they had always considered the national army of proactive warriors. However, it was a tool of the centralizing, 'modernizing' state, and increasingly

---

[12] On other institutions such as the judiciary: Aberra Jembere, *An Introduction to the Legal History of Ethiopia, 1434–1974*, Hamburg: Lit Verlag Münster, 2000; on religious institutions: Donald Crummey, *Priests and Politicians: Protestant and Catholic Missions in Orthodox Ethiopia 1830–1868*, Oxford: Clarendon Press, 1972; J. Spencer Trimingham, *Islam in Ethiopia*, London: Oxford University Press, 1952; Taddesse Tamrat, *Church and State in Ethiopia, 1270–1527* (Oxford Studies in African Affairs), Oxford: Clarendon Press, 1972.

displaced the process of dedicated sacrifice for self-assertive personal identification with land, people and borders. The rulers of the 'modern' state controlled the defence process and prioritized diplomacy over war. This unilateral decision-making about borders affected the presence of *fanno* and *shifta* in border areas. Nonetheless, it would not be far-fetched to claim that the history of individual political responsibilities and ancestral achievements has influenced contemporary pride in the resilience of Ethiopia's national identity and sense of independence. The warriors' socio-politically generated beliefs left a legacy asserting Ethiopian territorial sovereignty, including their ideals and practices concerning friends and foes within the northeast African region.

Of course, profoundly affecting Ethiopian society and survival was the country's geopolitical position. This had made Ethiopia a thoroughfare for trade between the African hinterland and the Red Sea and Indian Ocean, as well as with the Mediterranean and the so-called Middle East. Given the old slave trade and other exploitation, it can be said that the military settlements that the monarchs imposed on many had also increased the safety and security of local communities that the slavers had been exploiting.[13] Excluding foreigners from, or at least controlling them, on the trade routes and frontiers complemented the emergent warriors' ideals of everyone engaging in protection and defence, if only by encouraging the whole population to be on a war footing.

Though the self-trained warriors shared with the monarchs the privilege of defining friends and foes, the soldiers' definition involved either incorporating or distancing people as 'insiders' or 'outsiders'. The politico-military strategies they applied rested on ambiguous terms and ameliorative practices of coexistence. Evoking long views of history about the northeast African region, they spoke as many local languages as possible in borderlands and engaged in patron–client relationships, including fictive and marital ones, and child adoption. Aiming at making local people friends or 'insiders' (*wegen*), they also co-opted as many of them as possible as retainers and other functionaries. Their critical military strategy following co-option was to move the most important local leaders away from their localities, with the lure of rewards in land, military titles and ranks, so as to tie them to the hierarchy with the obligation of serving the *neguse negest*.

The concept 'outsider foe' referred to the totally alien enemy (*dina*), technically categorizing and distinguishing it from the enemy (*telat*). There were some cases where the label *dina*, or its equivalent, *felfeltu*, carried the sense of being supernaturally evil. Thus, oral tradition has it that the Jemjem would leave their territories and migrate away if

---

[13] Contemporary discourse on the political creation of ethnicity and nationhood, depicting self as 'nationals' and the subjected as 'others' shows how taxation marginalized some in the nineteenth century and resulted in certain social perceptions in the twentieth. See Hultin, 'Perceiving Oromo: "Galla" in the Great Narrative of Ethiopia', in P. T. W. Baxter, Jan Hultin and Alessandro Triulzi (eds), *Being and Becoming Oromo: Historical and Anthropological Enquiries*, Lawrenceville, NJ: Red Sea Press, 1996, p. 82.

the Sidama, whom they sought to distance, decided to move into their area. The status of hostility 'differentiated' (but neither distanced nor excluded) 'external outsiders' (*dina*) from local society by banning an exchange of blood money with them. In the case of some former foes, the term *dina* has become restricted to those who would remain excluded from the northeast African region, though it does not refer to contemporary sovereign states neighbouring Ethiopia. Probably as a result of experiencing European colonialism, the term has also come to suggest those who are totally alien to the region.

INFORMATION GENERATION, GATHERING AND DISSEMINATION

To hold the right political space, a leader had to engage in an elaborate system of announcing his intentions and asserting his power within the community and the state. Making himself a capable *balabat* who was indispensable to local affairs might gain him support from higher officials, even powerful monarchs, in the chain of command. He would be called upon to raise troops during general mobilizations such as in 1896. His views on, and commitment to, the wider Ethiopian landscape could be used to share and create linkages with similar-minded people. In particular, contestations against the agents of the 'king of kings' and his administration of justice, especially over land rights, could be passed around as songs, prophecies and other means of communication so as to influence public opinion.

Access to information was important for *chewa* use of land as their idiom of organizing society and the individuals within it. Full awareness of then current information, laced with a sense of its historical significance, contributed to the durability of *chewa* traditions. Would-be military leaders made history by uttering their views and circulating them in special ways. They ranted their views, opinions or threats through *zeraf*, and made sure these were relayed to their intended audiences.

Generating and gathering information at public and ritual centres, including markets and churches, and transmitting it, were vital tools for forming opinion. Local officials, such as governors, issued government decrees and orders known as *awaj*.[14] This was done by beating the *negarit* ('drum of authority'), first outside their official residence and then outside the courts of governors, often repeating them on market days for all the *gebeyategna* (shoppers).[15] Those who heard the *awaj* reported it back to

---

[14] For a discussion of the *awaj* as an institution, see Bairu Tafla, 'The 'Awāğ: An Institution of Political Culture in Traditional Ethiopia', in Sven Rubenson (ed.), *Proceedings of the Seventh International Conference of Ethiopian Studies*, Addis Ababa: Institute of Ethiopian Studies; Scandinavian Institute of African Studies, Uppsala; African Studies Center, Michigan State University, East Lansing, 1984, pp. 365–72.
[15] For examples of such texts in Amharic see: 'The mobilization against the Italian invasion of 1935', in Mahteme Selassie, *Memories of Significance*,

their communities in the form of news, and, depending on its urgency, village criers took the information around to hamlets and houses. Aspirants to power responded with their *zeraf*, either by rallying at the courts of 'masters' or at independent military festivals quickly organized for the purpose. Those who were ready to challenge authority made their own *awaj*, sometimes using drums or criers.

Announcements could be made in this way about land rights and certain other social transactions, such as important marriages.[16] Communities handled this information with care, and in the partly literate areas such as northern Ethiopia, Harar and Jimma, scribes or other individuals recorded it in the marginalia of prayer and other religious books. Periodically, communities collected information about their local areas, and vital information, such as that concerning land matters, was maintained verbally for generations because elders made children memorize them. Also, 'There is in each village, one hereditary officer that cannot be displaced', wrote Plowden, and 'this institution ... preserves some appearance of order, in the absence of all written documents, amidst the whirl of revolutions and the rapid succession of dynasties and governors'.[17]

Disseminating information was equally important. In times of war, people relayed messages spontaneously, sometimes by shouting across valleys. Those who travelled long distances from their own communities – itinerant students, beggars, hermits, hunters, soldiers, traders and minstrels – were expected not only to gather but also to transmit information. Indeed the communication they carried was so important that traditionally (as today) spies disguised themselves as one of these categories on the move. Those who regularly went to different places within a neighbourhood and kept constant surveillance of events were given critical attention. 'Children', women and other subordinate people who travelled far and wide were considered transmitters of serious information because they passed their days for most of the year in the open, including just outside a community's neighbourhood, where, as they collected firewood, fetched water or grazed small domestic animals, they could easily notice the presence of strangers or predators such as hyenas, slave raiders and vagabonds.

(contd) 1962 EC, pp. 105–28, 276–9. A summary version of the type given out in the provinces is in እምሩ ኃይለ ሥላሴ (ልዑል ራስ) ካየሁትና ከማስታውሰው 2002 (Imru Haile Selassie (*Li'ul Ras*), *From What I Saw and Recollect*, Addis Ababa: Addis Ababa University Press, 2nd edn, 2002 EC), p. 265. On the full text of mobilization against the invasion of 1896, see Guèbrè Sellassié, *Chronique*, 1930–32, Vol. I, pp. 373–4.

[16] Reports on such transactions are basic to the studies of both Habtamu and Crummey. See Habtamu, *Land Tenure*, 2011, pp. 192, 197–8, 207, *et passim*. On the use of records on transfers through the sale of land and other means, see Crummey, *Land and Society*, 2000, pp. 182–97.

[17] Plowden, Walter Chichele, *Travels in Abyssinia and the Galla Country: With an Account of a Mission to Ras Ali in 1848*, ed. Trevor Chichele Plowden, London: Longmans, Green, 1868, p. 138.

Domestics and shepherds boys aged eleven or twelve, accompanied by smaller boys and girls as young as seven (or even sometimes three) also spent most of the day beyond the local farms and homesteads, mainly in grazing areas and by streams.[18] In some places shepherds collected cattle, sheep and goats from the various houses, and grazed and watered them further afield. Being the first to note new people or groups coming into a neighbourhood, they would even run to impart the information, or raise cries of warning, if they thought the newcomers had hostile intentions. They reported unexpected events immediately, transmitting them through alarms known as the *u'uta* or *irrita*: long drawn-out cries heard in the immediate area of incidents. It was considered a serious transgression when large numbers of people, especially bands that might be organized rebels (*shifta*), appeared near marketplaces, in woodlands or along rivers without prior communication between their leaders and the local community. Village elders would investigate and communicate with such bands from 'beyond', by which they meant from unknown areas outside their localities.

Women collecting wood or water, usually in the early morning or late afternoon, stopped to chat and exchange news. In some communities, as late as the 1950s, only women undertook inter-communal trading – for fear of *dina*. Attacking women was considered shameful in most communities in southern Ethiopia, and men's desire to ensure the safety of their women and children locally made the women subjects of conflict. Women talked about news affecting the community during their cooperative work or over coffee. They discussed vital news heard from the 'children', and later passed it on to their spouses who also gave significant attention to their observations. Older shepherds shouted greetings and news at the doors of houses on their way back in the evening, while younger ones took back details to their families. Even nowadays, shepherds specialize in singing what some among them compose or what they themselves make up. Their role in gathering information is proverbial. In the past their information included outcomes of battles, the views of local leaders, *zeraf* poems or news of unusual social events.

Adult community leaders in particular looked out for hidden meanings in the messages sent or brought by those regularly visiting the social and political boundaries and contact points between communities. In Gojam, for instance, coded information on the exact nature of a new event was shouted across to those in the distance. In eastern Wellega, local hostility to strangers, such as troops moving in large numbers, was shown by small animals of contrasting colours, such as goats or sheep, being freshly killed and hung on trees along major highways. As people also looked out for omens and disturbances in the natural environment, more or less like hunters, such messages were taken seriously. Those intending to travel would at least change the

---

[18] This is still the practice in most parts of rural Ethiopia. For the variations in local practices, see Pankhurst, *Economic History*, 1968, pp. 32–5.

direction, if not the date and time, of their departure. Elders followed up on serious news, if necessary sending young men (their 'children') to investigate further, or going out themselves before formally informing the community of new developments.

Different communities had their own points of contact for collecting information. These included market sites, springs, rivers, religious sites, woodlands and large grazing areas. In traditional Ethiopia, and much of the whole region of northeast Africa, markets tended to be spaces in the open countryside that farmers and cattle herders controlled.

Renowned markets, in particular, were considered attractive to all, and were deliberately visited for important information as well as for their products. They were held regularly on the particular days of the week after which they were named. (In the Sidama and some other calendars a week has five days.) Some were so old that towns had grown around them. As the favoured means of disseminating information far and wide, markets were centres where people of all backgrounds and pretensions met, started friendships or hostilities, and exchanged information, ideas and news. In most communities in the south there were elderly men and women who did nothing but collect information, accompanying younger people visiting the marketplace. In the north, such elders would sit outside their village waiting for people to pass by on their way to or from market. Markets and grazing grounds were not infrequently sites of conflict between neighbouring communities. Lifecycle rituals were, and still are, performed in markets. Oromo youth going out on their initial militaristic expedition (*folle*) started their songs in the marketplace. It was in markets that Sidama and Walayta women, including potters, introduced new brides to the community, and publicly acknowledged prominent women as wives and mothers; and it was in markets that the Gedeo punished juvenile delinquents.[19]

Metaphorically, the marketplace was where people from far and wide mixed and barriers broke down. Symbolically, taking oneself or one's news and views to the marketplace meant bringing something or someone to public attention. The loud exchange of greetings and information or other activities of the marketplace even guided those lost in the countryside to the highway (*awera godana*). Serious information gathering involved going together to markets and deliberately seeking out and meeting others from different neighbourhoods. In nineteenth-century Ethiopia, as today, it was normal to feel such curiosity about social aspects of the market and about 'news from beyond'. Even those who had to travel far stopped with their pack animals at beverage places just outside the market where women sold *tella* (beer) either in huts or under trees. Before returning to their neighbourhoods, people would deliberately visit these women for information or to hear singers' compositions on topical issues. On returning from these markets, they brought news, sometimes indirectly through songs they had picked up. Rather like those returning from church and other

[19] Tsehai Berhane-Selassie, 'The Balabat and the Coffee Disease', 1978.

religious centres, neighbours would ask shoppers and other travellers for information, expecting to share the news they had gathered.

Similarly, vital sources of information were professional and long-distance traders (*sirara negade*), who owed their safety to the number of well-armed people accompanying them.[20] They were known to travel overland between places as far apart as Massawa (Mitsewa), Nairobi (Inerobi) and Mombasa (Bombasa).[21] They could be absent from their own neighbourhoods for periods of two months to two years. Along the way, some of their retainers (the *gorodoma*, perhaps similar to 'dragoman') were sent home, visiting different markets, bringing goods and, wittingly or unwittingly, dispensing information over wide areas. Long-distance traders were particularly significant transmitters of non-urgent written and oral messages, including information for state administrators.[22] With the distance they covered and the safety and security they provided, such traders also facilitated the mobility of ordinary individuals. People in their seventies in the 1960s and 1970s reported that if a girl was unhappy in her neighbourhood, or if a man was in debt, families would take special precautions to prevent them 'going off with the *negade*'.

Despite the importance of information, social bias excluded some members of society from gathering and circulating it. Though their livelihood depended almost exclusively on marketplaces, where they traded their artefacts, several restrictions firmly excluded crafts producers such as potters, weavers, tanners, blacksmiths, and silversmiths and goldsmiths from engaging in the circulation of vital information. Indeed in many communities, crafts producers were not allowed to buy dairy products, in the belief that they might cast the evil eye on farmers' cattle. Not only did farmers avoid exchanging information with crafts sellers, even in the marketplace, but buyers generally hastened to complete their transactions by neither gossiping nor exchanging serious information with them. It is still largely normal for the stalls of craftspeople to be on the outer corners of markets, and for customers to visit them rather cautiously, leaving their young ones elsewhere with friends for fear of the 'evil eye'.

Information relayed through these spaces served to forestall division and conflict, as well as to assert harmony. Acquiring and managing important information from any source allowed self-assertive initiatives in local politics. Though responding to provocations in the marketplace was an act of public censorship, battles could also start on the basis of received information. Crossing beyond certain markets implied going over both geographical and social boundaries, and here again, local communities took seriously news of such events as 'running away from the market' or 'crossing the river' to seek shelter or start a new life elsewhere.

---

[20] Pankhurst, *Economic History*, 1968, p. 347.
[21] Oral reports by members of my family who migrated from Minjar to Sidamo in the 1880s.
[22] Pankhurst, *Economic History*, 1968, p. 337.

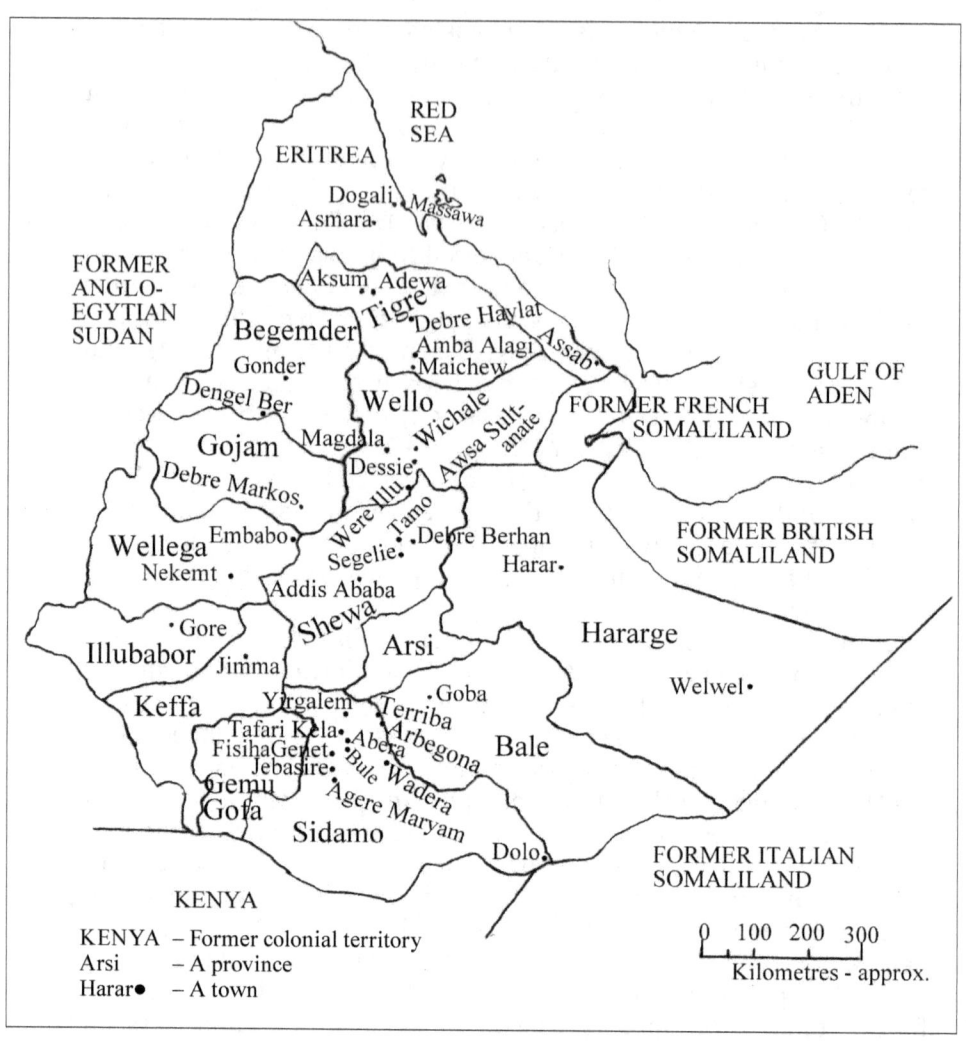

Map 1 Some of the place names referred to in the text (drawn by Peter Esmonde)

2

The Historical Context of Emergent Warriors

Historical setting is one of the key elements for understanding the socially rooted, popular, perpetually emergent individual warriors that the *chewa* were. This is because of their proverbial sensitivity to history, their loyalty to the local and national structures, and their practice of coalescing into cohesive forces across linguistic groups when faced with hostility. Pride in monarchs and regiments featured in their historical narratives, though most Ethiopians never strived to be literate in order to read about those histories. Nonetheless achieving titles and political positions in the hierarchically organized state was part of the *chewa* historical consciousness that remained a critical tenet for warriors' activities in the nineteenth century.

THE *CHEWA* AND THE *NEGUS* IN ANTIQUITY

The history of warfare in antiquity depicts a hierarchically organized Ethiopian state and society that used troops. Stone inscriptions and other ancient written sources indicate traditions in using terms such as *negus, neguse negest* and named military contingents. Sabaean inscriptions, probably from about the end of the sixth century BC, found in Axum, Yeha, Enda Ceros, Malazo, Matara and Kaskase, mention DMT and WRN dynasties (DMT and WRN are names found on stone inscriptions dating from a time when vowels were not used. Linguists continue to debate how they were meant to sound. I like to think of the first one as Damot, the name of a southwest region in medieval Ethiopia, and later also of a northwest region in current Ethiopia; but as a non-linguist, I have no supportive etymological evidence.) Military exploits of titled kings are mentioned in a Sabaean inscription dating from the fifth century BC in Yeha, in Greek, and later in Ge'ez inscriptions.

Titles designating monarchs and the names of regiments are two major features that should be noted with regard to subsequent history. A stone inscription from Adulis referred to a king who identified himself as a son of Ares, the war god, and described, among other things, his exaction of tribute from the people. He took half of their possessions for himself and allowed them to keep their lands as 'tributaries'.[1] His troops subjugated the pastoralist, commercial and warrior people along the Red Sea coast, and others in the region of Lake Tana and Gambella, as well as across the sea in parts of Arabia. Obviously confident of their loyalty, this king commanded the 'people of Solate' along the coast to guard it. Sergew notes that these conquests gained him control of valuable resources such as gold, incense and spices.[2]

Foreign writings, notably in Greek by Ptolemy III Euergetes (fl. 246–221 BC), depict Ethiopia as a well-known geographical location, although, not surprisingly, they are imprecise about its boundaries. Later, Strabo (c. 64 BC–c. AD 22), who called the source of the Nile Psebo, knew of Adulis, Axum and Berence. Attracted by the wealth of these cities, Augustus Caesar (r.27 BC–AD 14) tried to send an expedition. His great-great-grandson, Nero (r.AD 54–68), also had unfulfilled designs on Ethiopia.[3] Sources from the second and third centuries AD depict the growing power of the Agew-populated kingdom of Axum. According to Sergew, *The Periplus of the Erythrean Sea*, for instance, mentions a king of Axum, Zoskales (probably the Ze Haqile of the Ge'ez king lists) who thrived in AD 131–43. A stone inscription in Sabaean mentions another king, Gadar, this time using the term *negus*, rather than MLK (referring to *melek*) to mean king or overlord. The inscription indicates that Gadar was expanding his rule along the coast across the Red Sea around AD 130. This information tallies interestingly with that on Gadarat 'king of Habasites and of Axuman' in a later Ge'ez inscription narrating his military exploits taking territories there, reaching almost to Bab el-Mendeb.[4]

Equally clear in using the title was another Ge'ez inscription of an unknown date, but believed to be before AD 287. It is found in Deqe Mehari on the road to Keren (in present-day Eritrea), and reads:[5]

> King of kin
> Gs of Axumi
> Tes Great
> Sembrouthes came [and] set
> Up this stone in the year 24
> Of Sembrouthes the Great
> King.

There is no indication as to why this 'king of kings' entitled himself in this lofty manner. In any case, a famous Persian historian, Mani (c. AD 216–76), noted that Axum, ruled by Agew kings, was one of four

---

[1] The ancient historian (Cosmas Indicopleustes) who copied this inscription missed noting down the king's name. Sergew, *Ancient and Medieval History*, 1972, pp. 62–3.
[2] Sergew, *Ancient and Medieval History*, 1972, pp. 62–7.
[3] Augustus' expedition was diverted by the need to subjugate the Napatians on the way. See Sergew, *Ancient and Medieval History*, 1972, pp. 55–8.
[4] Sergew, *Ancient and Medieval History*, 1972, pp. 75–6 and p. 78.
[5] Sergew, *Ancient and Medieval History*, 1972, p. 12. The line breaks match those on the original inscription, reflecting the limited area of the stone in which it was carved.

great powers, the others being Babylon/Persia, Rome and China (Silis, according to him).⁶ Even as late as the eighth century, Ethiopia's king was depicted in today's Jordan as one of six major rulers of the world.⁷

It appears that the renown of Axum was waning by about the middle of the sixth century AD. Its kings faced serious rebellions that dominated the years between Ezana (r. in the first half of the fourth century AD) and Kaleb (r.c. AD 514–30). Rivalry between Kaleb's sons ended with one of them killed in a battle in Tigre. Earlier, in 543, Kaleb had to send two expeditions to quell an uprising against his viceroy, Esimiphaios, in Arabia. The rebel leader, Abreha, subsequently paid tribute to Kaleb in Axum, but made peace locally in Arabia and retained an autonomous status. He even attempted to expand his jurisdiction, making an unsuccessful attack against Mecca in 570 using elephants in his army. Though his sons succeeded him and ruled a few more years, other rebels allied with the Persians ended this last Ethiopian rule in Arabia.⁸

HISTORICAL NAMED TROOPS

The kings of Axum also used adjectives that might have been the names of clans or regions to which they originally belonged. Thus Aphilas, who ruled before Ezana, referred to himself as 'king of Axumites man of [Bisi] Dimele', and Ousanas referred to himself as 'king of Axumites man of Gisene'.⁹ Regiment names included *Mhaza, Mettin, Dakwen, Hara* and *Laken*. Interestingly, Ezana also called the captains of his troops *negest* (the plural for *negus*), and referred to several regiments by specific names including *Dakwen, Damawa, Falha, Halen, Hara, Laken, Maggaro, Mattin,* and *Sabarat Sena*. Probably as a general way of calling them 'his men', Ezana also used the term *sew* (here clearly meaning 'people' and 'human beings') to refer to his soldiers.¹⁰ Ezana sent out troops, whom he then followed personally, to punish rebels when the Serene of Afan attacked and killed a merchant caravan, according to Sergew. In this instance, he used other terms to describe the troops: '(ሠርዌ ሙሓዛት) [*serwe muhazat*] the young army of commandos so to speak;...ሠርዌ ዳክን [*serwe dakwen*] the elephant fighters; ... (ሠርዌ ሐራ) [*serwe hara*] the infantry'.¹¹ The word ሠርዌ (*serwe*) referring to the troops is reminiscent of the modern word ሠራዊት (*serawit*), carrying

⁶ Sergew, *Ancient and Medieval History*, 1972, pp. 81–2
⁷ Haggai Erlich, *Ethiopia and the Middle East*, Boulder, CO: Lynne Reinner, 1994, pp. 11, 193.
⁸ Sergew, *Ancient and Medieval History*, 1972, p. 145.
⁹ Sergew, *Ancient and Medieval History*, 1972, pp. 82–3; See Aphilas, in Michael Belaynesh, S. Chojnacki and Richard Pankhurst (eds), *The Dictionary of Ethiopian Biography From Early Times to the End of the Zagwé Dynasty c. 1270 AD*, Addis Ababa: Institute of Ethiopian Studies, Addis Ababa University, 1975, pp. 22–3.
¹⁰ Merid W. Aregay, 'Military Elites', 1997, p. 34.
¹¹ Sergew, *Ancient and Medieval History*, 1972, p. 95.

the same meaning. Some of these ancient kings who, according to Merid W. Aregay, gloried in their troops also referred to them as *ahzab*, a term that remained in use two hundred years after Ezana.[12]

FEASTS FOR ANCIENT TROOPS

Associated with these monarchic titles and military names were some depictions of weapons, festivities and tribute types. Drawing attention to this, Sergew notes that the Greek inscription at Adulis shows that the king (Cosmas was unable to decipher his name because of an eye problem) gained valuable resources such as gold, incense and spices, and that the monument he set up depicts 'spears, daggers, swords, axes and shields'.[13] These were possibly made from 'best quality' iron imported from India.[14] A coin of Endybis (fl. c. third century AD), one side of which shows his possible clan, Dakhy, and the other his effigy wearing an earring, is also of interest.[15] This decoration raises the question of its possible connection with the glory of hunting, as will be discussed concerning later times in Chapter 6. A possible link between the ancient world and another practice that was familiar in later centuries – that of feasting the troops – is offered in at least one inscription:[16]

ጽሕፈ ብዘት ንጉሠ
አጋቦ ዝሓውልት
ዚአሁ ስሒበ
ሕዝበ አጋቦ አተመ ቆዐት
በ፲፭ አለታት
ሡዋህ አሰየ ፭፻፳
ጽሕባት ወሕብስት አሰየ
፳፻፳ ወ፳፻፳.

Has written Bizet King of
Agabo [on] this stele
Of his own after he had subdued
The people in Qo'at
In fifteen days
And donated 520 jars of beer
And bread he gave
20,620.

According to some scholars, Axumite rule declined due to the loss of commerce, probably as a result of the diversion of Red Sea trade to the Gulf.[17] Merid attributes the demise of Axum to the frequency of

[12] Merid W. Aregay, 'Military Elites', 1997, p. 32.
[13] Sergew, *Ancient and Medieval History*, 1972, pp. 62–3.
[14] Sergew, *Ancient and Medieval History*, 1972, p. 73.
[15] Sergew, *Ancient and Medieval History*, 1972, p. 82.
[16] Sergew, who places this inscription early in the fourth century AD, also notes the lack of clarity on whether Bizet was a king under the 'king of kings' in Axum or the supreme king himself. Sergew, *Ancient and Medieval History*, 1972, pp. 89–90.
[17] In present-day Eritrea, Debarwa, Digsa and Asmara are cited as examples of cities that were replaced. Ayele Tekle-Haymanot, 'Le antiche gerarchie dell'Impero Etiopico', *Sestante*, 1965, Vol. 1, No. 2, pp. 61–7; Richard Pankhurst,

rebellions, notably pressures from pastoralist lowlanders.[18] A significant pressure that finally challenged Axum's power base was the rise of Yodit, Queen of the Bete Israel, about AD 940. Forced to abandon the established centre of power, the last monarch, Dil Nead, fled Axum and headed south. Anbesa Wedm, who arrived in Haik, made a town there. In neighbouring Lasta he may also have been the founder of Roha, famous for its monolithic architecture. Roha is considered to have been Ethiopia's capital under the Zagwe dynasty, which lasted until about 1270. Its importance has overshadowed the fact that nearby Adefa was their actual capital.[19] Two contingents stationed near Zobel to protect the new power centre, Lasta, were called *Jan Amora* and *Jan Qantaffa* (noteworthy for the use of *jan*, an Agew word meaning elephant, which is associated with the word *janhoy*, 'your majesty'). The dynasty saw the rise of these and other towns that became associated with the administration of settlements of military contingents, as will be discussed further below. Merid noted that Amde Tsion (r.1314–44) referred to most contingents according to their home bases in 'Damot, Saqalt, Gonder, Hadiyya, Tigre, Gojjam, Waggara, Korem, Beguna, Amhara and Shewa'.[20] This monarch also named some of his troops *Tekula*, *Qeste Nihib* and *Harab Gonda*[21] (respectively 'bee dart'; 'fox' and 'measure of'; 'top' or 'principled' troop). The word *harab* eventually became *arbegna*, 'patriot',[22] a designation for the resistance fighters of 1935–41, and *hadar*, like another troop name from the fourteenth century, *Damot Hadar*, seems to relate to the current word *wotader* for 'soldier'.

THE 'WANDERING MONARCHS'

The Zagwe dynasty led to a peripatetic existence for monarchs, who roamed with thousands of courtiers, soldiers and administrators. Hence the designation 'wandering capitals'. The monarchs travelled among different communities over wide regions to collect tribute, administer land tenure, and maintain and enforce their rule.[23] An instance of this is reflected in songs praising the success of Amde Tsion in the Gurage and Hadya regions. The wandering monarchs' military power relied on the loyalty of the soldiers seeking to attain high levels of authority. Nonetheless, they drew their legitimacy from the prescribed source and even engaged in creative genealogy to good effect to realize that purpose. They successfully incorporated people through their agents,

---

(contd) *History of Ethiopian Towns: From the Middle Ages to the Early Nineteenth Century*, Ernst Hammerschidt, F. Steiner, 1982, pp. 73–4.
[18] Merid W. Aregay, 'Military Elites', pp. 31–7.
[19] Sergew, *Ancient and Medieval History*, 1972, p. 268.
[20] Merid W. Aregay, 'Military Elites', p. 42.
[21] Merid W. Aregay, 'Military Elites' p. 43.
[22] Kidane Weld Kifle, *Book of Grammar*, 1948 EC.
[23] Crummey, *Land and Society*, p. 74; Ronald J. Horvath, 'The Wandering Capitals of Ethiopia', *Journal of African History*, no. 2 (1969) pp. 205–19.

making sure the fortunes of the emergent warriors related closely to theirs and paying them with their limited access to lands.

These monarchs had the express duty of removing or at least checking threats from external enemies. They brought their loyal soldiers to balance their admired political strategy of employing mercenaries (who could not be considered for the task of keeping out external enemies and defining the realm's territory) by settling them along the border areas. In this regard a national preoccupation that featured down the centuries was keeping open access to the port of Massawa and struggling internally against actual or assumed surrogates of *dina* along the Red Sea coast.

The monarchs had just a few small, scattered administrative urban centres.[24] Roha (later known as Lalibela), the capital of the Zagwe dynasty, was the last permanent capital for many centuries.[25] Defending the country from external enemies as well as controlling the expansive realm of the monarchs depended largely on the military contingents that followed them around, or those they had settled in the borderlands, both close to and far from their 'wandering capitals'. Loyal nobles who anchored the power of the state and ran its administration stayed in various regions drawing their livelihood from *gult* lands designated for administrative purposes. The *gult* they were paid reverted to the monarch at dismissal or death. The kings also paid the self-trained, loyal warriors for regular military services by giving them various forms of land grants specified for recruiting military servicemen, lands known as *maderya*, as will be discussed further in association with how the military related to land tenure. Subsequently, the settlements became instrumental in staking historical claims to borderlands and other territories in many parts of the region.

THE *KETEMA*

The monarchs of the 'wandering capitals' considered the scattered settlements of soldiers along Ethiopia's borders as guardians of country, king and religion. They even tried to use them to regain a foothold by the Red Sea. This soldiery asserted the authority of the peripatetic monarchs and offset the persistent rivalry between the ever-emerging warriors in society. An indication that the tide was turning in favour of these peripatetic monarchs came when they started building palaces and administrative centres. Also the campaigns of Amde Tsion (r.1314–44), reasserted his authority in the territories of Damot and Gafat in 1313, and Hadya, Sirka, Dawaro and Bale in 1332.[26] These centres of political and military operations were abandoned soon afterwards, supposedly for lack of food and fuel, which meant staying away for

---

[24] Crummey, *Land and Society*, 2000, p. 22.
[25] Crummey, *Land and Society*, 2000, p. 31.
[26] Jules Perruchon, 'Histoire des guerres de Amde Seyon, roi d'Ethiopie', *Journal Asiatiques*, Series 8, XIV (1889).

'not less than ten years'.[27] Over time, the peripatetic monarchs failed to sustain the link with the settled soldiers. It was almost a century afterwards that Zera Yaqob (throne name, Qostentinos I, r.1434–68) founded Debre Berhan in 1456. He lived there 'for twelve of the last fourteen years of his life, building an extensive palace and a number of churches'. His son, Be'ide Maryam (r.1468–78), stayed there for only the first few years of his reign.[28] This was the longest after Roha that the monarchs settled in a town. Berera, within present-day Addis Ababa, was sometimes the capital, e.g. for part of the reigns of monarchs from Dawit I (r.1380–1412) to Libne Dingil (r.1508–40), but it was destroyed by the *Imam* Ahmad ibn Ghazi, mentioned above. Gelawdewos (r.1540–59), who died fighting against Nur, the Adal *sultan* and successor to the *imam*, founded the city of Agraroha in Dawaro and another city in Waj. Under pressure from the Oromo migration, Sertse Dingil (r.1563–97) took his capital to Begemder (followed there by others such as the monk Bahrey from Gemu Gofa). For a brief period, Iyasu I (r.1682–1706) retrieved lands up to the Gibe River and Ennarya, campaigning from Gonder.

These monarchs and others after them strived to sustain their far-flung territories by continuing to plant military contingents. Their semi-permanent urban towns were followed by the founding of temporary administrative centres, in reality garrison towns, known as *ketema* – defence-oriented administrative centres. Within a century after Gonder was founded in 1636, government officials (*mekwanent*) began to live there and in other *ketema* permanently. In the third quarter of the eighteenth century foreign observers such as James Bruce of Kinnaird witnessed the residents of Gonder being fashionable, sophisticated, urbane and almost decadent. Leading its social life were the officials who were meant to anchor the power of the monarchs in the rural base. This urban-based administration led to serious challenges to the monarchs' prescriptive basis of power by the late eighteenth century. By the nineteenth century, stereotypes specified its distance from countrymen (*balager*) in such sayings as 'the children of the *chewa* [reside] in town', and the 'crude', 'uncouth' and even 'stupid' 'remain' in the country. In fact, abandoning control of the *chewa* settlements to live in towns intensively disconnected the state from its jurisdiction in the rural areas.

Similar *ketema* included Debre Tabor and Chilga in Begemder,[29] Adewa in Tigre[30] and later, Entoto in Shewa. Locally powerful warriors began

---

[27] Pankhurst, *History of Ethiopian Towns*, 1982, p. 41.
[28] Pankhurst, *History of Ethiopian Towns*, 1982, p. 41.
[29] Rosita Forbes, *From Red Sea to Blue Nile: Abyssinian Adventure*, New York: Macauley, 1925, p. 257; Henry A. Stern, *Wanderings among the Falashas of Abyssinia: Together with a Description of the Country and its Various Inhabitants*, London: Wertheim, Macintosh, and Hunt, 1862, p. 46.
[30] Henry Salt, *A Voyage to Abyssinia, and Travels into the Interior of that Country, Executed Under the Orders of the British Government, in the Years 1809 and 1810.* London: F. C. and J. Rivington, 1814, p. 424.

asserting themselves in these garrisons.[31] An example from the nineteenth century included *Dejazmach* Biru Goshu's hold of Jibela, a famous impregnable fortress in Gojam. When Tewodros II dislodged him from it, his wife reportedly refused to negotiate her husband's release, arguing that he should not have lost it in the first place.[32] Also significant were Ankober and the fortress in Tamo, both in Shewa. Bafena, then queen of Menelik II, contested Tamo when she rebelled against him, but she was soon forced to give it up.[33] In 1890 *Ras* Alula garrisoned Asmara, on top of the Hamasen escarpment, to keep out the Egyptians and British who had been making incursions there since the 1870s.[34] In the south too, the availability of firearms[35] increased the foundation of such garrison towns as Aberra on particularly prominent hilltops. Though this last was abandoned in favour of Agere Selam, most eventually developed into key urban centres, seats of power and political administration.

With increasing influx of firearms, the hilltops where the *ketema* were built served as prime defence positions during emergencies: people in hilltop and mountaintop settlements could 'relay messages by shouting from mountain to mountain'.[36] They attracted the self-trained, aspiring youth of rural society, who migrated to offer their services. Some showed off their military skills and reportedly achieved fame serving these urban-based 'masters', who organized games and frequent raids and counter-raids characteristic of the period. After the demise of the Gonderine court dynamics that had made space for autonomy and the Era of Princes, the contingents in the *ketema* played military roles similar to those others had played in the past. This was to change yet again when the emperors gained full control of the soldiers and marginalized the *chewa*, notably after the 1880s.

MILITARY CONTINGENTS

The practice of stationing named *chewa* troops in far-off regions, which took some peripatetic monarchs on campaigns for which they were glorified in their chronicles, probably influenced the formation of

---

[31] Guèbrè Sellassié, *Chronique*, 1930–32, Vol. I, pp. 170, 204.
[32] Stern, *Wanderings*, 1862, p. 72.
[33] Guèbrè Sellassié, *Chronique*, 1930–32, Vol. I. p. 135.
[34] Because of continuing fall-out from the chaos of the *zemene mesafint*, Asmara was already an easy target for contestation by the British and Egyptians in the 1870s. See Sven Rubenson, *The Survival of Ethiopian Independence* (Lund Studies in International History 7), London: Heinemann in Association with Esselte Studium and Addis Ababa University, 1976, pp. 333–4; Zawde Gabre-Sellassie, *Yohannes IV of Ethiopia*, 1975, pp. 60, 67–8; Pankhurst, *Economic History*, 1968, p. 693.
[35] Richard Pankhurst, *A Social History of Ethiopia: The Northern and Central Highlands from Early Medieval Times to the Rise of Téwodros II*, Addis Ababa: Institute of Ethiopian Studies, Addis Ababa University, 1990, pp. 277–95.
[36] Mesfin Welde-Mariam, *An Introductory Geography of Ethiopia*, Addis Ababa: Berhanena Selam, 1972, p. 178.

similar military towns. Said to have existed in the days of Menelik I, the first such soldiers were reportedly stationed at a place called Medebay. Troops carrying the same name were later found in Tigre, Semien, Tselemt and Wegera. Others, called Amara, were stationed in 1130 on the rural people of Wadla, Begemder, Saynt and Weleqa, host communities in the northern regions during the early Axumite and Zagwe periods, and as we will see, similarly billeted soldiers were mentioned through the centuries. These included units such as *Sellus Hayle, Badel Tsehai, Giyorgis Hayle, Senan (Seqeyat), Afro Aygeba, Aqetzer, Qurban, Wenbedie, Gendebel, Gondere, Kokeb, Bashbiziq, Legewon, Amhara* and many others.[37] A prominent cavalry regiment, the *Yehabeta*, lived within the kingdom of Ennarya in the west, ensuring that tribute flowed to the *neguse negest*. Members of this corps had been intermarrying with the local population of Ennarya and enjoying the protection of its kingdom at least since the thirteenth century.[38] A corps known as *Be Adal Mebreq* in Dawaro, present-day Bale and Sidamo in the south, was settled by the founder of Debre Berhan, Zera Yaqob (r.1434–68).

Nonetheless, oral information recalls some early contingents specifically as the 'origins' of clans in southern Ethiopia. An instance of this is the oral reports of the Gurage, which say that they came as soldiers from Gur'a in present-day Eritrea.[39] Similar recollections also appear in association with the kingdoms of the Gibe Basin, which came into existence on the ruins of Ennarya. The settlers appear to have facilitated the transmission of the ideals and influences of the state far and wide. To assert control of their military and political administrative lands, the warriors partly evoked local history and performed certain duties keenly, such as holding courts of justice and accessing information on land. Narratives of ruling families in Keffa, Welayta and pockets in Hadya also make similar connections with historical *chewa*.[40] The royal house of the kingdom of Welayta, which arose in the early thirteenth century on the ruins of old Damot and existed until 1894, claimed descent from a group of immigrants rather than settled soldiers, from either Gonder or Tigre.[41] This appears to have been known

[37] Bairu Tafla, *Aşma Giyorgis and his work: History of the Gāllā and the Kingdom of Šawā* (Äthiopistische Forschungen, Band 108), Stuttgart: Franz Steiner Verlag Wiesbaden GMBH, 1987, p. 139.
[38] Pankhurst, *A Social History*, 1990, pp. 295–6.
[39] W. A. Shack, *The Central Ethiopians: Amhara, Tigriña [sic] and Related Peoples* (Ethnographic Survey of Africa, ed. Daryll Forde, North-Eastern Africa, Part IV), London: International African Institute, 1974, p. 98.
[40] Eike Haberland, 'The influence of the Christian Ethiopian Empire on southern Ethiopia', *Journal of Semitic Studies*, Vol. 9, No. 1, 1964, pp. 235–8; Zawde Gabre-Sellassie, *Yohannes IV of Ethiopia*, 1975, pp. 5–6.
[41] Jacques Bureau, 'The "Tigre" Chronicle of Wollaita; A Pattern of Kingship', in Richard Pankhurst, Ahmed Zekaria and Taddese Beyene, *Proceedings of the First National Conference of Ethiopian Studies*, Addis Ababa: Institute of Ethiopian Studies, Addis Ababa University, 11–12 April 1990, pp. 49–64; Tsehai Brhane Selassie, 'The question of Damot and Wälamo', *Journal of Ethiopian Studies*, Vol. 13, No. 1, January 1975, pp. 37–46.

in the literature that the *chewa* accessed in the nineteenth century, and the soldiers' findings there included church ruins and relics that linked the place to the hagiography of a saint of Ethiopian Christianity – *Abune* Tekle Haymanot (c. 1215–1313), a thirteenth-century monk who had evangelized in Welayta.

The *Abe Lahm*, an ancient contingent that retained its Ge'ez name, survived and participated in the Battle of Adewa in 1896. Also known as *Weregenu* (Oromo), or *Gendebel* (which sounds Amharic), it was phased out in the 1920s. The *Werwari*, *Gondere* and *Barud Bet* were names of contingents that were similarly settled in the nineteenth century on lands where earlier monarchs had reportedly deployed corps of soldiers, the history of which became part of the long-term strategy that justified the territorial borders of western, southern and eastern Ethiopia.[42] In the southwest, south and southeast they became known collectively as Amhara, a catch-all term covering people speaking various languages from the central and northern highlands.

The capacity and loyalty of commanders and soldiers in the earlier, far-flung settlements compensated for the geographical distance between the monarchs and the regions they ruled. However, ecological pressure from the eastern lowlands, notably the Red Sea coast, appears to have undermined the power of the monarchs to control the troops settled in the regions. This culminated in two internal developments in the sixteenth century: the rise of the warrior *imam* from Adal who, as mentioned above, defeated the troops, and the rapid and steady migration of the Oromo from the south. The resultant weakness of the *neguse negest* was compounded by their failure to stem the erosion of their authority by exploiting religious divisions and rivalry for power among their courtiers. The monarchs, who were at first reduced to relying only on loyal soldiers nearer their camps, lost even this later in the eighteenth century.

These sixteenth-century events fractured and weakened the frontier *chewa* settlements in these regions, which eventually disappeared. Once the monarchs lost control of the contingents, their regime necessarily weakened, as the observant monk *Abba* Bahrey commented.[43] Already by 1565, Serse Dingil faced the problem of a contingent known as *Giyorgis Haile*, which first raided the Gurage and later attacked his camp. Another, called *Hamelmal*, sacked the monasteries of Endegebtan in Shewa. In what Crummey dubbed 'praetorianism', troops close to the monarch actually began to be involved in determining succession to the throne or, in one case at least, crowning their leaders.[44] Such occur-

---

[42] For a comprehensive indication of the names of historical contingents and the circumstances of various borderlands and associated military engagements, see Richard Pankhurst, *The Ethiopian Borderlands: Essays in Regional History from Ancient Times to the End of the 18th Century*, Lawrenceville, NJ: Red Sea Press, 1997.

[43] C. F. Beckingham and G. W. Huntingford, *The Prester John of the Indies: being the narrative of the Portuguese Embassy to Ethiopia in 1520, written by Father Francisco Alvares*, London: Hakluyt Society, 1961, p. 117.

[44] Donald Crummey, *Land and Society*, 2000, pp. 56–7.

rences signalled the breakdown of *chewa* traditions, and was probably caused first by the wars of Ahmed Gragn and then those of the Oromo, which had changed by the late sixteenth century from mere *gada*-based annual raids to sustained large-scale warfare known as *butta*.[45]

Though the monarchs, notably Gelawdewos (r.1543–59), tried to re-establish their authority, the loss of land-based resources was a serious blow. Also affecting the state reserves were the mistakes that Serse Dingil (d. 1596) made. He even had to pillage Tigre, Dembya, Gojam and Damot in order to support his troops who, according to him, were 'numerous, indeed innumerable'.[46] Among his strategies that further confused the system and its relationship with the monarchs' authority were the granting of *gult* land to someone as *rest* for his children, the transfer of lands reserved for supplying horses and honey to another private person, and gifts of other land to a private Muslim man, and to a woman, this time along with its tax and even its political jurisdiction.[47] His unpopularity intensified when, from his base in Dembya, he took 'all of its lands into his hands and established [*chewa*] on them'.[48]

The weakness of his reign, compounded by problems of succession and unrest among the troops, launched a crisis the following century regarding land–people relations. A *chewa* regiment called the *Qurban*, which Serse Dingil had established in 1575 in Dembya, asserted itself against the reigning monarch, Ya'qob, in 1603. Its commander, Ras ZeSelassie, who had been married to the king's sister in an attempt to placate him, exiled the king to Ennarya and crowned ZeDingil. However, ZeDingil managed to suppress this regiment and made a general call to raise troops who were personally loyal to him. Instituting a number of administrative reforms regarding these concerns, he issued an edict with the catchy phrase ሰብእ ሕራ መሬት ግዙር, the much-debated meaning of which Crummey accepts as 'Man is free; land is tributary'.[49] It promised farmers freedom from taxation (for instance in the form of labour) and their own land. Restricting the troops from using the farmers rather than their lands in taxation, the edict provoked one regiment, the *Qurban*, into rallying together to kill ZeDingil, which they did, and after considering abolishing the crown completely right there on the battle site, they brought back Ya'qob.

Although Crummey reports that the *Qurban* and their *gult* land administrator commanders constituted a class, the evidence from this one contingent in Dembya is probably insufficient for such a generalization. What made matters worse for the monarch was granting the Jesuits lands he had confiscated from the Ethiopian Orthodox Church in Dembya, Wegera and Gojam.[50] Susneyos (r.1606–32), who succeeded Ya'qob, started this discord, which intensified in the 1610s and 1620s,

[45] Crummey, *Land and Society*, 2000, p. 54, 56.
[46] Crummey, *Land and Society*, 2000, p. 57.
[47] Crummey, *Land and Society*, 2000, p. 61.
[48] Crummey, *Land and Society*, 2000, p. 57.
[49] Crummey, *Land and Society*, 2000, p.63–4.
[50] Crummey, *Land and Society*, 2000, p. 69.

when he (Susneyos) revoked the land grants that his predecessors, since the days of Yekuno Amlak in the thirteenth century, had been regularly confirming to local people.

Although this calmed with the expulsion of the Jesuits in 1632, the turbulence it caused augmented the rapid takeover by the Oromo of much of the territory previously guarded by settled regiments. Discussing this speedy process, several historians note that ecological and demographic forces may have pushed the Oromo and the Somali to 'dramatic prominence' and capacity in the early sixteenth century in order to challenge the monarchy of the *neguse negest*, and Donald Crummey suggests that such a conclusion 'awaits discovery'.[51] However, Bairu Tafla assertively attributes this speed to the Oromo assimilationist method of warfare.[52] An anthropologist details their socially rooted *gada* system, which expected their youth to engage actively in warfare annually and incorporate societies that they came across.[53] The socio-military practice around the *gada* system certainly grew further after the Oromo began acquiring horses around 1554–62[54] and later accessed firearms. Strengthening this argument is Mohammed Hassan's assertion that the politically disparate Oromo clans came upon a corps of settled soldiers, the *Yehabeta*, in semi-autonomous Ennarya in the southwest; and by the seventeenth century the Oromo, who had turned to settled agriculture, had become wealthy merchants trading in slaves, gold, ivory and civet; they also organized politically and increased their military capacity. This had gained them control of the vital trade routes to and from Ennarya.[55] Eventually taking over the ancient kingdom of Ennarya, they forced another *chewa* corps, the *Ilmegwazit Boran*[56] (whose name probably reflects earlier dealings with the Oromo) to seek help. *Ras* Se'ela Krestos and *Dejazmach* Buko, two officers of Susneyos (r.1606–32), withdrew this corps, settling some of its troops in Machakal, Mecha and Achefer, in present-day Gojam.[57] A branch of the Oromo reached Tigre by 1642 and established ruling families in Yeju a century later. This gave the Oromo (already speaking the court language, Amharic) a central role in the courts of the *neguse negest* in Gonder.

Susneyos, who had lived among the Oromo as a young man, accommodated some Oromo, organizing and settling them as contingents by taking away lands that were endowments to churches such as Bajana in Lay Armacheho – thus starting to integrate the Oromo into the *chewa*

[51] Crummey, *Land and Society*, 2000, p. 51.
[52] Crummey, *Land and Society*, 2000, p. 54–5; Bairu Tafla, *Aşma Giyorgis and his work*, 1987, p. 48.
[53] Asmarom Legesse, *Gada: Three Approaches to the Study of African Society*, New York: Free Press, 1973, pp. 8–9.
[54] Beckingham and Huntingford, *The Prester John of the Indies*, 1961, p. 115, fn. 4.
[55] Mohammed Hassen, *The Oromo of Ethiopia: A History, 1570–1860*, Trenton, NJ: Red Sea Press, 1994, pp. 64–9.
[56] Mohammed Hassen, *The Oromo of Ethiopia*, p. 69.
[57] Bairu Tafla, *Aşma Giyorgis and his work*, 1987, p. 761.

hierarchy. His successor, Fasil (r.1632–67), who established Gonder as his capital in 1632, re-established some church lands. His reign was noted for the construction of palaces and churches (including the restored Maryam church in Axum in 1655–6, to which the *tabot*, representing the Ark of the Covenant was brought back after an eleven-year exile); but it was fraught with rebellions by his son near his court, and in Lasta. His successful suppression of such risings meant a peaceful transition of power to his son Yohannes I (r.1667–82). For his grandson, Iyasu I (r.1682–1706), it ensured an ability to continue using *gult* to award contingent leaders and control parts of the south, for instance in the Gibe area, albeit for the last time for two hundred years.[58]

In addition to the corrosive religious arguments that had their roots in the proselytizing attempts of Portuguese priests in the sixteenth century, the power of the 'kings of kings' was further eroded by courtiers' chaotic manipulation of succession to the throne in the early eighteenth century. Thus, after Iyasu I abdicated in 1706 and retreated to a monastery, he was murdered by his son and successor, Tekle Haymanot (r.1706–8), who had taken a different side in the religious controversy. Other courtiers murdered this patricide, nicknamed 'The Cursed', and in a matter of twenty years they removed and replaced four out of five monarchs with their favourites. They brought in Tekle Haymanot's uncle, Tewoflos (r.1708–11), but he died in suspicious circumstances. His successor, another uncle, Yostos (r.1711–16), abdicated because of illness in favour of a third uncle, Dawit III (r.1716–21), whose replacement, Bekaffa (r.1721–30) ruled the longest of this family. Bekaffa removed most of the powerful nobles, trying to stop their interference, but his death launched another twenty years of continued rivalry over the succession. His eight-year-old son, Iyasu II (r.1730–55), had to rule under the regency of his mother, Mentwab and when Iyasu died, 'possibly poisoned by his sister Melmal',[59] his successor Iyoas (r.1755–69) ruled under another regency made up of a council of nobles.

This whirlwind sea change was followed by the appropriation of the monarchs' political power, initially by *Ras* Mikael Sehul who migrated from Tigre to Gonder in 1769. He killed two emperors within six months, including Yohannes II whom he had married to his granddaughter.[60] He gave the crown to Tekle Haymanot II, his fifteen-year-old great-grandson, son of Yohannes II. While Mikael Sehul was campaigning elsewhere, others replaced Tekle Haymanot II with Susenyos II, but the *ras* reversed this in late 1770. In 1771 a coalition of nobles (including *Dejazmach* Wend Bewesen, *Ras* Haile Yosadiq and *Dejazmach* Kenfu Adam) defeated this first kingmaker. By

[58] Crummey, *Land and Society*, 2000, pp. 81–4.
[59] Chris Prouty and Eugene Rosenfeld, *Historical Dictionary of Ethiopia* (African Historical Dictionaries, No. 32), Metuchen, NJ: Scarecrow Press, 1981.
[60] *Ras* Mikael Sehul deposed Iyoas and within days had him strangled, having already replaced him with Yohannes II, husband of the *ras*'s granddaughter and Iyoas' elderly uncle. He later had Yohannes poisoned. Crummey, *Land and Society*, 2000, p. 112; Prouty and Rosenfeld, *Historical Dictionary*, 1981.

then the thoroughly weakened monarchy was controlled by real political power than by the opportunity to show off status and wealth, and by manipulating the succession, the prescriptive rules of which they recognized. Using the wealth they controlled, the nobles still exercised the latent authority of the monarchy, and vied for the power to install and use the monarchs. The former government agents, who took on the local decision-making roles in the palace in Gonder, used their position as a springboard to power, and thus also started the rise of autonomous rulers of the *Zemene Mesafint*.

Ready to follow in the footsteps of *Ras* Mikael Sehul were Oromo nobles who had succeeded by then in setting up the powerful Yeju family in Wello. *Ras* Gugsa Merso, the first of this family to come to Gonder in 1789, used the nominal *neguse negest*, Gigar, to confiscate lands and provide new *gult* to his own favourites.[61] Gugsa increased his standing during 1800–25 by marrying his daughters to various titled officers, and establishing two of his competitive sons, Marye and Dori, in critical positions. These brothers are known in history for seriously debating with each other whether one of them should assume the *neguse negest* title and abandoning the idea after one of them replied 'Who will we claim gave it to us?'. Their implicit recognition of the prescribed source of power and authority of the *neguse negest*'s position, like the continuing use of Amharic as a court language, was almost the only sign of the continuity of the monarchy. The brothers were subsequently defeated by Sabagadis of Tigre, but one of the widows, Menen Ali Liben, regained power in 1831 and assumed the regency for her thirteen-year-old son, *Ras* Ali Alula. This *ras* removed Iyasu IV with his mother's help, and began installing Gebre Krestos on the throne, replacing him twice with Sahle Dingil, whom he also alternated five times with Yohannes III. He subsequently married the latter to his mother, who thus became Empress Menen.

The increase of personal economic and political power held by the nobles also led to the emergence of autonomous warrior leaders in centres such as Gojam and Shewa. Though these centres were inclined to support the position of the 'king of kings', the warriors' assertion of autonomy followed their personal aggrandizement, the scheme that had begun in Gonder. *Dejazmach* Goshu Zewde of Gojam (fl. 1825–52), for instance, asserted his claim as *mesfin* (prince), enabling his descendants to campaign outwards from their base autonomously. Those further south in Shewa similarly succeeded in increasing their political power. The *negasi* of Agencha, Shewa, the last official to take tribute to the already beleaguered Iyasu I, received the position *mer'ed azmach*, 'Commander of the Rearguard', and the right to beat twelve 'drums of authority', *negarit*.[62] He died in Gonder c.1703 without returning

---

[61] On the economic difficulties farmers faced during the period see Pankhurst, *A Social History*, 1990, pp. 75, 78, 80–1.

[62] Harold G. Marcus, *The Life and Times of Menelik II: Ethiopia 1844–1913* (Oxford Studies in African Affairs), Oxford: Clarendon Press, 1975, pp. 7–8, says that Negasi '...was invested as *ras* or *mer'edazmatch*, receiving twelve *negarit*...'.

to Shewa, but the recognition and title he received encouraged his descendants to be sole powerholders in Shewa in the south, and to see themselves, perhaps metaphorically, as the rearguard of the realm of the *neguse negest* with its centre in the north.

Some of these, namely Sebestyanos, Abiye, Amha Iyesus, Asfa Wesen and Wesen Seged (d.1813), made land grants to their followers and fought to forge links with the communities that had been farming there since the sixteenth century. Wesen Seged proclaimed himself a *ras*, and on the prompting of his mother, who claimed descent from the approved dynasty, even aspired to take the crown of *neguse negest*.[63] His son, Sahle Selassie, argued that he was descended from Emperor Libne Dingil (r.1508–40) and proclaimed himself *Negus* of Shewa, a title between *ras* and *neguse negest* in status. Typical of the regional nobles of the time, Sahle Selassie keenly cultivated foreign weapons traders and allies. The forces of his son, *Negus* Hayle Melekot, capitulated to the superior forces of Tewodros II in 1855, and his grandson Menelik was captured. Even after Tewodros's decisive campaigns, accumulating economic and political power continued to be a primary objective of anyone wishing to become *neguse negest*.

Two other monarchies set up by the Oromo, who displaced the *chewa* military contingents in ancient Ennarya, acquired political significance in the early nineteenth century. These were Leqa Lekemt and Leqa Qellem, both situated in what came to be known as Wellega. The stronger of these had relatively powerful leaders, with the rise of Bofu and then his son *Abba* Bagibo (r.1825–61). Others arose in the Gibe Valley: Limmu-Ennarya and Jimma-Kakka were set up through the efforts of *Abba* Magal and became even more significant under his descendants *Abba* Jifar (Sana r.1830–55) and *Abba* Reba (r.1855–9) and the latter's brother *Abba* Boko (r.1859–62). A sultanate that came into existence in Jimma in the 1830s also gained power by virtue of its control of trade from southeastern Sudan. The kingdom in Shewa had some relationships with these states from about the 1840s, but the *neguse negest* and their agents did not network with one another until the 1870s.

HISTORICAL FRIENDS AND FOES

Ethiopian monarchs were aware that political, religious, trading and other links had associated their country with the Arabian Peninsula

---

(contd) *Mer'ed azmach* was more a position than a title, and Negasi may have been invested with both this position and the title *ras*. Marcus refers to evidence that Negasi's son, Sebestianos, was *mer'ed azmach*, and states that his son or brother, Abiye, was officially made *mer'ed azmach*. On Negasi, see also Guèbrè Sellassié, *Chronique*, 1930–32, p. 56, fn. 6 and p. 83, fn. 10.

[63] R. H. Kofi Darkwah, *Shewa, Menilek and the Ethiopian Empire 1813–1889*, London: Heinemann, 1975, p. 17; Mordechai Abir, *Ethiopia: The Era of the Princes: The Challenge of Islam and the Re-unification of the Christian Empire, 1769–1855*, London: Longmans Green, 1968, pp. 150–1.

since antiquity. After continuing its strong presence in the Red Sea throughout the seventh century the Axumite navy attacked the Hijaz around 702. This attack was repulsed by Caliph Sulayman, whose successor, 'Abd al-Malik, also managed to take the Dahlak islands.[64] Sporadic Ethiopian attempts to reclaim control of the coastal region over the following three centuries were unsuccessful. Zeila and Massawa, which eventually attracted the Egyptians and the Turks, especially led the Ethiopians to engage in coastal contestations on the west side of the Red Sea. Arab commercial settlements slowly introduced a veneer of Islamic religion along the western shores of the Red Sea and the Gulf of Aden, and Tadesse Tamrat usefully shows this trend in terms of population mobility along the coast.[65] While this Arab presence introduced some Arabic language and Islamic scholarship, it also made the coastal region more vulnerable to Turkish claims, adding to Ethiopia's marginalization from the economic and political benefits of the region's commerce.[66] Later Ottoman and Egyptian political engagement in Yemen, the Hijaz and Aden, and their expansion along the Red Sea blocked Ethiopia's hold on the coast. The periodic association of internal rebels with this foreign presence on its coastline defined Turks, and to a lesser extent Egyptians, as *dina*.

This awareness was sustained also by the country's relationship with the Coptic Orthodox Church in Egypt, which sent bishops to Ethiopia over many centuries. Historians underline how Ethiopian monarchs were preoccupied with relating to this church.[67] Haggai Erlich argues emphatically that at least in early relations of Ethiopia with the Middle East, the responsibility for provocative military activities that threatened Ethiopia belonged predominantly to Egypt and the resurgence of Islam in the Arabian Peninsula.[68] Indeed, some monarchs threatened to block the waters of the Blue Nile (the Abay) for the purpose of helping the Egyptian church.[69] Around 1090, the Egyptians sent the Patriarch of Alexandria to appease the Zagwe dynasty over its supposed threat to divert the waters. There seems to have been similar activity in this regard during the time of King Lalibela (c.1185–1225?).[70] Threats were also sent by Yekuno Amlak (r.1270–85), and Amde Tsion (r.1314–44). Dawit (r.1380–412) even sent an army to Aswan, and Yishaq I (r.1413–30) sent letters to European kings offering an alliance against Egypt.

[64] Haggai Erlich, *Ethiopia and the Middle East*, 1994, p. 11.
[65] See Taddesse Tamrat, *Church and State*, 1972, pp. 74–94.
[66] Pankhurst, *The Ethiopian Borderlands*, 1997, p. 21. This is not to deny that Emperor Zera Yaqob established a post at Massawa – see Crummey, *Land and Society*, 2000, p. 18 – but it could not be sustained down the centuries.
[67] To understand the difficulties that the Egyptian Khedive Ismail posed, see details of nineteenth-century borderland negotiations with Egypt in, among others, Rubenson, *The Survival of Ethiopian Independence*, 1976, pp. 288–361.
[68] Erlich, *Ethiopia and the Middle East*, 1994, p. 11.
[69] Erlich, *Ethiopia and the Middle East*, 1994, pp. 23–5.
[70] The dates from the entry on Lalibela in Prouty and Rosenfeld, *Historical Dictionary*, 1981. Citing Egyptian sources, Erlich, *Ethiopia and the Middle East*, 1994, p. 23, gives Lalibela's dates as 1133–73.

Zera Yaqob tried at first to be positive towards the Egyptians, but he too threatened to block the Nile, and even resorted to imprisoning Egyptian envoys for two years.[71]

The monarchs effectively used this awareness of foreign pressures to overcome the isolation of their country. Internally, they couched their mobilizations in terms of the claim that *dina*, including Egyptians, had always wanted to take their country and attack their Christian religion. Egyptian events continued to influence the history of Ethiopian warfare even after the Mamluks lost power to the Ottoman Turks in 1517. The Ottomans began an aggressive policy along the coast, and even attempted to repulse the Portuguese in the Red Sea and the Indian Ocean. In later centuries, the uncontested use of the 'enemy' identity was transposed to the Ottomans in recognition of Arab and Turkish contestations for supremacy in Egypt, the Red Sea and along the Nile Valley.

In fact, several Ethiopian emperors found that their internal power was seriously affected by the long presence of the Ottomans in Egypt. This impact was felt in 1538 when the Ottoman pasha of Zabib in Yemen gave nine hundred trained fighters and ten cannons to *Imam* Ahmad ibn Ghazi, the Muslim leader of Adal in Ethiopia. Commonly called Gragn ('left-handed'), the *imam* used this help to consolidate a campaign (1529–43) to destroy the kingdom of the 'king of kings' Libne Dingil (r.1508–40).[72] In what is sometimes referred to as an internal *jihad*, he overran and devastated the realm at a time when, according to the monarch, the population had lost its will to fight. The *imam* was eventually defeated with the help of Portuguese soldiers, but his campaign led, in the short term, to the near-total demise of the *neguse negest*, and, in the long term, influenced the decline of the monarchs' internal power and the emergence of the Era of Princes.

The Ottoman aspiration to control the region as far as Zanzibar brought Ozdemir Pasha in 1557 to the port of Massawa and the hinterland capital, Deboroa. Two years later, *Baher Negash* Yishaq took back Deboroa and the Dahlak Islands, but he allied himself with Ozdemir's son and successor, Uthman, who defeated the *neguse negest*, Minas (r.1559–63) in 1562. Sertse Dingil (r.1563–97) dislodged the Ottoman Egyptians from Deboroa and reduced their presence to Massawa. Nonetheless, they later helped Ethiopia to expel the Portuguese missionaries who had converted Emperor Susneyos (r.1606–32) to Catholicism. The Ottoman presence continued to restrict the monarchs' control of trade routes to the Red Sea and the Nile Valley; though the establishment of Gonder as a permanent city brought some amelioration in this regard, their 'presence until the nineteenth century was efficient enough to continue Ethiopia's overall isolation from Europe'.[73]

Not surprisingly, Ethiopian military practices were also affected by the emperors' persistent contact with Egypt and its Mamluk rulers.

[71] Erlich, *Ethiopia and the Middle East*, 1994, p. 24.
[72] Erlich, *Ethiopia and the Middle East*, 1994, p. 32.
[73] Erlich, *Ethiopia and the Middle East*, 1994, p. 38.

In the days of Yishaq I, for instance, individuals who ran away from their rivals in Egypt helped reorganize the army, introduced the use of naphtha, and improved the arsenal of swords, spears and other weapons.[74] Judging by the general trend, it is possible that Ethiopia received the sickle-shaped sword, known locally as *ashmwatach*, at that time. Turkish and Portuguese involvement additionally introduced the use of firearms to Ethiopian warriors who were reportedly using 'cannons and muskets' by 1533.[75] The monarchs strived to import guns through the Portuguese, and later through the Dutch and British, who dominated the trade in the Indian Ocean and the Red Sea. Sustaining their access to firearms to the dawn of the Era of Princes, the rulers occasionally used Arab and Turkish individuals to operate cannon and other sophisticated weapons. Such contact is reflected in the vocabulary for these items.

EGYPTIAN HOSTILITY

Defining external hostile forces was partly rooted in *chewa* military experiences. Changes in weaponry improved, for instance, only when the troops of Yohannes IV captured advanced firearms in battles for asserting his mastery of the region against Egyptian invasions, which had resumed under Khedive Ismail.[76] The Khedive's troops captured Bogos in July 1872, Metemma in May 1873 and Adi Quala in July 1875. When this last force was destroyed in mid-November 1875 at Gundet, Yohannes's army captured 20,000 Maria Theresa dollars and 2,500 Remington rifles. These weapons were new to the Ethiopians, and Yohannes strengthened his arsenal by forcing *Dejazmach* Welde Mikael Solomon of Hazega to hand over the weapons he had captured to *Shaleqa* Alula. Offended by this, the *dejazmach* offered his services to the Egyptians, who made him a *farik* (equivalent to a full general in the Egyptian army), and he made himself a *ras*, and thus, a centre for other malcontents. Emboldened by this rebel and others that they bribed, the Egyptians marched to the Mereb River (7–9 March 1876). To stem their incursions, Yohannes gave Alula the title of *ras* and appointed him Governor of Hamasen in October 1876. Alula won a victory at Gura, but though this checked the Khedive's forces, he could not retake Massawa until July 1888.[77] Pursuing a policy of expanding Egyptian influence along the Nile and the Rift valleys, the Khedive also sent military missions to Zeila and Harar in 1874. Aware of this policy, Menelik notified Khedive Ismail that his military activities around Ethiopian territories were unacceptable.

[74] Erlich, *Ethiopia and the Middle East*, 1994, pp. 24–5.
[75] Richard Pankhurst, 'Linguistic and Cultural Data on the Penetration of Fire-Arms into Ethiopia', *Journal of Ethiopian Studies*, Vol. IX, No. 1, January 1971, pp. 47–8.
[76] Zawde Gabre-Sellassie, *Yohannes IV of Ethiopia*, 1975, pp. 50–3, 59–64.
[77] Zawde Gabre-Sellassie, *Yohannes IV of Ethiopia*, 1975, pp. 68–74.

EUROPEAN STRANGLEHOLD

The assertion of British military power in Egpyt in 1882 alerted Ethiopians to new foes, as well as new sources of access to better weapons. Indeed, the purported British purpose of ensuring their hold on the Suez Canal at the time became the so-called 'veiled protectorate', which lasted until 1914. A weakened subject of Ottoman Turkey, Khedive Ismail could only send his troops to the western frontiers of Ethiopia. The British and other Europeans developed a firm grip along the African coastline on the Red Sea and the Indian Ocean, replacing the Turks and their Egyptian subjects. The British and the French were also in connivance about rival ventures in the area. The French had already been in and around Djibouti (from 1864) and southern Somalia (1889–98); and the British, who having entered Ethiopia in July 1867, arrived eventually at the capital of Tewodros II in March 1868, and then withdrew, also established themselves in Somaliland (from 1869) and Kenya (from 1888).

In that political environment, Yohannes was unable to consolidate his victory at Gura and Gundet, but he used the captured weapons to fight off further Sudanese attacks. He sent *Ras* Alula to augment the troops of *Ras* Adal, who was engaged in repelling one such attack along the western frontier. Of course, the long absence of Alula from his governorate in Hamasen gave free rein to the Egyptians, by then conniving with British colonialists over an alliance in Sudan.

External threats and the need for weapons took Ethiopian politics back, as it were, to the time when powerful 'kings of kings' had tried to get the goodwill of faraway Europeans by soliciting their help against internal rebellions and nearby enemies. Among those who had tried to engage furtively with Europeans in order to acquire weapons was Tewodros II, who turned to soliciting a European Christian alliance against the Muslim Ottoman Turks ruling Egypt and initiated reforms regarding church lands despite potential Egyptian protests. He wrote to the British queen as a co-religionist, and Yohannes IV wrote in a similar vein. Yohannes IV and Menelik II, who brought regional rulers under better coordination and greater alertness, sought to develop formal relationships with 'Christian' European powers. In the period coinciding with Europe's increasing stranglehold on the Red Sea coast and the Nile Valley, Ethiopia's leaders were thus unaware that European colonial interests overrode religious loyalties. Of course, Yohannes IV continued to campaign against Catholics and Muslims, and Menelik used the name of Christian saints in various decrees. In the context of the dynamic changes in European power relations in the region, the emperors' somewhat anachronistic appeals to 'Christian' England or France against 'Islamic' Egypt bore no realistic diplomatic purpose.

However, by the 1880s, the Ethiopian monarchs had sufficient evidence that the European aim of colonizing northeastern Africa made the Europeans a new form of *dina*. In fact, *Ras* Alula had received a message from General Gordon, then scouting for British influence south along the White Nile, asking him to hold Massawa for him under a British consul, a request that *Ras* Alula turned down because he understood that the power of the British in Egypt sidelined even the hold of its Ottoman rulers, and by the late 1880s European emissaries, who had begun offering weapons, were also trying to impress the Ethiopians about the might of the various European countries. Some of these emissaries were ignorant of decent diplomacy, and their military activities were at best arrogant and at worst blatantly supremacist. Munzinger, for instance, served Egyptian interests while trying to give the impression of loyalty to Ethiopian ones.[78] Ethiopians came to realize that the Europeans, in competing with each other for domination of the Red Sea area and the Rift and the Nile valleys, were aiming to control Ethiopia. Ethiopian rulers agreed that defining their territories was a priority in the face of any external aggression, including European. From their perspective, pulling together Ethiopia's southern territories augmented the involvement of the wide range of ethnic and linguistic groups in the state.

European colonialists' attempt to use the religious card perpetuated their misconception of Ethiopia as a solely Christian state. European misunderstanding of the political use of religion in Ethiopia, which had long stereotyped Ethiopia as specifically a Christian land, added to a limited European understanding of the geography and history of the region. The view offered Europeans a vulnerable country, reduced to a conjectured locality that they chose to call Christian 'Abyssinia'. They used this to define the boundaries in the context of their colonial enterprise. Ethiopians were familiar with neither the term 'Abyssinia' as the name of their country, nor what it implied in the minds of colonialists. They officially called their *country* Ethiopia while informally referring to the *population* as *Habesha*, an Arabic word meaning 'mixed people', which a scholar claims to have appeared originally in writing in the days of Ezana.[79]

An interesting corollary to the religious colouring is the way in which Menelik II appeared to have symbolically confirmed a conceptual political bridge between religion and secular politics. In 1903, at his seventh-year commemoration of those who died in 1896, he played down the prayers and feasting associated with such a remembrance. He turned the occasion into a military display in which dignitaries and corps of soldiers from all corners of the land participated. His militaristic display of war booty and weapons acquired from Adewa confirmed Ethiopia's military orientation, and drew up the parameters of its foreign relations, and, symbolically, the country's state of being on a war footing against Europeans. The painting on the cover of this book is a popular example of how this conceptual bridge between religious views and secular politics was represented.[80]

---

[78] See, for example, Rubenson, *The Survival of Ethiopian Independence*, 1976, pp. 276–8, and Bahru Zewde, *A History of Modern Ethiopia*, 2001, p. 50.
[79] Sergew, *Ancient and Medieval History*, 1972, p. 94.
[80] The much-publicized Ethiopian paintings depicting the Battle of Adewa, such as the one on the cover of this book, show Italian faces in profile. This

CHALLENGING THE KINGMAKERS

Eventually, the power of the autonomous nobles and other rulers of the *Zemene Mesafint* broke, but it took the zeal and skill of four successive monarchs of *chewa* background to do this. They employed both the *chewa* and the wandering would-be soldiers to reassert the authority of the *neguse negest*. In the process, they also rendered landed property less useful in the political game of controlling local politics and the monarchy. Vying for the position of monarch from the grassroots was antithetical to the descent principle legitimized by the prescriptive source of authority, the *Kebre Negest* – the line claiming descent from Makeda (the Queen of Sheba) and Solomon, a biblical association giving it divine endorsement. While the widespread rivalry allowed some *mekwanent* to forge the Era of Princes, and become kingmakers, it was still persistent enough to enable the crowning of Emperor Tekle Giyorgis (r.1868–71), whose claim to the throne derived from the Zagwe, who claimed descent from Solomon's son by the handmaid of the Queen of Sheba.

The resurgence of the monarchy depended on a new resource: the importation of weapons, though for some nobles, control of the head of the Ethiopian Orthodox Church, whose responsibilities included officiating at coronations, was critical. Thus *Dejazmach* Wube Haile Maryam, who had in thrall *Abune* Selama III, the new archbishop who had arrived in the country at the end of the previous year, controlled the arms trade through Tigre; and with *Dejazmach* Biru Goshu from Gojam campaigned to overthrow *Ras* Ali. The *ras* (in fact a Christian) had only the nominal king behind him, and feeling threatened, he invited his uncle *Dejazmach* Biru Aligaz (a Muslim) and his cavalry force from Wello. This gave rise to what is somewhat simplistically seen as Christians fighting Muslims. In the ensuing battle at Debre Tabor in February 1842, Ali and Biru were losing the battle until a wing of theirs turned the tables on the other side and, capturing Wube, forced Biru Goshu to retreat across the Abay. Relieved, Ali gave the governorate of Daunt to Biru Aligaz, and Wube's territory to another ally of his, *Dejazmach* Merso. Calling on his uncle enhanced the perception that the *ras* favoured Muslims while these rewards offended his Muslim supporters in Wello, who reportedly resented being neighbours with Christians (in nearby Begemder).

Ras Ali eventually forgave *Dejazmach* Wube, gave him back his governorate and even allowed him to keep *Abune* Selama near him. Despite his ameliorative move, the *ras* appealed for help from the Egyptians, then consolidating their hold in Sudan, and this worsened the grudges against his perceived Islamic inclinations. Egyptian influence along the frontiers would contribute to stopping internal rivalry. Taking advan-

(contd) is said to portray them as evil, in the Ethiopian Christian sense, for encroaching on Ethiopian independence. This representation confirms the view that the feast was a conceptual bridge between religious views and secular politics.

tage, the resuscitating Egyptian–Turkish rulers engaged in expansion along the Nile Valley to exploit mineral resources in western Ethiopia. Turkish naval and land power had been overtaken by the Europeans in the eighteenth century, but the Ottomans in Egypt had long encouraged the expansion of Islam along the western frontiers of Ethiopia.

The long-held view of Turks as enemies of Ethiopia was confirmed by awareness of Ottoman presence in these areas. It was with this historical view that the governor of Dembya, *Dejazmach* Kenfu, reacted to an attack in a battle in 1837 at Wad Kaltabu, inside Sudan. Barely escaping with his life was his nephew, Kassa (the future Emperor Tewodros II), then operating as a *shifta* in the area and experiencing the Egyptian military performance. When *Ras* Ali appealed for Egyptian help in the 1840s, therefore, at least one internal potentate of the period, referring to Islamic powers, complained that Ethiopia was surrounded by *aremi*, a term that literally meant pagans.[81] However, as Islamic scholarship from Egypt had begun to take a serious hold among the Beni-Amer, this indicated knowledge of the political upper hand that Islamic power had externally rather than any religious animosity felt internally.

In 1875 the Egyptians sent an expedition that took Harar, killing its *emir*, and ruling for a decade before being overwhelmed and expelled by the rulers of Awsa, perhaps helped by the Oromo then in Harar. The resurgence of Egyptian ambitions to extend their influence from the Nile Valley to the Red Sea coast, using the spread of Islam as a stepping stone, aimed at skirting the Ethiopian borderlands in the southwest, south and east. Islamic influence was similarly felt in a series of small linguistic groups along the western sides of Illubabor, Wellega and Gojam. Affiliations with Islam along the western borders that developed sheikdoms, notably Beni Shangul, Assosa (or Aqoldi) and Guba, facilitated trading with states controlled by Sudanese Arab families, and in that sense contributed to Egyptian ambitions in the Nile Valley.

More directly influencing the *neguse negest*'s exercise of power were European commercial and later religious influences on Ethiopian courtiers and common people in the first four decades of the nineteenth century. Among new European visitors with scientific and ethnographic interests was James Bruce, who came to Ethiopia in 1770, met *Ras* Mikael Sehul and his protégé of the day, *Neguse Negest* Tekle Haymanot II, and visited the source of the Abay (the Blue Nile) before leaving two years later. The botanical and geographical explorer George Annesley (later Viscount Valentia), who arrived in Massawa in 1804, was keen to develop commercial links between Britain and the Red Sea coast.[82] Captain W. Cornwallis Harris visited the court of Sahle Selassie in 1841, as did Rochet d'Héricourt in 1843. Walter Plowden was received by *Ras* Ali in 1849. The Church Missionary Society was also active in

---

[81] See for instance, Rubenson, *The Survival of Ethiopian Independence*, 1976, pp. 49–50.
[82] [Annesley] George, Viscount Valentia, *Voyages and Travels to India, Ceylon, the Red Sea, Abyssinia, and Egypt, in the years 1802, 1803, 1804, 1805, and 1806*, London: William Miller, 1809, Vol. II, pp. 4, 49.

the country, and there was a new opening of Catholic missions – Lazarists in the north (from the 1830s) and Capuchins in the south (from the 1840s).[83] With such foreigners providing Ethiopians of the period with timely information on European technological and especially military advances, local leaders vied for their agency in the importation of European goods. The demands of Emperor Tewodros II (r.1855–68), the former Kassa Hailu, on missionaries to produce cannons and other guns were an expression of such consciousness.

An exemplary *chewa* warrior, Kassa Hailu's rise and career aptly illustrate various aspects of the warrior tradition. He attended school when his uncle *Dejazmach* Maru of Dembya placed him in a monastery as a child, but returned to Dembya in Begemder when the school was attacked and destroyed. Literate (although not a *chewa* requirement) and a soldier, he experienced warfare in his birthplace, the lowlands of Qwara, Dembya. His first participation in a battle was when *Dejazmach* Maru rebelled, fought and died at Kosso Ber in October 1827.

Fulfilling the processes expected of emergent warriors, Kassa aimed at inheriting Qwara, which was within a wider area known as *Ye Maru Qemis* ('Maru's savour'), once administered by his paternal grandfather, Welde Giyorgis, and his father, Haile Welde Giyorgis (popularly called Hailu). He then served *Dejazmach* Kenfu, the next governor of Dembya, whose attack on and defeat of an Egyptian army at Wad Kaltabu in 1837 gave Kassa a taste of guarding the border. As Kenfu did not recognize him as a potential successor to the lands that had belonged to his father, he abandoned him to serve *Dejazmach* Goshu Zewde in Gojam. Realizing that the authorities in Gonder were also inclined to bypass him regarding the inheritance on Kenfu's death, he withdrew his service to *Dejazmach* Goshu to retrieve his perceived heritage as a *shifta* operating in the lowlands of Qwara.

From there he cultivated the image of bravery, decisiveness in taking initiatives, and full strategic use of the landscape. Thus in many ways his early career followed the motivations and practices of ever-emerging warriors. Whenever he failed to gain high rewards, he accepted the conditions that benefited his subordinates. He also endeared himself to the inhabitants among whom he was engaged in rebellious defiance. Reportedly he shared captured grain and money with the rural people in Qwara, and 'told them to buy hoes and plant'.[84] He warned his intended adversaries by stating his intentions openly. His future skirmishes would show that he also punished his enemies ruthlessly.

Kassa's admired qualities attracted him a sizeable following. In the palace of Gonder his rising popularity alarmed *Ras* Ali II, Ali's mother, Menen, and her husband, the puppet monarch Yohannes III. Mother and son offered him the title *dejazmach*, the governorship of Yemaru Qims and Dembiya, and the hand in marriage of *Ras* Ali's daughter,

[83] Crummey, *Priests and Politicians*, 1972, pp. 59–60.
[84] Sven Rubenson, *King of Kings Tēwodros of Ethiopia*, Addis Ababa: Haile Selassie I University Press in association with Oxford University Press, Nairobi, 1966, p. 36.

Tewabech. Subsequently however, in 1847, they offended him and his wife by sending a portion of meat to wish him well over his discomfort after taking a purgative. This customary gift was an expected gesture, but the portion of meat was a symbolic insult to the dignity of a warrior of his status, which merited the gift of a live animal. In this most celebrated case, *Dejazmach* Kassa rebelled against his father-in-law, *Ras* Ali II, the last of the kingmakers of the Era of Princes. Tewodros reportedly complained: 'I am [honourable] enough to be given a [whole] ox; or else I should have been given a ram. Why am I given a *shint* [thigh] like a pot-bearer?' Incensed, his wife was said to have stirred him into action with the words '*Tateq! Ager yelehim!*', meaning: 'Arm yourself! [Have you] no country [to retire to]? Let's go!' Tateq became his 'horse-name' from that moment onwards, thus bearing witness to her connivance in his rebellion against his in-laws.[85]

He angrily retired again to his home base in the lowlands of Qwara. As he was a *dejazmach* declaring himself in direct conflict with the powerholders in Gonder, warriors immediately rallied to his cause, and later followed him in a series of skirmishes. Using the *chewa* politico-military traditions of asserting control over one's ancestral lands – in this case his father's lands in Qwara – he also used the practice of giving, withholding or withdrawing personal and communal support to (or from) the most powerful. In 1848, he was wounded in a skirmish against Egyptian troops at Debariq, but because he emerged successful, albeit barely escaping with his life, his reputation increased. Understandably, his in-laws waited until the new season of warfare began after the rains, and *Ras* Ali fielded troops on 27 November 1852. In this battle at Gur Amba, Kassa killed the leading *dejazmach*, Goshu Zewde of Gojam: none other than his former patron. Proceeding to fight his way to Gonder, he successfully beat four *dejazmach* at the Battle of Takussa on 12 April 1853, including Biru Aligaz, and Gwangul, the son of *Dejazmach* Wube Haile Maryam of Semien. The following *zeraf* couplet by his soldiers captured his continuing reputation for bravery:

> አራት ደጃዝማቾች የደገሱውን
> የካሳ ፈረስ ጠግቦ በቻውን
> The feast organized by four *dejazmach*,
> Kassa's horse alone consumed it.

Fresh troops sent to fight him at his fortification at Dengel Ber, just north of Gojam, were too scared and simply passed the rains in Dembya. By September, the traditional time of new appointments, *Ras* Ali gave *Dejazmach* Kassa's governorate to *Dejazmach* Biru Goshu of Gojam, whom he ordered to move against the rebel. Kassa boldly left his fortified position and offered battle in the plains. In the ensuing full day of fighting, both sides suffered heavy casualties, but Kassa's men forced

---

[85] ተክለ ኢየሱስ [ዋቅጇራ] አለቃ፤ *የኢትዮጵያ ታሪክ፤* ሕተታ በሰርገው ገላው 2002 (Tekle Iyesus [Waqjera], *Aleqa: History of Ethiopia*, perhaps 1917 EC; introduction and annotation by Sergew Gelaw, Addis Ababa: Berhanena Salem Printing Press, 2002 EC), p. 101.

Biru's to flee south into Gojam, and Biru himself to retreat to the mountain fortress of Jibela, overlooking the Chamwaga River valley.

By 1853, Kassa's personal bravery had become established. He used *zeraf* to announce his intention to depose the nominal emperor, Yohannes III. Typical of war preparation at the time, this immediately provoked insults from the nobility. Empress Menen herself decried him with:

> የሄ ቀዋሬኛ
> የፍየል አረኛ
> This one from Qwara,
> This goatherd.

A singer in the camp of *Dejazmach* Wondyirad, a loyal courtier, referred to Kassa's purported lowly roots:

> ሺህ ብረት ከሀዋላው ሺህ ብረት ከፊቱ
> ሺህ ነፍጥ ከሀዋላው ሺህ ነፍጥ ከፊቱ
> የሄን ሳታይ ሞተች ኮሶ ሻጭ እናቱ
> በሸዋ በትግሬ የተቀመጣችሁ
> በጎጃም በላስታ የተቀመጣችሁ
> አንድ ዛላ በርበሬ መንቀል አቅትዋችሁ
> ቆጥቆጦ አንገብግቦ ለበስ ይፍጃችሁ
> A thousand 'iron' in front, a thousand 'iron' behind him,
> A thousand rifles in front, a thousand rifles behind him,
> His *kosso*-vendor mother died without seeing this!
> Those in Shewa and Tigre,
> Those in Gojam and Lasta,
> Unable to uproot a single pepper plant.
> It burns, scorches and scalds you to extinction!

Mother, son, courtiers and supporters attacked Kassa at the Battle of Ayishal on 29 June 1853, but when he defeated them, Yohannes III immediately acknowledged him. Clearly well informed, Kassa punished those who had thrown insults at him in their *fukera* (presentation), reportedly obliging the captured empress to grind beans, and *Dejazmach* Wondyirad to drink large quantities of the purgative that was purportedly the source of livelihood of Kassa's mother. His ruthlessness showed further when he rhetorically asked the male singer what he had sung about him, and by way of pleading mercy the singer replied:

> አፍ ወዳጁን ያማል የሚሰራውን ሲያጣ
> ሻመል ይገባዋል ያዘማሪ ቀልብ አጣ
> A careless mouth gossips about friends.
> A forgetful singer deserves [a beating with] the walking stick.

The singer had possibly counted on his earlier acquaintance with Kassa, but he found that his poetic words condemned him literally to death by beating. However, Kassa forgave and sent away a female singer who had joined in insulting him because she humbly replied:

> እርሱ አይሰማም ብዬ አንደት በጉድ ወጣሁ
> መንጠልጠያ በገኝ አሰማይ በወጣሁ
> መውረጃ በገኝም አምድር በገባሁ
> What difficulties for me – thinking that he might not hear!
> I would climb into the sky, if I had a ladder!
> Or into the earth, if I had the steps!

Despite Kassa's success in Gonder, Biru Goshu of Gojam left his mountain fortress of Jibela in March 1854, wanting to avenge his father, Goshu Zewde. Kassa's men, however, captured and incarcerated him on another mountain fortress west of Chilga, where he stayed for fourteen years. Chagrined, Biru's wife surrendered Jibela with its arsenal on condition that she would not be reunited with her disgracefully defeated husband. This left Kassa free to pursue his well-armed, powerful rival, *Dejazmach* Wube Haile Maryam of Semien.

Kassa, refusing to accept Wube's attempt to restore the former Emperor Sahle Dingil, determined to remove the *Zemene Mesafint* form of exercising power. In fact, he captured Wube, distributed the wealth he had stored to his own soldiers and obliged the archbishop, *Abune* Selama, to crown him *Neguse Negest* Tewodros II.

RESTORING THE 'KING OF KINGS'

Having removed the top powermonger, *Ras* Ali, Tewodros successfully challenged the new landowner families, simultaneously encouraging extensive use of the emergent warrior tradition and foot soldiery among the displaced population in order to end the practice of wealthy nobles ruling from behind the throne. Controlling those loyal to the descent principle but evoking its rules, he announced his lineage from Fasiledes (r.1632–67), and thereby from the approved dynasty. This truly potent combination – espousal of the descent principle of the *Kebre Negest* after blazing his own trail in the tradition of Ethiopian warrior kings – was the ultimate achievement for *chewa* warriors. By the time of his coronation, he was the epitome of a popular and capable warrior 'master'. He further increased his capacity by rewarding his numerous troops with appropriate feasts, weapons, titles and loot from more and more regions and power centres. Within a year he controlled Tigre and Wello, and, setting up his capital on the mountaintop of Mekdela, he marched to Shewa a year later. He took the kingdom by storm and carried away its heir, eleven-year-old Menelik, whom he later married to his daughter.

In his zeal to increase his power, he made requests, notably to Britain, to acquire weapons technology. This was specifically couched in terms of asking for instructors, but as it drew no response after two years, he took out his frustration against Europeans then residing in the country. He incarcerated missionaries and commercial agents in 1864, and, suspicious that the British were allied to Egypt, arrested diplomats, including Consul Cameron and his staff. He recognized the role of missionaries, allowing them to hold religious services, but he also expected them to repair muskets and produce weapons and ammunition. Two years later he released the prisoners, but allowed only one missionary, Flad, to leave the country.[86]

[86] Rubenson, *The Survival of Ethiopian Independence*, 1976, pp. 237–49.

Incensed by Tewodros's handling of its diplomats, Britain sent a large invading force from India under Lieutenant-General Robert Napier in 1867.

Tewodros burned Debre Tabor and retreated to his mountaintop capital, Mekdela. The British stormed this capital in April 1868, using their superior breech-loading Snider rifles. They were assisted by local rebels to whom they had promised supplies of weapons. Deserted on all sides, Tewodros committed suicide, ironically shooting himself with a pistol Queen Victoria had sent him earlier. Part of his warrior upbringing enabled him to face up to the unexpected possibility of falling into enemy hands. His suicide continues to represent the traditional spirit of practising, evaluating and transmitting the ideals of the brave. When the departing British expedition rewarded one of the rebels, the future Yohannes IV (r.1872–89) with a cache of old and outdated weapons for having helped them, they boosted Ethiopian awareness of European military technology, these weapons being less outdated than Ethiopian firearms. It made them more conscious of being short-changed by arms traders.

Tewodros is said to have left the nation as divided as he had found it, mainly because of the desertions he faced in the end. In continuing to break down the *raison d'être* for regional autonomy, his successors followed his example. Emperors Yohannes IV and Menelik II managed to unify the country by imposing their power to grant military titles. Tewedros's immediate successor, *Wagshum* Gobeze, crowned as Emperor Tekle Giyorgis II in 1868, invoked the descent principle, albeit from 'the lower ranked dynasty' of the Zagwe. He then quickly set about subjugating the potentates of Tigre, Gojam and elsewhere. After he was defeated in January 1872 when he tried to capture Adewa, then capital of Tigre, the local victor, Kassa, had himself crowned at Axum as *Neguse Negest* Yohannes IV. There were fewer rebels under Yohannes IV compared with their prevalence under his two predecessors, and those with pretensions to Begemder, Gojam, Wello and Shewa individually held larger areas. In other words, with more firearms in the hands of the powerful, and the threat they felt from Egypt, it was no coincidence that he and his successor Menelik II benefited from a decrease in local rebels.

When dealing with rivals, Yohannes used political skill. His major rival Menelik of Shewa, who was claiming royal heritage acceptable to the prescription in the *Kebre Negest*, had given himself the title *neguse negest* soon after the demise of Tewodros. In the old fortress of Mekdela in Wello in 1875 Menelik replaced Mestawat and her son, *Abba* Wattew (Amede Liben), with their rival, Mohammed Ali. He further asserted his claims to these areas north of Shewa by founding a town, Were Illu. However, Menelik faced internal dissent as he supported one side in a doctrinal dispute in the Ethiopian Orthodox Church, and those opposed to this called for the intervention of Emperor Yohannes, who marched against him in 1878. Yohannes had armed his forces well under *Ras* Alula, and was joined on the way by Menelik's ally, Mohammed Ali of Wello.

With this far superior army, he marched to Leche in Menz, but Menelik prudently submitted, thus preventing the destruction of his realm.

After a major conference at Boru Meda on 26 March 1878, Yohannes facilitated the successful resolution of a long-standing division within the Ethiopian Orthodox Church and began converting local Muslims to Christianity. He stood as godfather to Mohammed Ali, who took the baptismal name Mikael, and he gave him the title *ras*. Yohannes forced Menelik to drop his claims to the title and position he had assumed, and gave him the lesser title of 'king' (*negus*). The meeting resolved the larger religious divides within Ethiopia, and lessened the effects of the threat of 'Islamic' Egypt. Yohannes imposed political limitations on Menelik, taking away the part of Wello he had taken earlier and giving it to *Ras* Adal. He ordered Menelik to build churches and expel missionaries from his kingdom. Menelik obeyed, although the last requirement meant reduced external links not only with Muslims but also with Catholics, Protestants and other foreigners who might have enabled access to the importation of weapons.

Yohannes IV died in 1889, killed by a retreating wing of the vanquished enemy who accidentally came across him after a successful personal campaign he led against an Egyptian-supported Mahdi attack at Metemma on the Sudanese border. Significantly, what took effect then was Yohannes's political achievement: an order of seniority between potential successors. Menelik II succeeded as *neguse negest*, fulfilling the unification ambitions of his three predecessors.[87]

CHANGING THE PRINCIPLES OF WARRIORHOOD

The reforms of Tewodros had brought in significant changes in the relationship between soldiers and monarchs. Beyond getting rid of the powerholders of the Era of Princes, he closed the communication gap that had arisen between the rural population and the monarchs. He modified the principles with which the monarchs' exclusive prescriptive rights could be balanced with the processes that ordinary *chewa* warriors followed. He challenged the warrior traditions by disciplining his loyal troops. He also restricted the local progress of emergent warriors. Said to have been inspired by his experience of the Egyptian troops during his border clashes against them, Tewodros instituted a hierarchy of military titles, thus imposing a rule that proceeded within a single chain of command under the *neguse negest*: *asir aleqa*, *hamsa aleqa*, *meto aleqa*, *shaleqa*: literally, commanders of, respectively, ten, fifty, a hundred and a thousand (soldiers). The title *shambel* ('captain'), which falls between *meto aleqa* ('lieutenant') and *shaleqa* ('major'), was also included.[88]

Initially applicable to those under him, this chain of command elevated the status of the overall 'master' in command of the army

[87] Marcus, *Life and Times*, 1975, pp. 7–10; Darkwah, *Shewa, Menilek*, 1975, pp. 6–7.
[88] Bahru Zewde, *A History of Modern Ethiopia*, 2001, pp. 28, 31–3.

to the larger setting of the whole country. It also meant that ordinary people whose military achievements had gained local social recognition could not contemplate challenging and excluding the authority of the 'king of kings'. Under the direct command of the 'king of kings', the new hierarchy of military officers started to play down the importance of social recognition. This began to change the traditions of personal aggrandisement that the emergent warriors had relied upon in order to join the political hierarchy.

The new chain of command discouraged the rise of autonomous regional potentates. Their political roles became dependent on the goodwill of the monarch, whose control of the line of command gave him the sole privilege, power and authority over the appropriate symbols of power. In time, his restrictions were in no greater evidence than the threat they posed to regional titleholders who claimed their positions on the basis of descent from *mesafint* and *neguse negest*. The right to titles such as *baher negash* in Tigre, or *wagshum* in Lasta were to be sought afresh from the *neguse negest* by every generation. Shewa no longer carried the title and authority of *mer'ed azmach*, 'commander of the [nation's] rearguard', designated by Iyasu I (r.1682–1706).

Tewodros's other reforms, particularly regarding land, were frustrated, probably due to his haste in dealing with both secular and church land administration.[89] When he found it difficult to overhaul the land tenure system while still extracting tributes, he resorted to burning, maiming and displaying overall ruthlessness. Only a few attacked him openly in protest. The majority succeeded in stemming his overweening exercise of power by their passive resistance. Many warriors defected from his camp and potential taxpayers ran away to join key rebel *chewa* leaders. Needless to say these responses inflamed his unpredictable and at times irrational behaviour, a trait already mentioned in the case of his response to the two critical singers.

Tewodros's three successors followed his military reforms and discipline by reducing the emergent warriors' drive to dominate the structure of the state. Tewodros's example in limiting the challenges to the monarchy helped his successors redirect the focus of fighters towards standing against external threats. The monarchs enhanced their power through increased importation of firearms. They accompanied this acquisition by reconciling their historical claims to the breadth and width of the country with nineteenth-century political realities.

By acknowledging the importance of Yohannes IV as the *neguse negest* and owner of the most weapons during the period that coincided with a pronounced presence of European colonialists, the monarchs appropriated the sole right to define and defend the borderlands. This resulted in assuming the power of distinguishing 'insider' from 'outsider', and giving it an altered social meaning. Thus, for instance, *dina* was an ongoing reality with reference no longer to local communities but to Europeans. Even the semi-autonomous *fanno* along interna-

[89] Crummey, *Priests and Politicians*, 1972, pp. 124–5.

tional borders came increasingly to depend on the monarchs' appointees for their safety and security. Borderland potentates who had sought foreign support, especially from Egypt, in the hope of gaining access to weapons appear to have been equally impressed, at least temporarily.

Early in the century, the *chewa* rulers of Gojam, just to the north of the Abay River, and Shewa, in the centre of the country, were campaigning in the neighbouring principalities to increase their economic and political power. Some of them had been turning their attention to regaining the territories 'lost' since the sixteenth century. In fact, in the 1870s and 1880s *Ras* Adal of Gojam and *Negus* Menelik of Shewa, who had managed to acquire mountain guns, were already intensifying their predecessors' campaigns and settling their troops in those 'lost territories'.

The 'retaking' of 'lost lands' had begun to intensify in Shewa when Sahle Selassie campaigned against the Oromo in western Shewa. The reclaiming of areas across the south, east and west of the country was in full swing by the late 1870s. The areas stretched from the Red Sea coast to the middle Awash in the Rift Valley, and to Harar, Arsi and Bale. Surviving in parts of the ancient Dawaro kingdom in the centre were smaller states such as Hadya, Kambata and Gurage. Further southwest from the Rift were the Konso, practising terrace agriculture, and others such as the agro-pastoralist Hamar, Mursi and Gelab. Keffa and Welayta to the north of these had relatively long-standing and highly organized, powerful monarchies that dominated the long-distance local trade running on a broadly north–south axis. In many of these places a religious colouring evoked the ancient presence of Christianity. During the campaigns in Welayta in 1894 and Keffa in 1897 such references were made in ways that resembled the use of 'Israelite origins' to justify the dynasty approved in the *Kebre Negest*. In the areas where the Oromo had a firm hold by the late nineteenth century, an association was made by claiming a Christian presence in earlier times. A narrative had the marriage of an Ethiopian *weyzero* (a pre-mid-eighteenth century title for a high-ranking woman), who had fallen on hard times, to a cattle herder named Lalo, a subject of the governor of Bale. According to this symbolic history, the governor had lost his province in the thirteenth century to Lalo, whose children lost their Christianity because the 'cow ate their book', leaving the Oromo since then to read cows' entrails, especially when trying to make decisions on matters of war. A similar association is made with the ruling family of Adal, which was said to have descended from an Ethiopian captive prince, who became a Muslim. Gragn Mohammed, the sixteenth-century challenger of the 'king of kings', as already mentioned, was also said to be the son of an Ethiopian priest and a Muslim woman.

In practical terms, successive rulers engaged in the process of reclaiming the 'lost territories' referred to the sixteenth-century invasions of Gragn Mohammed and the migration of the Oromo, who were said to have cut off the *neguse negest* from the troops they had settled in these areas.[90] Most battles fought following the historical precedence of military settlements were in the south. Menelik's troops, led by *Ras* Gobena, took the lands of the Gurage and the Oromo to the west. *Ras* Gobena had even set up the gunpowder-making units, the *Barud Bet*, by 1875.

The troops of Gojam and Shewa clashed in 1882 at Embabo, as we will see below, and Menelik took the upper hand in this rivalry. The rulers of present-day Wellega and Illubabor submitted to him in 1882, while *Abba* Jifar of Jimma did so in 1883. Menelik campaigned in Bale and Arsi, with *Ras* Dargie taking a major part, and succeeded in incorporating them by 1886, and also captured the city of Harar in 1887 with *Balambaras* (later *Ras*) Mekonnen. Well established directly to the south, corps under *Dejazmach* Beshah Aboye campaigned in Sidamo in 1891. Most of these leaders in the region followed Menelik when he undertook a personal campaign to subjugate Welayta in 1894. In 1897, the same *chewa* corps enabled *Ras* Welde Giyorgis to campaign successfully in Keffa, and *Fitawrari* Habte Giyorgis to do likewise in Borana. Menelik's strong economic and political power had enabled him to become *neguse negest* when Yohannes died in 1889.

The beginning of these reclamation processes was facilitated partly by reduced conflicts and diplomatic compromise between internal rivals, a policy that Yohannes IV pursued while being vigilant to the presence of Egyptians and others along the Red Sea and the Nile Valley. An instance of his internal policy was his attitude towards Adal Tessema of Gojam, who was once loyal to his predecessor Emperor Tekle Giyorgis. Adal bitterly opposed Yohannes's appointee Desta Tedla, son of Tedla Gwalu (famed as a rebel against Tewodros), defeating him in July 1874. A few months later Yohannes confirmed Adal as *ras* and governor of Gojam. Adal proved his loyalty by campaigning in Begemder to assert the emperor's supremacy. Of course rivalries and campaigns still provided battles (which were sometimes at agreed venues), in which warriors could hope to prove themselves.

Another action defined and sealed the political right of the *neguse negest* to decide the status of the rival regional potentates and the territories where they were billeting their troops. Playing one rival off against another, Yohannes permitted *Negus* Tekle Haymanot (the former *Ras* Adal) to continue expanding his territories south of the Abay River, in areas where Menelik's troops were already campaigning. He then brought Menelik and Tekle Haymanot to a political meeting with him in 1882, and held them to account for their disobedience in clashing at Embabo without his 'permission'. Persuading them to accept his authority even extended to arranging succession to his throne: he secured the marriage of Menelik's daughter, Zewditu, to his son, *Ras* Araya Selassie. When two regional kings (*negus*) accepted the authority of Yohannes IV, and rightly, as the 'master' in command of the most weapons, it meant

---

[90] For similar reasoning, see Mahteme Selassie Welde Meskel, *Memories of Significance*, 1962 EC, pp. 108–9.

that valiant warriors recognized the militaristic position of the *neguse negest*.

Thus going beyond a show of military force, Yohannes's political moves concerning the two rivals gave fresh prominence to the principle of rule by the *neguse negest*. What Tewodros had started by disciplining his troops had resulted in reducing the potential of emergent warriors and their leaders to assert local power against the agents of the *neguse negest*. Nonetheless, control by the 'king of kings' was enhanced by their connections with Europeans, and the access that gave them to a relatively large quantity of weapons imported into the country by traders, travellers and diplomatic missions. Such empowerment enabled them to make a significant policy change to reduce the importance of other tools, such as resources in the frontier lands or access to communal land ownership.

3

Military Lands and Power Politics

Emergent warriors and political leaders commonly held land as the core of symbolic identification with their ancestral people and places. Such identification meant pure ownership rather than the 'holding right' that rural people were given by legal instruments that the state generated.[1] The fighters protected communal ownership once they achieved social approval for their competence to do so. Seeing land as their metaphor for 'country' and its borders, they engaged in national defence on their own initiative, or under rebels or monarchs. Counter to this perspective was the theoretical ownership of all land by the 'king of kings'. The most senior titleholder among the *chewa*, the monarch, used land as an award to meritorious loyal warriors, for *maderya*, payments for military services rendered, or as *gult* in lieu of salary for administrators. Rights to *gult* lands reverted to the crown on death, and the *maderya* could be confirmed to family members if they volunteered to continue to serve as soldiers. In both regards, land for the monarchs was their tool for centralizing state power and legitimacy.[2]

Land use, also an all-important political and economic base for the *chewa*, divided society perceptually into professional soldiers, clergy and private farmers (some of whom worked on their own lands and others on state lands). Women and members of occupational minorities were not awarded grants of lands reserved for military service, and other land grants occasionally made to them did not entail military titles and honours. A rare exception of women holding titles and

---

[1] Emphasis here is on the customary beliefs of communal ownership, and not on history-specific legal provisions on land in Ethiopia. For a recent study on legal provisions see, for example, Daniel W. Ambaye, *Land Rights in Ethiopia*, Springer International Publishing Switzerland, 2015.

[2] On the power and legitimacy of the monarchs see Messay Kebede, *Survival and Modernization, Ethiopia's Enigmatic Present: A Philosophical Discourse*, Lawrenceville, NJ: Red Sea Press, 1999, pp. 118–19. The strategy of the monarchs asserting their authority by making and unmaking appointments as they saw fit is referred to also by Markakis, *Ethiopia: Anatomy*, 1974, pp. 37–40. Contrasting the monarchs with nobles from different eras, Pankhurst also argues that 'appointments and dismissals' were important indicators of the relative strengths of the kings. See his *State and Land in Ethiopian History* (2nd edn), Hollywood, CA: Tsehai Publishers, 2006, pp. 9, 18, 34.

even appointments to administrative posts occurred in the reign of Emperor Zera Yaqob (r.1434–68), who appointed his two sisters to provincial governorates (but later hanged them for disobeying his orders to stop participating in a spirit worship cult). In the seventeenth century, Emperor Serse Dingil granted land and certain jurisdictions to some women. Others of high rank received the new title of *weyzero*, the local version of the Turkish vizier, and though the duties it entailed at the time are difficult to establish, powerful men in the nineteenth century claimed the crown on the basis of being descendants of the *weyzero*. Any titles or status women received, however, did not generally modify their access to land grants until government reforms specified land ownership as usufruct rights that could be inherited; but this was only in the late nineteenth and early twentieth centuries.

The military and administrative concerns of land use represented the conflicting power of the monarchs and local people over land. Over time, they affected how the individual related to land and how the deeper processes of local boundaries and national defence were perceived. In the warrior tradition, participation in military activity, whether voluntary or not, was theoretically open to warrior men and women. However, meritorious political power for military service was strictly open only to men. During 1769–1855, even this was undermined when perfidious recipients manipulated and purloined their *gult* grants. Their action displaced local landowners from their communal lands, and weakened the 'kings of kings', who thereby could not access the soldiery or raise administrative resources.

When the monarchs regained their power in the latter part of the nineteenth century and engaged in the project of reclaiming 'lost territories', they were able to lure warriors by offering them land rewards for military service. The project involved moving participating trained warriors out of their rural home communities to settle permanently elsewhere. They were no longer defending their communal lands, and those left behind were discouraged from engaging in warriorhood. Significantly, by the time that tax in cash for 'measured' land (*qelad*) was introduced in the first two decades of the twentieth century, rural owners of communal land had lost the bargaining instrument with the state and its agents that land had been. The defensive engagements, as they perceived them (restoring to the state what it had lost), brought warriors directly under a monarchical state that took over sole responsibility for defending territorial Ethiopia.

TAKING AWAY THE KING'S *GULT*

The process of depriving local communities of their rights in this regard had started earlier when some titled nobles reneged on their loyalty and challenged the theoretical rights of the 'kings of kings' by taking over *gult* lands and turning them into private holdings to pass on to their descendants.³ These powerful nobles abandoned the regions they were meant to administer on behalf of the monarchs and became either kingmakers or autonomous rulers of the so-called *Zemene Mesafint* (Era of Princes). This provoked the emergence of new centres of power in the late eighteenth and early nineteenth centuries.

The changes in land tenure followed the challenge that *Ras* Mikael Sehul of Tigre had initiated in 1769 in Gonder, and were intensified by the nobles who came from Yeju. Confiscation of rural lands spread to the rest of Begemder, and to Tigre, Eritrea, Gojam, Wello and most likely Shewa, directing the transmission of economic power away from the state and the monarchs to urban dwelling recipients of *gult*. Like those in Gonder, *gult*-holding nobles in these areas vied to increase their access to land with which to pay their private fighting forces. The *gult* system that had once facilitated the survival of the state with the 'wandering capitals' thus became a source of the near-demise of the monarchy. This led to the rise of autonomous and disparate centres of power, with some even rejecting the authority of the *neguse negest*. The pauperized monarchs lost their prescriptive ownership of all land – their source of personal income and their means of raising and rewarding loyal servicemen. Only occasionally did the enfeebled 'kings of kings' at the centre of these new developments demonstrate any modicum of military strength. An outstanding example was Tekle Giyorgis I, who, during one of his spells on the throne (1779–84), headed south to receive allegiance from Asfa Wesen of Shewa, who discreetly paid him tribute.

It was not only the monarchy that suffered. The changing ownership of lands meant the transmission of economic power to private hands, challenging the inalienable right to *rest* and the right to local inheritance known as the *atsme rest* (literally, skeletal land ownership, i.e. personal access to communal land). This process generated landless labourers of a category called *zega*, without rights and privileges, and entirely excluded from political rights inherent in communal lands.⁴ It disrupted their social organizations and their skilful management of local land rights. As *zega*, landless farmers either had to comply with slave-like servitude or flee the claimant's jurisdiction. If they remained in their former communal lands, they became providers not only of farm products but of personal services.⁵ Many migrated in search of employment as soldiers, retainers or servants in disparate centres of power. As the increasingly drifting individual *zega* had grown up as self-trained warriors in the *chewa* tradition, they found employment as retainers and soldiers (*wetader*) with 'capable masters'. Their private employers organized them loosely into coordinated military forces to

---
³ Crummey, *Land and Society*, 2000, pp. 194–7.
⁴ Habtamu, *Land Tenure*, 2011, pp. 202–12. The word *zega* is neither in the text nor in the title of the French translation of Menelik's chronicle, Guèbrè Sellassié, *Chronique*, Vol. I, 1930, p. 196, presumably because the translator, Tèsfa Sellassié, did not see its significance as a category. It appears in a title (on p. 99) of a published Amharic version (to which I currently have no access).
⁵ Habtamu, *Land Tenure*, 2011, p. 208.

which they promised land rewards, thereby increasing the frequency of raids during breaks in agriculture cycles. This development was what Caulk aptly described as the 'predatory' means of collecting tribute by the nobles.[6]

People in communal lands were rendered powerless and landless. Losing the rights pertaining to ownership, they were left with nothing to use as a political counterweight to unjust 'masters'. Their condition laid the foundation for distancing the relationship between Ethiopian monarchs and the public. The difficulties of these country people, including children, in unexpectedly having to search for employment is depicted by a singer, *Azmari* Sahle, who ran away from a 'master' because the chores of cutting grass, tethering the mule and closing the gates to the compound overwhelmed him as a child. Later employed by a travelling singer to carry his musical instruments, he experienced people giving him food and other gifts, and more importantly, the man taught him his art. In fond memory of this mentor, Sahle therefore opened all his own entertainments with the following couplet:

ለጌታ ማገራ ማበዴ ማበዴ
ሳር ኣጭጄ ሃዳ ጣም እሬ ሆዬ
Taking service under a 'master' – madness, madness!
Having gone to cut grass, my stomach went empty in the night![7]

The couplet first recalls his childhood under his thoughtless 'master' and his exhaustion from cutting fodder grass for the animals of guests. By referring to the stomach, idiomatically the seat of thoughts, secrets and intentions, it also expresses the futility of making sacrifices to benefit those who live off the poor.

The contradictions inherent in the *chewa* capacity to tax local lands generated systemic tensions during most of the nineteenth century. Land tenure, the basis for recruiting and organizing a loyal army that the monarch could call up for general defence, did not deter local people from training as *chewa* soldiers in defence of their local communal lands. Whenever the *neguse negest* asserted local land rights and holdings as part of a general scheme of taxation, it contradicted the political use of *wegen* that was at the core of *chewa* ideals of local defence. Local people constantly rivalled each other in either support or defiance of government officials. In many places, locally emerging warriors, in the 1840s, for instance, contrasting themselves with urbane *chewa* who were not necessarily from the immediate locality, were not constrained from engaging in warfare on their own initiative. As Plowden wrote, 'A whole province of cultivators, in times when the military are engaged elsewhere, will meet by accord, and some thousands of them will attack another province, destroying, burning, and bequeathing feuds to distant generations.'[8]

---

[6] Caulk, 'Bad Men of the Borders', 1984, pp. 201–27.
[7] Oral information on *Azmari* Sahle came from my mother, *Weyzero* Workaferahu Haile. She recalled this man as an elderly singer in pre-war Sidamo.
[8] Plowden, *Travels in Abyssinia*, 1868, p. 135.

To challenge those from outside their community, emerging warriors in the period rallied social support and built up and maintained local fighters. Raising sufficient personal followers meant accessing wealth to shelter, feed and clothe a large number of people, and land plots with which to make rewards. It meant having many domestic women produce foodstuffs, and engaging blacksmiths and artisans to forge spears, swords and other war materials, and weavers to make the clothes – all of which had vital symbolic value for political and military events. Self-sufficient leaders had to have cattle, crops and houses to accommodate some of these producers as their dependants, and more significantly to provide for the self-trained warrior farmers to display their martial skills. These were the conditions under which local 'masters' or leaders who enjoyed social support could formally consider their local communities as their *wegen*, or 'allies'. They could not call upon them for political and military support without these preconditions, and would be seen as their own 'masters' and even 'father of the country' if they had access to such resources. Having a large number of followers to lead against external 'blood' enemies (*dina*), or to rally in defence of country and crown when called upon to do so, would make them accomplished 'masters'. Such capacity and successful organization by local leaders mirrored the military structure supporting the monarch, and had serious significant social and political implications.

DEFENCE OF BOUNDARIES

Communal boundaries were traditionally demarcated by brooks, bushes, trees, permanent stones, man-made trenches, ditches and banks, while long-enduring sites within communal *rest* lands, notably the burial places of ancestral bones or umbilical cords, personified human identity. The boundary markers, *cheqa*, carried both metaphorical and real meanings for villages, personal holdings and local markets, symbolizing the singularity of a rural community within them. *Rest* was a fundamental socio-legal criterion representing holdings that recognized communal ownership ideals and control of inalienable rights. The ideals defined the limitations of the emergent warriors' belongingness and defence. Trespassing over the boundaries of *rest* holdings caused clashes between neighbouring communities, while violating the right to personal entitlements of access to plots within *rest* caused frequent murders.

The markers were recorded in writing and orally, including by informing young children about the demarcations. 'When land or houses are sold numerous little children are called to receive a handful of peas, and are useful afterwards as witnesses from those juvenile recollections.'[9] These one-off presents aided memory in those living all their lives in their villages. Stories accompanying the relevant markers

[9] Mahteme Selassie, *Memories of Significance*, Addis Ababa, 1962 EC, pp. 138–49.

inculcated in such children the sense of ownership of local land holdings, accompanied by inalienable rights of belongingness in the communal *rest*. Opening their minds to recognizing their rights of participation in local politics, the stories encouraged awareness of the importance of collecting knowledge of local events. Drawing their attention to transactions involving the buying and selling of houses or land helped prepare the community's children to develop into well-informed elders. When this knowledge combined with hunting expeditions, as we will soon see, boys gained ritual and symbolic attachment to their communities and lands.

Euphemistically, the word 'land' (*meder*) stood for 'tolerance' – as in the earth idiomatically 'tolerating all creatures' – or for broad-minded human beings. The soil itself was perceived to link the ancestors with the living and the children to come. Soil from ancestral lands and grave sites was attributed with spiritual potency, symbolizing control over death and life. Should those who inherit plots in communal lands quarrel, none of the parties might bring into their house soil from the grave of the person who had passed on the inheritance to them. It could cause death. On the other hand, a traditional medical textbook prescribes 'the soil from the grave' for inducing a barren woman's fertility.[10] That is, bringing 'soil from the grave' was a way of giving and receiving life from the earth. In the generic sense, ownership of a plot within *rest* lands, the minimum property a human being could have, was associated with the sense of belongingness to the permanent factor of earth – the marker of human continuity and permanence. Even though land ownership was a criterion by which status was broadly differentiated, this attitude towards soil influenced such social categorization as the distancing of crafts producers who mysteriously burn soil for their creativity. Basically, that is, the *chewa* principle of identifying people with land in their own communities was not extended to their ownership elsewhere – except during attacks from outside Ethiopia. This explains why, when a governor was assigned to work elsewhere, the whole military and civil retinue followed him, leaving their landed positions to the new governor and his followers. Within their own communities, the same *chewa* principle also marginalized crafts producers, often even preventing distinguished hunters or warriors among them from being rewarded with land grants.

Warriorhood implied willingness to 'die for' the place where ancestors' *atint ena gultmit* ('bones and fragments of bones') 'were crushed', where their 'blood was spilled', and where one's own 'sweat was shed'. In that sense, *rest* land was the bearer of the defensive sacrifice of both ancestors and their living descendants – a mark of human continuity and permanence. In some areas, such as Wello and Shewa, the earth itself was a respected, almost venerated entity in its own right. People were discouraged from aiming at the naked earth when practising

[10] Tsehai Berhane Selassie, 'An Ethiopian Medical Text-Book Written by Gerazmach Gäbräwäld Arägahäñ Däga Damot', *Journal of Ethiopian Studies*, Vol. 9, No. 1, 1971, pp. 95–180.

javelin throwing or shooting. Though this was not entirely unknown, they normally practised on other targets such as trees.[11] An orally transmitted complaint against the invasion of 1935–41 was on Italian aerial bombing of the earth 'for no reason at all' – the earth that had done them no harm.

This minimal ideal of the power of communal land ownership and belongingness was also transmitted in how people saw themselves. All descendants of an original *abat* ('ancestor') of a community were collectively known as *balabat*, 'owners of father', irrespective of their engagements in cultivating, livestock herding, soldiering, weaving or pottery making. Broadly speaking, such a community spoke the same language, related to the same social circle and owned plots in a defined area. In this sense, the insult *yetabak!* or *yetabash!* (literally, 'which father of yours!') is a very serious challenge – one that insults a person as a nonentity, without social roots anywhere on earth. Moreover, to speak of someone 'with a father' (*bale-abat*) was a political adage that expressed pride in being local and relating to the rest of the community.[12] This wider meaning may be at the root of using *balabat* as the term for the lowest local official.

Customarily, individuals had the right of access to specific plots, *meret* (a word that literally meant 'the earth' or 'soil'), and of passing these on to their descendants or selling them. However, any sale could occur only with the explicit permission of those others descended from the common ancestor. Even the powerful were expected to consult with siblings and other local members over this. Those from outside the community who owned land through purchase or inheritance from vulnerable people could do so mainly because they were not socially rooted there. An Amharic expression, that *rest* 'would come back to its owner even after a thousand years', accommodates changes that could happen through purchase or gifts or inheritance from elderly or other vulnerable people without relatives. The saying strengthens different means of acquiring private plots. It is also a reminder that the right to ancestral communal lands that made any person its *balabat*, literally assumed that nobody was without land, and that no land was without its owners.

Owning personal plots (becoming *bale meret*) ensured belongingness in such protected communal lands. It also asserted the permanence of land as an economic asset. Controlled access to personal land ownership prevented control of the local communal *rest* by those who were considered 'non-related' (*ba'ed*), sometimes even distancing rulers as 'strangers'. Losing one's land, therefore, was akin to losing a sense of belonging somewhere – the sense of belongingness that was strengthened by customary law that discouraged transfers. This perception

---

[11] Of course there were games of throwing javelins at a point on the ground. See Marcel Griaule, *Jeux et divertissements abyssins abyssins* (Bibliothèque de l'École des Hautes Études, Sciences religieuses, Vol. 49), Paris: Ernest Leroux, 1935, pp. 92–3.
[12] This sense of the word is generic, and differs from its use as an office or position for government officers.

even inhibited accomplished local fighters from using military force to take land. To resist military-driven control of community-oriented land rights, many voted with their feet or engaged in face-to-face battle.

Defence of so-defined local lands brought forward self-trained, socially approved and popular warrior individuals prepared to die for their communal boundaries. Known as *yegobez aleqa*, literally 'chief of the brave', the military power of such leaders ranged from the broad categorical term of 'family circle' (*wegen*) to the wider community. They could choose to exercise political and military privilege by convincing local people to accept the government or reject the exercise of its power, and their wives replaced them in their absence. Resultant frequent battles and interpersonal rivalry often confused the process of distinguishing the 'local' from the 'outsider', but combatants used self-identifying codes, at least in the 1916 Battle of Segele, as we will see below.

DYING IN DEFENCE[13]

Defending ancestral home and family, including spouse, parents, community and posterity, or 'dying for them', was identical to defending one's country. Famed leaders of communities that owned the local *hager* were socially rooted potentates who were expected to exclude external enemies (*dina*). Vigorous defence of a socially supported ancestral homeland underpinned *chewa* military practices of organizing an army. Emergent warrior leadership of local defence did not entail loyalty to a central 'master' located elsewhere, but a leader could take up political space in the wider setting. However, the local boundary markers were used for purposes of tribute collection, and this caused contestation and even rebellion against government troops, who tried to control local lands in the name of the *neguse negest*. Defending land on that account meant that farmers were not the docile underdogs of powerful rulers and governors. Nonetheless, the possibility of others accessing local lands was a political issue that led to constant reconceptualization of the 'insider' (*wegen*). Engaging local people to either support or reject the government was also a political matter, especially along border areas.

'Dying for land' was a nineteenth-century emergent warriors' expression of local politics that concerned the defence of communal lands. It meant taking up the vocation of warriorhood, and anyone who undertook to do so was a *wetader* – now a technical term for 'soldier'. The word derives from *watto*, 'staying out', or *wato*, 'roaming', and was strongly associated with mobility. It meant one who 'roams', 'lives [his or her] nights out in the open' or is 'without a fixed place of work'. Idealized association of the same word with bravery, manhood and

---

[13] i.e. of one's land, country, monarch, 'master', wife, honour, self, religion and a host of other issues.

masculinity signified courageously facing danger in order to defend communal lands. A brave soldier was spoken of in the feminine in everyday Amharic. This is strictly to denote admiration and deep respect verging on fear is clear from referring to a brave woman as 'man of a woman', and to a cowardly man as 'he is not a man simply because he has it dangling'.

Linguists do not seem to have paid specific attention to the gendered use of Amharic in the military system. At least one linguist, who also refers to findings by others, asserts that 'the language relies heavily on the natural gender', has 'definite masculine and feminine markers', 'the vast majority of animate nominals have the same root for both males and females', 'the default marker' is masculine, and that gender inversion of words in Amharic is circumstantial.[14] Battles, warfare or clashes are certainly always referred to in the masculine, signifying the 'default'. 'Feminized' words denote a relatively diminutive size such as meagre resources, small village-like towns or a short distance yet to be covered. As we will see below, mothers who have lost several children in infancy refer to their surviving offspring in the opposite sex for the purpose of 'hiding them from death', a tendency similar to hiding monarchs' identity on the battlefield by wearing similar clothing. Any connection between the symbolic, metaphorical hiding of infants from death by changing their gender pronoun and the strikingly common citation of brave and heroic warriors in the feminine can only, however, be conjectural.

In *zeraf* sessions, in which the enemy was often belittled, expressions of superiority did not apply gender inversion. During the training of warriors, hunters disparaged those who failed strictly for their cowardice, and lauded the successful for their brave achievements, but here too there was no gender inversion. The ultimate object of *chewa* warfare and defence – 'Ethiopia' – is referred to in the feminine, and she is called 'the motherland' for the purpose of expressing affection and attachment. Sayings such as 'one sent by a woman fears no death' were empirical expressions of the practice of women encouraging men participating in battles. Despite pervasive gender inequality,[15] it should be noted, *chewa* parlance used neutral words properly to defend and emphasize any male or female warrior who is brave (*gobez* or *jegna*), loyal (*tamagn*) and a patriotic lover of country (*arbegna*). A courageous individual was a person who was not afraid of death, and was not distracted by material gains. Such a brave person firmly stood up for the 'master', the land, the spouse and other dependants, collectively called *wegen*. He or she did 'not hold his or her soul in a piece of cloth'.

Displaying these ideals, especially the qualities of courage and obliviousness to danger, contributed strongly to self-advancement. Local and

---

[14] Ruth Kramer, 'Gender in Amharic: A Morphosyntactic Approach to Natural and Grammatical Gender', July 2012.
[15] For recent studies on patriarchal denigrations in Amharic phrases, proverbs or sayings, see Aschalew Bililigne, 'Female Disempowerment: some expressions in Amharic', Addis Ababa University, 2012, an MA thesis in linguistics.

social ties, real or affected, were critical elements in attracting brave, loyal and 'manly' retainers. Gaining respect and rising to leadership, for whatever cause, through such local endorsement, irrespective of the size and constitution of followers, meant achieving recognition for one's prowess from the local community. For the most part, however, real bravery was resistance to outside pressures. Revenge killing was 'bravery' only in some communities like the Oromo of Rayya, Yeju and parts of Gojam. Killing a personal enemy (without a court decision) – literally *nefs* or *sew matfat* (Amharic) – tantamount to 'killing the soul', was murder and punishable by law. Some communities were considered 'brave countries' for sheltering murderers or revenge killers from neighbouring communities. Keffa and Welayta were 'brave countries' for resisting domination, while Gojam was considered 'brave' for refusing to accommodate tax collectors from time to time.

Indicators of political authority were seen as meaningful only in the context of communal interest. 'Personal bravery', *jebdu*, was appreciated only during military expeditions outside one's locality, or when setting off on a military career on behalf of one's immediate community or *wegen*. Thus a brave warrior who became an alternative rallying focus was selected leader to uphold the notable values of standing up for land, family and 'master'. Even in that context, it was necessary to report to elders on matters affecting local communities before starting military activities. Otherwise it would be resistance to social authority, and doing this, especially regarding matters vital to the community, was frowned upon and considered *jebdegninet*, hollow bravado.

The presence of active soldiers increased the status of a local community on the defensive, and, depending on the occasion, its capacity to form alliances with neighbours. Organizing for unexpected battle being no small matter, a local leader with the largest *wegen* would be seen as an influential elder, *abat* or *ya abat*, 'father' or 'father of father', respectively. Equivalent to the *aba dula*, 'father of war', of the Oromo or the Sidama, to whom local communities gave social endorsement, such noted, important men (*teleq sew*) advanced their status by taking initiatives in leading the community in its local cause, especially during such crisis times as 1935–41.

There were several views on the frequency with which independent soldiering led to fights. Despite the social support they had, local people could be critical of those with different political views, and even battles could draw amusement. When autonomous power centres, such as *Dejazmach* Wube's and *Ras* Ali's, fought during the Era of Princes, a farmer asked a soldier returning from the battlefield: 'How did the battle end?' The other replied: '*Dejach* Wube was defeated and *Ras* Ali ran away!'[16] 'Come on, be in order!' said the listener, and the soldier replied, 'They were not in order themselves; how can I be!'[17] Such commentaries

---

[16] *Dejach* is colloquial for *dejazmach*.
[17] Bairu Tafla, *Aşma Giyorgis and his work*, 1987, pp. 443, 641. Bairu uses 'seriously' rather than 'order' in the translation, necessarily for the compatibility of the nuance in English. I have used the word 'order' so as to give the wider

on this unusual outcome of a battle censored disorderly leaders. Even long-term group battles were stereotyped. Thus, *Aleqa* Tekle Iyesus, for instance, attributed revenge warfare and internal fighting among Oromo clans (*gosa*) of Shewa and Wellega, which were common, to the simple pretext that someone from the neighbouring group beat a pet dog, creating quarrels lasting generations.

One who attempts to create an organized military following without sufficient social backing was called an *amba-gennen*, 'one with mountaintop fame': that is, one famed for the landscape rather than for the people. This was an attribute of rebellion against local society, and implied that the leader had yet to garner acceptability by explaining his cause and seeking social backing and authority. It was not unusual for such leaders to emerge and attract support from elsewhere, say a neighbouring community, and several such leaders were collectively known as leaders in the *amba* and the *gora* ('mountaintop' and 'valley'). Their presence indicated widespread rebellion, and often led to chaos. Especially in times of widespread war, therefore, local socio-political relationships encouraged political awareness, for instance discouraging government service that would allow access to land tenure.

Government soldiers from lands designated for military service took all issues of land primarily as their responsibility. Soldiering was only another seasonal occupation for the farmers, priests, traders and others, but engagement in local issues was basic to military activities and was not to be left to the army or the highest political authority. Answering to government calls did not mean abandoning matters of social self-identity and communal responsibility. After all defending ancestral lands and communities was a responsible step that led to the highest echelons of society and military rank, with or without involvement in the government army. Warriorhood was part of local life, and partly as a result, the protagonists of the frequent conflicts could draw on a constant supply of men. Thus, it was easier to take these to raid outlying border areas to extract tribute by force, and eventually to assert their association with those places.[18]

Leaders and retainers had similar training. As Plowden commented, 'it must ever be remembered, that between the chief and the most ragged of his followers there is no distinction'. Attributing this to a lack of difference in education, orientation and thinking, he evaluated '[t]he Abyssinian' as an 'equal of his chief, frequently far more elegant in his humility than the latter in his arrogance'. Plowden also contrasted the 'Abyssinian' soldier with the English, who were more

---

(contd) meaning referring to the militaristic behaviour that, I believe, was appropriately intended in the conversation. See also ተክለ ጻድቅ መኩሪያ ዐፄ ተዎድሮስ እና የኢትዮጵያ አንድነት ኩራዝ አሳታሚ ድርጅት 1981 (Tekle Tsadik Mekuria, *Emperor Tewodros and Ethiopian Unity*, Addis Ababa: Kuraz Publishing Agency, 1981 EC), p. 100.

[18] See Caulk, 'Bad Men of the Borders, 1984, pp. 201–27; Irma Taddia, 'Land Politics in the Ethiopian-Eritrean Border Area', 2009, pp. 58–82.

concerned with class distinction.[19] As socially approved soldiering and participation in military activities were instrumental in an individual's self-advancement, all soldiers aspired to achieve the potential or real status and capacity to award retainers with hierarchical military titles. However, the capacity to give titles of the military hierarchy to their followers, a capacity that was in practice limited to relatively few, distinguished successful warriors from others.

Emerging warriors' familiarity with the necessary politics also meant organizing themselves into a fighting force on the same pattern as the army under the *neguse negest*. The similarity meant that individuals could join the retinue of a nearby army of a powerful titled officer recognized by the local population and find ways of initiating their military career. In other words, warriors seeking access to high political space could join government leaders and authorities who were capable of rewarding them. They could take employment in any capacity, from grass cutter to shield bearer, from spearman to staff bearer and gunner. Such men, of course, risked being taken away from their land tenure-based obligations, or having their services and land designated as reserved for military purposes.

MILITARY OFFICIALS, BILLETED SOLDIERS AND POLITICAL POWER

The assertion of holding lands and communities through *tesari sarawit*, 'billeted troops', since Axumite times has left a historical legacy of military reserve lands whose owner warriors were loyal to the monarchs. Sometimes described as whole 'countries', these lands were in the northern regions of Gojam, Begemder, Saynt, Wello and Tigre.[20] In these provinces, the 'kings of kings'' appointees, namely *gult-gez* officials, could call up the inhabitants of such lands for combat. It seems that the monarchs brought from elsewhere *teseri serawit* (billeted soldiery) to live among the *balager* (country people). This strategy of billeting outmanoeuvred local notions of holding on to ancestral lands. The monarchs and their agents were supposed to seek advice on accessing local resources from the *balabat*, whose duty it was to ensure acceptable levels of relationship with the government. Leaving local people with much reduced rights and privileges, it often caused the rise of warriors who challenged local authorities. Such warriors were designated *shifta*.

Billeted soldiers, their leaders and the *gult-gez* officials replicated the same beliefs in territories that they set out to 'reclaim' in the nineteenth century, notably in the south, as will be shown below. In these areas, the government-appointed low-level *chewa* official, the *balabat*, was answerable to the governor, even though he was supposedly to

---

[19] Plowden, *Travels in Abyssinia*, 1868, p. 60.
[20] Imru Haile Selassie, *From What I Saw and Recollect*, 2002 EC, pp. 130–1.

seek and acquire permission of the landowners to secure their lands for the notionally temporary use of higher officials.[21] In the north, the title *balabat* was given either to a locally senior authority or to the warrior with the most social and military ties. In the south, both the *balabat* and his duty to mediate between the local *rest* owners and the billeted soldiers were more or less imposed on the local community. Leaders of billeted soldiers supposedly had the obligation to consult with him about 'extra' (i.e. vacant) plots on which they could billet their retinue. However, the billeted soldiers reduced or at least ignored his power, especially in communities considered to have fought valiantly against the billeting, thus making the local people subservient to them. In Welayta, Jimma and Wellega, where formerly supreme rulers were exceptionally powerful, raising and collecting taxes was left entirely to them. Appointing a *balabat* eased the appropriation of land because the local population tolerated them. Such officials were supposed to collect only land-based tax rather than the labour of the population, but were also accused of irregularities in this regard in the 1920s.

In the 'reclaimed' territories, titled governors or provincial kings were appointed to command *reste-gult* land and other local resources to sustain military officers and retainers. These 'masters' and the billeted soldiers drew their maintenance from the *gebbar*, literally 'taxpayer in kind' (from *gibir* 'tax' or 'tribute'), which made the local *balager* carry the burden of providing both military and domestic service to the local officials rather than to the state.[22] Till the end of the 1870s, the dispossessed soldiers from the north even expected to appropriate local *rest* lands and transfer the local *atsme rest* to themselves by cajoling and pressurizing the *balabat*. After the land reforms that began around 1894,[23] therefore, the rights of communities were invariably overshadowed by the new *rest* owners' duties to collect taxes, administer justice, maintain peace and manage landed property. In the first decade of the twentieth century, the billeted soldiers passed on this privilege as a personal inheritance. On top of making people subservient, they challenged the traditional forms, sizes, permanence and, of course, identity of ownership of plots. This allowed those soldiers and their descendants to transform local land rights into their personal ownership in the post-1941 period.

In the 1890s, providing military service had symbolic importance

[21] Crummey, *Land and Society*, 2000, pp. 23–49.
[22] Bahru Zewde, *A History of Modern Ethiopia*, 2001, pp. 14–15 and 92, has presented this as part of the surplus extraction mechanism the warriors employed, and says that the words *gebbar* and *balager* are interchangeable. He illustrates that such tax extraction prevailed in the north as well by quoting Plowden, who travelled in northern Ethiopia. Markakis emphasizes that it refers mainly to the south. See Markakis, *Ethiopia: Anatomy*, 1974, pp. 79, 110–11.
[23] Land tenure rights and obligations, systematized since about 1894, are detailed to some extent in Mahteme Selassie, *Memories of Significance*, 1962 EC, pp. 69, 105–32.

to members of the households of 'masters', whose higher status meant they could keep ownership of lands allocated as *maderya*. This imposition of military service with such lands established and enhanced the authority of the state, especially in the south. The burdens of local farmers in the south increased every time the government changed its administrators. The departing official and his retinue collected additional resources, while the newcomer simultaneously appointed a temporary *asash*, 'surveyor', who prepared the collection of similar revenue. This practice of *chewa* administrators was officially contested in the 1920s by local people in Gurage and Kambata who successfully appealed to the central government to regularize the acquisition of goods and other materials from local taxpayers.[24]

FUNCTIONS OF MILITARY LAND GRANTS

Not all plots on communal lands were allocated for military purposes. Strictly speaking, living on military lands distinguished soldiers from other members of a local community, and their survival in office depended on the power of the commander to organize *rest* (inalienable communal land) and *atsme rest* (personal access to communal land) for military purposes. Supreme commanders could threaten to expel soldiers and *rest* owners if they failed to serve in the army during general mobilization of the 'country'. Commanders might receive either a defiant or a positive reaction, and very often the latter during general crises and mobilization.

Military officers could offer and give military land grants to anyone, except in Tigre, where traditionally Muslims 'were not allowed to hold land'. Yohannes IV's decree of 1875 against Islam brought about temporary grants to converts to Christianity who, after returning to Islam, were able to keep their land grants.[25] This was partly said to be in reaction to war with Egypt and the consequent suspicion of Islam. Foreigners who rendered crafts production services received land grants too.[26] Women, who had not been involved in formal administration since the fifteenth century, did not qualify for grants of military lands, at least not in their own right. In Tigre and Serae, Yohannes IV improved women's rights to inherit landed property from their fathers.[27] Elsewhere too, they could inherit such property from their fathers, or on the illness or death of their husbands, and could often act as regents or guardians of male minors entitled to succeed their fathers.[28] However, after 1941, elders and high military and state officials frequently diverted such inheritances of females to male relatives or even to themselves.

[24] Imru Haile Selassie, *From What I Saw and Recollect*, 2002 EC, pp. 180–2.
[25] Pankhurst, *Economic History*, 1968, p. 147.
[26] Pankhurst, *Economic History*, 1968, pp. 142.
[27] Pankhurst, *Economic History*, 1968, p. 147.
[28] Pankhurst, *Economic History*, 1968, pp. 135–7, 148–9 and 548–52.

There were five forms of land grants in the category of *maderya* that enabled military officers to recruit warriors and exact tribute from the locality. In the late nineteenth century, the *maderya* known as *milmil meret*, 'recruits' land', sent a fixed number of youths to a sector of the military called *milmil*. Those of the 'water-ration land', *wiha senqu*, were responsible for tents and other effects in the supplies unit. Those of the 'convoy land', *gindebel meret*, served in the baggage units of the state army on the march, and each household on such lands in normal times fed and maintained one or two horses for army use. Those on 'cavalry land', *balderas*, kept large numbers of horses and other pack animals while the *abne-lam meret* (Amharic for 'cattle-keepers' land': namely the *tsehafi lahem*, the 'scribe of cattle' or *abne-lam* 'responsible for cattle' in sixteenth-century Ge'ez records, or *werre-genu* in the Oromo language) were responsible for army livestock, as already noted.[29]

High-ranking officers such as *dejazmach*, including *yewech dejazmach* ('provincial') and *balenegarit dejazmach* ('drum-beating') *dejazmach*, and *ras* were appointed over areas called *mar agar*, 'honey land', where farmers kept bees to pay them tribute in honey. Such officers had the privilege of brewing the celebrated *tej* (honey mead), to drink themselves or to reward the bravest of their soldiers. Inhabitants of other areas paid in kind, including household effects and food items for the state army during its mobilization, campaigns or expeditions. In western Shewa, for instance, people reportedly paid minor kitchen utensils and food items as tribute, mainly from their private supplies.[30] Plots known as *metkeya-menqeya*, literally 'with which to supplant-remove', were given, on a very temporary basis, to retainers with military prowess. They were intended to provide officeholders with income for the period of their appointment. Giving such plots within communal *rest* areas was often, but not always, the privilege of military leaders with responsibility for distributing titles and appointments on behalf of the state. After the land reforms and the introduction of 'modern' institutions, including the fledgling state army set up in the 1920s, it was sons of such officials who were recruited into military service.

Making military land grants was known as *mireet*, literally 'guiding' or 'allotting' lands. Officials known as *abegaz* assumed such rights over whole territories that became 'countries of the *abegaz*'.[31] Their privilege ended when they were demoted. Such administrative regions existed in most parts of the north, and the local people were permanent military

---

[29] The sons of such landowners were recruited into the 'modern' army that was set up in the 1920s. On the sons of the *Gendebel* who were recruited into the bodyguard, for instance, see Mahteme Selassie, *Memories of Significance*, 1962 EC, p. 111. See also the last chapter of the current book on other recruits.
[30] Mahteme Selassie, *Memories of Significance*, 1962 EC, p. 116.
[31] Until the mid-nineteenth century, rulers in Gurage country were locally known as *abegaz*, and at least one of them as *negusu*. Dorsisa, who held the title *negus*, was said to have lived in the early 1800s. See William Shack and Habte-Mariam Marcos, *Gods and Heroes: Oral Traditions of the Gurage of Ethiopia*, Oxford University Press, 1974, p. 84.

service providers. In the southwest they included Jimma and Wellega, where billeted soldiers from the north were not given *gebbar* (literally 'tribute payers') but extracted produce from allocated lands worked by someone else they employed for a fixed share. As neither the office nor the status was expected to be hereditary or of long duration, the *abegaz* were not entitled to pass the land to their descendants or anybody else. However, some administrators used their position to help their troops transfer local land to others.

This irregularity, coupled with the turnover of officials assigned to administer the grants, mirrored the volatility of the military personnel. The grants of plots known as *maderya* (literally 'on which to live') illustrate the impact of this volatility on the local population. Sometimes, leaders of expeditions assumed the right to institute *maderya* even for local warriors who opted to follow them. A 'master' would give such grants as part of *qeleb*, literally 'something to eat' or maintenance, in lieu of salary on a temporary basis, to his 'servant', 'child', retainer, soldier or other dependant, until they could establish themselves as independent 'masters'. The grantees had to find and keep their own *chisegna* ('tenant farmers') until the end of the grant period, or the end of their active service in the case of billeted soldiers. In practice, these rules were expanded in most of the southern regions where exploitation of the *rest* owners included appropriating their lands. Much litigation arising from this in many parts of the south at the turn of the twentieth century was still unresolved by 1975 when a 'revolutionary' government nationalized land.

The monarch's self-allocation of private and communal lands as *madbet*, kitchen, to feed the household troops was equally alienating. Wolayta, for instance, was appropriated as *madbet*, for use by the court of the *neguse negest* or by government armies that might pass through. As this was designated strictly as a resource for personal maintenance (*qeleb*) after victory in battle, it was supplemented by another land-based resource, the *gane-geb*, literally 'that which goes into the pot'. People on *gane-geb* lands were expected to provide supplies for special guests whose movements the authorities wanted to control, and generally served the needs of commanding 'masters', who escorted the guests and retainers sent to them by the *neguse negest*. This process asserted state political control of land rights, even where former rulers were allowed to continue to use their old titles. These included *Kao* Tona of Welayta, *Sultan Abba* Jifar of Jimma and *Moti* Kumsa Moroda (known also as *Dejazmach* Gebre Egziabher) of Leqa Lekemt in Wellega. Informally designated *balabat*, these generally had higher status and genuine duties, even beyond areas they had formerly administered. Sooner or later, however, most were kept either in the capital or under strict surveillance in their home areas.

Designating a region as *madbet*, usually made on lands on which people had resisted becoming tribute payers, showed the high status of those making the designation. Officers appointed on such land facilitated taxation and the maintenance of fighting troops, including those who would be available to march at any time for the state. The ordinary soldiers billeted on *madbet* plots kept their rights, but, if inherited, every generation had to seek confirmation that they owned the land from the original designator of the *madbet*, namely the superior state official or his successor. Local people suffered deprivation of personal property, even if temporarily, and the maltreatment of women. They tilled the land in rotation and stored the harvest for the monarch. They even worked for the military leader or 'master', despite his being appointed only as governor. Worse in perpetrating such abuses were marching soldiers under a disgruntled 'master', though powerful 'kings of kings' could hold them accountable. Unlike the relatively more permanent *gane-geb* in eastern Shewa, the status of *madbet* ceased when the monarch decided that the region had paid enough for having resisted.

THE SUPREMACY OF MONARCHS

By the fourth quarter of the nineteenth century, the monarchs were able to use the *chewa* to defend the legitimacy of their reforms in land tenure, and to establish political balance. Menelik II especially succeeded in controlling the right to determine land matters, and to consolidate this right with regard to making decisions about the outer territorial limits of the country. His victory at Adewa gave him sufficient political and economic means to employ more emergent warriors than before. For this reason, he bypassed local socio-military control of communal lands, and reformed land tenure by measuring plots, imposing taxation accordingly; he used the warriors to impose the new system irrespective of local practices. For the rest of his reign, therefore, military achievements and identification with land and society were barely considered privileges open to all men.

The growing power of the monarchs also meant reducing the regional identities of local powerholders referring to the long view of history. Among such regional potentates only those in Gojam and in Shewa had achieved the status of *negus*. In both regions, warrior leaders had been increasing their economic and political power since the late seventeenth century. Their rivalry for resources was conducted independently from the mid-1870s with the purpose of reclaiming the territories that had been lost to the state. After 1881, however, the incumbents, *Negus* Tekle Haymanot and *Negus* Menelik, accepted the supreme status of one *neguse negest*, Yohannes IV, and continued to 'reclaim' territories under his aegis.

This project of reclaiming the 'lost territories', it has been claimed, was in reality one of acquiring lands and resources so as to be better able to reward soldiers. This went well with one of the major aims of those who served various regional officers: to join in stretching the hold on lands and people they considered Ethiopian. Most soldiers were among those who had been disinherited through land grabs and appropriation of government lands by those who had inherited the practices of the Era of Princes. Many such soldiers went to eastern Shewa to join Menelik and were eventually planted on communal lands. Among them were those protesting against Tewodros II's attempt to introduce new forms of disciplining troops. Also attracting the warriors to those regions was the presence of rebels (*shifta*) and hunters (*fanno*), whose activities in border areas rivalled their potential to become local authorities, but also helped open up the areas to them.

Negus Tekle Haymanot and *Negus* Menelik had organized *fitawrari* commanding their advance into areas 'that had not yet been straightened out' (*yalkena*). As these approached local people, they either magnanimously spared the communities or cruelly punished them for their 'hostility'. Most local communities resisted the onslaught of advance troops (*werari*), some in Jibat, Mecha and Arsi and Wolayta holding out for a number of years. The Sidama and Hadya responded with immediate submission, not least because they were shocked by the sound of gunfire. Some others brought whatever tribute (*gibir*) was required of them to stop the attacks and accepted *chewa* appointees. The advance commanders were expected to forge ameliorating political relationships with local leaders, appointing them as *balabat* with local responsibilities alongside as many loyal *chewa* warriors as possible.

In most cases, however, the *chewa* moved the local leaders, along with their retinue, to areas where they required fighters. For instance, they recognized the leaders of Gurage and Kambata as *balabat* and turned them into *chewa* officers to be deployed elsewhere as loyal soldiers responsible directly to the *neguse negest*. They also organized the mass of the former retainers of these leaders, creating such named corps as the *Barud Bet* or gunpowder makers. This, like other named corps, was billeted elsewhere to perform *chewa* military duties. It was later sent on campaigns for recovering the 'lost territories': Sidamo (1891), Welayta (1894), Harar (1891) and Keffa (1897). Those in Bale, Arsi and Hararge were mostly known as the *Gondere*. The operating contingents in Wellega and Illubabor in the west were predominantly called the *Werwari* (literally, 'throwers'). Those in the Sidama lands of old Dawaro, and in Gemu Gofa and Keffa in the southwest were mainly the *Barud Bet*. The local leaders who were removed lost the political clout they had had in their home bases, but their new status as *chewa* titleholders elsewhere entailed privileges that were higher than those of the local powerholders over whom they had command. Thus what began with removing local powerholders and co-opting them and their retainers as loyal subjects elsewhere in the 'lost territories' ended with asserting the political control of the *neguse negest*. The local people referred to all the billeted soldiers and their 'masters' as 'Amhara', irrespective of origin.

By the end of the nineteenth century, the presence of the named corps of soldiers settled over the previous two decades helped to bypass the right of the local *balabat* to govern the population. Some commanders enhanced their personal power by reporting directly to the *neguse negest*. Former powerholders qualified for rewards of high titles, lands and other privileges.

There were atrocities, especially perpetrated while demanding or raiding and forcefully extracting tributes of cattle, grain and slaves from target communities. The commanders of the contingents incorporated local communities in the jurisdictions of their overlords, mainly to enforce tribute collection. The ease with which this was done depended on the local official acknowledged as *balabat*. His role of working with a military counterpart was not easy, as in many cases he was given only vague administrative powers. In the north such persons had to emerge first as socially approved warrior leaders, whereas in the south they had to be pre-existing leaders appointed to support the *chewa*. What made it difficult was the introduction by billeted *chewa* soldiers of turning local people into labourers. This is attributed to their experience mainly in their home bases in Gonder, Gojam and Tigre, where, as we saw, corruption of the *gult* system during the Era of Princes, when the Yeju branch controlled palace politics, reduced landowning communities to the status of the *zega*, as the landless were called. The practice in the south reinforced a new definition of *gebbar*[32] (literally 'taxpayer'), in which *rest* owners' tribute payment made them not only taxpayers but also personal service providers.

Reminiscent of the days of the 'wandering monarchs', these billeted contingents manifested population mobility similar to the Oromo migrations. That is, the settlements of *chewa* contingents, from at least the last quarter of the nineteenth century, longer in some places than others, contributed to a southward population movement. Thus, in a developing pattern, *chewa* from Begemder, Tigre, Gojam, Wello and Selale, replaced others in Gurage, Wellega and Illubabor. In turn, those from Wellega and Illubabor moved, replacing still others in Sidamo, Wolayta, Keffa, Bale, Arsi and Hararge. Those incorporated until the early 1880s were at both the emitting and receiving end, and the domino effect, continued by recruitment of newly landless soldiers, was halted only when the recovery project came up against the European acquisition of territories along the borders.

By the turn of the twentieth century, the commanders of the various contingents had been appointed provincial governors ruling directly over the local population – but solely in the name of the 'modernizing' *neguse negest*. During the last quarter of the nineteenth century the commanders had contributed to raising the prestige and control of the *neguse negest*. As they had significantly increased the power of the state, their titles, jurisdictions and status were considerably higher than those of similarly titled earlier officials serving the monarchs nearer 1868, the time of Tewodros's death. Within his last decades, however, Menelik instituted means of suppressing potential rivalries among the *chewa* in these regions. He reclassified some military service lands by measuring them into *qelad* and instituted in them troops called

---

[32] Habtamu, *Land Tenure*, 2011, p. 211.

the *Dembegna*, literally 'legal' military service providers. Each contingent of this corps was under a *shaleqa*, 'commander of a thousand', most with the rank of *fitawrari*, but some as high as *ras*. Though they did not stop the *chewa* from using existing military lands as their heritage, their presence counterbalanced the older corps.

BATTLEFIELD PRACTICES

The warriors fired up in preparation for battle, challenging the other side, and, as necessary, also their own leaders. The commanders, on the other hand, played to the gallery, but with a political panache that also achieved the implementation of only their own decisions. Details of these battle practices are illustrated here with reference to three engagements: a battle of rivalry in Embabo (1882), a campaign of subjugation in Welayta (1894) and a battle at Segele (1916) over bringing back on track and reifying the succession to the highest military title – that of *neguse negest*. The military practices and strategies in battles fought with the express purpose of reclaiming 'lost territories' during the later decades of the nineteenth century were largely similar. By then the wandering warriors who had lost their own lands had been recruited in large numbers, and become aligned under two commanders, *Negus* Tekle Haymanot and *Negus* Menelik, both essentially loyal to the *neguse negest*. In the idealized history of the *chewa*, the presence of these troops contributed to bridging the gap that had been breached between the *neguse negest* and the territories settled prior to 1520. The internal processes of the battles they fought also show that leaders and retainers operated within *chewa* traditions. Though the monarch was later to challenge their traditions the soldiers were committed to the establishment of an overall *neguse negest*.

THE BATTLE OF EMBABO, 7 JUNE 1882

Embabo, in present-day northeastern Wellega, was the site of the battle between rival protagonists, *Negus* Tekle Haymanot of Gojam and *Negus* Menelik of Shewa. The immediate excuse for their clash was control of trade routes from the southwestern and western parts to the north and east. Both had been in power in their respective areas for at least a decade prior to their clash. Having sent troops to reclaim 'the lost territories', each was claiming precedence in them. Though Menelik won militarily, Yohannes IV, whom both recognized as *neguse negest*, scored the final political victory.[33]

---

[33] In exploring the warrior concepts of the time in this section, I have used mainly two sources: Tekle Iyesus, *Aleqa: History of Ethiopia*, and Bairu Tafla, *Aṣma Giyorgis and his work*, 1987. The other resource is my unpublished article, 'Biography of *Ras* Gobena Dachi'. This is based on a close review of an incomplete Amharic ms: ነጋድ ፡ የራስ ፡ ጎበና ፡ ዳጭ ፡ ታሪክ (Negede, 'Biography of *Ras* Gobena

Negus Tekle Haymanot was a grandson of Biru Goshu and started his military career as a *shifta* (rebel) by repulsing Desta Gwalu, the appointee of Tewodros II. When he submitted to Tekle Giyorgis II (r.1868–71), he was created a *ras* and ruler of the whole of Gojam. He was also granted 'permission' to campaign in the 'heathen lands neighbouring his territory'.[34] During this emperor's three-year rule, therefore, as *Ras* Adal, he led repeated expeditions in the Mecha region south of the Abay. When Yohannes IV took over, *Ras* Adal confronted and defeated his appointee as well, and paid direct homage to the emperor. This led Yohannes to reconfirm him in his title, position and privileges.

His rival, *Negus* Menelik, once a child captive of Tewodros, had escaped from Mekdela with support from some warriors from his home base of Shewa. They had wanted him to reclaim his father's position, and as they escaped they deliberately left behind his wife, Tewodros's daughter Altash. In their haste they failed to announce Menelik's arrival in Shewa. Not surprisingly, Tewodros's appointee there, *Ato* Bezabeh, and his supporters put up resistance. On the advice of one of Menelik's councillors, a famous *azmari*, Enat Awaj, used the following *shilela* to remind the border guards who he was and ask them to refrain from using their weapons:

ማነው ብላችሁ ነው ጦሩ መሰበቁ
ማነው ብላችሁ ነው ጋሻ መወልወሉ
የጌታችሁ ልጅ ነው አረ በስማብ በሉ
Who do you think is [coming] that [your] spears are sharpened?
Who do you think it is, that [your] shields are polished?
It is only your master's son – say your prayers!

On hearing this, the country people abandoned *Ato* Bezabeh and followed Menelik to Ankober where they installed him, and, in a well-known saga, his courtiers apprehended and tried Bezabeh for treason. Taking first the title *abeto* and then *negus*, titles that his father and grandfather had held during the Era of Princes, Menelik actively initiated himself as a warrior by killing an elephant in Selale (just north of the present capital, Addis Ababa), thereby acquiring his first trophy as a hunter. Like *Ras* Adal Tessema, he also acquired Emperor Tekle Giyorgis's permission to control additional regions, in his case towards the Beshilo River in Wello to the north and Arsi to the southeast of Shewa.

He also attracted warriors from the north, including Tigre, and from Agewmeder in Gojam. Some of these had served *Wagshum* Gobeze (later

(contd) Dachi', n.d.). The twenty-page ms was lent to me by *Weyzero* Mamite, a granddaughter of *Ras* Gobana, but I gave this ms back around 1990 (unfortunately without keeping a copy) to another member of that family, the late Dr Berhanu Abebe of Addis Ababa University. Intensive studies of the Battle of Embabo have been made by, among others, Alessandro Triulzi, 'The Background to Ras Gobana's Expeditions to Western Wallage in 1886–1888: A Review of the Evidence', in *Proceedings of the First United States Conference on Ethiopian Studies 1973*, 1975, pp. 143–56, and Tarafa Walda Sadiq, 'The Unification of Ethiopia (1800–1935): Wallega', *Journal of Ethiopian Studies*, Vol. 6, No. 1, 1968.
[34] Tekle Iyesus, *Aleqa: History of Ethiopia*, p. 151.

Emperor Tekle Giyorgis), Kassa Mercha (the future Yohannes IV) and Adal Tessema. Menelik organized them as corps collectively called the *Gondere* and *Werwari*, and billeted them first in rural Shewa. On drawing complaints from the local people through Enat Awaj, who sang against Menelik's gift of his father's land to the *Gondere*, he used the people to increase his wealth. He sent them on annual expeditionary campaigns, as his forebears, especially Sahle Selassie (r.1813–47), had done.[35] Lamenting his 'spear for spear and horse for horse' personal campaigns among the weak and divided Arsi clans, he also resolved to accumulate firearms. He later sent the above corps to Arsi, Bale, Wellega and Illubabor, spreading them in several directions, reportedly to forge alliances, make friendships and develop relationships in advance of his campaigns to reclaim the 'lost territories'.[36]

Menelik initially placed the troops under his most able warrior, *Ras* Gobena Dachi, an Oromo said to be of the Tulama clan. He had recruited Gobena reportedly after his excellent performance in *genna* games. Conducting expeditions 'from the borders of Ankober to the Mecha Oromo lands', Gobena went on to earn increasingly high titles, and was given the nickname 'window to the west'.[37] Incorporating the people in these lands as part of his soldiery, he took the Gurage chieftains, for instance, to the present-day Sudanese border, and to the waters of the White Nile beyond, where he marked territorial claims by cutting a live tree into the shape of a cross – by 'the River of the Areb Shanqela beyond Beni Shangul'.[38] Spurred on by Menelik's enthusiastic call in the 1870s, he even formed, as we have seen, the *Barud Bet* corps by using some of the Gurage to specialize in making *barud* (gunpowder).

For many years, the rival troops of *Negus* Menelik and *Negus* Tekle Haymanot had been obliging local people to support their respective claims over lucrative trade routes.[39] Some of the territories that Gobena's forces overran had been sending gifts and tribute to Shewa since the 1840s.[40] Menelik's side finally gained support for control of trade passing through the kingdoms of the Gibe basin, including Jimma, after his submission in person to Yohannes IV following the Battle of Embabo.

The forces of Gojam and Shewa encountered local Oromo whose infighting they took advantage of, and formed relationships with various groups. In an example cited with reference to *Ras* Adal's campaigns in

[35] Bairu Tafla, *Aṣma Giyorgis and his work*, 1987, p. 757.
[36] Guèbrè Sellassié, *Chronique*, 1930–32, p. 175; Tsehai Berhane Selassie, 'Biography of *Ras* Gobena Dachi', n.d. For his use of religious idioms that sound rhetorical, Tekle Iyesus, *Aleqa: History of Ethiopia*, p. 151, attributes this campaign to the religious zeal of *Negus* Menelik and *Negus* Tekle Haymanot.
[37] Bairu Tafla, 'Three Portraits: Ato Aṣmä Giyorgis, Ras Gobäna Dači and Ṣähaf Tezaz Gäbrä Selassé', *Journal of Ethiopian Studies*, Vol. 5, No. 2, 1967, pp. 133–50.
[38] Negede, 'Biography of *Ras* Gobena Dachi', n.d., p. 18; cf. Bulatovich, *Ethiopia Through Russian Eyes*, 2000, pp. 175, 178, 390 fn. 12B.
[39] Bahru Zewde, *A History of Modern Ethiopia*, 2001, p. 60.
[40] Bahru Zewde, *A History of Modern Ethiopia*, 2001, pp. 60–2.

present-day Wellega, a story highlights how he 'saved' a child slave and had him brought up a literary man and painter in his court. This man reports also that the *chewa* warriors of Gojam valiantly fought the 'heathen', whom he also saw as using morally incorrect strategies: 'Among all' the Oromo, he wrote, 'none are as difficult as the Kutay [clan]'.[41] Also,

> when they heard the approach of *Ras* Adal, they [the Oromo] rallied their troops and came in neighbourhood, [from] the lowlands [*qolla*], mounted on their horses, according to their youth-leaders [*loga*], putting their *gudo* [knife] around their waist and swinging their *tchere* [a type of spear], three for each of them. At that time, the Oromo were afraid to fight at close quarters because they did not know of firearms. They would enter at the reflection of the camp-fire at night and kill, thus becoming a nuisance. They did not spare those who were at the back [*dejan*] or those who went beyond the *fitawrari* [advance guard].[42]

The Oromo battle formation, armed with *tchere* ('three spears to each warrior'), was in contrast to the Gojame with firearms. Some Oromo warriors, for example Kedida, leader of the Jimma Kakka clan, showed particular bravery: entering *Ras* Adal's camp pretending to submit he was caught trying to assassinate the *ras*. Realizing he was about to be executed, he sent runners to an old rival, Abasha Garba, telling him to submit like him, ostensibly to trap Abasha Garba into suffering the same fate. Abasha continued to resist and even transfixed a pursuer and his horse to a tree using a spear, and the Gojame later 'tested their muscles' by trying to pull out the spear. Besides, the Oromo did not engage in face-to-face fighting but applied such ruses as night attacks. Abasha Garba and his followers even stripped the Gojame warriors of their *jano* (toga of honour) and turned up in their midst pretending to be *wegen tor* ('allied troops') in order to cause havoc. The ruse of night attacks, attempts to cheat an old rival, and wearing the toga were morally wrong, according to the scribe, and contrasted with the 'right and proper' way of *chewa* fighting, face to face and in daylight. Despite the heavy casualties his troops suffered, *Ras* Adal defeated 'thirty-one kings… [among the Oromo]… just as [the biblical] Joshua had defeated thirty-one kings'.[43]

In January 1881 Yohannes IV designated *Ras* Adal 'Tekle Haymanot *negus* of Gojam and Keffa'. This allowed Tekle Haymanot to confer the title *ras* on two of his officers who continued campaigning in the same areas. One of them, *Ras* Dereso,

> … started off with the Kutay. Wherever his horse ran, however his heart thought, [and] wherever his eyes could see. In Gudru, Amoru, Horro, Nonno, Jimma, Yibantu, Wallega, Guma, and Gera, he waged war, collected civet and tusks, and leaving these at Ennareya and Limmu, he galloped on to Keffa …[44]

He stopped when he clashed with *Ras* Gobena, who 'campaigned in Darra, Borru, Galan, Salale, Abote, Jarso, and Mecha, and on arriving

---

[41] Tekle Iyesus, *Aleqa: History of Ethiopia*, pp. 144–5.
[42] Tekle Iyesus, *Aleqa: History of Ethiopia*, p. 144.
[43] Tekle Iyesus, *Aleqa: History of Ethiopia*, pp. 144–5.
[44] Tekle Iyesus, *Aleqa: History of Ethiopia*, p. 151.

at Ennareya and Limmu, captured the tusks and civet that the Gojame had left there'.[45]

Ras Dereso, of course, resisted handing over the booty, but Ras Gobena appealed successfully to the agents of Yohannes IV who were then trading in the area. Ras Dereso accepted their verdict and handed over the elephant tusks and the civet, and Ras Gobena's soldiers sang:

> እንግዲህ ጎጃሞች በምን ይስቃሉ
> ጎቤ ጥርሳቸውን ወስደ ይላሉ
> How will the Gojame smile now?
> Gobe is said to have taken away their teeth [tusks]![46]

The others insulted Gobena:

> ሊጋዛ ቢመጣ ከእንጦጦ ጎስጎሶ
> በዮሃንስ አምላክ አሰኘው ደረሶ
> He galloped from Entoto to rule.
> Dereso forced him to appeal 'By Yohannes's God!'[47]

Yohannes IV sent a warning to both sides not to fight, but his letter to Negus Tekle Haymanot was intercepted by a shifta on the banks of the upper Abay,[48] and that to the negus of Shewa arrived too late. After showing deference to the emperor by taking their confrontation over the haul of civet and elephant tusks to his agents, Ras Dereso and Ras Gobena sent messages to their respective masters. Ras Dereso also retreated towards the Abay River and on to Gojam. Ras Gobena pursued him expressly to force him to relinquish his claims to the region.

Ras Gobena boasted to Menelik that he 'had made them vow never to return', and also pleaded humbly: 'I have written to you, negus, so that you do not accuse me of fighting without permission.'[49] The pertinent claims and counter-claims eventually generated differences of opinion among historians. A rumour was even circulating in Menelik's capital that the Oromo of Jimma had written asking to be rescued from their Sultan's oppression. The historian Zewde Gabre-Sellassie, Yohannes's great-great-grandson, points out that various Oromo groups had already been in correspondence with Menelik's ancestors before the Gojame appeared on the scene. Menelik regretted that Yohannes had permitted Negus Tekle Haymanot 'to trespass' and campaign in those lands as this reduced his growing influence in the area.[50]

Meanwhile, angry at being challenged, Negus Tekle Haymanot sent his son Bezabeh to support Dereso. Menelik abandoned his unsuccessful campaigns in Arsi and rushed to help Ras Gobena, accompanied by Mestayit, Queen of Wello, and her cavalry. This was probably

---

[45] Tekle Iyesus, Aleqa: History of Ethiopia, p. 151.
[46] Tekle Iyesus, Aleqa: History of Ethiopia, p. 151.
[47] Tekle Iyesus, Aleqa: History of Ethiopia, p.152
[48] Tekle Iyesus, Aleqa: History of Ethiopia, p. 152.
[49] Bairu Tafla, Aṣma Giyorgis and his work, 1987, p. 727.
[50] Zawde Gabre-Sellassie, Yohannes IV of Ethiopia, 1975, pp. 101–2, 104–5.

a face-saving exercise given his failure in the Arsi campaigns. *Ras* Gobena met *Negus* Menelik at Lega Anan, and together they burned the *ketema* ('garrison town') of *Ras* Dereso in Gudru on 14 April. It took them six days to reach Wellega where the chiefs paid them tribute. Apparently astounded at such a quick march, and hearing that Menelik had already begun the battle, *Negus* Tekle Haymanot mobilized too (as the narrator of the battle on the Gojame side notes[51]), but by the time he crossed the Abay, Menelik and *Ras* Gobena had already advanced well into Wellega, and sent *Ras* Dereso's soldiers under escort 'to their country via the Abay'.[52]

The two sides soon began exchanging *zeraf*, the wordings of which underline how closely they followed *chewa* tradition. According to his chronicle, Menelik told Dereso's men:

> What government do you have on this side of the Abay? I, for love and friendship, gave *Negus* Tekle Haymanot Amoru, Borru, Gudru and Gendiberet, the land of Kedida. You went beyond that and started to wage war on other countries. The proverb 'the beggar becomes the *rest* owner if he stays long' is coming true with you. I have taken back the lands I gave him. Go across the Abay to your master! If your master comes to fight for the countries I have taken back from him, I give you leave to come with him.[53]

Menelik's message suggests that flexing his muscles at the rising power of the kingdom in Gojam was important. We learn of Tekle Haymanot's response from Menelik's side:

> Before the war he sent a verbal boast, unsatisfactory to Christ [and] insulting to *Negus* Menelik of Shewa, through his bold servant Yigzaw Meko. [The messenger was] without a letter. These were the words: 'Why I am not sending a letter, why I am sending only verbal messages, is because I think you are a coward and you will look at the letter, tear it up and run away. If it is verbal, you will be forced to face me for the sake of not being disgraced by all your army who will hear the message.'[54]

The 'bold servant', Yigzaw Meko, and his party asked to see Menelik in person and delivered this message in front of courtiers. Menelik is said to have responded: 'The "house of *Negus* Tekle Haymanot" has courageous [*gobez*] councillors, but not intelligent reconciliatory elders ("*shimagelle*").' He sent them away giving each twenty dollars for their trouble, and, according to the same source, with a message to the *ras* saying:

> I will not rely on my strength and my army, like you. My power is Christ. Let us be reconciled if that is possible. Let not the people perish. If you force it, I will wait for you as you come.[55]

A slightly different emphasis is given in Menelik's chronicle. Using a term of respect for Menelik, his chronicler reports the message from *Negus* Tekle Haymanot thus:

---

[51] Tekle Iyesus, *Aleqa: History of Ethiopia*, p. 153.
[52] Tekle Iyesus, *Aleqa: History of Ethiopia*, p. 153.
[53] Guèbrè Sellassié, *Chronique*, 1930–32, Vol. I, p. 103.
[54] Tekle Iyesus, *Aleqa: History of Ethiopia*, pp. 152–3.
[55] Tekle Iyesus, *Aleqa: History of Ethiopia*, p. 152.

Why are you always disrespecting me? You once destroyed my country, Gojam. Do not go away now. I am coming! Choose an open plain from Gudru, Horro, Jimma [or] Cheleya, and wait for me. I am not sending you a letter in case you see it on your own and run away as though you have not heard anything. If your servants hear this verbal message and you run away, they will disrespect you.[56]

Menelik reportedly said: 'You are liars because you have not brought a sealed letter. These are not the words he entrusted to you. He must not send verbal messages if he claims to be a king.' When the messengers replied that they would be punished if their words were false, he retained one of them and sent back the rest to bring a sealed letter in five days as he would not wait further with the impending rains. He also entrusted them with a verbal reply asserting that he would fight the *negus* but that he would not write him a letter 'of which you are contemptuous already'.[57]

These reported *fukera* from each side show that both parties were paying attention to the higher authority of the *neguse negest*, as historians have shown.[58] The exchanges, especially in the use of the name Adal, also reflect the writers' sympathies with the advantage of hindsight. Of songs reflecting public opinion, examples from Menelik's camp are:

> ይህ ግርግር ያዳል ሴራ ነው
> ጠቡንም ፍቅሩንም አንዱን አጣነው
> This to-ing and fro-ing is Adal's plot;
> We cannot tell his friendship from his hostility!

And the women sang:

> ሴቶች ተሰብሰቡ እንርገጥ ዳንኪራ
> ክርክር አይቀርም ከዚያ ከሰው ጋር
> Come together women, let's dance!
> Hostilities are sure to start with that man.[59]

Menelik's scouts (*selay*) under *Dejazmach* Welde were 'surprised' to find that *Negus* Tekle Haymanot had already crossed the Abay and was camped close by.[60] The scouts saw the tents of the *negus* and of the *tabote Tsion*[61] pitched, and the soldiers were on standby. Menelik's councillors advised blocking Tekle Haymanot's advance, but, apparently waiting for an attack, he reviewed his troops instead. As was the usual practice for a commander, Menelik's tent (forming the *gedam*) was in the centre of his camp. On his left were Mestayit, Queen of Wello,

---

[56] Guèbrè Sellassié, *Chronique*, 1930–32, Vol. I. p. 104.
[57] Bairu Tafla, *Aşma Giyorgis and his work*, 1987, p. 735.
[58] Zawde Gabre-Sellassie, *Yohannes IV of Ethiopia*, 1975, pp. 104–5; Darkwah, *Shewa, Menilek*, 1975, p. 55.
[59] Both *Fukera* supplied by my mother, *Weyzero* Workaferahu Haile, who heard them from a member of her parents' household. This person had previously been in the service of *Azmari* Tsadiqe, a famous female battlefield singer, whom he had the obligation to accompany to battle.
[60] Guèbrè Sellassié, *Chronique*, 1930–32, Vol. I. p. 179.
[61] Guèbrè Sellassié, *Chronique*, 1930–32, Vol. I. p. 179. This refers to any ark representing the Ark of the Covenant, and was brought by the priests.

and her cavalry. Deployed as *fitawrari*, 'advance guard', because he was already on the spot, *Ras* Gobena was ready to implement a characteristic strategy of throwing a cordon of fighters around the rear of Tekle Haymanot's troops.[62] Menelik's chronicle provides these details but hardly mentions the arrangements in the Gojame camp.

Reporting with zeal, the historian from Gojam asserts that 'because God had strengthened' their leader 'in order to punish his people', the Gojame hastened to initiate battle; they were doomed to fail even before they started. When Menelik appeared with an army 'as numerous as the stars in the sky', he reports, *Negus* Tekle Haymanot released his mountain guns like 'lightening in June'. With these and his *sabew, merbut* and *sinader* guns he dispersed Menelik's army:

> ... like the clouds affected by a strong wind current. The smoke from the guns covered the population. At the same time, *Ras* Dereso and *Dejach* Seyoum fought, standing on dead bodies, and pushed on to the *gedam*, right in the center [of Menelik's camp]. The army of Shewa was overcome by the bullets [*arar*] so that they started to fight with their faces down to the earth.[63]

Initially the Gojame had the upper hand, particularly in capitalizing upon their defences. Menelik's *Chronicle* highlights the lack of success:

> They started battle at the fifth hour of the day. However, you, the king, were in the *gedam*, right in the centre, with your household servants. At this time, the mounted gun (*madef*) of *Negus* Tekle Haymanot started to fire. It shot twice, and on the third, the machine broke down and fell. They were shocked when they saw that; they realized that God had parted from them ... Thus, you [Menelik] closely surrounded and captured the wounded *Negus* Tekle Haymanot in less than two hours.[64]

As though Menelik himself had reached the *gedam* of Negus Tekle Haymanot, Tekle Iyesus writes: 'When *Negus* Menelik saw the strength of the troops of Gojam he mounted his horse called Dagnaw, dismantled his tent, and felled the canopy bearer.' Also:

> Seeing the cruelty of *Ras* Dereso and *Dejach* Seyoum, he [Menelik] released the hidden cavalry of Wello under Mestayit. With the dust standing like an avalanche from a cliff, these attacked the men of Gojam. They smashed them; they broke them with their *afa* [spears]. *Negus* Tekle Haymanot, with his household servants, shot from his *gedam* until his thumb was bruised ...[65]

Pressure from *Ras* Dereso and *Dejach* Seyoum appears to have forced Menelik to deploy the cavalry that reached *Negus* Tekle Haymanot's *gedam*:

> But God heard *Negus* Menelik's sorrow, so that in the end, He gave victory to the Shewe. And *Negus* Tekle Haymanot seeing that things were not going well wanted to give himself up of his own accord, reasoning 'I must not fall into the hands of a cruel man and be manhandled'.[66]

---

[62] Guèbrè Sellassié, *Chronique*, 1930–32, Vol. I, p. 153.
[63] Tekle Iyesus, *Aleqa: History of Ethiopia*, p. 153.
[64] Guèbrè Sellassié, *Chronique*, 1930–32, Vol. I, p. 179.
[65] Tekle Iyesus, *Aleqa: History of Ethiopia*, p. 153.
[66] Tekle Iyesus, *Aleqa: History of Ethiopia*, p. 153.

Tekle Iyesus credits the soldiers of *Ras* Gobena and the Wello queen, Mestayit, 'who were ruthless', for obliging the Gojame to negotiate directly with *Ras* Gobena and his soldiers to avoid *Negus* Tekle Haymanot 'being trampled under horses' hooves'. After receiving a wound in the armpit, the king sent for a horseman, Mengesha Atikem, whom he recognized as 'a son of *Dejach* Goshu's officer' but was a 'servant of *Negus* Menelik' by then, and handed himself over to him: 'Mengesha Atikem came, arranged his clothes in order [showing respect for the king], and bowed saying [a formulaic] "Your hands in sash" [using no hand cuffs], and took him to *Negus* Menelik.'[67] This young captor, Mengesha Atikem (who became a *ras* within a decade of this), was one of those who had joined Menelik's camp soon after Tewodros's death, expecting him to take the crown and title of *neguse negest*. His symbolic and verbal chaining of *Negus* Tekle Haymanot was in contrast with the capture of the *Tato* of Keffa, whose hands were reportedly put in gold chains[68] when he was taken to Menelik as a prisoner.

The battle did not end with *Negus* Tekle Haymanot's capture because *Dejach* Dereso and *Dejach* Seyoum, fought on, defying their leader's drum ordering them to stop. Supported by *Memher* Welde Giyorgis in charge of the priests and the *tabot*, they said: 'There is no king other than Yohannes. We refuse. Go on fighting! He [Menelik] will bring back whom he has taken!' Tekle Iyesus points out that these leaders were defeated in the end 'because their resistance was haughty and without sorrow ... The men of Gojam were neither able to kill nor to run away because they were surrounded by the troops of Shewa'.[69] Menelik's chronicle concludes his narrative by quoting in Ge'ez a biblical maxim that one rewards evil with kindness, pointing out that Menelik visited the battlefield the following day, and had the dead buried and the wounded collected, magnanimously, from both sides. Three days later, he pardoned the troops of Gojam, saying he had nothing against them even though they had fought against him without provocation.

Tekle Iyesus quotes the following *zeraf* poems on the fate of emasculated Gojame fighters:[70]

> ገሌሌ! ደሞም ገሌሌ! ደሞም ገሌሌ!
> የጎጃሜ እናት አትዘኝብኝ
> እኔ ምንላርገው አፋው በላብኝ!
> Gelele, again Gelele
> Don't blame me, Gojame mother!
> I couldn't help it; my spear did it!

Gobena's *Biography* has:

> እንግዲህ ጎጃሞች በምን ይሽናሉ
> ጎቤ ቀላቸውን ገሽለጠው አሉ

---

[67] Tekle Iyesus, *Aleqa: History of Ethiopia*, p. 154.
[68] According to information I was given in early 1971 (but silver chains, according to Bahru Zewde, *A History of Modern Ethiopia*, 2001, p. 66).
[69] Guèbrè Sellassié, *Chronique*, 1930–32, Vol. I, p. 179.
[70] Tekle Iyesus, *Aleqa; History of Ethiopia*, p. 154.

> How will the Gojame urinate now?
> Gobe is said to have slashed off their penises.

The vanquished *zemach* (expeditionary force) from Gojam was attacked by the Oromo while travelling back across the Abay, and lamenting the hardship of their friends, the survivors sang:

> የት አድርጎት ኗሯል [ኦሮሞ] ብድሩን
> በሰፈረው ቄና ከፈለው ቄሙን
> የዘመተው ዘማች ሚያለቅስለት ቢያጣ
> ቅል ወርዶ አሞራ ፊት ነጭቶለት መጣ
> Where had the 'Oromo' kept their loans?
> They have paid it back measure for measure!
> Seeing no one lamenting for the *zemach*,
> Birds went to the valley and tore off their faces![71]

After this battle, the question of collecting trophy by emasculating the enemy, dead or alive, was addressed officially for the first time. It is reported that Menelik and *Negus* Tekle Haymanot were 'shocked' when they saw that soldiers who were used to emasculating 'the heathen' were emasculating Christians too. Before he left the site of battle, therefore, Menelik ordered warriors to stop emasculating captives and prisoners 'whoever they were'. Referring to 'the law of kings', he stipulated in his proclamation that 'those found with the *seleba* ["trophy"] will be punished'.[72] At least theoretically, this was meant to stop the practice, which nonetheless kept resurfacing later, for instance during the Italian invasions of 1896 and 1935–41.

Taking his rival prisoner, Menelik returned to Shewa in firm control of the contested area 'that had been paying him tribute since 1875'. He billeted the wounded Gojame on the Jarso Oromo, charged *Ras* Gobena with escorting the rest to the Abay River and confirmed him governor of the western provinces. The *ras* continued to campaign further west as Menelik travelled back to his capital Entoto, reviewing his troops at Guddo Robbi and displaying the guns and goods he had captured. His chronicler lauds Menelik for personally washing the wounds of *Negus* Tekle Haymanot, to underline his charitable act. Reportedly Menelik asked his captives, who had presumably pleaded for his mercy, what they would have done to him had they won. The Gojame replied that they would have torn him to pieces, but that it was 'fit to be ruthless when a fighter and benevolent when a victor'!

Back at Entoto, he built a church to house the captured *tabot*, and appointed a *baldereba* to attend to the needs of *Negus* Tekle Haymanot and his *mekwanent* ('nobles') and their retainers, allocating to them

---

[71] Tekle Iyesus, *Aleqa: History of Ethiopia*, p. 155.
[72] Guèbrè Sellassié, *Chronique*, 1930–32, Vol. I, p. 181. The annotator De Coppet, fn. 6, notes that the practice of collecting trophy was witnessed, among others, by Arnauld D'Abbadie, *Douze Ans dans le Haute-Éthiopie (Abyssinie)*, Paris: Librairie de L. Hachette, 1868, p. 224; see also Plowden, *Travels in Abyssinia*, 1868, p. 53; Vanderheym, *Une Expédition avec Le Négous Ménélik (Vingt Mois en Abyssinie)*, Paris: Hachette, 1896, p. 171; Lincoln De Castro, *Nella terra dei Negus, pagine raccolte in Abissinia*, Milan: Fratelli Treves, 1915. Vol. I, pp. 154–5.

rations and clothes appropriate to their ranks. In welcoming him, some priests called on Menelik to claim Keffa, a region to which Yohannes had authorized *Ras* Adal's expeditions.[73]

It is noteworthy that, with the impending rains and in fear of Yohannes's punishment, Menelik did not follow up his victory by subjugating Gojam. Indeed, he immediately sent a message to Yohannes, who had already set out on an expedition southwards, inviting him to stop and pass the rains in his area of Were Illu in Wello until he came to see him there, 'now that Your Majesty is so close!' Yohannes was already in Saynt when he received this message, and summoned Menelik, ordering him to bring his captive. Though it was the month of August, and the rains were at their heaviest, making rivers impassable, Menelik went to Were Illu to hand over his prisoner. Attributing the outcome only to the subsequent decisions of the *neguse negest* to punish both protagonists, neither Menelik's chronicler nor Tekle Iyesus recount how Yohannes settled their controversies.[74]

An interesting glimpse elsewhere shows that Yohannes resorted to diplomatic face-saving devices that accommodated all the *chewa* rivals, including him.[75] Menelik's counsellors had advised him to show only the minimum of deference when meeting the emperor, given that Yohannes was about to force him to drop his claim to the title and position of *neguse negest*. Menelik, indeed, kept his *shemma* (toga) over his head when he approached the emperor, and Yohannes turned to the priests by him to complain, not about this mark of disrespect, but saying that Menelik 'was not interested in reconciling me' with *Negus* Tekle Haymanot for having fought at Embabo 'without my permission'. This way round the matter allowed Menelik to present a case on behalf of his prisoner, *Negus* Tekle Haymanot, thus giving Yohannes the upper hand of arbitration over both, side-stepping confrontation and forgiving Menelik now that, as it were, he had come to know who the culprit was (*Negus* Tekle Haymanot).

Yohannes did not stop at Menelik and Tekle Haymanot's submission; he reorganized their internal relationships. He took away Tekle Haymanot's territory of Agewmeder and gave it to his trusted general, *Ras* Alula. Also proceeding to cut Menelik down to size, he ordered him to give back the arms and ammunition he had captured from Tekle Haymanot. He then appointed over Wello his adopted son *Ras* Mikael, a son of Workit, a rival queen to Mestayit who, as we have seen, had been on Menelik's side at

---

[73] Guèbrè Sellassié, *Chronique*, 1930–32, Vol. I, p. 180–1.
[74] Tekle Iyesus, *Aleqa: History of Ethiopia* devotes space to an investigation of a *shifta* who had intercepted a letter Yohannes had written to Tekle Haymanot. This man was apprehended and hanged. His widow, surprisingly, came to the camp of Yohannes to seek justice concerning her husband's hanging for stealing the emperor's letter, but, unsurprisingly, neither Yohannes nor his courtiers was interested in the affair. Even intercepting the imperial message became insignificant once the addressee was vanquished, and those responsible for punishing the *shifta* received no rewards for their efforts.
[75] Bairu Tafla, *Aşma Giyorgis and his work*, 1987, p. 675.

Embabo. Menelik had no choice but to accept. As we saw in Chapter 2, the emperor had crowned as *negus*, Adal, who took the throne name Tekle Haymanot in 1881. After the Battle of Embabo, Yohannes crowned Menelik as *negus*, thereby forcing him to forfeit the title of *neguse negest* that he had assumed. This settled the matter of precedence between Tekle Haymanot, Menelik and Yohannes, the last high-level rival *chewa* of the period. The emperor further ensured Menelik's loyalty by suggesting that he give his six-year-old daughter, Zewditu, as wife to his twelve-year-old son, *Ras* Areya Selassie, along with (as part of cutting him down to size) the province of Wello as a wedding gift. The child bride joined Yohannes's household, along with everyone familiar to her. Menelik's chronicler enthusiastically records the marriage to the heir of the 'king of kings', seeing it as an honour.

Indeed, the marriage signalled that Yohannes took Menelik as the stronger party and ally (relative to Tekle Haymanot), and that he clearly planned to use Menelik's daughter to ensure the continuity and increasing power of the office of *neguse negest*. Despite the intended increase in Menelik's prestige, the scale of the wedding proved an economic burden that significantly depleted his economic resources. The whole episode of the submission and the wedding annoyed *Ras* Gobena, who raided southern Wello and retreated in disappointment to Shewa without seeking Menelik's permission. Yohannes's arranging the marriage of his son to Menelik's daughter established a pecking order of succession among the most powerful regional contenders. By the time Yohannes IV died while fighting against Mahdist attacks on the Sudanese border in 1889, therefore, the number of powerful contenders to the throne of *neguse negest* had been reduced to just two: his own heir and Menelik of Shewa. With the death of *Ras* Araya, and with Embabo behind him, Menelik was without a rival in both reclaiming the 'lost territories' and the prospect of one day filling the position of *neguse negest*.

THE CAMPAIGN IN WELAYTA

By the time of Yohannes's death, Ethiopians had generally shifted the category 'enemy' away from the Turks towards the Europeans, who, with the Italian drive south from Asmara, were engaging them in battle, as we will see below. With this in the background, Menelik declared in April 1891 his historic right to all land 'beyond the "Oromo"' south 'to Lake Nyanza' (Lake Victoria), which he intended to strive to capture, 'if God gives me the strength'.[76] With this statement he clarified the extent of 'lost territories' that the *chewa* could claim. Told to campaign 'as far as your horse takes you', his troops were determined to follow in the steps of *Ras* Gobena.

[76] See 'Letter of Menelik to European powers', in Ignazio Guidi, 'Documenti amarina', *Rendiconti della Reale Accademia dei Lincei*, Vol. VII, 1891, p. 294.

One of their targets was the autonomous kingdom of Welayta, which had been resisting annual *chewa* attacks, reportedly for seven years. It had emerged in the thirteenth century on the ruins of Ennarya and Damot. Welayta oral historians, interviewed in the 1970s, echoed the existence of King Motolomi who, they said, had been a Christian in the early period of the kingdom. Other accounts mention that kings of that time were overthrown by 'Tigre' kings with Christian names.[77] Travellers reported seeing an ancient church ruin.[78] The French journalist Vanderheym, and others who accompanied the expedition, claimed that Welayta had at one time accepted Catholicism too.[79] In the 1970s a local oral historian cited as evidence of past Christianity the recitation in Ge'ez of the Lord's Prayer ('Our Father') by non-Christian Welayta who knew neither its significance, nor, less surprisingly, its meaning.

Be that as it may, the rulers of Welayta had been using such strategies as digging trenches and holes in which poles, with sharpened tips pointing upwards, were fixed to trap invading cavalry and foot soldiers, *werari*, and releasing ground red pepper to be blown in their direction. Welayta's dynasty of kings, known as the 'Tigre', was, according to oral tradition, founded by an immigrant from the north. The dynasty had increased its power by capturing mercenaries it called Boyna-Tigre, 'farmer Tigre', from surrounding areas. From about 1887 the areas for drawing mercenaries from had been reduced to only Kullo and Konta. The mercenaries were formed into Welayta's cavalry and used as foot soldiers. The last king, *Kao* Tona, used them to resist the *chewa*, who had been making incursions from all directions except Keffa.

Kao Tona, who succeeded his grandfather in 1890, married the daughter of the *sultan* of Jimma and was trying to make alliances with the rulers of Kullo and Konta, Arsi, Kambata and Hadya. He relied heavily on the trenches and holes,[80] a system that was reportedly started by a late eighteenth-century *kao*, Oggato, who, according to oral tradition, had predicted even the coming of the Amhara.[81] However, by the time of Menelik's personal expedition, most of Tona's allies were under Welde Giyorgis (the future *ras* and *negus* of Keffa). Aware of becoming

---

[77] Tsehay Brhane Selassie, 'Menelik II: Conquest and Consolidation of the Southern Provinces', senior dissertation, Haile Selassie I University, Addis Ababa, 1969, pp. 31–6; Tsehai Brhane Selassie, 'The question of Damot and Wälamo', 1975, p. 43.
[78] R. P. Azaïs and R. Chambard, *Cinq Années de Recherches Archéologique en Éthiopie*, Paris: Geuthner, 1931, p. 273.
[79] Vanderheym, *Une Expédition*, 1896, p. 163.
[80] In 1972 I saw a trench about a metre wide and two metres deep, overgrown with bushes. These were also seen by several travellers, including Vanderheym in 1896, Welby in 1898, and Azais and Chambard in the late 1920s. See Vanderheym, *Une Expédition*, 1896, pp. 158–9, 178; M. S. Welby, *'Twixt Sirdar and Menelik: An Account of a Year's Expedition from Zeila to Cairo through Unknown Abyssinia*, New York and London: Harper & Brothers, 1901, p. 141; Azaïs and Chambard, *Cinq Années de Recherches*, 1931, p. 273.
[81] Tsehai Brhane Selassie, 'The question of Damot and Wälamo', 1975, p. 44; Welby, *'Twixt Sirdar and Menelik*, 1901, p. 141.

largely encircled, Welayta strengthened its trenches and holes. Its warriors were armed with spears and curved knives (*qonchora*) and prepared hides to be beaten and impregnated with pepper for release towards would-be attackers. The Welayta and others in southern Ethiopia reportedly melted down firearms they captured, and metal from other sources, to make knives and ploughshares.

Menelik's plan to campaign in Welayta in person after the rains of 1893 had been postponed[82] until 1894. As usual, the preparations that started during the rainy season were effected only in November. He announced his impending expedition to Welayta in August 1894, 'when the farmers [his soldiers] had finished sowing their seeds'. Underlining the 'lost territory' cause, his chronicler emphatically refers to the *Hagiography of Tekle Haymanot*, a thirteenth-century saint who reputedly evangelized in Welayta:

> *Atse* Menelik, having heard this story, and saddened that in Walamo [Welayta], where *Abune* Tekle Haymanot had accomplished many miracles and had baptized Motolomi, religion had been destroyed, was waiting for a suitable time to straighten it out. As it [the Bible] says 'God's Will be done', and when the time came for it to be straightened out, the Holy Spirit aroused you to take those of your soldiers close at hand and you went to campaign in Walamo, in the Year of Luke, 1887 (Ethiopian calendar).[83]

Menelik mobilized his household officials, namely *Fitawrari* Gebeyehu, *Dejazmach* Welde Ashagre (governor of Efrata), *Dejach* Webe Atnafseged (his daughter Zewditu's second husband), Haile Maryam Wele (cousin of the empress), *Bejirond* Balcha, the treasurer, and Abate his *liqe mekuas* (the monarch's impersonator). He also enrolled *Ras* Mikael, his son-in-law and subordinate (after Yohannes's death), whose Wello troops could not ford the rivers for some time and reached Addis Ababa on 1 November.[84] Others, *Dejach* Welde Giyorgis (who had taken Kullo and Konta), *Dejazmach* Beshah Aboye (governor of Gurage), *Dejazmach* Tessema Dargie (of Arsi and Kambata) and *Sultan* Abba Jifar II (of Jimma) waited on standby and joined later on his orders.[85] Some, for instance *Dejazmach* Lulseged, governor of Sidamo and Darassa (now Gedeo) further south, were to support the 'master' campaigning near them; they therefore reported only when Menelik reached the battlefield area.

Menelik arrived at Shone, a *kela* (a border and customs post) at Welayta, a fortnight after starting from his capital. He used the forest and water holes in the area to review and deploy his troops cautiously, first sending spies to study the conditions. The spiked trenches and holes obstructing Menelik's horses and foot soldiers also contributed to the stopover.[86] Past those, the soldiers 'discovered' the ruins of a church

---

[82] Richard Caulk, *'Between the Jaws of the Hyenas': A Diplomatic History of Ethiopia (1876–1896)* (Äthiopistische Forschungen, Band 60), ed. Bahru Zewde. Wiesbaden: Harrassowitz Verlag, 2002, p. 414.

[83] Guèbrè Sellassié, *Chronique*, 1930–32, Vol. I, pp. 360–81.

[84] Vanderheym, *Une Expédition*, 1896, p. 138; Guèbrè Sellassié, *Chronique*, 1930–32, p. 362.

[85] Vanderheym, *Une Expédition*, 1896, p. 158.

[86] Vanderheym, *Une Expédition*, 1896, p. 158; Tsehai Brhane Selassie, 'The

they ascribed to the famed thirteenth-century saint, Tekle Haymanot. Menelik deployed *Ras* Mikael by his side, and *Ras* Welde Giyorgis and Aba Jifar II (the latter under the auspices of the *ras*) flanked his main army towards the Omo River in the south. With *Liqe Mekuas* Abate and *Dejazmach* Lulseged on the opposite side in the east, his encirclement left open only Borodda in the south.

From Shone, Menelik sent a message to *Kao* Tona asking him to submit in words that his *Chronicle* paraphrases as: 'Do not have your people massacred, and your country devastated. Bring your tribute and submit!' Presenting *Kao* Tona's response similarly non-verbatim, Menelik's chronicler phrased it as arrogant defiance: 'But he, having never seen a Christian army replied, "No Christian is to come into my country. I will not submit. I will fight!"'[87] While this reflected his underestimation of the forces ranged against him, the phrasing served to underline the perception in Menelik's army that not only had the Welayta lost their Christianity but that their ruler was preventing contact with Christians by creating spiked trenches and holes to keep them out!

Menelik passed a day at Shone because it was Sunday, ordering his *werari*, under *Dejazmach* Haile Maryam, *Fitawrari* Gebeyehu, *Liqe Mekuas* Abate and *Ras* Mikael, to fill in trenches and holes and prepare the way. Three days later, Menelik was still supervising the road-clearing when he learned that, in his absence, 'a few soldiers had engaged in a skirmish without being ordered to do so'. Vanderheym noted that the men of *Ras* Mikael of Wello had come across Welayta horsemen and foot soldiers in battle order, and had used cannons to force them to refrain from initiating more attacks. Menelik stopped *Ras* Mikael's men from mounting further attacks, and deployed *Liqe Mekuas* Abate and *Bejirond* Balcha from his own household. These arrived at Qontela the following day and captured some people who became his guides to Tona's capital, Dalbo. Narrating a later stage of the attack, the chronicler writes:

> Noticing the fertility of the land and the number of the population and the cattle, and in sympathy with the country and its people, so that they might not become destroyed, he sent word to the *balabat* saying thus: 'It is difficult to reconstruct a country after it has been destroyed. And money, unless it is forced out, will not be finished if given willingly. Do not have your country devastated. Bring your tribute and submit.' But he [*Kao* Tona] stayed away refusing to submit.[88]

By calling *Kao* Tona the *balabat*, the chronicler intended to downplay his status. Menelik pursued Tona up to Damot, the mountain 'where *Abune* Tekle Haymanot had baptized Motolomi' in the thirteenth century, and then sent advance troops to attack right and left. The *kao* fled to Borodda but one of *Ras* Mikael's men captured him wounded in the neck. The rest of the population came to submit with large numbers of cattle and children. The women and children approached with fresh

---

(contd) question of Damot and Wälamo', 1975.
[87] Guèbrè Sellassié, *Chronique*, 1930–32, Vol. I, p. 362.
[88] Guèbrè Sellassié, *Chronique*, 1930–32, Vol. I, p. 363.

grass in their hands to show respect, salutation and submission, a common practice they shared with the Sidama to the south. The expedition was over within one day of passing the defences at Shone, and at the end of the campaign Menelik camped at Wanza, a place that *Negadras* Fullas eventually enclosed as a garrison.[89]

Oral tradition reports that many country people (*balager*) who were taken as domestic slaves became carriers of tents and provisions to the battlefield of Adewa in 1896. The large number of cattle from the Welayta expedition were distributed in the rest of the country to compensate for the 1888–92 cattle epidemic and famine. Historical studies have correctly asserted that obtaining economic resources was the main purpose of this expedition. Declaring Welayta his *madbet* or 'kitchen' was part of the ameliorative overtures that established Menelik's direct control of the territory. In other words, instead of appointing newcomers he appointed a local man, *Fitawrari* Kurfa, as *abagaz* (military governor), recognized Tona as the *balabat* still with his title of *kao*, and promoted other notables to the status of cattle chiefs (*sanga-dagna*) with the title of *fitawrari*.

Before he left, Menelik had Tona and his closest relatives baptized, with himself as their godfather, and gave the rest of the family to other Christians for instruction. Menelik favoured *Kao* Tona by appointing a *bejirond* (treasurer), *Negadras* Fullas, to represent his authority alongside the *abegaz*. According to oral tradition, the *kao* was on familiar terms with his godfather, Menelik, and referred to Menelik's daughter, Zewditu, as 'baby daughter' (*mamitie*). Menelik's courtiers, except the *kao*'s father-in-law, Aba Jifar II of Jimma, rose whenever Tona appeared in court.

Having thus incorporated Welayta, the expedition helped Menelik centralize his political control of land and people in most of the south. In taking control of independent rulers such as the *Kao* of Welayta in 1894 and the *Tato* of Keffa in 1897, the victor expropriated not only their personal property but also the local military establishment. He thus deprived them of access to the country (*hager*) that had generated, promoted and supported them. The *Tato* of Keffa, Gaki Sherocho, was even kept prisoner, in the custody of the highest *chewa* commander who captured him, till the end of his days.

Kao Tona and *Sultan Abba* Jifar of Jimma, who appear to have enjoyed more personal freedom than *Tato* Gaki Sherocho, were subsequently reinstated to their former positions. However, they ruled their population by proxy while living under close surveillance of the victor and his court. The population was eventually said to have accused *Kao* Tona of distributing local people as slaves to *chewa* officials in the capital and elsewhere. As they pleaded with him for a new ruler, Menelik appointed *Ligaba* [Mayor] Beyene in his place, and, summoning *Kao* Tona in 1903, he retained him in his court. As we will see below, that later period coin-

---

[89] According to Vanderheym, soldiers who had never had the chance to better themselves took the opportunity to do so in the following three days, *Une Expédition*, 1896, p. 171.

cided with the government's final phasing out of the *chewa* as a military force and Menelik's introduction of direct personal rule along the lines of 'modernity'.

THE BATTLE OF SEGELE, 1916

The most important impact of Menelik's strong political acumen in controlling the *chewa* military structure was first his introduction of 'modern' institutions, and secondly ensuring that the monarchy after him remained at the centre of power. After suffering a stroke in 1909 he designated his fourteen-year-old grandson, *Lij* Iyasu (1895–1935), as heir to his throne under a regent, *Ras-Bitweded* Tessema Nadew. When the regent died two years later, the sixteen-year-old was left to his own devices, resulting in certain inevitably hasty actions and perhaps gullibility. Reports that were coloured by subsequent political developments make it difficult to distinguish his own beliefs and real politics from those of others, including the diplomatic community. Of particular interest is the façade of internal opinion at the time that influenced the politics of the Ethiopian state and led to *Lij* Iyasu's removal from office. His supporters and antagonists fought at the battle of Segele over whether to wrench the position of *neguse negest* from his grasp. In addition, the historiography of the battle is dominated by a well-known saga in which issues pertinent to how *Lij* Iyasu conducted internal administration revolved effectively around foreign interests that were driven by World War I. Though *Lij* Iyasu's position as Menelik's successor was confirmed, the allegations of impropriety made against him in the context of those interests make the battle the first internal affair, but not the last, to reflect international interests.

Menelik continued to suffer strokes but, persisting in his work, he promulgated the private property law that abolished state ownership rights and set up a council of ministers, appointing *Fitawrari* Habte Giyorgis Dinagde as its head, a position he held until 1915.[90] Differences over conducting internal administration while Menilik was ill, starting with palace politics, directly impeded or even confused *Lij* Iyasu's exercise of power. Missing at the beginning of his reign were ritualized symbols of power that should have been displayed during the absence of Menelik from public affairs. Of course, Menelik had named *Lij* Iyasu as his successor to ensure a smooth transition of power, and had nominated *Ras-Bitweded* Tessema Nadew as regent to his heir. He made the announcement about this to his ministers and to the nobles and foreign legations in 1908,[91] and then to the public in an edict in 1909. Menilik's queen, *Itege* Taytu, however, took advantage of Menelik's deteriorating health and started to engage in governmental matters, chairing the council of ministers, and virtually running provincial administra-

---

[90] Marcus, *Life and Times*, 1975, p. 213.
[91] Marcus, *Life and Times*, 1975, p. 231.

tion, making many appointments especially in the northern provinces. When some nobles in Wag and Tigre rebelled, the government authorized *Dejazmach* Abate to suppress the protest, managing to draw cooperation from all fronts to sustain harmony. The empress tried to stop the successful *dejazmach* from marching back to Addis Ababa from the north. The other members of the council, who were confident that the transition of power would go according to Menelik's choice 'neutralized' her influence.[92] Soon afterwards, on 15 April 1910, *Lij* Iyasu appeared in public walking under the sovereign's red canopy and sat on Menelik's throne to receive *Ras* Abate, who presented himself triumphantly at the palace.[93] Over the following months, fresh appointments and realignments defused various factional divisions, and *Ras* Tessema took steps to inform foreign legations not to communicate with the empress on state matters. It appeared that the regency would function with full authority. Despite this, however, *Lij* Iyasu was not allowed to use either the title of emperor or even his own seal.

Besides, it was said that his defiance of the regent made the latter so distraught that it contributed to his death in May 1911.[94] Reluctant to name another regent, and with Menelik too ill to appoint one, *Lij* Iyasu asserted his chairmanship of the council of ministers. He was soon said to be taking counsel from the wrong or inexperienced people and opportunistic foreigners. He was restless, changing his residence from the house of one noble to another. When the ministers confronted him about this and other issues, he promised to consult them.

Allegations highlighting Iyasu's personal morality soon surfaced, including shunning or disrespecting nobles, courtiers and senior government officials, even insulting some as his father's fattened sheep. He was said to have wickedly forced *Fitawrari* Habte Giyorgis, who suffered from arthritic legs, to walk long distances with him,[95] and to laugh at *Dejazmach* Abate (later *ras*) who, after mounting a mule on *Lij* Iyasu's suggestion (because he knew that it was one that kept bucking), fell off and was badly hurt.[96] A few days later, *Ras* Abate was said to

---

[92] Marcus, *Life and Times*, 1975, p. 237.
[93] Marcus, *Life and Times*, 1975, p. 246.
[94] Some oral reports imply that this *ras* had been harassed along with his young charge and family, making his illness worse. After his death, his son and his family were thrown out of his house, and his property was confiscated: ይከጥፉ የነበር ወላንሳ ስጋጃ /ያራስ ተሰማ ቤት አበቀለ አ ሙጃ (The carpets of silk and beauty / *Ras* Tessema's house, overgrown with grass!). Though silent on the fate of *Ras* Tessema's house, which became the residence of *Lij* Iyasu for a time afterwards, his nephew, *Bitweded* Mekonnen Enalkachew, mentions the harassment of the brother-in-law, *Ras* Abate. See his ቢቷዴድ መኮንን እንዳልካቸው፤ መልካም ቤተ ሰቦች፤ አዲስ አበባ 1949፡፡ አሥመራ የኩሪየሪ ኤሪትሬያ ማህበር ማተሚያ ቤት፡፡ (Mekonnen Endalkachew (*Bitoded*), *Fine Families*, Addis Ababa: Asmara Corriere Eritreo Association Printing House, 1949 EC), pp. 68–70.
[95] Richard Pankhurst, 'The Reign of *Lij* Iyasu – as Avedis Terzian Saw it', in Éloi Ficquet and Wolbert G. C. Smidt (eds), *The Life and Times of* Lij *Iyasu of Ethiopia: New Insights*, Zurich and Berlin: LIT, n.d. [2014] (pp. 91–100), p. 93.
[96] Mekonnen Endalkachew, *Fine Families*, 1949 EC, p. 62.

have addressed the council of ministers saying that *Lij* Iyasu should be put in a school and a regent should be appointed to care for him and the government. He followed this by marching a troop to the late regent's house, but *Fitawrari* Habete Giyorgis and the others ignored his move, his armed followers dispersed when they saw the lack of support and the incident passed off peacefully. Still, the deliberate dissemination of incidents highlighting the prince's immaturity and lack of a sense of responsibility left him open to criticism from those rivalling each other to influence him, by becoming at least his regent, if not monarch.

Lij Iyasu, who was staying in *Ras* Tessema's house at the time, soon left it. He moved to *Fitawrari* Habte Giyorgis's house, and then to *Afe Negus* Nessibu's. Such restlessness started to create an image of an impulsive person incapable of running the affairs of state on his own. Aside from Menelik's still being alive (although not working), this public image precluded the heir presumptive's work of confirming the transition of power through a normal coronation at which he could display appropriate military pageantry or issue the formulaic edict 'We are the one who is dead and we are the one who is alive!'

In fact the most telling of the allegations of *Lij* Iyasu's disrespect concerned his attitude to his grandfather, probably arising from what Harold Marcus has aptly termed 'the politics of the body and death of Menelik'.[97] *Lij* Iyasu's disconnectedness from the scene of palace politics probably distanced him from opportunities to fill the vacuum created by the emperor's absence from public engagements. Wanting to take the crown, *Lij* Iyasu attempted to force his way into the palace, but when the guards protecting the royal couple in their palace barred him, he laid siege to the troops, and even to messengers who had gone out to collect supplies. A shoot-out occurred, but was prevented from escalating by the intervention of the prelate, *Abune* Mattewos.

Menelik died on 12/13 December, 1913, after over four years of absence (since 28 October 1909) from public engagements, and Iyasu had 'emerged as the undoubted leader of Ethiopia' when the regent died (on 10 April 1911).[98] To enhance his status, Iyasu took the title of *abeto*, last held by Menelik after his escape from Mekdela and probably in imitation of his grandfather's status as a young man. That however did not stop the accusations of misdemeanour, allegations of disrespect and even a claim that *Lij* Iyasu went to play *guks* (Ethiopian polo) only one day after Menelik died. His subsequent silence on the matter of holding a memorial for his grandfather was taken as a lack of political sagacity.

Continuing to assert himself, *Abeto* Iyasu's involvement in internal administration also became unpopular. He furthered his prerogative as a *neguse negest* in 1914 by sending Menelik's crown to his father, *Ras* Mikael, whom he appointed as *negus* of Wello and Tigre. A year later,

---

[97] Marcus, *Life and Times*, 1975, pp. 230–44, discusses these events of 1908 to 1913 in considerable detail, also helpfully using documentation from foreign and written sources.
[98] Marcus, *Life and Times*, 1975, p. 251.

Gojam and Begemder were added to *Negus* Mikael's jurisdiction,[99] but he seems not to have been in a position to do much about it. It is not clear if *Abeto* Iyasu was trying to build up a chain of regional kings over which he would be 'king of kings' (*neguse negest*). A recent study of documents from the time confirms that this coronation gave his father political space in central administration, and that he may have been engaged in consulting on wider issues. It seems, however, that the role of the *negus* was neither in the open nor clearly spelt out. One high official in the ministry of foreign affairs appears to have insisted that his position be approved by *Negus* Mikael.[100] Indeed, such a role was implicitly acknowledged at the time by the nobles, who claimed to have written to the *negus* asking him to restrain *Abeto* Iyasu's unbecoming behaviour.

Inflaming accusations against him seems to have been his way of conducting internal administrative matters. He made impromptu appointments and dismissals of officials, and had a habit of visiting the regions by persistently leaving the capital suddenly and without his government's knowledge, and without consultation or discussions concerning the political implications. Concealing his intensions created uncertainty, though the officials were said to have become used to the unpredictable timings of his departures. Disastrously for his image, he undertook a slave-raiding expedition to the Gumuz, in southwestern Ethiopia, and returned with about ten thousand slaves. The expedition gave rise to accusations of his 'immoral hunting expedition', and, though most sources are quiet about this, the accusations fuelled a rumour that he despatched some troops, mainly Muslims from Jimma, to help the Germans in east Africa.[101] Perhaps such projects arose from misguided attempts to assert his authority as *neguse negest* and prove his valour as a warrior. A statement attributed to him by an observant historian and literary man, Mers'e Hazen, reveals his self-perception in that regard; he told the old nobles that they were too far past their prime for active participation, so should not be following him around wherever he went but should stay behind and perform their duties.

Continuing resentment escalated regarding the eastern province of Hararge and over appointments, including jurisdictions that Iyasu gave to his father. One of his sudden trips, this time to Hararge, took him into the outstretched arms of Ahmed Mazhar, a Turkish consul appointed to Ethiopia in 1912. A finding by Haggai Erlich details how this romantic visionary had convinced himself of his capacity to involve *Abeto* Iyasu in a scheme of having a Somali–Ethiopian jihadist state run from the

[99] Mers'e Hazen Welde Kirkos, n.d., p. 17 (a short manuscript I read in the 1980s at the University of London's School of Oriental and African Studies); Wolbert G. C. Smidt, 'The foreign politics of *Lij* Iyasu in 1915/16 according to newly discovered government papers', in Ficquet and Smidt (eds), *The Life and Times of* Lij *Iyasu*, 2014, p. 109.
[100] Wolbert G. C. Smidt, 'The foreign politics of *Lij* Iyasu in 1915/16', in Ficquet and Smidt (eds), *The Life and Times of* Lij *Iyasu*, 2014, p. 110.
[101] An interview I conducted in 1973 in Jimma, Keffa, with an elderly man who claimed to have been one of these troops.

town of Harar. Mazhar's plan revolved around a Somali revolt led by Sayyid in the European colonies of the Horn of Africa, in association with the Arabs in the Turkish-held areas of the Hijaz and Yemen. In June 1912, Iyasu left the capital on a tour of Wello, eastern Shewa, and the 'fringes of the Ogaden, and enabled Abdallah al-Sadiq to impose in Harar what the British consul called "*a reign of intrigue*", further undermining Tafari by building a new police force in Harar based on "*a collection of undesirable Arabs*"' (italics in original).[102]

Iyasu appeared to be cautious about involving himself in Ahmad Mazhar's scheme in 1915, but he engrossed himself in it in 1916. Despite Turkish losses in the war, and colonial British and Italian propaganda that had made the Somali leadership's interest peter out, Iyasu thought he would hit the goal of heading an Islamic state from Harar by his efforts alone.[103] He returned to the capital in April 1916, only to leave it again in July. Historian Shiferaw Bekele outlines the intensive activities in which Iyasu engaged that summer, in the last year of his reign.[104] He departed by train to Harar on the night of 28/9 July, accompanied by *Negadras* Tessema Eshete and *Negadras* Abubeker Ibrahim, and bringing with him the displaced nobles, *Ras* Lulseged Atnafseged, *Dejazmach* Kebedde Mengesha, *Fitawrari* Mekonnen Tewedbelay and *Ligaba* Beyene Wendim-Agegnehu. Iyasu did not inform anyone of his departure, not even Harar's governor, *Dejazmach* Tafari, whom he had summoned to Addis Ababa and who was waiting for permission to return. He did not stay in the palace in Harar with his niece, the wife of Tafari. Instead, he stayed in Dire Dawa with a merchant, the Turcophil Hasib Ydlibi, a close ally of Mazhar, thus increasing worries about his preferred alliances in World War I.

However he continued to use his power to summon the nobles of state, appoint and dismiss its officials and use its financial resources. On 5 August he ordered disgraced nobles to return to the capital and made appointments and demotions. He took the train to visit Djibouti on 7–10 August, with his personal attendants, Ydlibi and his daughter and *Negadras* Abu Beker. His unannounced visit took the colonial government by surprise. As if that was not enough, he held a meeting with Afar and Issa chiefs without seeking the authorities' permission or presence. After his return to Dire Dawa on 13 August, he removed *Ato* Yosef Zegelan, a long-standing Ethiopian consul in Djibouti, and Mersha Nahusennay, governor of the Afar region since the 1880s, replacing the latter with *Negadras* Abubeker, appointed *Hajji* Abdallah al Sadiq governor of eastern Hararge and made Ydlibi *Negadras* of Harar

---

[102] Haggai Erlich, 'From Wello to Harer: Lij Iyasu, the Ottomans and the Somali Sayyid', in Ficquet and Smidt (eds), *The Life and Times of* Lij *Iyasu*, 2014 (pp. 135–47), p. 139.

[103] Erlich, 'From Wello to Harer', in Ficquet and Smidt (eds), *The Life and Times of* Lij *Iyasu*, 2014 (pp. 135–47), p. 139.

[104] Shiferaw Bekele, 'Dirre Dawa, Harer and Jigjiga in the weeks before and after the overthrow of Iyasu on 27 September 1916', in Ficquet and Smidt (eds), *The Life and Times of* Lij *Iyasu* 2014 (pp. 151–63), pp. 152–6.

and Dire Dawa, thus enhancing the status of this merchant among foreigners in the area. He removed the governor of Hararge, *Dejazmach* Tafari, and appointed him to Keffa, which was seen as a demotion.

Continuing to rally support for his scheme, he went to Jijiga in September and held a meeting with a large number of Somalis and their chiefs. On his return on 7 September he stayed in the palace in Harar, from where he urged Tafari to depart to Keffa. He urgently summoned ten nobles, including *Dejazmach* Balcha, *Dejazmach* Habte Maryam and *Afe Negus* Tilahun, and kept them under close scrutiny in Harar. Apart from fuelling his inclinations to side with Turkey and enhance the power of the Islamic Middle East, Iyasu's socio-politics created religious tensions in Hararge, raising concern in the capital. Recent documentation reveals how the Christians in Hararge were cowed by the Oromo and Somali Muslim troops that *Abeto* Iyasu was raising and arming. Though marriage was a political device of political alliances and religion a serious idiom of inclusivity in their tradition, the courtiers embedded both schemes to highlight *Lij* Iyasu's 'moral' politics. Ahmed Hassen Omer also accuses the Ethiopian Orthodox Church of amplifying *Lij* Iyasu's 'association with the daughters of Muslim chiefs' and 'the intimacy he extended to the Muslims' in Harar, Dire Dawa and Jijiga, and attributes later disturbances in Arsi, Bale, eastern Haregre, and among the Afar to their resentment of the removal of *Lij* Iyasu, who had promised them favours.[105] Haggai Erlich's research into Middle Eastern sources has generated evidence of Iyasu's close liaison with the Turkish consul, who promised him a sea port and French and other Somali territories in return for an Islamist and jihadist Ethiopia.[106]

Nonetheless, a British diplomat, W. G. Thesiger, who discussed the matter with *Abeto* Iyasu on 21 June 1916, learned that the prince did not hide his sympathy for Muslims, including Turks, and that though he had been alarmed at hearing that Turkey had declared a *jihad* he had feared for Muslims in Ethiopia and 'he was merely playing with the Mullah in order to keep him quiet and far from Abyssinia' – he never entertained changing his religion.[107] British and other diplomats who feared an Ethiopian alliance with Turkey even circulated photographs of the Ethiopian flag with Arabic letters that *Lij* Iyasu had purportedly used to please the Turks. *Lij* Iyasu's consultation with two individuals on how to divide Hararge, which he refers to as 'Muslim country', into administrative regions over which he would 'appoint Muslims from Wello and Shewa'[108] also appears political.

---

[105] Ahmed Hassen Omer, '*Lij* Iyasu', in Ficquet and Smidt (eds), *The Life and Times of* Lij *Iyasu*, 2014 (pp. 81–9), p. 88.
[106] Erlich, *Ethiopia and the Middle East*, 1994, pp. 83–91.
[107] See a conversation of June 1916 in Hugh Drummond Pearson, *Letters from Abyssinia: 1916 and 1917, With Supplemental Foreign Office Documents*, ed. Frederic A. Sharf, Hollywood, CA: Tsehai Publishers, 2004, pp. 112–13.
[108] ተክለ ሐዋርያት ተክለ ማርያም ፊታውራሪ፥ ኦቶባዮግራፊ 1999 (Tekle Hawaryat Tekle Maryam (*Fitawrari*), *Autobiography*, Addis Ababa: Addis Ababa University Press, 1999 EC), p. 273.

Iyasu's neglect to inform his government as to his motivations was tantamount to developing secret policies that he would expect them to accept. He justifiably explained his association with Muslims as his way of promoting equality among his subjects, but he did not follow such confirmation to foreigners by announcements to his public. Though his position availed him of government facilities in the capital, his frantic activities appeared to be conducted from the margins. Certainly, going it alone in making personal links with cross-border populations of the southeastern regions of northeast Africa was as unpalatable to them as his hunting and slave-raiding expeditions in the southwest. Though he assured a British diplomat that his apparent favouritism towards Turkey without any explanation to his ministers was only a passing game, the persistent image he gave was of cross-border coordination of Muslims. His neglect of those at the centre of political activity led to varied interpretations, making it difficult to disentangle his political and religious motives. Perhaps Iyasu's attempt to create a political integration of Muslims in the Horn of Africa from Harar was based on a desire for a socio-political power base of his own in a local community.

Of course, Iyasu's sincere attempts to push the scheme to aggrandize his territorial hold on his own, at the risk of giving a religious colour to the allegations, brought the confusing impressions on himself. Among scholars who considered why *Lij* Iyasu was acting personally from the margins, rather than from the government at the centre, Haggai Erlich plausibly concludes that the prince was trying to find ways of incorporating Islamic communities into the wider Ethiopian setting. However, his association with Ahmed Mazhar and Ydlibi at the height of World War I was a miscalculation of the extent of his own charisma and political power. Like his hunting expedition to Dizi in the southwest, and his search for a socio-political base even in colonially held territories, he appears to have been following a project of expanding the Ethiopian state: he was upholding a potentially old-style *chewa* military practice anachronistically.

Commenting nearer his time, Gebre Hiywot Baykedagn asserts that even schemes Menelik initiated did not challenge the traditional political system the nobility knew, but *Lij* Iyasu tried to change that. However, on reassessing his initiatives, historian Ahmed Hassan highlights the positive side of his invitation to Ydlibi – namely developing Dire Dawa as a model town that could be imitated in other Ethiopian towns.[109] Referring to Mers'e Hazen, Bahru Zewde also cites the 'guaranteeing of property and a more equitable system of *asrat* [tithe] collection', introducing a municipal police force known as *Trimbouli* (from Tripoli in Libya whence its first recruits came), and firmly getting rid of the *leba shay* institution in preference for starting a police force.[110] A *leba shay* was sent to each province with *maderya* land grants, but their practice of drugging boys who would then 'detect' thieves was

[109] Ahmed Hassen Omer, '*Lij* Iyasu: A Reformist Prince?', in Ficquet and Smidt (eds), *The Life and Times of* Lij *Iyasu*, 2014, pp. 81–9. 86–7.
[110] Bahru Zewde, *A History of Modern Ethiopia*, 2001, pp. 121–2.

criticized.[111] Other reforms *Lij* Iyasu carried out occurred during his visit to the west when he removed the *Gondere* corps from Wellega and settled it in Getema town in Arjo, also in Wellega.[112] He also settled 1,785 captives he brought from his raids in the west in what later became Yegimira Sefer in northern Addis Ababa.[113] Systematizing accountability regarding palace property was an additional effort, but this implicated some nobles in inappropriate drawing of cash from the palace treasury and later drew hostility to him.[114]

The main cause of reactions against him was his absence from the capital, the centre of state administration. Anonymous pamphleteers, describing themselves as 'the Ethiopian people', campaigned against him, interestingly referring to foreign diplomats' concerns about *Lij* Iyasu's alliance with Germany, and how this jeopardized Ethiopia's place in international politics.[115] They judged his trips to Djibouti and the bordering areas, including British Somaliland, in light of neutrality being in the national interest. Leaving no stone unturned, they also insisted that his Islamic inclinations were evinced in his liaisons with Muslim girls and his visits to mosques while neglecting the churches in Dire Dawa.

When informed of a plot to overthrow him, *Lij* Iyasu reportedly boasted that the 'son' of Menelik was 'invincible', but he also made phone calls to the capital to deny that he had changed his religious belief.[116] On 27 September, the nobles in the capital declared him deposed, using 'the opportunity of his absence' to bring in Menelik's daughter, Zewditu, and crown her 'queen of kings'. The courtiers claimed that they had written twice to *Negus* Mikael asking him to discipline his son, and a third time to inform him of Zewditu's coronation.

It is said that the last letter precipitated *Negus* Mikael's initiative to reinstate *Lij* Iyasu. *Lij* Iyasu rallied the *Gondere* and *Werwari* troops in Hararge and sent them along the Awash valley, allegedly due to the half-hearted support of their leader *Dejazmach* Gugsa Aliye,[117] who delayed their departure.[118] These forces were to march on Addis Ababa from the north, the northeast and the east, and one of them clashed but was defeated in a skirmish with a contingent despatched from the capital. In addition to his father, one of his young boon

[111] The *leba shay* were descendants of three brothers from Minjar who had been practising for about five generations before *Lij* Iyasu stopped them. My mother recalled that they protested the loss of their *maderya* land grants, and a few continued to practise their art clandestinely until the eve of the 1935–41 war.
[112] Mers'e Hazen Welde Kirkos, *My memories*, 2002 EC, p. 96.
[113] Mers'e Hazen Welde Kirkos, *My memories*, 2002 EC, p. 97.
[114] Mers'e Hazen Welde Kirkos, *My memories*, 2002 EC, p. 127.
[115] Smidt, 'The foreign politics of *Lij* Iyasu in 1915/16,' in Ficquet and Smidt (eds), *The Life and Times of* Lij *Iyasu*, 2014. Though there was no anti-European perception in the country as concrete as held by the campaigners of 1916, such an attitude towards foreigners intensified in the 1920s and 1930s.
[116] Tekle Hawaryat Tekle Maryam, *Autobiography*, 1999 EC, pp. 275–82.
[117] Tekle Hawaryat Tekle Maryam, *Autobiography*, 1999 EC, pp. 312–19.
[118] Mers'e Hazen Welde Kirkos, *My memories*, 2002 EC, p. 156.

Photo 1 Queen of Kings Zewditu (Source: R. Pankhurst & Denis Gérard, *Ethiopia Photographed: Historic Photographs of the Country and its People Taken Between 1867 and 1935* (Kegan Paul International, 1996), p. 66; by kind permission of Richard Pankhurst's family and Denis Gérard)

companions, Abraham Ar'aya, voluntarily rallied to Iyasu's cause.

Lij Iyasu himself left Harar for Dire Dawa where he gave his followers what he could find in the treasury and the customs office. Sending some to Djibouti with Ydlibi and Mohammed Yaahya, he took the rest by camel-back and departed to meet up with his father in Wello. *Negus* Mikael, who had mobilized without wasting time, bringing his household troops and the *melmel* (recruits), sent word to all in his jurisdiction to join him as he was rushing to crown his son in Addis Ababa. While his telephone operator hastened the officers in the province, the *negus* sent a branch of his forces through Aheya Faj, an approach over the mountains to the north of Addis Ababa, and led his main force through the low plains to the northeast. At Koremash, a town founded by Menelik in Menz, he received a runner from *Lij* Iyasu urging him to await his arrival.

This campaign, which *Ras* Tafari announced was 'neither for territorial expansion nor loot', did not display the characteristic exchange of *zeraf* messages. Instead, the Minister of War, *Fitawrari* Habte Giyorgis, 'pretended to conduct negotiations' with *Negus* Mikael until troops from Addis Ababa could rendezvous with the *Barud Bet*, who were coming from Sidamo. Led by *Ras* Lulsegad Atnafseged, this contingent arrived earlier than those from the capital and positioned itself on a hilltop at Tora Mesk, where the larger contingent that *Negus* Mikael had sent suddenly came upon it. In less than two hours, the *Barud Bet* was overwhelmed and *Ras* Lulseged and his main commanders were killed. A lamentation dirge for Lulseged made him a hero:

> ወይ በሰውነት ያለ መከራ
> ሉልሰገድ ሞተ እንዲያ ሲያስፈራ
> Woe for the troubles of being human!
> Lulseged is dead, though he was so awe inspiring![119]

Meanwhile, *Negus* Mikael who had been pressing forward, received another message from *Lij* Iyasu instructing him to await his arrival as he was then on his way. *Negus* Mikael reportedly replied, 'It is fit to wait for one's child with food but not war; I will continue with what I am doing!' By now, his troops understood that their leader was definitely on a war footing. He therefore issued an *awaj* saying that his aim was to locate *Lij* Iyasu, whom he had lost. At the time, *Lij* Iyasu had been reportedly raising troops among the Afar, and was resting at Hara Weyn from his hurried escape from Harar. According to an informant who was then his camp attendant, *Lij* Iyasu's advisors suggested approaching the French or another of the colonial powers for help. He replied that they were 'going by what is temporarily convenient', for if he were to sign an agreement with any of them he would be 'selling his country'.[120] He clearly understood the international implications better than those around him.

Another message from *Fitawrari* Habte Giyorgis to *Negus* Mikael, this time with priests as negotiators, asked for reconciliation. The *negus* wanted to give this a chance, but his advisors, his sister included, pointed out that this was only a ruse, given that his camp had cost the lives of high officials such as *Ras* Lulseged. He therefore sent back the priests without a response, but holding back the main messenger, and began taking up position at Segele. *Dejazmach* Balcha's troops alone were left in charge of the capital and the queen-elect. As information came that looters among *Negus* Mikael's marching troops looking for hidden treasures ('alleged Muslims') had desecrated Sahle Selassie's grave and thrown about his bones, priests in Addis Ababa were armed to guard the churches in case the *negus* marched in victorious. *Dejazmach* Balcha hanged seven looters, making examples of those who were inclined to create disturbances.

The troops from Addis Ababa were from virtually all the provinces, except Wello, and some arrived after the battle was over. Their leaders included the new crown prince-designate, Tafari, now titled *ras*, and all the newly appointed ministers. On 27 October 1916, *Ras* Tafari placed troops all around the battlefield at Segele, some hundred kilometres north of the capital. Continuing his ruse, *Fitawrari* Habte Giyorgis placed only a few soldiers where the advancing troops of *Negus* Mikael could see them. Trapped, and seeing even those close to him falling,

---

[119] An oral couplet my mother recalled.
[120] Mers'e Hazen Welde Kirkos, *My memories*, 2002 EC, pp. 165–6.

Negus Mikael gave himself up. He was first brought to *Ras* Tafari who received him with dignity, leaving him his own tent. Seeing this, soldiers complained that they had gone to great trouble 'only to find that "father" and "son" were friends'! The *negus* was therefore transferred to the camp of *Fitawrari* Habte Giyorgis. Back in the capital, where the queen received both victors and vanquished at a parade, *Ras* Tafari, *Fitawrari* Habte and the others bowed in front of her and sat at places allocated to them. *Negus* Mikael, who was riding a mule like the other dignitaries, was made to dismount and pass by. Later, under guard at *Fitawrari* Habte Giyorgis's, he was tried for treason and committed to prison, where he died. *Lij* Iyasu was captured in 1921 and imprisoned near Harar until his death in 1935. The battle was the culmination of several recent engagements in which *chewa* nobles fought each other to sustain the monarchic tradition.

On accepting the crown, Zewditu agreed to restrictions such as not seeing her husband, *Ras* Gugsa Wele, governor of Begemder, and accepting a regent, *Ras* Tafari. According to the regent's autobiography, she came to consider him, not surprisingly, as her 'son'. Observers at the time composed a sarcastic ditty:

> ዘውዲቱ መኒልክ ልጅ የላትም ሲሉ
> ተፈሪና ብሩ በድንገት ብቅ አሉ
> While they said Zewditu Menelik was childless,
> Tafari and Biru have suddenly come forward![121]

The council's consensus to promote a woman to the throne was a historical landmark. Powerful women in the past – notably Empresses Eleni, Seble Wengel, Mentwab, and Menen – held their political offices as regents for minors. These, like other women and as much as men, were repositories of *chewa* ideals as we will see in the resistance to the 1935–41 invasion. In an apparently remarkable reversal, this well-established married princess, Zewditu (29 April 1876–2 April 1930), was placed under a regent, *Ras* Tafari (23 July 1892–27 August 1975), who was sixteen years her junior. The campaigners had presented Zewditu to the public in terms of their respect for Menelik, highlighting that she paid appropriate attention to her 'mother', Empress Taytu, with whom she stayed by Menelik's deathbed, and later mourned her father. They depicted her as a devoted daughter, willing to give her father, the 'motherly' Menelik, appropriate mourning and a decent burial, a pious Christian paying attention both to the 'poor' and the *mekwanent* (nobility). These images were meant to contrast her with *Lij* Iyasu. In that perspective, she was a compromise candidate through which the country could be extricated from the supposed alliance that Iyasu had been forging with Turkey and the Islamic Middle East. They saw her as custodian of the crown of *neguse negest*, in whose person the prescribed and the *chewa* processes of succession could be safeguarded.

---

[121] Information from my mother, *Weyzero* Workaferahu Haile. The reference is to Biru Welde-Gabriel, later *ras*.

Personalized tales of individual heroes and villains from the period have also sustained some kind of mythology around the 'sons' of *Lij* Iyasu and other 'descendants' of Menelik. Coming into the limelight during 1935–41, at least three of *Lij* Iyasu's children achieved some significance as rallying points for fighters against the invaders, showing the persistence of *chewa* tradition at the time. Partial interest in them re-emerged again in 1973–4, when one of *Lij* Iyasu's natural sons was seen as a possible monarch instead of Haile Selassie. Similarly inconsequential events that have become prominent over the decades since 1916 seem to have transformed the childhood relationships between *Lij* Iyasu and *Ras* Tafari into political rivalries. Among these is Iyasu's marriage to six-year-old Aster Mengesha, who was said to have been betrothed to Tafari. *Lij* Iyasu was said to have compensated Tafari by marrying him to his cousin, Menen, already wife to *Ras* Lulseged. Presumed to fear *Ras* Lulseged, therefore, *Ras* Tafari allegedly delayed sending contingency troops that could have saved his life. A similar politicization of events relates to the supposed enmity between Wello and Shewa. In 1936, the population along the Dessie road were said to retaliate over the imprisonment and death of *Negus* Mikael by attacking troops retreating from the northern front during the second Italian invasion.

Lij Iyasu's absences from duty, his alleged inclination towards Islam, and his entangled conduct of the country's international politics in relation to World War I still generate controversy. If using marriage as a political device explains his widespread 'marital' contracts, creating fictive relationships justifies his engagements with the clans in the northeast African region. Perspectives of warriorhood could explain his absence from the base of central administration, and perhaps his belief in creating a traditional socio-political base for himself. It should be noted too that *Lij* Iyasu's rejection of prevailing court behaviour, which some have put down to immaturity, was addressed by the rebels' claim to be retrieving Menelik's love and influence by replacing him with Zewditu.

Be that as it may, the protagonists in the Battle of Segele ignored the fact that 'modern' institutions, including the monarchy, could not be personalized. They failed to make the transition between prescribed succession to the throne and the 'modernity' that Menelik had envisaged for the state. Subsequent events, notably the constitution of 1930, were to show that their choice opened the way for the throne to belong to the line of Haile Selassie alone. Their struggle also resulted in a serious change with regard to the defence of the country. Their focus on foreigners' attitudes was inevitable during World War I, but the precedence ushered in a fundamental shift that made international politics central to Ethiopia's defence policy. The reigns of Empress Zewditu (r.1916–30) and Emperor Haile Selassie I (r.1930–75) enshrined deference to foreign views and attitudes. As we will see, paying attention to the principles of the League of Nations partly influenced Emperor Haile Selassie's conduct of resisting the second Italian invasion of 1935–41. Of course, Ethiopia's lack of appropriate armaments, the ruthlessness of the fascistic invader and the international betrayal the country faced did not help either.

Map 2 Some rivers and peaks of Ethiopia (drawn by Peter Esmonde)

4

Ecological Roots of Local Leadership

The features of the Ethiopian landscape were among the inclusive principles that for *chewa* defined the country (*hager*). Deeply appreciating them as part of their ancestral heritage, warriors familiarized themselves with the rivers that were frequently impassable, the mountains that were strongholds, the forests that were inhabited by outlaws and wildlife, and the 'deserts' and low-lying areas that were perceived as distant. In much the same way as when they defended personal and communal lands, the *chewa* sought acknowledgements of courage, stamina and excellence in knowing and overcoming the challenges posed by the topography. Youth committed to experiencing these land features achieved symbolic transition towards adulthood, while adults received recognition for their good political judgement. *Chewa* warriors were committed to 'die', both for the lands and the people inhabiting them at the risk of their own livelihoods. The capacity to use ecological frontiers to determine Ethiopia's friends and foes gave the warriors, whether in training or qualified, lifelong experiences that defined Ethiopia and its people in the wider region. Rubenson challenged Toynbee's assertions that Ethiopia owed its survival to its landscape.[1] Indeed Ethiopian warriors attributed defence to the qualities of their warriorhood in the various features of the landscape.

LANDSCAPE FEATURES

The warriors experienced the practicality of militaristic principles and duties while living as hunters, overcoming the mysterious and ambiguous dangers posed by illegal traders, outlaws and external invaders. In that sense, surviving in inhospitable riparian areas was also considered among *chewa* military feats. Rivers, lakes and forests were almost 'no-man's lands' in political and military terms. Dervla Murphy experienced the dangers in the 1960s,[2] and Mesfin Welde-Mariam points out: 'when crossing most river valleys one may not see a single person,

[1] See Rubenson, *The Survival of Ethiopian Independence*, 1976, pp. 1–2, 407–8.
[2] Dervla Murphy, *In Ethiopia with a Mule*, London: John Murray, 1968, pp. 155–7.

unless one is unfortunate enough to encounter *shiftas* or robbers'.[3] Some of these features were historical territorial markers that were not to be crossed. Sending a message to people living by a river of one's intention to drink from its waters was a threat, and speaking of the death of a foe 'while facing away from the river' indicated impending victory.[4]

Spiritual and temporal attributes gave additional and deeper meaning to the topography. The savants of the Ethiopian Orthodox Church, for instance, attributed a sense of the idyllic and the heavenly to the highlands, which they contrasted with the discomforts of the *kolla* or *bereha*, the lowlands. Not surprisingly, everybody feared the lowlands because of such dangers as malaria and other fevers. In the nineteenth century and early in the twentieth, travellers often found it difficult to hire 'Abyssinian' carriers and guides to these zones.

Caves found on mountains, in valleys, along rivers, in forests and in virtually all parts of the country were equally significant in defining land and people. While various sizes of caves have long been transformed into religious sites, some substantial ones were strongholds and hideouts for people, cattle and grain facing threats, including marauders and invaders. An example is Bullo Worne ('cave of gold'), which local people said had gold hidden in it and was inhabited by devils.[5] As a traveller remarked, 'Many caves are capable of containing a whole village, and in them they often take refuge'.[6]

Likewise, forests were home to outlaws, murderers, thieves, disgruntled political opponents, professional hunters,[7] and, at least in the late nineteenth century if not earlier, to slave dealers. Forests were found in the foothills of mountains, in valleys and lowlands, and in riverine areas. Viewed as far from human settlements and mysterious, they even symbolized a confidant to whom secrets could be entrusted, meaning that one could hide everything in the deep recesses of their minds. Forests were to be explored and brought under control, along with their contents. As rebel hideouts, they were springboards for most nineteenth-century local conflicts, notably for *shifta* intending to turn into *chewa*. Authorities, therefore, often reduced them in most parts of the north. Forests were also territorial markers, mostly in the south. Borelli recorded that forest boundary markers were known as *moga* in Oromiffa,[8] and remarked that there was law and order in it. Mérab too

[3] Mesfin Welde Mariam, *Introductory Geography of Ethiopia*, 1972, p. 54.
[4] Guèbrè Sellassié, *Chronique*, 1930–32, Vol. I, p. 290; C. H. Walker, *The Abyssinian at Home*, London: Sheldon Press, 1933, p. 181.
[5] C. W. Isenberg and J. L. Krapf, *Journals of the Rev. Messrs. Isenberg and Krapf, Missionaries of the Church Missionary Society, Detailing their Proceedings in the Kingdom of Shoa, and Journeys in Other Parts of Abyssinia in the Years 1839, 1840, 1841, and 1842*, London: Seeley, Burnside, and Seeley, 1843, pp. 275–6.
[6] Plowden, *Travels in Abyssinia*, 1868, p. 21.
[7] Alberto Denti di Pirajno, *A Cure for Serpents: A Doctor in Africa*, trans. Kathleen Naylor, London: Andre Deutsch, 1955, pp. 170–80.
[8] J. Borelli, *Éthiopie Méridionale: Journal de mon Voyage aux Pays Amhara, Galla et Sidama, Septembre 1885 à Novembre 1888*, Paris: Ancienne Maison Quantin Librairies-Imprimeries Réunies, 1890, pp. 224, 274, *et passim*.

heard that 'Abyssinians' got people to cut or at least remove branches as marks of subjugation. Menelik ordered the trees in what is now Addis Ababa to be cut down and burned to avoid his soldiers being ambushed.[9] In about 1913–14, Menelik's heir, *Lij* Iyasu, ordered the residents of the capital to remove the leaves of the eucalyptus trees on his return from his wild expeditions to see if he would be obeyed.[10]

In the post-World War II period, the foregoing attitudes to trees unfortunately developed into the idea that forests were not only woodlands but *taff*, that is, unutilized and unoccupied lands inhabited by wild animals. In the 1960s, therefore, the 'modern' development sector considerably reduced forest cover regardless of the effect on existing users, claiming simply that forests were taking up space that could be used for cultivation.[11] During the unsettled period since 1991, people have been heard saying that removing the forest cover deprives them of their sulking grounds.

Chewa warriors made their centres of administration churches or permanent houses away from 'dangerous' landscape features. That is, mountaintops, the brows of tablelands, and raised ground were the preferred sites for defence and political activity. Indeed, Johnston said that it looked as though almost every hill, surrounded by cultivated lands on all sides, was 'the perching place of a little hamlet or town'.[12] Harris described the residence of a governor of Wello as 'built on top of a hill, which forms a complete mass of rock ... There is only one way ... and this is attended with great difficulties ... No Abyssinian force is able to conquer this stronghold.'[13]

POLITICAL GEOGRAPHY

In the perspectives of seeing 'country' as a geopolitical land in a non-delimited and expansive region, territorial Ethiopia was what the warriors controlled either by cultivation or some other activity, both historically and contemporaneously. Near their home bases, they used land features to define borders in order to ensure their land rights, and in faraway frontier lands, to define their responsibility towards the people in them. According to their ideals, warriors thought of a popula-

[9] Mérab, Paul, *Impressions d'Éthiopie*, Paris: Ernest Leroux, 1921–9, p. 240.
[10] Mérab, *Impressions*, 1921–9, p. 252.
[11] Tsehai Berhane-Selassie, 'The Socio-Politics of Ethiopian Sacred Groves', in Michael J. Sheridan and Celia Nyamweru (eds), *African Sacred Groves: Ecological Dynamics and Social Change*, Oxford: James Currey, 2008, pp. 103–16, pp. 110–11.
[12] Charles Johnston, *Travels in Southern Abyssinia, through the Country of Adal to the Kingdom of Shoa, during the years 1842–1843*, London: J. Madden, 1844, p. 469.
[13] Cf. William Cornwallis Harris, *The Highlands of Æthiopia, described, during eighteen months' of a British embassy at the Christian court of Shoa* (3 volumes, 2nd edition), London: Longman, Brown, Green and Longmans, 1844, Vol. II, p. 327.

tion inclusively, and as a consequence, made identity differences on the basis of living in a region or ecology inconsequential for defining Ethiopia. This view facilitated seeing the country as ancient and expansive. Along with their sense of people-focused borders and non-delimited space of 'country', it enabled the playing down of internal rivalry and difference.

Asserting control of the expansive space across ecological zones had a bearing on ethnic and other differences. The warriors ameliorated these by imposing ambiguous practices of delimitation along borders, and in the relationships between victors and the vanquished, or insiders and outsiders. These pertained along borders of local communities, provinces or international territories. To exclude people along physical lines drawn on the ground was alien to this conception of defining people and borderlands. Of course, recruiting local people within the border meant incorporating significant local leaders in the system of ever-emerging warriorhood. Besides, the practice of evaluating warriors for political and military purposes did not include relinquishing other forms of identity such as ethnicity. Indeed, inclusive recruitment encouraged the diversity of warriors who were in the defence system by their own efforts. It was this system that contributed to the puzzlement of Europeans (with their divide-and-rule expectations) over Ethiopians' ability to suspend their local conflicts during external invasions.

The principles of exclusion worked differently within neighbourhoods and across topographical zones. Deliberate exclusion was social, just as belongingness was relative to the immediate context. The status of local 'country people', or *ageree*, contrasted with that of newcomers who had neither kinship nor para-kinship ties. Members of the local community saw themselves as 'child of man' and their slaves and other domestics as 'child of the house'. All these local persons were protected. The 'unrelated newcomer' was exposed, extraordinary and lonely; he or she was someone 'whose whereabouts were unknown'.

These principles meant that, for distancing outsiders from the local community, the warriors held categories of hierarchical relationships. Concepts of social boundary or *gedeb* attributed a narrow and polite rendering to the word 'human being' (*sew*) and placed hierarchical belongingness on the excluded. This is best illustrated in the differences between foreigners and locally excluded manual workers.

Potters and other crafts producers who were local, distanced but much sought after as ritual and medical experts and crafts producers, were relegated to marginal lands within the local communal area. These specialists gave symbolic significance to these lands by ritually controlling and managing places such as forest, water and other primordial environmental features. Their lands contrasted with the choice areas of the dominant farmers or cattle herders, and even of foreigners. For all legal and social purposes, however, the dominant rural farmers or cattle herders considered that they owned the lands that crafts producers occupied. Of course, although many in this category changed their status through geographical mobility, and even joined the soldiery, their efforts had limited practical effect on their acceptance by farmers and cattle herders.

The dominant society acknowledged occupational groups as descendants of senior sibling ancestors who lost their right to local land ownership. Consequently, the logic goes, they could not be incorporated in the local kinship system through marriage or symbolic association of belonging to the 'house'. It is interesting to note that many occupational groups explained their endogamy by seeing non-craftspeople as essentially 'without work' and less worthy. The dominant group also attributed to them the 'evil eye', and such feared qualities as powers of communicating with both evil and benign spirits lurking in marginal lands – esoteric attributes that distanced them from good land and from local and state politics.[14] Some, like the Bete Isra'el (Felasha) of Begemder, engaged in weaving, but most were potters, beekeepers, blacksmiths or tanners. Such groups among the Sidama considered the Hadicho as descendants of an 'older' brother who 'lost his land' for eating forbidden food. Others were the Weyto among the Amhara and Oromo, or Wata as they were known in the south, the Fuga among the Gurage, and many more elsewhere. Even in urban areas, manual work made people almost non-entities despite their subsequent transformation to another status over a long period. For instance, during the first three or four decades of the twentieth century in developing, urban Addis Ababa, Gurage engaged in trade and in menial work were seen as acceptable only gradually. The strong prejudice against them pervaded the economic and political system, leading some scholars to categorize them as a caste. Whatever reasons were given for circumscribing their status, occupational groups were still considered members of the local community.

Likewise, the foreigner, who was thought of as having his or her own 'country', albeit somewhere else, could be alleged to have the 'evil eye' (*buda*) like the artisan.[15] The unrelated foreigner was known as *yesew ager sew* or 'man [or person] of the country of [other] man' – one who was part of the general category of humanity but who did not belong even in terms of symbolic kinship. The foreigner was set apart from the local society, and though to be tolerated (as we will soon see) as a subordinate, was denied protection beyond that which local 'owners' of the 'country' could concede to someone not belonging to the 'country'.

However, though carrying as strong a social stigma as having leprosy or certain other diseases, a foreigner was not to be confronted openly on the subject of identity. Relationships with the foreigner were preferably left as vague as possible. Indeed, in major towns, where the local community was seen as relatively unstable, a common saying lamenting the lack of empathy for or defence of the 'stranger' was: 'Everyone is a child

---

[14] Tsehai Berhane-Selassie, 'The Socio-Politics of Ethiopian Sacred Groves', 2008, pp. 106–7.
[15] John Camden Hotten (ed.), *Abyssinia and its People; or, Life in the Land of Prester John*, New York: Negro Universities Press, 1969 [1868], p. 134.

of man in his own country'. As a traditional rhyming couplet with double meaning has it, no newcomer should be exposed:

> የሰው አገር ሰው በሺተኛ
> አትቀስቅሱት አርፎ ይኛ
> አት7ላልጡት አልበታል
> አገርሽቶት ይሞታል
> [አገር ሽቶት ይሞታል]
> Man of the country of man, the patient!
> Do not disturb him; let him sleep.
> Do not expose him, he is sweating!
> He might die of relapse
> [i.e. he might die pining for his country]

HABESHA ALONG THE ETHIOPIAN BORDERLANDS

'Country' (*hager*) had different meanings in various contexts, though it was basically conceived of as encompassing belongingness in a society that gave protection, opportunities and rights. Large-scale forced outward migration (due to famine or war) meant profound crisis – being set adrift from all that 'country' had to offer. Conditions of such a major natural calamity or of socio-military disturbances that warrior leaders could not control were described as the 'unmaking of people and their country'. To speak of the 'country' turning out at major events (such as funerals or religious festivities) designated only people. Referring to a specific territory such as Begemder or Ethiopia as *hager* contrasted it with other 'countries' of people with comparable standing. To speak of belonging to topographical features demarcating boundaries such as named rivers like the Abay, or lowlands such as Netch Sar *bereha* and the Red Sea coast, did not imply internal exclusion from the named 'country', Ethiopia.

Within Ethiopian territory, *hager* had meanings in terms of exclusivity and inclusivity, while the word *Habesha* encompassed ethnic and linguistic variations. Said to come from an Arabic word meaning 'mixed' people it did not imply merely genetic mixture. At least in the nineteenth century, *Habesha* consisted of ethnic and other classificatory groups whose identities were named groups with territorial affiliations. To the state leaders and the popular culture that generated the self-trained warriors, such threats as nineteenth-century European colonialists evoked hostility. While colonialism challenged the national order, rivalry over trade routes to the Red Sea or the Mediterranean caused internal disruption. However, the *Habesha* justified their hostile relationships or alliances by asserting their manhood in defining Ethiopia within the topographical zones. The use of the term *Habesha* for such an assertive defining of Ethiopia was core to the warriors' military self-conceptualization.

It is important to note also that ethnic terms, descriptions and lands have shifted in different historical times. Thus, the names of ethnic groups distinguished early in the nineteenth century as Amhara,

Oromo, Tigre, Welayta (then referred to as Welamo), Weyto, Sidama, Keffa, Adere, Somali, Adal, etc. carried different meanings. For instance, Oromo (then designated by a different word) stereotypically identified any non-Christian people or 'country' as Sidama, whereas Amhara and Tigre were said to be Christians in the 'Christian country'. Describing a given people as Christian or Muslim on the basis of ethnic nomenclature has added emphasis to the historical *chewa* narrative of 'were-Christians' by which the Adere, the Somali and the Adal, for example, were 'formerly Christians' whose lands were lost to Islam during the Gragn invasions (1520–40) and to the Oromo after that.

Examples of identity changes referring to linguistic and ethnic terminologies include that of the Oromo. Having spread from southern Ethiopia to Lake Tana and Wello from the sixteenth century onwards, their migration was accompanied with changes in ethnic and clan nomenclature (probably not for the first time). In time, taking the seat of power in Gonder through the Yeju clan, they adopted Amharic, the court language, and the Yeju then referred to people south of them with the old term for Oromo. When the Tigre from near the western shores of the Red Sea became powerholders, they referred to all land they came across in religious terms. Thus, Emperor Yohannes IV (r.1872–89), for instance, whose court used Amharic, insisted on everybody converting to Christianity.[16] This resulted in identifying the *chewa* as Christian and Amhara, and the rest as either Muslim or pagan for some time afterwards.[17] Another way of thought of *chewa* power politics, the standard and inclusive position of seeing many as Christian or formerly Christian, overlooked religious group differentiations for official purposes. When Menelik II was expanding his jurisdiction by 'reclaiming the lost territories' in the southern regions from around 1875, *chewa* in his service officially spoke Amharic; they were mostly Christian but included some Muslims. Ethnically, they were mainly Amhara, Tigre and Oromo from the north, namely Gojam, Begemder, Wello and eastern Shewa. They incorporated Gurage, Welayta and Kembata as they proceeded towards the Sidama, Guji, Derasa (or Gedeo) and Borena lands. In the last three decades of the nineteenth century, everyone in government office (i.e. the civil service) was labelled 'Amhara' irrespective of their ethnic or linguistic base. After three generations the term Amhara appears to have overtaken its former ethno-linguistic and political references. By the dawn of the twentieth century, its people had become detached from their ancestral localities. As part of such political self-assertion, identifying with the Amhara was used, for instance, by freed and often Christianized slaves too.

This changing use of the term Amhara has historically generated interest in defining the word. Kidane Weld Kifle in his *Ge'ez Amharic Dictionary* claims that the word is derived from the root verb *memmar*, to learn, and other Amharic written sources give its meaning as 'free,

[16] Zewde Gabre-Sellassie, *Yohannes IV of Ethiopia: A Political Biography* (Oxford Studies in African Affairs), Oxford: Clarendon Press, 1975, pp. 96–100.
[17] Mérab, *Impressions*, 1921–9, p. 160.

clear and clean people'. However, despite the people called Amhara being freedom-loving, nothing but the sound similarity with the word *amare* ('has become beautiful') justifies the supposition that *'amhara'* entails such an interpretation. The Italians used the word Amhara in 1935–41 negatively, designating it as 'enemy' – an unprecedented meaning with unfortunate long-term consequences. Used at the time by the Italians to distance the *chewa* from the population in southern Ethiopia, this definition built implicit linguistic and political meanings into the word *'amhara'*. An example of negativity was the much-touted 'expansionism of the Amhara', which imputed to the actual ethnic group alone the overall emergent, warrior-led phenomenon – that of incorporating 'lost territories' of people and lands within the Ethiopian political system. Other Europeans referred to Amhara in conjunction with Tigre and identified the imagined territory they referred to as Abyssinia with Christianity.

The ongoing debate on Amhara as an ethnic identity first appears as early as 1841,[18] when Issenberg noted that the 'real' Amhara were in Amhara Saynt, a small area above the confluence of the Adabay and Mofer Weha rivers.[19] Though probably descended from a *chewa* contingent placed there by the peripatetic monarchs, it appears that the Amhara of Amhara Saynt have had no control of central government (if they ever had) since the Zagwe dynasty was overthrown in 1270. Historical documents show that in the sixteenth century this area was overrun by the Oromo and 'ethnically' dominated by them thereafter. Interestingly, despite the general perception, the Amharic-speaking Amhara in Gojam, Begemder, Wello and Shewa never asserted that they were pure Amhara or any ethnic group. Indeed, they describe themselves as people of Shewa ('Shewe'), of Gojam ('Gojame') or of Begemder ('Gondere'). If pushed, they easily admit that they have been mixed with Oromo and other migrants to their areas since the sixteenth century.

In the *chewa* warrior politics of the late nineteenth century, that is, 'Amhara' designated any Amharic-speaking group that engaged in government service, and possibly in the military activities under discussion. Particularly with changes in identity, the lack of stability makes attributes of language or descent untenable criteria for defining people. The frequent historical wars and population migrations since the sixteenth century, and even before, and continuing beyond the nineteenth century, complicated the historical process of changing nomenclatures. In the political structure of the widest region, the appellation came next to *Habesha* in its inclusivity of local identities in sharp contrast to foreigners. Using Amhara as an ethnic term and applying it, as the Italians did deliberately, mainly to the emergent warriors (originating from many backgrounds), is a misconstruction, erroneously

---

[18] Charles William Isenberg, *Dictionary of the Amharic language in two parts: Amharic and English, and English and Amharic*, London: Richard Watts, 1841.
[19] Augustus B. Wylde, *Modern Abyssinia*, London: Methuen, 1901, p. 403, describes these rivers. The Adebay joins the Jema, which flows into the Abay (see the map at the end of Zawde Gabre-Sellassie, *Yohannes IV of Ethiopia*, 1975).

imputing that their motive for warfare was to assert ethnic identity. The broad concept of *Habesha* as 'mixed people', referring to a unitary whole within Ethiopia, included the local ethnic and other categories. It denoted a political meaning that was wider than religious, occupational or linguistic identities.

People were central in the geopolitical territory that the *chewa* defined as 'country' and the *Habesha*-inhabited 'country' was not merely the length and breadth of local space, but a combination of land and people. The warriors' territoriality reconfigured people with such border-linked inclusivity, rather than internal hostility. Borders were always what Ethiopians could reclaim on the basis of 'always having had them in the past' – for any number of reasons, including local people paying tribute to their rulers, hunters' long-term presence and *chewa* soldiers' historical settlements. On the popular level, people and land defining each other in specified territories ideally resisted the challenges external to the region, including new ideas and forces concerning identity. The translation of 'country' by the formal political structure defined by the mobile warrior population conceptualized a spectrum of Ethiopia and *Habesha* as a single territorial term. Populations could reclaim plots of land anywhere, but were not to allow the giving away of parts of the 'country' (to foreign powers) that the *chewa* had previously held and protected.

LOCAL ECONOMIC POWER, AUTHORITY AND SOLDIERING

Integral to controlling lands and the mobility of local people, information gathering was considered highly virtuous, as it gave access to economic power and authority. Sharing information with others indicated close social and political ties, and using the marketplace was therefore vital in local nineteenth-century political and military initiatives. A particular method was *aqrari masnesat*, that is 'to prompt a singer to sing *qererto*'. The word *qererto* (*gerara* in Oromo) referred to 'military war songs' that transmitted serious threats to rivals or expressed political views, as we will see below. The singer (*aqrari*) would sing in a high-pitched voice for all to hear, relaying the *shilela*, i.e. the wordings that spelt out the intended message. Military leaders, or would-be political campaigners, used them quite frequently in their local markets, their own hamlets and elsewhere, especially in the early part of the nineteenth century. As we have seen, the activity of singing out and relaying military messages, for example during purposely organized feasts, constituted the *zeraf*. It was an integral part of the *chewa* politico-military tradition by which leaders started voicing local politics. Perhaps partly in fear of that tradition, governments since 1960 have tried to stop ordinary people's interest in asking about and exchanging political information.

The self-trained emergent warriors who aspired to take political power were inhibited neither by the local community nor the changing power of governors and their institutions. They would invite similarly spirited warriors to resist the unjust manipulation of their ancestral lands, including by those in government office. Popular community leaders, and those who designated themselves as *balabat*, or 'fathers of the country' in the so-called Era of Princes, could raise political issues in public gatherings or in their homes and call for decisions. Acquiring local political space enabled them to call for military or social help from neighbouring communities, for instance to discuss the sudden appearance of a new governor, or a band of soldiers in local woodland, and to take initiatives in relation to the outsiders. Despite local ideas of politics differing in many ways from those of state agents, such popular local leaders could carry out government orders to collect increased taxes. In such instances, the appropriate and timely use of their local social popularity could catapult the individuals into state political positions.

Once in social power, individuals interwove their activities with the annual cycles of farming and war. Their recruitment of local help directly impacted on local relationships. In other words, local people who joined the local soldiery responded to government calls to arms only 'after the rains', when farming activities eased. Though important people participated in leading the political processes, including promoting themselves and assisting the state to organize and reorganize local lands, they could draw rural people only into part-time military service.

HAGER

Notwithstanding the challenges of the terrain of mountains, forests, lowlands, rivers, gorges and caves, the *chewa* conception of people in it formed a significant aspect of what 'country' (*hager*) meant. Warrior leaders' definition of 'country' and territory – far more for people under their jurisdiction than in the physical localities and boundary markers – informed the various circulars and documents[20] that they wrote to foreigners. They repeatedly identified Ethiopian territory, formally *hager*, as associated with the people inhabiting the natural features. Reflecting this, an Amharic reader for schools, produced in the 1950s, wrote of *hager* thus:

> *Hager* is part of the world where a people tied together in language, customs, hopes, pleasures and sorrows live together. It is where the ancestors were born and brought up to perform heroic defence against external enemies, gave useful services to the public and the state, replaced themselves with their children, and hid in the hole in which they were buried. Because they found unity with it through their umbilicus and their bodily remains, the soil is where the people live. God recreates from the seeds of the Earth, and *hager* is the mother who suckles and nurtures and whose bone-penetrating love is

[20] See for instance, several entries in Rubenson, *Correspondence and Treaties 1800–1854*, with Getatchew Haile and John Hunwick, Evanston, IL: Northwestern University Press; Addis Ababa: Addis Ababa University Press, 1987. Acta Æthiopica, Vol. 1.

indelible. The ancestors grew from childhood and worked for life and death, imprinting themselves in the local rivers, mountains, plains, the low lying and high grounds. *Hager*, therefore, is [imbued with] memories of love and longing when in exile. *Hager* is father, mother, relative, food and jewellery; working for it to death, even in times of poverty and oppression, is a strict ancestral legacy.[21]

The topography and people in the local and wider landscape centred inseparably on the soil. The topographical claim of highland massifs and associated lowlands metaphorically reflected the popular song on getting voices heard, as exemplified in the following 'wax and gold' poem:

> ያደኩባትን መሬት
> ማነው ሜዳ ናት ያላት?
> እኔ ልናገር የማውቀት
> አገር የጋራ ናት፣ አገሬ ጋራ ናት
> The *meret* (land) I grew up in,
> Who is calling her plain?
> Let me speak, who knows her best
> Land is for all; land is mountainous!

This poem laments divisiveness, and illustrates how unity is to be perceived in relation to the country's social and political surroundings. The 'wax' meaning here is: 'Who said the land I grew up in is flat country? I know it is mountainous.' The 'gold' meaning, and the serious message, is: 'Who is accusing my country of being common and base in the way she handles her children? I grew up, that is, I climbed the social ladder in my country. Nobody has the right to tell me to keep quiet. Let me speak out: "country" most highly belongs to all.'

These significant sociological, spiritual and political attributes, with which the warriors classified and defined the politico-military relationships, recognized barriers between people in the broad topographic features. That is, farmers and cattle herders considered crafts producers and those whose livelihoods were hunting and fishing in another ecological zone as less civilized, or even dangerous and treacherous. These 'marginal' people considered the dominant farmers and cattle herders as good-for-nothing 'non-workers'. Such differences across localized ecological zones were tempered by adoption or shelter provision for the vulnerable. Millennia of constant conflicts, however, have added to barriers across large-scale topographical features. Thus, men in one ecological zone appear to have developed a tradition of symbolically defining their manhood by emasculating the 'other' from a different zone. Those in the Rift Valley regions, for instance, took glory in emasculating any highlander wandering unaccompanied into their ecological area, and, vice versa, the highlanders engaged in the same practice. In a telling reflection of this state of hostile relationship across major zones, Harris noted: 'everyman's hand [in the lowlands]

[21] ማህተመ ሥላሴ ወልደ መስቀል *(ባላምባራስ)*፡ የቀድሞው ዘመን ጨዋ ኢትዮጵያዊ ጠባይና ባሕል፡ መጋቢት ፳፭ ቀን ፲፱፻፶፰ ዓ.ም 1958 (Mahteme Selassie Welde Meskel (*Balambaras*), *Ethiopian* Chewa *Character and Culture of Former Times*, Megabit 25, 1958 EC).

was armed for strife. The peasant carried spear and shield, and wore the shield girded to the loins; and ... his habitation had been carefully selected ... as a precaution against attack and invasion'.[22] When his expeditionary force of 'five hundred horse and foot' was mistaken for 'an eruption of Aroosi', 'cattle were driven off with all expedition to the summits' of the mountain, and villages were 'vacated in an instant'; and 'their inhabitants were to be seen clustering on the inaccessible heights in the momentary expectation of attack'.[23]

These instances across the wide landscape were not eased by such externally induced disturbances as Arab slave trading over the river valleys, foothills and scrubland towards the Red Sea, which afflicted the region for at least a millennium. As noted earlier, this influenced internal classification and gave rise to the conception of the historical 'enemy'.

---

[22] Harris, *The Highlands of Æthiopia*, 1844, II, p. 216.
[23] Harris, *The Highlands of Æthiopia*, 1844, II, p. 264.

5

Social Localities of Emergent Warriors

THE SOCIAL FABRIC OF *CHEWA* HIERARCHY

The social fabric of the society that uses land to organize itself shows the centrality of narrowly perceived physical markers – the *adbar* and its analogous social person, the *teleq sew*, 'big man'. Both were primary markers of a territorial entity that was accessible to all, against which hostilities were counterpoised across ecological features. Pivotal to the neighbourhood as physical symbol of local stability and internal cohesion, the *adbar* was often a tree, a church or an open and accessible field endowed with the benign spirit of belongingness. The population made settlements near such a physical feature and related to it, though people normally avoided erecting houses near a water surface such as a river or a lake. The 'big man' or the locally important leader networking with individuals and the wider community was seen to have the same qualities as the *adbar*.[1] The hamlet of such a person metaphorically represented neighbourhood permanence.

Perceived as benign, these features of a neighbourhood served as public and communal activity places. Endowed with a welcoming spirit, the *adbar* was expected to be accommodating towards newcomers, foreigners, complete strangers or newly-weds. Conceptualized as permanently present, it made residents and land part of a social aggregate, and gave symbolic anonymity to strangers. When a newcomer had not fared well in the place, the normally welcoming *adbar* might be seen as having 'quarrelled' with the person. In areas where the worship of a female spirit prevailed, accommodating or discomforting all categories of people in a village, town or neighbourhood was attributed to this deity, which was said to be the *adbar*.

The *teleq sew*, or 'big man', was referred to as *adbar* in the expectation that he had responsibilities to be a rallying point. This was reflected in

---

[1] Relationships of individuals with the wider society are now different from how they were in earlier days. Remarkably, over the latter half of the twentieth century in Addis Ababa, which was founded in 1891, the *adbar* was the courtyard just outside people's own houses. Prior to 1975, some thought of the monarch as the *adbar* for the country, or even provincial governors for their jurisdictions.

dream interpretations or complimentary statements that invested the person at the height of power with responsibility and, by extension, a welcoming socio-political leadership. Expected to accommodate a large number of dependants, including adopted and foster children and friends, and capable of attracting a substantial following, he was also the richest farmer, owning large tracts of land. Such a person organized the neighbourhood during peace and took leadership initiatives during war. In both cases he would be known as a *sebsabi*, literally 'gatherer' of people, conceptually mirroring the shade of the *adbar* tree where people assembled.

These expectations from the 'big man' practically idealized him as an organizer of patron–client relationships, linking people and their location in a permanent co-existence. Someone 'who was as inclusive as the *adbar* tree' developed and managed patron–client relationships and even made his house a physical landmark. In some senses, he was thought of as spiritually endowed and was even attributed with esoteric power. He could be seen to cause bad luck, fate, or ill health, or the opposite. This was similar to what was said of the marginal artisans, or even of newcomers whose sources were unknown, and these qualities extended his powers beyond his narrow social circle. His residence could not exclude those who were otherwise referred to by terminologies of exclusion. Thus he was expected to accommodate even the 'man of the country of man' (*yesew ager sew*). Seen to be different from the 'non-related' (*ba'ed*), this category included long-distance merchants, those potentially waiting to be included, artisans who were prescriptively excluded and strangers to the region. In this regard, his importance was beyond that of the *balabat*, here understood as the local community with claims to local lands.

His defence responsibilities for local people and their 'lands' meant organizing both the socio-politics of the ownership of communal property and his personal fighting capacity. As we have seen, in nineteenth-century Ethiopia a man who was such a strong rallying point had to bring up young men, providing them with the necessities for training in the martial arts, and, along with his other dependants, coaching them in political leadership. Beyond building up such an inner circle of dependants, he elevated his status by joining work and social networks. He attained political recognition by forging marriage, kin and fictive relationships, which contributed to his leadership of as many people as possible.

To give his dependants the valuable sense of belongingness and to raise their consciousness of the idealized accomplishments of fighters, he facilitated marriages for his protégées. Weddings ritually recognized men as defenders and women as their subordinates. Forging and managing their marital relationships gained the 'big man' the symbolic honour of distinguishing 'alien intruders' (*dina*) from 'those who belonged' (*wegen*) locally. This served a politico-military purpose, as it gave his dependants belongingness in a community of emergent warriors. His inclusiveness of 'those who belonged', though gendered,

Photo 2 A common scene outside a governor's residence, Jijiga, shown in an old photograph from c.1901 (Source: Commander C. N. Robinson (ed.), *The Navy and Army Illustrated* (Hudson and Kearns/George Newnes), Vol. XII, 8 June 1901, p. 268)

ensured him a ready fighting force at his side – ranging from his marital and other family members to his political supporters.

The desire to achieve the *adbar* status was so pervasive that men throughout society could be said to have been preoccupied with becoming a 'big man'. The network and circle of such a *teleq sew* rallied together during important military feasts (*gibir*) that displayed his power and elevated position, allowing him to acknowledge and promote warriors – of his household and outside it – and fulfil the obligatory redistribution of wealth. In militaristic terms, any material gains that accrued to him were of secondary importance. Local crafts producers would also rally to his call on the basis of asserting the inalienability of land and people, and their presence would simply be seen as his 'wealth in people' rather than the result of extraction of labour and economic resources.

THE HAMLET OF THE *CHEWA*

At the end of the nineteenth century, the hamlets of community leaders still served military and associated socio-political purposes, and characteristically distinguished different social categories in most of the highlands. A local leader's hamlet was his permanent residence. Constructed to accommodate as many local dependants and constantly expanding family circles as possible, the hamlet of a *teleq sew* contrasted him sharply with the impermanent ordinary soldier, the *wetader* (literally the 'homeless wanderer') enrolled under him, or those newcomers seeking and gaining employment as soldiers. His hamlet accommodated any non-local person temporarily, just as they would sleep in his camp during campaigns. To have many blood or other kin showed that the hamlet owner was a 'child of man' (*yesew lij*). In ensuring that he was not 'person poor' (*yesew deha*, i.e. relative-less or support-less – a serious defect indicating the lowest social position), creating real and fictive children broadened his social ties.

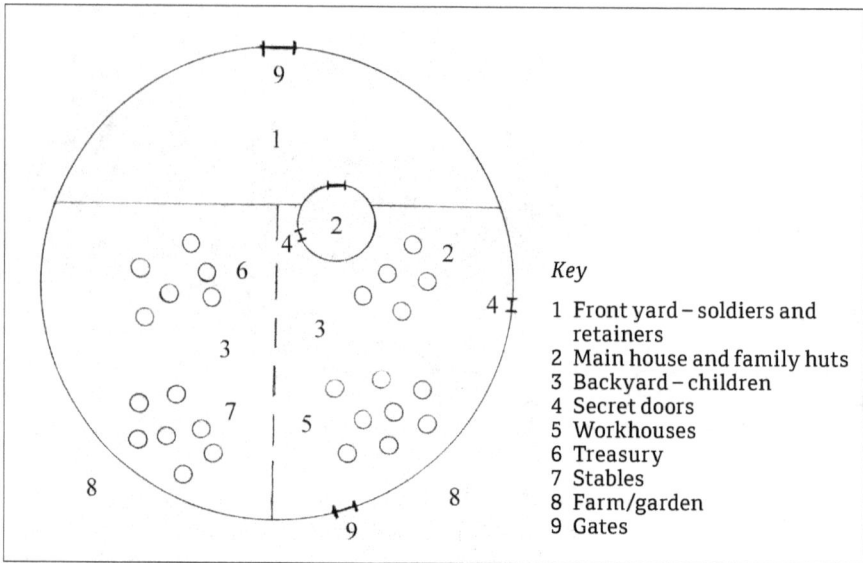

Figure 1 Plan of a hamlet (Adapted from a drawing by *Balambaras* Berhane-Selassie Yigeremu)

It was usual to boast of one's *wegen* and social circle as being of genealogical renown (often more fabricated than real), and many aspiring individuals' strategy for achieving this status was to assume a position in the household of the *teleq sew*. Recounting genealogies back at least seven generations, ambilineally in all directions, and claiming to belong to named historical social origins were useful. Tracing proper genealogies so far back in history was necessary when marriage was under consideration, and discreet investigations would determine falsification and lead to serious challenges.

It was at the discretion of the *teleq sew* to qualify visitors as 'children of man' by making them his 'children'. He could exclude close kin from descriptions of 'those who belong' (*wegen*) or those with marital kinship, or disqualify illegitimate children while qualifying slave-children. Of course, slaves qualified better than the free and non-related (*ba'ed*) others who did not belong locally. Overall, ensuring that his family kin and number of dependants were ever increasing, the 'big man' ensconced himself in social and work associations and engaged in appropriate marriage arrangements (for himself and others). In that sense, the hamlet of a popular local leader signified self-definition and self-assertion, leading to politico-military capacity.

The construction of traditional highland houses and their positioning in a hamlet showed this particular military purpose. Houses were generally round with steep thatched roofs, but the larger houses were sometimes rectangular. The walls were made of any material available in the locality – stone, wood, mud and wattle – and were often plastered with mud mixed with straw. Irrespective of shape and material, houses were called *bet*, meaning 'house' and/or 'home'.

Described according to size, they were 'small house' (*gojo-bet*) or big and 'spacious house' (*seqela bet*) and 'king-size or very large house' (*bete-negus*).[2] The bigger ones, occupied by those of high status, were often distinguished by the topping of the roof, known as the *gulelat* ('finish'), sometimes with ostrich eggs or elaborate designs made of clay, wood or iron. Unlike small houses, these had tiny openings just under the roof to allow in air and some light[3] and at least one door front and rear.

The central pillar, a stout pole supporting the roof, was symbolically the most important part of the house. Unsurprisingly, a 'war pillar' metaphorically expressed a valiant or courageous warrior.[4] In round houses, the central pillar was used to measure distance to the wall for placing furniture and other facilities in the house. In the simplest houses the beams, radiating from the pillar, were used for keeping seeds to be sown in the coming season, or other items that needed to be dried and kept out of the way. Often utilized to divide the single-roomed house into different compartments, the pillar was also used to tether chickens, goats or sheep awaiting slaughter in the kitchen.

Hierarchically positioned in relation to one another, the houses in a hamlet had fences of poles, stones or hedges, with two entrances serving as the 'front gate' (*fit ber*) and the 'back gate' (*yegwaro ber*).[5] Not infrequently, a third door, the *serkosh ber*, meaning 'secret' (literally, 'theft') gate, opened into an obscure part of the surroundings. A number of houses served as rooms, their type, size and position designating the relative status of their users. This collection of 'rooms' formed the hamlet (*wudemo* or *hudemo* in Amharic and Tigrigna respectively; *mansera* in Oromo). It was not difficult to detect that the *chewa* hamlet was markedly different from non-military houses.

> When I married and moved from my parents' house, I noticed a big difference in how people in the household behaved. In the house of my father, who was a *yenesta dagna* (a judge in the '[slave] freedom court'), there were guards but everybody came and went as they pleased to see either of my parents or anybody else. In the house of *getoch* ('master', i.e. my husband's father) who was one of the commanders of the *Barud Bet*, visitors had to refer to his *agafari* before they could see any one of us. We, the female relatives (daughters-in-law, unmarried sisters and others) had to be at specific places at different times of day, and on holy days, weekends and other days. Generally in the mornings, we would be in our own quarters. Then we would be invited to be with *emete* ('mistress', i.e. my mother-in-law), and remain with her the rest of the

---

[2] Ignazio Guidi, *Vocabulario amarico-italiano*, Rome: Casa editrice italiana, 1901.
[3] Théophile Lefebvre, et al., *Voyage en Abyssinie exécuté pendant les années 1839, 1840, 1841, 1842, 1843*, Paris: Arthus Bertrand, Libraire de la Société de Géographie, 1845–1851. Vol. 3, p. 273.
[4] Guidi, *Vocabulario amarico-italiano*, 1901.
[5] Lefebvre, *Voyage en Abyssinie*, 1845–1851, Vol. 3, p. 272; Mansfield Parkyns, *Life in Abyssinia: Being Notes Collected During Three Years' Residence and Travels in that Country*. London: John Murray, 1853 (New York: D. Appleton, 1854), I, pp. 353–5.

day, sitting and working on cotton processing, or, depending on the day of the week, receiving visitors or being entertained by singers.[6]

Small houses were roughly divided into two or more parts by a curtain or a temporary division using furniture or wicker-work, with about one-third of the house extending from the door to the pillar, an empty space known as the *adarash* or 'reception area'.[7] On either side of the door into this area was a raised platform of mud and clay, the *medeb*.[8] Covered with pillows and throws ranging from leather to cloth material, the *medeb* was used for seats during the day or bedding at night. As small houses lacked a separate bedroom, near the *medeb*, in an alcove separated by a curtain or a partition, was the bunk bed proper (*qot*)[9] of the head of the house. Only special guests were allowed into that part of the house. In daytime, women and children of the house sat on another *medeb*, sometimes below the main one. The small opening of the *serkosh ber* (secret door) nearby, hidden from view, enabled the master and mistress of the house to enter and leave unnoticed.[10]

Next to the bed area in the smaller huts were the storage space and kitchen, used only for cooking and storing utensils, such as pots and jars. The hearth, consisting of three stones,[11] was opposite the front door so that the fire received a constant stream of air. Servants and other dependants, and sometimes children, might have to sleep there. The millstone was in the kitchen, next to which was sometimes the storeroom.[12] There, the wall was lined by *zelenga*, shelves for crockery, vessels, grain, flour, and cooked food and drinks.[13] Across from the storeroom, and therefore opposite the bedroom of the larger huts, were the stables for the mounts.

The personal possessions, furniture and general appearance inside and outside any house also indicated the way of life and relative status of its occupants.[14] The walls of an *adarash* displayed the instruments used by the master of the house. While whips and other farming equipment indicated the home of a farmer, guns, spears and shields

---

[6] My mother, *Weyzero* Workaferahu Haile, September 2012.

[7] Parkyns, *Life in Abyssinia*, 1853, I, pp. 553–8; Lefebvre, *Voyage en Abyssinie*, 1845–1851, Vol. 3, p. 271; Frederick J. Simoons, *Northwest Ethiopia: Peoples and Economy*, Madison, WI: University of Wisconsin Press, 1960, p. 59; Augusto Franzoj, *Continente nero: note di viaggio*, Turin: Roux e Favale, 1885, p. 26.

[8] Parkyns, *Life in Abyssinia*, 1853, I, pp. 210–1, 357–8; Franzoj, *Continente nero*, 1885, p. 26.

[9] Franzoj, *Continente nero*, 1885, p. 26.

[10] Parkyns, *Life in Abyssinia*, 1853, I, p. 358.

[11] G. A. Lipsky, *Ethiopia, its People, its Society, its Culture*, New Haven: Human Relations Area Files, 1962, p. 151; Lefebvre, *Voyage en Abyssinie*, 1845–1851, Vol. 3, p. 271.

[12] Guidi, *Vocabulario amarico-italiano* 1901; J. Doresse, *La Vie Quotidienne des Éthiopiens Chrétiens aux XVIIe et XVIIIe Siècles*, Paris: Hachette, 1972, pp. 237, 253.

[13] Doresse, *La Vie Quotidienne*, 1972, p. 253.

[14] Parkyns, *Life in Abyssinia*, 1853, I, p. 211.

were evidence of his involvement as a soldier. The 'work-house' in the backyard of a well-to-do family man was simply regarded as the makeshift rest quarters of slaves and their families, or of other domestics, who would have no possessions visible on their walls. These quarters might consist of thirty to fifty huts. Depending on the work, various items, for example grinding stones, would form the most important part of their furniture. In a military commander's hamlet, these would be under the constant surveillance of the *azazh* (head of personal and household troops), whose own hut in the area might be bigger but otherwise no different from the others. A little removed from these huts, and occupying the area to the left of the rear gate, would be the stables (see Figure 1). Cattle and other domestic animals, brought in and out through the front gate of the main house, were overseen by shepherds and others, who slept on a platform over the animals. In daytime, shepherds normally looked after the animals outside the hamlet; but milch cows and beasts of burden or personal mounts for the family were kept in the stables, where grass was brought to them. The personal mounts of individuals in the 'work-house' were kept separate from those of the master and mistress. The butchery, also in the 'work-house' area, kept and processed the necessary cattle, sheep and goats for the kitchen. The exception was the animal that had to be killed in the *adarash* on certain occasions. As we will see below, this was slaughtered in front of respected guests as an important part of the *gibir* ('formal military banquet').

Not far from these huts, and somewhat closer to the 'work-house' area, was the 'smoke house', or kitchen. With its own huts for cooking, this section could also be large or small depending on the requirements of the hamlet. Several of these huts were internally adapted to the functions they served, and were under strict guard.[15] Further from the 'work-house' and the stables were the *bejirond* and the *elfign*. The houses of the *bejirond*, the treasurer,[16] stored weapons, gold, money or other valuables that the master of the house might possess, and honey mead (*tej*), meat, grain and flour. Some huts had meat on hangers; others had mead in huge pots. Invariably, the woman working under the treasurer was head of the kitchen. The number of huts depended on the amount stored, and some also housed people working under the treasurer. Thus, the backyard was not only a place of refuge but also a kitchen and 'work-house' area providing vital services to the family and the hamlet's military retainers.

In the area inside the compound (the *gibbi*, a term applicable also to the grounds of a palace), fencing divided the complex of houses in the hamlet into two parts, distinguishing the 'big man's' family circle from the rest of the community. The front yard, the gate and the area immediately outside belonged to the male members of the household. The master of the house, his male and official guests, his personal retainers,

[15] Parkyns, *Life in Abyssinia*, 1853, I, p. 354.
[16] Parkyns, *Life in Abyssinia*, 1853, I, p. 354; Doresse, *La Vie Quotidienne*, 1972, p. 253.

prisoners and usually his saddle animals occupied and used this part. Considered as *dej* or 'outside', and larger than other such spaces in the hamlet, it was actually a public area, and therefore 'on show'. The area nearer the back gate, in contrast, including the backyard and the space immediately outside it, contained smaller huts, with only one or two of the bigger type. Female members of the family, children, visiting friends, unmarried sons and domestic servants were found there, the occupants thus being the most intimate. Thus, the backyard, *gewaro*, accommodated most of the activity of family life.

The compound had three main divisions: the private family area contained the largest house, the *elfign*, with sleeping and reception areas; the second largest huts, the *bejirond*, contained supplies and stores and resembled farmers' huts; the *sera bet* (literally 'work-house') was the living quarters of slaves and other domestics, and their working areas. Located parallel to the treasury or *bejirond*, the *elfign* had a base raised above ground level, and its top decorated in some fashion.[17] Unlike others, this had two rooms inside it: the *elfign-adarash* ('hallway') and the inner room or *gewada*.[18] Along the inside of the wall on both sides of the door were raised platforms known as *alga*, 'bed'. Opposite the door was a raised bed that the master and/or mistress of the house used as a divan chair. This bed had a lower level, the 'dwarf bed', which was used partly by the master and mistress as a leg-rest, and partly to seat guests of subordinate but respectable status. On the right of the bed (looking outwards), about a third of the way from the door, was a separate room, either curtained off or separated by a wall with a curtain at its doorway. This had a bed for the master and mistress to sleep on.[19] The house was warmed by an open fireplace in its centre. Behind the *elfign*, and opposite the *bejirond*, a group of similar but smaller huts served the same purpose for junior members of the household as that provided by the *elfign* to the master and mistress. Accommodated here were newly married sons, grown-up youths and divorced kinswomen. These huts were near the 'theft' or 'secret' gate of the hamlet so that the occupants could move about freely without drawing public attention from visitors or senior men in the front yard.

The appearance and place of the main gate, opening inwards, and frequently left open, also indicated the politics of space in the hamlet. In this politics of space, the area outside the front door of the *adarash* was left open for retainers, servants, and supplicants seeking employment or justice to stand and wait for the master. The number and size of huts and retainers to the right of the front gate on entering it[20] indicated the significance of the owner of the hamlet. From the *adarash* to the front gate and outside it, male and senior members of the household displayed their power of protection, showing their skills at traditional games appropriate to the time of year, and singing challenges

---

[17] Parkyns, *Life in Abyssinia*, 1853, I, p. 356.
[18] Doresse, *La Vie Quotidienne*, 1972, p. 253.
[19] Franzoj, *Continente nero*, 1885, pp. 26–7.
[20] Parkyns, *Life in Abyssinia*, 1853, I, p. 363.

to their 'master's' enemies. Members of the inner part or the backyard over-extended themselves, as it were, by being seen in this public space, though boys could practise throwing spears and javelins, archery, and use swords there. Horses were exercised in a nearby field.

Mentioning that many enclosures contained quite a number of buildings, Wylde says: 'The doors of these outer enclosures are generally very strongly made.'[21] The owner's importance was enhanced by the heavily guarded 'secret gate' that allowed only intimate family members to come and go unnoticed, and by the almost empty *adarash* to which only selected visitors would be admitted to receive the attention of the 'master' at his discretion. Indeed the backyard was often surrounded by a growth of bushes, or at least faced a stretch of farmland, while the exposed parts of the front yard faced the main thoroughfare.

An *elfign* that opened into the front yard in a well-provisioned hamlet was laid out to receive as many suitable visitors as possible. Some *elfign* doubled as bedroom for the master and daytime living room for the respectable ladies of the household. In the bigger hamlets of important military leaders, the reception room, the *elfign aderash*, was relatively empty of furniture and household articles. The master of the house as well as the mistress prayed in that room. The lady stayed on the divan (also called 'bed') in the centre, and, depending on her status, was surrounded by children and adult attendants. If her status was not really high, she did the necessary spinning and basket weaving in a different room of similar size and significance. Supervision of the kitchen or other areas of the compound was left to domestics.

The activities in and just outside the *adarash* expressed the status and occupation of the owner. Only lady visitors, close kinsmen and respected guests were allowed into the *elfign*. The lady of the house joined her husband in the *adarash*, which might also be a separate 'reception-hut' just outside the *elfign*, to receive honoured guests. The divan bed was in the central part of the wall opposite the front door, and shorter beds on either side of this accommodated respected guests and favourite dependants. The divan beds were supplemented by benches.

Significantly, whether in the *adarash*, the storeroom or the 'work-house', these sections of the hamlet, and objects such as the bed and the divan beds, represented privileges to intimates and special members of the family. Bed, the most respected place, was even used interchangeably with the word for 'throne' (*zufan*) which also means, in a broad sense, the crown of a monarch. Likewise, use of the inner part of a house indicated intimacy and seniority, and, like the word *adbar*, designated how places distinguished insiders from outsider 'others'. Used as the main banqueting hall for all occasions, though the master might or might not eat in it all the time, the *adarash* was the place for the mandatory *gibir* that leaders with the title *fitawrari* and above gave to their retainers and important persons. If their guests were their

[21] Wylde, *Modern Abyssinia*, 1901, p. 227.

superiors, 'masters' entertained them and their retainers in tents larger than the *adarash*.

Thus patterned to keep various members of the household, family and dependants in their proper places, the *chewa* hamlet, and the housing layout in particular, imposed a classification of people in relation to the owner. The household provided protection and shelter. With the senior members occupying the central and well-protected parts, and the juniors the back part, which was considered even safer, visitors were allowed into the different areas in line with the privileges accorded them. According to oral reports, and from some evidence still visible today, the parents, their 'children' and real sons and daughters, servants, unmarried, divorced, widowed or widower siblings, other relatives (fictive or real), and close friends and constant visitors and, traditionally, slaves, were entitled to the protection of the 'inner room'. For the emergent warriors, dependants were inevitably also deeply involved in the affairs of the family. Boys below the age of ten rarely came to the front yard, but those designated by the technical term *ye bet lij*, 'child of the house', frequented the front yard. These included young shield and or gun bearers of the master, and other military service providers training as emergent warriors. They were 'kin' and were understood as *ye saw lij*, 'child of man', a term that contrasted them with *ye bet weld*, 'house born', a word referring notably to slaves, other domestics and subordinates in the backyard.

The importance of having many 'children' meant that mothers would ideally space their real children three years apart. Giving birth more frequently would be seen as 'God's gift'.[22] Parents who lost children in their infancy went to great lengths to hide the gender of their surviving children. To 'confuse death' and 'to protect them' from the attention of evil spirits or perhaps evil people, they recategorized the gender of their new born, and referred to them and clothed them in the opposite gender until they were more grown up. In a way, this symbolic change appears to have contributed to diverting attention for the sake of protecting the vulnerable. Indeed, those going to battlefields referred to the camp of accompanying wives and domestics as that of the 'children' and, sometimes, of the 'women and children'. The *liqe mekuas*, 'impersonator', is used along similar lines of confusing or throwing off the enemy from targeting the monarch whose fall on the battlefield would cause disarray.

EXPANSIVE SOCIAL NETWORKS

Though the hamlet was significant, varying degrees of communal and state-level relational differences guarded against undermining the importance of its kin-based social relationships. The social networks

---

[22] Infertility was also seen as the will of God, and never as any physical problem of couples.

and associations around the hamlet were, ideally, gender specific, and they demarcated local communal cooperation. In order to organize these relations and private property, important local leaders used blurred kinship and relational terminologies. One way of doing this was to stop specifying relations within the *beteseb*, 'family circle', by avoiding formal distinctions among collateral *yesega zemed*, 'flesh relative'[23] or blood kin, within a range of up to five to seven generations. Descendants of a common named ancestor did not necessarily belong in the same family circle (*beteseb*) as physical and temporal distance might disqualify some from the status. The discreet and ambiguous gender gap in the networks of power also blurred specific references to members of the immediate social circle of powerholders. This probably gave rise to an anthropologist's misapprehension that the Amhara 'have no terms by which to designate distant lineal or collateral kinsmen'.[24] Regardless of the specific and exact definitions of these categories, local *chewa* related to one another either as *wedaj*, 'friend', *wegen* or sometimes *zemed* (strictly speaking 'blood kin'), interchangeably using the terms to refer to any politico-military 'relative' or friend.

The blurring was made practical through such sayings as 'relatives and medicine, in days of trouble seek them'.[25] At times *zemed* were 'appealed to in days of trouble'. They were called upon to exact revenge and defend family honour, for instance. These socially specific terms implied that friend (*wedaj*) was interchangeable with *wegen* and also identified degrees of relationships with in-laws. Generally known as *amat* to the husband and wife, who in return were called *amach*, the terms for in-laws extended to all other relatives on respective sides of the couple. When required for legal purposes, the terms for daughter-in-law (*mirat*) and son-in-law (*ye-lij-bal* literally 'child's husband') could be used. The wife of a brother or husband of a sister was known as *warsa*, the sister of a wife or brother of a husband as *ayut*, a wife's sister's husband as *betayut*, and so on. These terms were sometimes stereotyped with negative moral attributes of character, and their use could lead to unsavoury assumptions by relatives; only legal or inheritance needs made their specific use acceptable. Indeed, using the categorical terms to address one another was said to distance relationships and was tantamount to creating hostility.

More acceptable terms for these 'relatives' were simply sister, brother or child (*lij*) depending on the relative age of the speaker. Elderly people used the word *lij* when speaking to their young in-laws, except in legal cases. Until the 1970s elderly people applied the term and title *lij* not only to young men of 'aristocratic' origin, but to any young man they respected.[26] Speaking in terms of 'parent–child' relationships was most

---

[23] Lipsky, *Ethiopia, its People*, 1962, pp. 75–6.
[24] Shack, *The Central Ethiopians*, 1974, p. 29.
[25] Lipsky, *Ethiopia, its People*, 1962, p. 75.
[26] To see the ease with which the title *lij* had begun to be used by the first two decades of the twentieth century, see መርስዔ ሃዘን ወልደ ቂርቆስ፣ የሃያኛ ክፍለ ዘመን መባጫ የሆነን ታሪክ ትዝታዬ፣ ከየካተና ከሰማሁት፣ አዲስ አበባ፣ ዩኒቨርሲቲ ፕሬስ፣

widely accepted, especially among close relatives. The word 'child' signified the age of a person relative to the speaker, and might be specified as a male or female child, and big or small to reflect the order of birth. In an important person's household, the pervasive 'parent–child' relationship, including fictive kin and clients, underlined the speaker's high status.

Significantly, terms of affection towards elders carried hierarchical and sometimes militaristic meanings. Thus, when young family members referred to each other and those they considered *zemed*, 'relative', they addressed their elder 'brothers' as 'my shield', 'brother-shield', 'brother-pleasure', etc., and elder 'sisters' as 'my [own] sister', 'my flower', 'my sugar-cane', etc. Whether used with or without personal names, references to aunts and uncles who appeared older than the speaker suggested affection. People of one's parent's generation were addressed by the terms used for the parents, and categorical terms (aunt, uncle, etc.) were avoided in verbal address, though personal names of those involved were added, unless the issue was about confirming pedigree in which case specifying the names was necessary.

The inclusivity that pertained in social and familial settings was also reflected in military contexts. Using personal names in the *chewa* military camp showed absolute equality between fighters or an expression of patronage by their commanders. *Chewa* addressed each other by title rather than their personal names, and in an informal setting this also reflected a sense of equality and mutuality rather than rank and hierarchy. Such ambiguity applied even in describing military loyalties as exemplified in the couplet composed by soldiers in the camp of Tewodros II. Uncertain of his reaction to the death of his rival and rebel 'brother' (in fact, cousin), they lamented:

> ጋሬድ ሞተ አንከዋን ተቀብሬ
> ወንድምህ ነውና እንፈራው ነበረ
> Gared is dead; good, and he is buried!
> We used to fear him as your brother![27]

The militaristic and hierarchical attitudes within families in the network of *chewa* leadership encouraged their large followings. Furthermore, children did not necessarily have to be the natural offspring of their parents. If the marriage proved childless, husbands would usually defy the law of monogamy and have concubines or go elsewhere to get a child. Barren wives would traditionally 'give' one of their household

---

(contd) 2002 (Mers'e Hazen Welde Kirkos, *My memories of what I saw and heard of the history of the beginning of the twentieth century*, Addis Ababa University Press, 2002 EC). By referring to their wives as their 'children' the Sidama, and to some degree the Oromo, indicate junior status, especially that of their women.
[27] Tewodros's cousin, Gared, described as his 'brother' in the poem, was killed by *Liqe Mekuas* Bell when he went to avenge the killing of his friend, Plowden. The same ambivalence is also reflected in Rubenson's view that Bell's death by a spear thrown from the rebel's camp may have tempered Tewodros's possible anger over his cousin's death. See Rubenson, *The Survival of Ethiopian Independence*, 1976, pp. 188–9.

slaves to their husbands if they could afford 'the luxury' of begetting children.[28] Even without the consent of the legal partner, extra-marital children would be brought to the legal wife to bring up, with the appropriate order of birth and sex status. The offspring and the identity of the natural mother would be kept secret, and disclosure would be a serious breach of confidence, even leading to divorce. With the Oromo, who generally adopted only infants, the natural parents were kept completely out of the picture, and the children were considered the real children of the foster parents. Among the Amhara, once such a child came to know at an appropriate age their real parentage, they came and went between the houses of their natural and adoptive parents. Despite this ideal welcome, however, evidence shows that illegitimate children would be known as 'bastards' (*diqala*), and, often despised even by both parents, their status was lower than the 'real' children born within the marriage. However, as an acute observer reported at the beginning of the twentieth century, illegitimate children were not excluded from property inheritance.[29]

Other ways of increasing the number of 'children' in the *chewa* family included fostering, adoption and patronizing. Elder brothers or sisters of good social, economic and political status would adopt the children of their real or fictive 'sister' and preferably would not tell them about their natural parents. For 'a sister's child is one's own even if one did not beget him/her', as the saying goes. Of almost equal status to the 'sister's' child was the 'child in trust' (*ye adera lij*), given to the *chewa* by any friend or a relative, usually on the deathbed of the real parent, along with their property. Where property was involved, foster parents informed such children of their parentage; failing that, their own blood kin, who were free to visit, would make sure that they knew. The foster parent took care of child and property until the child's maturity, when he or she would be at liberty to do as they chose. Those who lacked economic and social means, for instance tenant farmers, widows, slaves or servants and any poor subordinates, might 'give' their children to be brought up by adoptive parents.

So bringing young children to be brought up in the household of emergent warriors meant placing them in the latter's kinship relationships. *Chewa* foster parents did not distinguish practically between these and their 'children' in a family circle, and a 'child in trust' could even expect to inherit property from them. The purpose of parent–child relationships between natural, adopted, fostered or enslaved people and the *chewa* was to build up the *chewa*'s status by assuming responsibility for 'bringing up' (*masadeg*) others. This involved preparing the children, irrespective of gender, to 'conduct their personal affairs independently' (*rasen mechal*), so that they could establish and promote their lives in society. Whatever the children achieved or failed to achieve later in life, those who brought them up took either the credit or the blame. Foster

---

[28] Walker, *The Abyssinian*, 1933, p. 37.
[29] Mérab, *Impressions*, 1921–9, pp. 157–8.

children were therefore supervised and trained even more strictly or 'properly' than natural children.

Though a much sought-after position, parenthood was not limited to relationships between children and grown-ups. Nor was it a case of bringing up children into adulthood in the literal sense. Frequently, parenthood included becoming godparents, achieved through baptism or other rituals. Men and women would initiate such relationships with their social equals to strengthen existing friendships between adults. Parents would sometimes choose the same couple for all their 'children', and even encourage other families to choose them as well. The parents and godparents referred to each other as 'father of child' (*abe lij*), and shared the responsibility of the religious upbringing. In such patron–client relationships, those considered seniors would readily accept the invitation to be godparents, but they would not consider 'giving' their own children to their subordinates, unless the intended relationship was seriously religious. That is, Christians and non-Christians might perform a ritual to forge relationships with the family of the dominant faith. In all cases, the relationships were said to be a means of increasing the number of very close 'family' members.

The 'breast-father/mother' (*ye tut abat/enat*) and 'breast-child' (*ye tut-lij*) relationship was a more direct form of sponsorship often contracted between adults. Initiated by prospective children and sometimes by friends or even blood relatives, the formal ritual was performed only after careful selection. The would-be 'child' initiated such a relationship through intermediaries. It was sealed in a private ritual of suckling honey from the thumb of the 'parent', and witnessed by only the go-between. An individual could have as many such 'children' as he or she wished, but the 'child' could only seek and belong to one such parent. Characterized by relationships between social superiors and inferiors, there was a strictly observed giving and receiving of certain social obligations, mainly of support, and the 'client' always became a member of the family circle. It was thus intended to lead to further promises of mutual help between adults.[30]

RETAINERS AND SLAVES

In such arrangements the 'parent' had to carefully avoid involving other people's slaves whose lot he or she could not improve. A telling indicator of undertaking responsibility for people in this category (as well as for those likely to be embarrassing in terms of their character) is the following saying:

> አይውሉ ውዩ
> ተባረያ ጡት ተጣብች
> ለያው ብሄድ ታስር
> ለስፈታው ብሄድ ተገንዘ
> I associated with one I should not,

[30] Guidi, *Vocabulario amarico-italiano*, 1901.

'Breast-suckled', with a slave.
When I went to visit, in chains he was.
On returning for his release, in shrouds.

Slavery perhaps encapsulates best almost all that was significant in such patron–client relationships. Owning slaves, of which Ethiopians seem to have had large numbers, was justified on the grounds that Old Testament people had had them. Especially in rural areas, households preferred to maintain slaves at a high cost rather than employ servants for much less.[31] Their conditions, described as 'good in Christian families', were also 'confuse[d] with domestic servants', who were considered 'as the children and members of the family'. The children of slaves were treated better than their real parents, 'because', content to accept their surroundings, 'they were considered more trustworthy, loving and obedient'. They passed their time freely with the master's children 'developing familiarity with them'.[32] Generally, they were reportedly treated with loving care, and though for that matter beating a slave, or anybody else, was seen as nobody else's business, killing a slave, like killing anybody else, was considered homicide punishable by law.

Key distinctions existed, however, between slaves and other 'children'. The term 'children of man' excluded prescriptive marginal people, namely craftspeople and long-distance merchants. These belonged to the general class of humanity, and the term was applied to them in religious terms only. Like slaves, they were not acceptable in the *chewa* social circle and network. However, slaves were, as already indicated, 'children of the house', and, as part of acquiring 'wealth in human beings', they were trained to a significant level in the art of war, including hunting. Like those brought up by fictive parents, they too swore in their masters' names. However, they were different from such 'children of man'. Whenever they were called, for instance, slaves answered with a fixed couplet of praise that rhymed their names with words reflecting the social attitudes, personal aspirations, hopes and fears of their owners. As property, slaves were given as gifts to churches, entering church as free people. They were also used as their masters' farm labourers.

Slaves became free when their masters died, and sometimes inherited landed property for their lifetime. Their names, which had meanings like practically all other names, made their former status as slaves easily identifiable; but their names were usually changed by socially understood principles that ensured their freedom and respectability. Slaves who worked exceptionally hard in *chewa* military terms could acquire social acceptance, including by the various means of fictive kinship described above. Probably in that sense, it has to be added that soldiers, especially *yabet lij*, applied the term 'slave' (*bareya*) to themselves when they expressed absolute loyalty to their superiors. Only occasionally were they actually former slaves.

[31] Mérab, *Impressions*, 1921–9, p. 32.
[32] Mérab, *Impressions*, 1921–9, p. 160.

The status of being a retainer was the most explicitly political of patron–client relationships embedded in parent–child associations within families. As we have seen earlier, the latter encompassed a wide socio-political network of significance to the *chewa* military structure. Sons of dependants, such as tenants and other farmers, fictive and real kin, and retainers and slaves, focused their belongingness on the central figure of the 'master/mistress' who patronized them, and, in the case of slaves, owned them. They considered the 'parent–child' relationship a means of creating closeness between them. As the 'children's' personality supposedly reflected back on that of the masters, they were taught and trained in social manners. They formed the core of the retinue (*ajeb*) around *chewa* individuals, and their numbers reflected their patron's social standing. They rallied to the 'master/mistress' whenever they travelled or required a large show of support. In times of war, women and girls were included as part of the retinue, often with their husbands, and performed such duties as grooming horses or even engaging in battles in the absence of their spouses.

COMMUNAL INTERDEPENDENCE: SOCIAL AND WORK ASSOCIATIONS

The privileged and exclusive hamlet, and the social relationships it accommodated, was not intended to exclude the *chewa* master from the rest of the local community. The owner was drawn into the affairs of most members of the community because of the work association networks and the marital rituals that upheld the ideals of men as warriors. As the accepted authority figure, he acted as an arbiter when the need arose, and his skills in managing the seemingly light socio-politics of the society contributed to the perception that he was prepared to organize local defence.

The associations that characterized networks within neighbourhoods were relatively formal. Those for self-help, farm work and fund-raising, for instance, had prescribed rules and optional membership; they needed little input from the *chewa* or the church authorities. The *debo* or *jigi* (an Oromo word in current use), meaning 'work community' or 'self-help', were productive groups, with individuals providing feasts to facilitate farming or other activities such as house construction. Neighbourhood women came together to process cotton and spin, and formed work associations called *wenfel*. There were also ephemeral flexible feasting associations known as *mahiber*, a Ge'ez word denoting a club. These were formed by men and women of the same neighbourhood, and were more common and more undifferentiated by gender. They were encouraged by the church in traditionally Christian areas, and often involved potlatch-like feasts on occasional Sundays and periodical named saints' days linked to parish churches. Christians sometimes started or joined such associations in return for favours from their patron saints.

As they promoted networking for socio-political purposes, *chewa* masters recruited social and political followers during these feasts. There are two types of *mahiber*: the *senbete* and the ordinary *mahiber*, and though church based, they were influenced by the local *chewa* master. The *senbete* was held in the church courtyard, usually nearest the west gate reserved for the purpose. Where the church was well endowed and organized, money collected from the parishioners maintained the storerooms in which the church kept bread baskets, cutlery, drinking vessels, candles and other items. Equipped with benches and tables fixed to the ground, the main hall was more or less similar to the reception area of a hamlet, its size depending on the wealth of the parish members. Depending on the contributor's wealth, two sizes of unsalted bread baked from the sacred grain, wheat, and optionally, *enjera* and specialized and varied *wet* (sauce), were taken to the church. The *bejirond* and the secretary of a *chewa* master's hamlet ensured that his contribution every Sunday maintained certain standards of food and drink for distribution after the church service. A number of other people took turns to contribute a fixed value and amount of bread and roasted grain, as well as local beer for the *mahiber* feasts. Minors were very rarely actual *senbete* members, but the poor were never left out of handouts.[33]

Everyone at church was expected, theoretically, to partake in the feast in the hall and attendance was to the advantage of the 'master'. On days when the *senbete* occurred, distribution of the food would be part of feasting the poor, including beggars who usually lived in and around the church compound and were first to arrive. In reality, the only times beggars were admitted into the hall was during the rains, the excuse at other times being that the feast was really for the association members. Priests and deacons were *de facto* participants, coming in large numbers and without inhibition. Travellers staying in the locality, usually in the church courtyard, were freely admitted into the hall and seated after the church ministers. People with social pretensions preferred to give priority to the poor, whose children they would allow into the hall either because they belonged to the clergy in some way or other, or because they were adventurous. Last to come were the 'students' living at the expense of the priests and considered 'children', whatever their age might be.

Though members of a community formed the *senbete* associations voluntarily, church authorities conducted and promoted these feasts. One of the priests, designated as the *muse* or 'leader', blessed the food and started the food distribution by dividing the bread into four parts and handing a quarter to the person whom the members nominated to be next in the rota to bring the food. All the food was to be consumed, and the members shared the bread and roasted grain, seeing both as sacred, and distributed the portion they took home to family members

---

[33] Donald N. Levine, *Wax and Gold: Tradition and Innovation in Ethiopian Culture*, Chicago: University of Chicago Press, 1972 (1965), p. 224.

and other visitors, whom the women would call upon to help prepare the next feast. Of course, not everybody was served from the quarter taken home, and not all those who received the pieces were invited to the feast. As will be shown below, food distribution was significantly pertinent to the exercise of power, and in that context, even church feasts mediated social networking between categories of people in the neighbourhood.

A noteworthy point is that the expectation 'to feed' ensured co-membership with governors, *balabat* (other nobles), local family heads and anyone else in the *mahiber*, thereby helping to maintain a sense of solidarity between different levels of society. While they were expected to go into the church hall to feast, their presence was often political. In large communities in semi-urban and urban areas where churches might accommodate multiple *mahiber*, important families tended to belong to several associations. They sent representatives to find out when their turn was to be and to deliver the food and drink accordingly. In areas where the whole community belonged to only one such association, important persons took advantage of everybody's presence to increase their popularity.

Though cautious, membership and attendance of a *mahiber* proverbially stood for the intimacy of any two people in a neighbourhood. Idiomatically, to denote that two people drank at the same *mahiber* was to show that their interests were identical not only in terms of venerating the same saints but also in the respect and responsibility they showed each other. Members of a *mahiber* looked out for one another's welfare and interests, and even afforded each other shelter and protection in case of need. They also sponsored each other to cope with major life crises, participating on such occasions as births, christenings and funerals. If two members quarrelled, the rest acted as intermediaries to resolve their problems. A function of their membership was helping to marry off each other's children, or being present whenever the scale of attendance would enhance their prestige. More important still, members showed favour towards each other in cases of litigation with non-members. By their nature *mahiber* are impermanent and rarely survive the lifetime of the initiator.

Such a sense and display of belongingness, togetherness and internal solidarity was also expressed in local communities' *jigi* or *debo*, 'farm work association'. Unlike the *mahiber*, however, most work associations were seasonal. They largely followed rules similar to those of women's spinning associations. Whatever the type of land tenure, the provision of beer and roasted or boiled grain was the minimum a farmer should provide, and depending on the distance to the plots to be worked on, the food and drink would be carried to the field. All the farmers brought their own implements and oxen, and worked on the plots of one of their number, who fed the members until all the work was done. Not surprisingly the most common associations prevailed during the ploughing and harvesting seasons, essentially helping individuals in their farming or gardening work. The participating farmers went from plot to plot, ploughing the whole area together, and the work might last only one day in the case of a poor farmer. The food provided was expected to reflect the size and type of land, with the poor expected to provide only beer and boiled grain. Wealthier farmers with larger plots requiring several days' work provided food throughout. Those living on plots called *hudad*, 'land on which one has the obligation to work' (principally government land), ploughed them with the rest of the community for a fixed number of days in a season. The official responsible would ask all the farmers around to work on *hudad* and provide similar sustenance as with *jigi*.

There were of course limitations. The general wealth in an area could limit the number of plots worked through an association. Those who could not afford to give the minimum food and drink would have to do all the work themselves. In areas where land tenure was strictly communal, the community might provide sustenance on behalf of the poorest among them. In practice, all poor people got help, especially if their poverty was attributed to supporting a large family of small children 'who are old enough to eat, but not big enough to work'. Expected to come without the prospect of food, farmers left poorer people's plots until the last. Some farmers promised future feeding, thus putting themselves in debt to the community.

Spinning associations (*wenfel*) met throughout the year, tellingly reflecting women's proverbial never-ending work. A woman with lots of cotton to work on took the initiative to organize the *wenfel*, going around the neighbourhood asking the other women to help, and expecting responses according to their pressure of work. She took her cotton to them at the various stages of its preparation prior to its being spun into thread: deseeding, fluffing and smoothing out. All neighbourhood women participated, reportedly eagerly, in return for similar favours. Except in households of rich women, like the example above, the participants took and processed the cotton in their own homes. Old women especially, and those with many domestics, helped in making the thread, the most time-consuming and skilled part of the work.

In these domestic associations, like in farming, anybody could take an initiative, irrespective of age or means of livelihood. Slaves of different households, when they existed in the society, shared with each other such work as grinding grain, preparing pepper and churning milk. Elderly women with no one to care for them participated, exchanging their labour for yarns of cloth. Men without their own plots of land or strangers stranded in a locality helped in ploughing or harvesting in exchange for grain. (Mutual self-help groups that involve fund-raising to assist individuals' cash flow are still held weekly. Work associations still persist in the countryside; but in urban and semi-urban areas where people from different backgrounds support each other's interests, the *mahiber* predominates.) Work associations went on operating irrespective of their membership, which was flexible in line with the main focus of activity, and their size depended in part on members' capacity to provide food for those participating in the work. Because associations did not keep records their historicity has been open to some discussion.³⁴

These informal community organizations were a means of developing closer ties between members who assumed equality and mutual support beyond such times as they saw one another. Those who lost contact, but who found each other again later in life, felt a mutual sense of obligation and solidarity from having been in the same association(s). Besides, the interdependence of members of the same *mahiber* was carried into all aspects of life; members might help each other out even on the battlefield. Key to *chewa* relationships, membership of such associations was a socio-political system of sealing friendship over time. Irrespective of where they found themselves geographically, former members initiated and sustained the *mahiber* of those who had grown up in the same neighbourhood, experienced the same hunting expeditions or somehow shared the same military activities. In the nineteenth century, most successful individuals acquired membership of such associations theoretically, along with privileges and rights to political space. All in all, the concepts of personal mutuality expressed in the structure of the hamlet, kinship, voluntary association membership and communal belongingness categorized individuals, giving them status and enduring social relationships.

GENDERED WARRIORHOOD, ADULTHOOD AND MARRIAGE

Chewa warriors were expected to be networked and socially rooted individuals who had matured into adulthood, retaining their community-oriented place during war or other disturbances. Women might participate in warfare, though not in the military training men received during peace time. They were considered vulnerable and protected, and fighting in battles did not entail conferring on them the transformative status of adulthood and responsible 'parenthood' that it did on men. As we will now see, womanhood was instrumental in defining men as adults and this was recognized at their marriage. At marriage, a critical consideration was the contribution of men's conjugal status to their communal belongingness and access to land

---

[34] It has been claimed that such associations are new developments, dating from the 1960s, but the evidence shows otherwise. See *Kebre Negest*, p. 142. Guidi, *Vocabulario amarico-italiano*, 1901, defines *mahber* as a congregation, explaining the usage of *mahber tatata* as a periodical reunion for a banquet, and in this particular, he refers to his own work of about a decade earlier. As well as oral tradition on associations, mention is made of Menelik II as belonging to a *mahiber* of ten members (Walker, *The Abyssinian At Home*, 1933, pp. 128–9), including the chief justice, Wube Atnafseged. Self-help associations, such as the Alem Gena to Welamo Highway Building Association, in which members contributed money towards building a public road, is a modification of the tradition. Indeed, it was actually the population's familiarity with the concept that helped the socialists of the post-1974 period to promote work associations.

tenure. This influenced the history of various strands of women's political importance.

Any trained man who proved himself was duly rewarded with titles and land, and even administrative posts. Opportunities existed for this in the turbulent history or armed factional confrontations and rebellions that made all members of society in most areas of Ethiopia into professional fighters. At times of major crisis with large internal conflicts, such as after the end of a monarch's reign and during international wars, women, normally excluded from political roles, might assume them, often as dowager queens. There was no strict prohibition on women's participation as fighters in their own right. Especially when there were no brothers (or they were too young) to inherit the military lands their fathers might have had, women could enrol in military service. In the northern and central highlands, they could also take menial jobs. Several observers of northern Ethiopian societies commented on the abundant women grooms of warriors' horses during nineteenth-century internal conflicts. Some women even learned to handle war equipment and voluntarily participated, but the rules of *chewa* service excluded them from owning military lands.

Most communities of southern Ethiopia report myths of gender relationships in which women lost their right to rule or to participate in political or military leadership. For example, a myth, prevalent mostly among the Sidama and Oromo communities of the south, has it that a female ruler, Ako Manoye, once declared war between the sexes. This is held to have resulted in Sidama men, for instance, still having to force their women to comply with their demands. There were women local chieftains among several other linguistic groups, but their participation in warfare, while a theoretical possibility, appears to have been quite restricted.

By the nineteenth century, the control of power in Ethiopian politics was very much part of men's day-to-day activities and lives, especially those of the *chewa*. While boy children played paramilitary games during the rainy season, girl children proclaimed the advent of peace at the beginning of the dry season; they thus marked seasonal periods of transition. This seeming initial equilibrium between boys and girls disappeared when the boys began taking part in activities outside the house. The girls remained behind until the parents quietly married them off. It was through the wedding celebration that a girl was given sudden adulthood, along with the entitlement to handle her affairs, including matters of property. A man achieved the status of qualified warrior by his first 'kill'; a woman achieved the status of being 'like her mother' through the marriage rituals. While the man's warriorhood qualities were symbolized by the number of animal and human enemies destroyed by the warrior-hunter, a quality required of him as a soldier whatever his age and marital status, the true warrior-hunter was someone who had succeeded in attaining responsible adulthood. Besides, adult men who engaged in sporting and paramilitary activities presented trophies, as we will see below, to women as well as to their military commanders. The adult women posed as arbiters on those occasions, often influencing the judgement as to who was more heroic among the competitors. The consequences of these military exploits and socio-political control were differing conceptualizations of the adult status of men and women. A man's adulthood and social recognition depended in large measure on the adult women who gave these to him. In order to confer this status, a woman had to achieve her own transformation from childhood to adulthood. For an emerging *chewa* warrior the achievement of adulthood did not happen just because he had qualified as a warrior by his first 'kill', or simply because he had got married. Besides the hunting rituals, that is, the hunter-warrior needed to gain sufficient social recognition to gain a social base of dependants and followers. Thus, though initial serious hunting could be seen, to some extent, as a 'rite of passage' to warriorhood, it was not a marker of adulthood, which had to be earned over time.

Marriage was arranged between the parents of the young couple, with the boy's father approaching the girl's parents, following a common friend's recommendation. Once the two sets of parents agreed in principle, the boy's father would let his son know of his designs, and then choose an elder to engage as the 'father of cases arising' (*ye-neger-abat*). The negotiator arranged the date of the wedding and the signature of the marriage contract by the parents in front of a judge, who would come to the bride's house to preside over this ceremony. Once the documents for the betrothal of the future bride and groom were formalized, the girl was known as the wife of her fiancé, but neither performed the role of wife nor had the status of a married woman. In her parents' house the girl's wedding was talked of as 'her parents giving away a daughter' while the fiancé would be said to 'bring in' a bride. The mediator remained neutral to the two families but important in the lives of every married couple. Engaged as a negotiator until the wedding, he would later conduct any litigation that the couple might have between them. He was also proxy for the parents.

If the marriage contract was not to be signed until the wedding day, the young couple were not brought into focus. Both were considered children, and their parents spoke of the approaching festivities only in terms of *ye lijoch guday*, 'the children's affair', without informing the couple. The young girl was not supposed to know anything about it until the preparation for the feasts was well under way, while the young man was taken to see his bride a few days before the wedding. Neither was allowed to make further ado about the choice.

Wedding songs before the wedding ceremony praised the mother for such a fine child, the father for putting on such a grand show, the parents for such good fortune of beautifying a daughter they would give away, the parents and their *chewa* family for their great political and social merits in this 'home country'. The girl's young friends and relatives would start to sing of her approaching departure two or three days before the wedding. She was treated not just as a child throughout the semi-ritualistic negotiations and preparations, but almost as an invalid. She would be given purgatives a week before the wedding, and would be fed well so that she would look plump and at 'her best' at the wedding. A female relative would give her a bath on the morning of the wedding day itself, her mother would apply make-up to her face and young friends would help her into her wedding dress, and, depending on resources, gold jewellery and an embroidered cape. The girl cried, as it was usually said, according to an 'honoured custom' (*weg*), about 'being a young girl and not knowing what she was going to face in her future life in a different family'.

On the wedding day, the negotiator would lead the bridegroom and the best men (*mize*), with as many friends as he could muster, to the house of the bride's parents. They would be met by a group of young female friends of the bride who would be singing, and an elderly relative of hers who would engage the negotiator in the following mock negotiation:

Relative:	What do you want? Why are you standing there?
Negotiator:	We have come to be your children!
R:	What do you have in your hands?
N:	Rolls of silk and rolls of gold!
R:	Count them and hand them over!
N:	We have such-and-such pieces of land, this amount of cattle, sheep and goats, so much money, this number of slaves and servants, and we have brought clothing and jewellery for the bride.
R:	That is not enough! Our daughter is neither a servant nor a slave; she will not go for that. Not our daughter!

At that first sign of rejection, the negotiator would consult with the bridegroom and his father, both standing behind him with other friends, who would augment their offers. This would go on for some time until the bridegroom named a guarantor for 'giving' more at a future date, thus securing their entry into the bride's house. Their entry was the cue for mock resistance and horseplay between the young people of both sides. The bride's group would block the way, telling the other party to stay out (occasionally even engaging in serious fights).

The entry of the bridegroom would bring two persons into the ceremony, the principal best man and the *ye-neger-abat*, the person who would guarantee the handing over of the bride's promised property (of gifts or dowry, depending on local custom) at a future date. The principal best man would be taken into a separate room where the bride was waiting for him to carry her out on his back to the assembled guests and the bridegroom. Placing her beside the bridegroom, he would produce a necklace (*mateb*) and put it around her neck, vowing to be her brother and protector. A priest or a judge would then join the hands of the couple and the marriage would be completed with the signing of the marriage contract, if the parents had not done this already.

Meanwhile, refreshments would be brought. During the entertainment singers would continue to praise the beauty of the bride and the great celebrations that her marriage had caused – repeatedly asking who had put on her cosmetics, and announcing that the whole world was trying to see the bride. After the main meal they would address the bridegroom, saying how he was a lucky man who should take care of his negotiator for life, and provoke his best men, saying they were dull and without songs, even after they had eaten, and that they were poor, without perfume to spray on the guests to honour the new bride and groom. Both parties of guests would compete in dancing and singing, leaving the couple sitting together.

This signalled that the married couple were about to depart to the house of the groom's parents. Relatives and invited guests prepared to see the bride and groom off. Important family members, including the bride's parents, came forward to sit in the centre of the company, where the bride and groom would pass them on their way out. The number of people sitting with the bride's parents was intended to satisfy the invited guests regarding the standing of her relatives. While female singers sang – 'but where to?' – indicating that they were about to depart, the newly-weds would kiss the bride's relatives and receive their blessings. All would rise and try to follow the couple by way of seeing them off. The guests would stand in the open space outside the house, assisting the singers in wishing the bride that the *adbar* of the husband's home village would accept her.

As the bride and groom were on the way out, the singers would turn their attention to her mother and perform one more ritual. One of the women would throw a new pot off her back to break it. Said to represent a child, and perhaps symbolic of the end of the bride's childhood, this act might also signify the destruction of the social restrictions on the female child, now an adult who was no longer treated as a non-sexual child but almost as the equal of the male. The entertainers would then return to the house singing that they had seen off the older one and was there a younger one still to go? Was there any more food that this wonderful mother could give them as she sent the younger one away?

Meanwhile singers at the young man's house, accompanied by relatives and friends, would be praising his family, their son and brother, and would be saying that they could not wait to see what he brings back. With the arrival of the bridal party, the whole atmosphere would become that of a returning hunter. As the songs made the bridegroom feel alone among the relatives of his bride, so now his bride would be made to feel the same in his parents' house, except for her newly acquired 'brother'. On their arrival, the bride and groom would step over a sheep slaughtered at the door of the house.

After arriving in the middle of the invited guests and pausing for a while, the bride and groom would be invited to their nuptial chamber, a new hut built for the occasion. They would consummate their marriage before emerging for dinner. This part of the marriage established that the 'hunter-bridegroom' was a virile man and that his wife was his patron in his hunting and warriorhood.

The best men (*mize*) would announce that the groom had broken the silver armlet and that his wife had been transformed into womanhood. The *mize* would tie the hunter's sash around their heads and sing the hunter's songs, while female singers kept asking for the evidence. The principal best man would then present them with a sash dipped in blood, or a rose bud. (Where the young man happened to be impotent, or the girl had not been a virgin at the time, the principal best man would cut his finger in order to dip the sash in blood.) Bringing the bloodstained sash to the parents of the groom as though it signified a 'kill', the best men would congratulate them on the heroism of the son who had broken the 'silver armlet'. Breaking the virgin's hymen, metaphorically 'the silver armlet', showed the young man's virility, and, significantly, symbolized his acquisition of the armlet, which a warrior's patron would give to his protégé in the hunting context. The principal *mize* and his friends would take the same evidence to the bride's parents the following morning, announcing that their daughter had 'untied her belt', a polite expression meaning that a girl was no longer a virgin and that their daughter has now become 'like her mother'. The singers taking the rose bud or the sash around would receive money from guests, parents and relatives in both houses, which they later gave to the bride, pointing out that this was her special day. In some cases, the money was seen as the couple's start-up fund.

The wedding ceremony underlined the advantages of marriage for men. It also enhanced another aspect of life – that of the symbolic acceptance of the couple into society. Their invisibility during the various ceremonies that kept bridegroom and bride as family 'children' broke down after they had consummated their marriage. On the third day, the couple would both be invited to the bride's parents' house for the ceremony known as the *mels*, 'the return', and more festivities would follow. This ceremony supposedly marked the time when the bridegroom could return the bride to her parents' house if he did not like her (which does not happen). The climax of the festivities was usually on the fifth day, when the two sets of parents jointly entertained their respective relatives and guests together, usually in the house of the groom's parents. Known as *qelqel*, 'mixing', this introduced the relatives of both sides of the couple to one another.

During the following few weeks all significant relatives would invite the couple to *mels* feasts, with the same or supposedly similar intentions. This made the wife now welcome into these houses as an adult, and the married couple were declared worthy persons on the social ladder of their two families. Families would claim responsibility for a marriage that turned out to be a good one, but not for one that went wrong, for that had supposedly been willed in heaven before the partners were born. Though blame would also be imputed to the go-between who initiated the marriage, he kept the peace between the man, who retained the status of hunter, and the woman, who retained that of mother. After the *mels* feasts both wife and husband were expected to stay indoors and not to cross any river or other body of water until forty days after the wedding. (The same restriction was observed by people who wore certain medicinal amulets.) In cases where the bride could not afford to engage help within this time, or where the female relatives of the groom were unable to help, the bride though would engage in household activities and even go to the market.

Because of the wedding ceremony where he was declared to have broken the silver armlet, a man could stop looking for hunting trophies unless he wished to prove himself as an exceptional hunter. The symbolism that transformed the girl into the status of maturity as a 'parent' made her the patron of her husband's overcoming of his *mera*, i.e. having his first 'kill', thus achieving the 'silver armlet'. Her passage into adulthood defined her not on the axis of military power but simply on that of fully-fledged membership in society. For the man it underlined his status as a hunter-warrior, strengthening his potential reputation with his peers. As we will see below, unmarried men would have to collect more armlets to reach the status of 'breaking' past this or that hunter's order before being rewarded with the silver armlet.

Marriage itself symbolically committed the man to the defence of the local land and community to which it now fully obligated him. Thus the social meaning of marriage was the cause for the necessity of mentioning one's mother and wife in *zeraf* poems, as in the following, sung out with fury:

>የማን ቤት ፈርሶ የማን ይቀራል
>የማንንስ ሚስት ማን ያንገላታል
>የማንን እናት ማን ይነካታል
>ወንድ ልጅ አላት ይሞትላታል
>Whose house will burn and whose will stand!
>Who will desecrate whose wife!
>Who will touch whose mother!
>She has a male child who will die for her!

6

Military Training in Sports, Horsemanship and Hunting

From childhood, sporting activities gave physical prowess and mental agility to farmers committed to sustain the military system. They learned war-like strategies and leadership. Hunting (*aden*), for instance, enabled youth to kill wild beasts, some of which were thought to represent hostile human beings, and therefore the enemy. In the process they underwent rituals similar to rites of passage, and passed from childhood towards adulthood. They also learned notions of leadership and bravery, and became acquainted with faraway hunting grounds and people in the Ethiopian landscape. Horsemanship brought them skills like handling weapons and executing battlefield manoeuvres. Later in life excellence in these led them into adult military duties, and thereby into fulfilling society's expectation of proving their worth as community leaders. Such self-trained rural farmers formed the *chewa* fighting force, whose members, as noted earlier, were recruited and promoted to senior positions so as to be on constant standby for military action in the Ethiopian politico-military system, if necessary at all seasons of the agricultural cycle.

CHILDHOOD GAMES

Boys' childhood games developed aspects of leadership, such as sharp wits and a politico-militaristic sense of obedience, loyalty and self-sufficiency, as well as the ability to move in political society. Peers played games throughout the year as part of everyday and seasonal life, with strict rules preventing adults playing violent games with children. There were huge regional and even local variations and the players adopted them to local practices, but generally the wet season games trained the young in mental agility, witticism, military skills and politics, while the dry season ones helped them develop physical prowess.[1]

Boy children learned team formation (*budin*), control and humility, and made lifelong friends. Even nominating their team leaders and

---

[1] See Griaule, *Jeux et divertissements*, 1935, p. 2.

dividing into random parties of equal numbers, regardless of their social positions, especially 'master–servant' status, taught them correct conduct. Team leaders, 'fathers of the team' (*budin-abat* or *ambel*), cultivated the capacity to develop patron–client relationships while interacting with the players with a sense of self-censorship, communal responsibility and propriety.

Responsible parents encouraged children by firing their ambitions and supporting them in their games. Among the Tigre, Amhara and Oromo of the nineteenth century they deliberately prepared the conditions for their boys' participation. Neighbourhood elders, military authorities and other adults watched and evaluated the children playing paramilitary games. A good reputation from these stayed with them for life. It was key to eligibility for marriage and to becoming a 'full person', *mulu sew*. In that sense, the saying that everything about children is unknown and that hidden forces guide them was perhaps part of the rationale for the games.

Akandura (darts), for instance, which an anthropologist called *jeux d'adresse*, a game of 'skill and cunning',[2] trained children during the rainy season in witticisms and challenge. Emphasizing the necessary verbal witticisms emulating war, it was also a game of conquest in which players, using the seasonal long, thick leaves of *tult* (dock leaves, *Rumex* genus),[3] competed for the opponent's leaves. Each player would have an agreed number, say a hundred, and was equipped with darts made of wood, metal or horn. They threw their darts into the opponent's pile of leaves to pierce as many of them as possible. The winner had to take all the leaves speedily while trying to control his opponent's movements verbally. Accompanied by witty exchanges that insinuated taking a war-prisoner into slavery, players competed to say the right words before their opponent did, and pretended that the leaves they pierced in rapid succession were enslaved soldiers. Phrases like 'That I take her by the horse's neck!', referring to the capture of war captives as slaves by tying them to horses' necks, tested players' alertness and quickness right to the end. Adroitness in saying the words rhythmically while throwing the darts and removing the leaves was the aim. A player losing too many leaves had to replace them quickly while verbally indicating his opponent's dumbness in letting him do so. With the last few leaves the weaker player would quickly convince his opponent to throw his dart from a longer distance, saying 'That I measure against you!' (*bilekabih!*). If the stronger player pierced leaves despite this, he could say 'I have emasculated you!' (*selebkuh!*), or he would put down his leaf saying 'the louse has nit-picked its third!' (*qimal sisowan!*), claiming that (though as slow as a louse) his defeated

---

[2] Griaule, *Jeux et divertissements*, 1935, p. 105. Kidane Weld Kifle has this word as *akandura akhdar* (Arabic for 'green') and relates it to the Ge'ez word for *akeder*, greenery and leaves. See Kidane Weld Kifle, *Book of Grammar*, 1948 EC.
[3] Griaule, *Jeux et divertissements*, 1935, p. 106. On p. 258 he identifies *tult* as *Rumex steudelii*. (Various authors say the name *tult* is also used for *R. nepalensis*, and sometimes *R. hapalensis*.)

opponent had defended himself to the last. The winner could play with another of those waiting his turn, by saying 'That I pull you in!' (*bewust bagebah!*), thus making the point that, as a winner, he was taking him away from his partner by co-opting him.

The speed and alertness of the players' exchanges was a decisive feature of this game. Some words appeared to be meaningless waffle, while others rhymed only to provoke, insult, cajole or lull the opponent into defeat, but the words simulated mock battles and taught boys to throw provocative challenges. A version recorded in Gojam actually pretended cavalry was galloping on the battlefield, another that tax collection was in progress, yet another announced cattle rustling. Themes depended on the players' skill and experience.[4] A version that simulated a battlefield had one player saying the first line and his opponent the next, thus:

> A: Invasion!
> B: Fast horse!
> A: Lining up!
> B: Maddened!
> A: Battle!
> B: She is galloping!

Suggesting that the slow-witted player was like a mother who kept being kind however much her children offended her, a player could show benevolence to his opponent saying: 'A mother does not hold grudges, go on!' The unexpected word 'mother' could change the theme of the exchanges, forcing the opponent to continue thus:

> A: Abandoning her skull cap!
> B: For your sake!
> A: Sharpening my spear!
> B: Cabbage!
> A: Peaceful on the outskirts![5]
> B: The *sora* [a type of bird]!
> A: God's work!
> B: They say 'you' [feminine]!
> A: Bad-odoured Haylu!

Now 'mother', taken as a nun, uses her symbol of respect, the skull cap, and the player is forced to start a new theme: 'for your sake', which returns the game to the battlefield theme. The word *sora*, which refers to the feathers that hunters and warriors used and is introduced to simulate hunting, is dismissed as only 'God's work', thus provoking the other to lose his patience and respond with a forthright insult. The winning player takes his last leaf from his opponent calling it *yemotech*, 'the [feminized] dead one', insinuating that the defeated opponent's defence was dead.

[4] Griaule, *Jeux et divertissements*, 1935, pp. 105–16, records examples of such games.
[5] Griaule, *Jeux et divertissements*, 1935, p. 107, translates *daraman* to mean a parent or someone 'who has given away someone else in marriage', but 'cabbage', a fasting season food that had no place in feasts at the time, is a challenge to the other speaker. It is made up of two words, *dar* and *aman*, meaning 'peaceful on the outskirts'.

In an example from Damot a player pretended to force the opponent to be a taxpayer (*gebbar*) and invited him to try and impose conditions for extracting tax, 'with her tip'! (*bechafiwa*), placing his leaves with the tips facing out, thus making it more difficult for the other to pierce them. Victory would be in sight if the opponent imposed his own conditions, turning the leaves to face inwards and saying 'with her root' (*besirwa*), thus making it easier to pierce the leaves. Should a player succeed in piercing the leaves, he would chant the following proclamation, *bush talalala* (in the following instance), as if he were already a 'master':

> *Bush talalala!*
> From that herd!
> From that bull!
> Separated you [in the feminine] this way!
> *Bush talalala!*
> Let it be your [in the feminine] code.[6]

He insinuated that he was addressing the booty he had enslaved, ordering its constituents, belittled as feminine, and giving them a code for recognizing each other, as if they were in battle.

Such games were evaluated critically by adult onlookers, who associated reputations with the players in accordance with their wit and craftiness.[7] They passed their observations to the growing children, reminding them about the changing of themes and ways to win. These assessments were considered vital early clues of personality, reputation and social support, and mattered in the players' continued development as hunters, warriors and subsequent political leaders.

'WHIP' (*JIRAF*)

The game of 'whipping' (*jiraf*), played towards the end of the ploughing season around late August, was appropriate once highland farmers stopped using their ploughing whips and large numbers of children and older boys were freed from helping them. Though more significant in certain neighbourhoods than in others, it was a serious game of mock-battle played annually before New Year celebrations, which began on 11 or 12 September. To commemorate the light of the Transfiguration of Christ (25/26 August), children stopped playing *akandura* and lit torches, staying late outdoors for a few days cracking whips. Older boys made whips sound like gunshots. Coinciding with children's celebrations for the Transfiguration, popularly known as *buhe*, the cracking sounds extended the dry season games of battles (which began in September, the first month of the year) to the end of the rainy season. Mothers, aunts, older sisters, neighbours and other influential people in the neighbourhood made a point of giving the children *buhe* bread. All unmarried children could expect to receive this bread every

---

[6] Griaule, *Jeux et divertissements*, 1935, p. 110.
[7] Mahteme Selassie, *Memories of Significance*, 1962 EC, p. 885; Griaule, *Jeux et divertissements*, 1935, pp. 105–10.

year, even when there had been no contact between relations and neighbours during the year. If they failed to send this very important gift, real or adopted parents and distant relatives would at least offer explanations, such as poverty or distance.

The cracking sound of the *jiraf* and the fun of collecting loaves of bread attracted neighbourhood children in groups. In the old days, each group of players also constructed a small house just outside their neighbourhood. The bigger boys formed groups and selected leaders on their side of the local river, hill or mountain, and picked quarrels by challenging those on the other side, shouting insults like 'wait making my trousers for me' and 'I will make you put on your trousers!'[8] Intended to throw doubt on the manliness of their opponents, these verbal insults were similar to adult warriors' *zeraf*. At its most conspicuous, this obliged the boys to slash each other with their whips.

They also reached out to the neighbourhood before engaging in the games, each group of boys going from house to house of the 'masters' and 'mistresses' singing the militaristic *hoya hoye*. The lyrics teased and begged for their 'usual share' (*leket*) of bread and attention. The lead boy evoked a banquet organized by the *agafari*, the usher in court, in which he would gorge himself and lie back on the divan of honour (the *dink alga* or 'dwarf bed'). In the double meaning, the *dink alga* meant the throne, and the singer expressed an aspiration for it, although it could not accommodate more than one person at a time. When they received their *leket* of bread or an animal to slaughter and eat in the wild, the singers complimented and blessed the households, wishing them good harvest, plenty of children and well-being. They retaliated against those who refused to give them anything by cursing and even burying their effigies. The curses were much feared, as children were believed to possess supernatural powers that made their curses or blessings effective.

Under the control of the leader, who was recognized as self-made, the children stored the bread and other gifts in their specially made huts for final distribution. At the end of the games, the winners sang the *assiyo belema*, a song looking forward to a pleasant season. Some groups kept this up every night during the following few days, with a message of assertiveness being led by the leader. People still watch boys cracking their whips while begging for gifts and asserting themselves:

> *Assiyo belema!*
> Oh, ho ho!
> Say *ahay!*
> *Assiyo belema!*
> I say *belema!*
> Oh, ho!
> Say *ahay!*
> *Assiyo belema!*
> I for my own tricks!
> Oh, ho!
> Say *ahay!*
> *Assiyo belema!*

---

[8] Griaule, *Jeux et divertissements*, 1935, pp. 120–4.

Challenges were realized in the fiercest version of this game, in which the players whipped their opponents' faces without hurting them anywhere else. On those occasions, the game was large and drew whole neighbourhoods or 'countries' against each other. Team formation was dictated by tradition, and in some places the mock challenges and facial whipping were sustained by the belief that the 'country' needed to spill blood in order to avert disease and pestilence.[9] Legal resort was considered a transgression of the harmony expected to prevail between neighbours. That is, the aggressive challenges and harm to eyes or any part of the face were not to be reported to the courts, and vengeance was not to be sought even in the event of death. Underlining that the games were not to be used for political confrontations, elders on both sides defended those who slashed their opponents. The only intervention that might happen was the wealthy providing bullocks and more loaves to the winners to celebrate their success. The players were expected to 'part as friends', arranging a rendezvous for the following year.

Despite such precautions, traditional hostility flared up occasionally, even between 'countries'.[10] An example, involving the strongest and most violent grouping of the *jiraf* game, was known as the *woyane*. This was prevalent in some northern areas of Yeju in Wello, as well as Agame in Tigre and Merhabete in Shewa. In these areas Menelik was reportedly embarrassed when he failed to ban this version of the game after elders persuaded him to retract his edict, which nonetheless halted the proliferation of the game. The violence in the *woyane* game was variously attributed to the consumption of the potent meat of a small antelope (*feqo*),[11] also eaten by hunters, or to a bishop's curse. Probably relating it to the Ge'ez *wein* ('vine'), *woyane* is attributed to the effects of alcoholic drinks.[12]

DRY SEASON GAMES

Turning the games towards direct rather than mock battles, adults in general and soldiers in particular engaged in military training as soon as the rainy season sports ceased around 11/12 September. Groups of young girls collecting tall yellow daisies from the fields, and singing from house to house distributing small bunches of them, launched the dry season games. People would give them money and small gifts that each group leader kept and shared out equally within her group. Of course, the nearest their songs came to military-like activities was the competition to excel in the amount of money and other gifts they collected. However, their songs proclaimed the passing of the rainy

---

[9] Griaule, *Jeux et divertissements*, 1935, p. 124.
[10] Griaule, *Jeux et divertissements*, 1935, p. 120; Plowden, *Travels in Abyssinia*, 1868, pp. 55–6; Kebede Tessema, *History Notes*, 1962, p. 22.
[11] Griaule, *Jeux et divertissements*, 1935, p. 124.
[12] Kidane Weld Kifle, *Book of Grammar*, 1948 EC.

season and the coming of the New Year. Though they did not express it as such, their season hailed the transition from childhood games to those of adult warriors. While children played war games from the backs of donkeys or of each other (*fendidosh*, 'bending over'), parents vied to provide their older children with horses and fields.

Guks and *genna*, respectively similar to polo and hockey, were played in the dry festive, harvesting season in the months of Teqmt (late October/early November) and Hidar (late November/early December). As this season also coincided with the traditional annual periods of raids and counter-raids, the sporting activities sometimes gave way to real, or at least mock, battles. Mounted groups engaged in deliberate cattle raiding expeditions against each other, thus launching the season of games on horseback at the time that synchronized with the traditional annual cycles of actual battles, including light local raids and skirmishes.

Characterized by spear throwing from horseback, war games did not involve boys aged below ten. Practising youth showed off their prowess and horsemanship, and adults judged their suitability for battle and leadership. The most common war games, *guks* and *genna*, trained men in speed, physical prowess and horsemanship. Popular among adults, they were also played during weddings, and in association with religious festivals, after which they were sometimes named. *Guks* was played at most festivals of the year, beginning around *Meskel*, the Feast of the Finding of the True Cross (28/29 September), and in January around the celebrations of the Lord's Baptism,[13] when *genna*, also meaning Christmas, was more frequent.

The rules of *guks* differed from place to place, but it was commonly played between two teams, often starting with a simple competition to hit a ball first, or with the team leader calling 'heads or tails', so to speak, with a wet flat stone, or throwing a ball three times saying 'defend!' (*mekit!*), proceeding at the fourth. The players aimed their ball at a goal (*gib*), or their javelins or spears at trees or other fixed targets (*elama*). In one version, each player was armed with three smoke-seasoned staffs to throw at someone they could take prisoner, who defended himself with his shield.[14] It was a great feat of achievement to 'throw their staffs and pierce shield, man and horse, targeting the head or the back of the player'.[15] The soldiers showed off their marksmanship, horsemanship and military status during *guks*, while their servants competed to collect their staffs (*zeng*) for them.[16] As in the *jiraf* games, deaths or other mishaps were not to be avenged, legally or otherwise, although culprits would be banned from further *guks* games.

In a variation on *guks*, supposedly representing a 'system of fighting to the life', players used blunt sticks and 'lives were not infrequently

---

[13] Walker, *The Abyssinian*, 1933, p. 84.
[14] Griaule, *Jeux et divertissements*, 1935, p. 64.
[15] Mahteme Selassie, *Memories of Significance*, 1962 EC, p. 880.
[16] Plowden, *Travels in Abyssinia*, 1868, p. 211.

lost'.[17] Normally, horsemen without leaders but armed with shields and one or two stout bamboo canes, 'kept their horses moving constantly "as in battle"'.[18] They made feints, 'all shouting their war-cries'.[18] The players rode together 'quietly up and down, instead of always riding at full speed' and other men shot 'with powder at the advancing horsemen, and then ran like devils'.[19] As if on the real battlefield, they played according to fixed rules of flight and pursuit, but also used ruses and made retreats as part of the rules.

A traveller witnessed the selection and division of players into competing groups in the camp of Yohannes IV, who was watching it as a 'martial exercise'. The competing sides 'circled around each other, delivering their javelins at suitable distances and opportunities; these were caught on the shield, or avoided by stooping'. They engaged in mock battles using swords and practising checking the horses 'in full career'. Finally about twenty players 'mingled together ... attacking each other indiscriminately'.[20] Although, like *genna*, known to be a war game, *guks* was also an opportunity for exercising both man and horse. Afterwards, players would give their horses to their servants, and return home on their mules: 'an ambling mule has more honour than a horse'.[21] As raiding expeditions were to follow, the conclusion of the games was often used to display local military might to invited guests and agents of those to be challenged. Presenting 'a picturesque and wild appearance',[22] players wore full military attire, their commanders displaying their military strength; 'No-one of course throws at the master himself'.[23] Though a young *chewa* officer would join the game, a governor would be represented by his *balderas* (an officer in charge of the cavalry).

Foreign travellers referred to *genna* as 'Abyssinian hockey'. It was played on foot. As in *jiraf*, players divided according to their neighbourhood, allegiance or trade, so that merchants could play against a governor's retainers, one age group against another, household heads against each other, married men against unmarried youth. It was one of the occasions that allowed the *chewa* to mix with everybody else around them. Older men defeating younger ones was a good omen; losing was a bad one. *Genna* was traditionally played in the field outside the hamlet or camp of the military leader. Any number of players in two groups would start the game, with their elected leaders (*ambel*) throwing a ball thrice into the air and competing to hit it into their opponent's side from a small hole in the centre of the field. The number of times the ball crossed the line determined the winner.

[17] Plowden, *Travels in Abyssinia*, 1868, p. 211.
[18] Plowden, *Travels in Abyssinia*, 1868, p. 210.
[19] Plowden, *Travels in Abyssinia*, 1868, p. 210.
[20] William Winstanley, *A Visit to Abyssinia: an account of travel in modern Abyssinia*, London: Hurst and Blackett, 1881, pp. 240–41.
[21] Walker, *The Abyssinian*, 1933, p. 84.
[22] Plowden, *Travels in Abyssinia*, 1868, p. 211.
[23] Plowden, *Travels in Abyssinia*, 1868, 210–11.

Aspects of *guks*,[24] *genna* and other games carried social meaning that almost resembled a ritual that transformed young men, for example at their weddings, into responsible adults. Ordinary soldiers noted for their performance were promoted to a status higher than was warranted by their local political importance. In a most frequently quoted example Menelik II, while watching *guks*, recruited Gobena Dachi, whom he eventually raised to the status of *ras*. Masters took the opportunity of the *Meskel* festivities, which coincided with the time for reviewing troops, to make new appointments and demotions and to assess and discern public opinion regarding their decisions on the performance of individuals. If those they demoted went away sulking, 'masters' took it as a lack of loyalty. If their appointees failed to attract retainers and followers straight away, it revealed to 'masters' a lack of leadership capacity.

Team leaders took credit and praise for winning and blame for losing, suffering jeering and teasing. Teasing after *genna* games resulted in 'masters' and servants insulting each other, and the social impression, especially the jeering that followed the game, remained for a long time, exaggerating players' actual prowess or weakness. In some contexts, the insults signalled that 'masters' and servants were relaxed with each other over these war-like confrontations, and the insults became challenges or threats to their enemies. Poems touching on the looks, social background or character of people spared neither team leaders nor emperors. Though a 'master' might allow his retainers to insult losers on his behalf, he had to show benevolence and prevent any retaliation at the taunts thrown at him. Insults included calling losers 'priests', and as such classificatory references bore nuances of threat or exclusion they infuriated soldiers and led to scuffles. A famous insult thrown at Menelik referred to his protruding teeth and played on the name of his queen, Taytu, whose name means 'the sun:'

> በሰማይ የሚጸድቅ በምድር ያስታውቃል
> ተከንፈሩ ዘልቆ ጥርሱ ጣይ ደሞቃል
> You can tell someone who is going to heaven
> His teeth pass his lips to enjoy the warmth of the sun.

Insults such as this were also punctuated by a reminder:

> በገና ጨዋታ
> አይቆጡም ጌታ
> In the *genna* game,
> Master does not get upset.

As with *guks*, it was decidedly bad form to hold grudges for injuries sustained, and, at worst, players could only be banned from further participation. Even if players hit each other's legs in an effort to hit the ball into the opposite camp,[25] the rules precluded culpability for injury.

---

[24] Walker, *The Abyssinian*, 1933, p. 84.
[25] Kebede Tessema, *History Notes*, 1962, p. 22; Mahteme Selassie, *Memories of Significance*, 1962 EC, p. 884.

Marksmanship and weapons handling were specifically mastered through the competitive game of throwing the javelin (*gite*) or the spear (*tor*) at a target (*elama*). Played at Easter and the week after, players brought their own three spears or javelins made of light wood. They aimed to hit a designated tree or tree trunk brought for the purpose. In one version, each would try to hit the target without running forward, and the fewer throws a player took to hit the target the better was his score. Alternatively, the spear or javelin would have to pass through a rolling wheel made of creepers or bark. The target was placed about twenty metres away,[26] or a distance measured by a player's paces or by a javelin thrower's 'throw'.[27] The team with the greater number of players hitting the target was the winner. By the end of the 1970s, only the words for target (*elama*) and team (*budin*) had survived this obsolete military game.

HORSEMANSHIP

Young men acquired horsemanship, the most serious and socially conspicuous of the martial arts, first by familiarizing themselves with riding unbridled horses (*leta*). As their experience increased, they readied their horses to reflect their personality, acquiring saddles, decorations and other paraphernalia. The Ethiopian horse of the martial arts, measuring about 13.3 hands, specially bred since antiquity,[28] was very carefully selected for agility, speed, strength and usefulness in the mountainous landscape, and was the preferred choice for the Ethiopian 'mode of fighting'.[29] A relatively larger and stronger horse, known as *megazha*, was used for transporting goods, as were donkeys.

In the nineteenth century 'Most men pretending to anything like gentility' had mounts noted for surefootedness in the craggy landscape – the horse or the mule. (The latter is also said to have been bred in Ethiopia since ancient times). The horse used for display 'is never used on the road, but led before his master ... while the owner follows on an ambling mule'.[30] Lands known as *yeferes mekomiya* were allocated to maintaining horses for the state cavalry. In markets where horses were bought and sold, sellers would intoxicate them to make them unusually swift.[31] The mule was a normal, leisurely and prestigious means of travel. Due to the respect and attention warriors had for their horses, they sometimes kept them indoors even at night. The following couplet that underlines the stamina, speed and durability of both horse and

---

[26] Kebede Tessema, *History Notes*, 1962, pp. 21–2.
[27] Griaule, *Jeux et divertissements*, 1935, pp. 92–4.
[28] They are said to have been taken in 1861 to a British stud that tried to breed them. See www.equinekingdom.com/breeds/light_horses/abyssinian.htm, accessed on 27 January, 2014.
[29] Plowden, *Travels in Abyssinia*, 1868, p. 72.
[30] Parkyns, *Life in Abyssinia*, 1853, Vol. II, p. 31.
[31] Oral information from my father's friend, *Ato* Jigsa Habte Maryam.

rider expresses both respect for the horse and its use in establishing military reputation and lasting identity:

ፈረሱን ገደለው ቼ ብሎ ቼ ብሎ
ከመቃብር በላይ ስም ይቀራል ብሎ
He raced his horse to its death.
Saying [one's] name survives beyond the grave.

The *balderas* led the horse before its master and his retinue, and onlookers would recognize its master's military status and wealth by its highly ornamented livery.[32] Sometimes, the headstall of a horse would be of white or red leather, and a 'strap, ornamented with circular plates of brass, was placed down his forehead and nose, reaching from his forelock to his nostril'.[33] Occasionally decorations of the horse were of silver or gold instead of brass:

> The bridle is usually of round plaited leather, nearly an inch in diameter, and covered with scarlet cloth ... the horse's throat is slung round with a set of eight fine copper chains to which hangs a small bell, and occasionally with a broad set of leathern charms, alternately red and green.

The saddles, covered with scarlet green or red cloths almost touching the ground, were of wood. They were described as a box, with the pommels high and protruding inwards rather than outwards, 'thereby endangering the stomach of the awkward rider'. Until the 1920s, men, mules and horses were unshod. For stirrups there were 'small iron rings, through which the great toe, or, at most, the first two toes are passed'.[34]

During military parades when everyone displayed their horsemanship, wealth and strength of retinue, warriors showed off their horses' manoeuvrability in galloping (*gilbiya*) and in parading (*somsoma*). Managing horse, shield and spear, while charging and retreating as necessary during a fight was admired. Warriors guarded their horses' hind feet and forehead with their shields. The accomplished charging horseman would exchange his lance and shield from hand to hand to parry attacks. The epitome of the art was to spur on the horse and throw the lance while carrying a gun and a shield. Good military strategies in battles meant rarely charging more than two hundred yards, and then turning sharply and suddenly by throwing the horse on his haunches, or wheeling him off in a half-circle when at full speed, showing the swiftness and obedience of the horse and full command of the bit.[35]

The social development of 'horse-names' symbolized riders' performance during the games of *guks* and *genna*, or the military parades around *Meskel* and Easter. Men created their own horse-names or were given them by family, household members or friends. With rider and horse seen as identical in most paramilitary games, owners, retainers and admirers used these strictly personal names during warfare, other

---

[32] Information from my father, *Balambaras* Berhane-Selassie Yigeremu.
[33] Parkyns, *Life in Abyssinia*, 1853, Vol. II, p. 32. See also Plowden, *Travels in Abyssinia*, 1868, pp. 71–2.
[34] Parkyns, *Life in Abyssinia*, 1853, Vol. II, pp. 31–3.
[35] Plowden, *Travels in Abyssinia*, 1868, pp. 72–3.

military activity, or whenever the need arose for using terms of endearment. The horse-name, with its prefix *Abba*, 'Father of', indicated ownership, control, aspiration, character, or mission desired and intended in warfare. Rather like oxen among the Dinka,[36] horses represented their owners' identity. Horse-names acquired in youth remained for life, irrespective of what happened to the original horse. Sometimes children vied for the most outstanding horse-name, especially those describing good warrior qualities. Sibling rivalry for a father's horse-name, and likely his office and military position, was fierce and frequently needed arbitration by household members, who imposed names that described only the colour of the horse.

Added to a man's 'world' and 'baptismal' names, his horse-name asserted his high qualification as a warrior. Warriors' horse-names were used in the lengthy war songs (*shilela* and *qererto*) commonly sung during festivities, training, parades, preparations for war, *en route* for battlefields and during battles. In the war chants (*fukera*) on these occasions, soldiers evoked their master's horse-name, or their own or that of their favourite warrior to emphasize their allegiance to a cause. Retainers and 'servants' used them to indicate their allegiance or subordination, and 'masters' to announce their intentions in the battle. The following couplet by Emperor Tewodros II is an example of using one's own horse-name to impart political intentions to one's followers:

> ታጠቅ ብሎ ፈረስ ካሣ ብሎ ስም
> አርብ አርብ ደሽበራል ኢየሩሳሌም
> 'Arm yourself' for a horse-name, and Kassa for a name!
> Jerusalem trembles [with fright] every Friday!

The high value attached to horses and horse-names resulted in specialized songs such as *che belew*, which encouraged men in both peace and war. In this song the music imitated galloping hooves, and was punctuated by pertinently onomatopoeic words; the lyrics admired the colour, size and elegance of the horses' tails and manes, and, of course, identified the riders. In other songs praising heroes, horse-names were frequently dropped or alternated with the father's name (normally a person's second name). As indicated in the random list of famous horse-names in the table opposite, they expressed aspirations such as combat, welfare or responsibility.

HUNTING

While horses shared an identity with their individual owners and members of society, wild animals received human attributes in general, and provided their hunters with social recognition, military titles and the esoteric qualities worthy of skilled individuals. Associating with wildlife enhanced the personal qualities of warriors, especially their

---

[36] Godfrey Lienhardt, *Divinity and Experience: The Religion of the Dinka*, Oxford: Clarendon Press, 1961, pp. 13–16.

Table 1 Nineteenth-century horse names

Historical personalities	Horse names	Meaning
Sahle Selassie, *Negus* of Shewa (+1847)	*Abba Dina*	Father of Enemy
Tewodros II, *Neguse negest* (+1868)	*Abba Tatek*	Father of Arm Yourself
Yohannes IV, *Neguse negest* (+1889)	*Abba Bezibiz*	Father of Plunder
Haile Selassie I *Neguse negest* (+1975)	*Abba Tekil*	Father of Engulf / Roll in
Welde Gabriel, *Ras*	*Abba Seytan*	Father of Satan
Mekonnen, *Ras*	*Abba Kagnew*	Father of Protagonist
Tessema Nadaw, *Ras*	*Abba Kemaw*	Father of Snatch
Tekle Giyorgis, *Neguse Negest* (+1871)	*Abba Jihad*	Father of the *Jihad*
Iyasu, *Lij* (r. 1913–16)	*Abba Tena* *Abba Gragn*	Father of Health Father of Discipline
Darge, *Ras*	*Abba Girsha*	Father of Recurring Impediment (i.e. impeding the enemy). *Girsha* is literally 'relapse', as in illness
Balcha, *Dejazmach*	*Abba Nefso*	Father of the Soul
Menelik II, *Neguse Negest* (+1913)	*Abba Dagnew*	Father of Justice
Gobena Dachi, *Ras*	*Abba Tegu*	Father of Patron
Habte Giyorgis, *Fitawrari*	*Abba Mechal*	Father of Tolerance
Abate Bwayalew, *Ras*	*Abba Yitref*	Father of Bounty
Welde Giyorgis, *Negus* of Gonder	*Abba Segud*	Father of Commandeering

familiarity with the landscape. The experience of youth as 'killers' (*geday*) of wildlife in the hunting grounds, and their ritual-like isolation and training in humility and the ways of the wild that accompanied it, enhanced their transition into adulthood and increased their prospects of marriage.

Wild animals were killed for eating, for mere sport and for *gedday* ('the kill'). Elephants, lions, buffalo, rhinoceros and giraffe were the most important for the 'kill' as they were regarded as representing hostile human beings. Killing as many of them as possible was seen as a feat of military achievement, even earning the hunters military titles. The perceived parallels between wild animals and human beings signified admired military characteristics. Thus, 'lion' and 'elephant' featured as names of several historical regiments. Live lions were kept as royal symbols, considered dignified, brave and daring, and their preoccupation with privacy was seen as supporting these qualities. A saying goes, 'The lion hides its kill just as a human being hides his stool'; and in polite conversation, the 'lion's couch' designated a retreat, a place of dignified privacy – 'the place for relieving oneself'.

Attributes of magnificence and grandeur made the elephant admirably equal to humans. Pereira, who gives the words for elephant in various languages (including *negie*, *negeye* or *negeyat* in Ge'ez), points out that the word *janhoy*, 'your majesty', 'comes from *jan* for elephant in the Agew language'.[37] Several words reportedly described the type, size and age of elephants. By the nineteenth century and perhaps earlier, the words *degaga* or *mana-ilka* were used for the largest elephant; *kemer* or *mana-kwachar* was reputed to be temperamental and a dwarf; *elmole* was a young one; *mangure* was young but older than *elmole*, and *manguro* was an adult.[38]

The Ethiopian sense of dignity, honour and respect connecting warriorhood with the elephant goes back to classical times. References in Egyptian pyramids indicate hunting for ivory, as does an inscription on the stele of Pithom dating from around 264 BC and another in Adulis on historic Ethiopia's coast from around 246–222 BC. Sporadic evidence suggests that wild animals were present in and around the courts and the military set-up as early as the fourth century AD. The use of an elephant to pull a royal chariot in Axum in that period not only

---

[37] Fransisco Maria Esteves Pereira, 'O Elephante Em Ethiopia', 1868, pp. 4–5. Accessed in the library of the Hiob Ludolf Centre for Ethiopian Studies, University of Hamburg, Germany. For translating this from Portuguese to English I am indebted to Ms Irene Rioticiani, whom I met at the Hiob Ludolf Centre for Ethiopian Studies in 2013. In Pereira's opinion the Ge'ez word for elephant probably originated from Sanskrit and was brought by Indian merchants – an unlikely event, given that the African elephant is of African origin. Whatever the link between Sanskrit and Semitic languages in antiquity, his conjecture reflects the nineteenth-century belief in a single origin of civilizations, that is, Orientalism, that does not take into account the dynamics of local languages in Africa itself.

[38] Antoine D'Abbadie, *Dictionnaire de la Langue Amariñña*, Paris: F. Vieweg, 1881.

indicates that elephants roamed the northern mountains of Ethiopia, but also that they were being tamed. Travellers saw herds of them in the same area in the mid-sixth and early seventh centuries. As already mentioned, an Axum inscription mentions a military regiment called *serwe deken*, probably because it used Indian elephants,[39] and an army used them in the Year of the Elephants, when a general led an expedition to suppress a rebellion in the final years of Axumite rule across the Red Sea.[40]

There appears to have been a formalized man–animal association at least as early as the days of Emperor Amde Tsion (r.1312–42), who reorganized the judicial system, reportedly institutionalizing several offices of judges. One of these was the *ba'ala harafa*, 'who is also *Dej qalbas*, he is *sahasarwe* with a ring of gold which is called *belul agambake*; he guards the lions'.[41] The guardian of the lions was also overseer of the king's coronation, according to a letter from Emperor Libne Dingil (r.1508–40). Animals were designated as at least symbolic officers with political significance, even if the specific forms are now difficult to ascertain. Reversing Amde Tsion's orders, Libne Dingil hinted at such political use of animals in his letter:

> ... and that the arrogance of their [the rebels'] hearts might be destroyed and their glory humbled, he [Amde Tsion] set over their land [Emba Saynt, in Eritrea] beings who were not of the race of Adam and Eve, whose name was *halastyotab* or in the language of Tegray [the tongue known as Tigrigna] *ahbay* [baboon] ... But from this time the Ra's Zenay and also his successors shall be called *seyum* of Emba Saynt ... And these *halastyo* shall be killed and their memory shall not remain, as I Libne Dingil, have ordered.[42]

Perhaps Libne Dingil's order coincided with the time the army was reorganized, as there was an obvious scarcity of trained personnel. In the days of Sertse Dingil later in the century, an observant monk, *Abba* Bahrey, complained that only about a tenth of the population was involved in the army.[43]

Encouraged and facilitated by the arms trade and expansive cultivation, hunting big game was limited to dangerous and challenging ecologies. The buffalo was considered fast and quick-tempered, the rhinoceros ruthless and oblivious to danger, and the giraffe beautiful and remarkable for surviving in flat, hot, low-lying areas. The leopard, hyena and fox were not considered 'kills'. Crop pests such as wild boar, baboons, apes, birds, and ever bothersome scavengers like

[39] Pereira, 'O Elephante Em Ethiopia', 1868, p. 9.
[40] Sergew, *Ancient and Medieval History*, 1972, p. 152.
[41] G. W. B. Huntingford (trans. and ed.), *The Glorious Victories of Amda Seyon, King of Ethiopia*, Oxford: Oxford University Press, 1965, p. 13.
[42] Huntingford, *The Glorious Victories*, 1965, p. 13.
[43] *Abba* Bahrey divides the number of able-bodied men of his time by ten in order to explain that only one-tenth of the population was involved in military activities. Bairu Tafla, *Aṣma Giyorgis and his work*, 1987, pp. 460–5; ጌታቸው ኃይሌ፤ የአባ ባሕርይ ድርሰቶች ኦሮምን ከሚመለከቱ ሌሎች ጋር፣ ኮሌጅቪል ሚኒሶታ፦አዲስ አበባ 1995 [2003] (Getatchew Haile, *The Works of Abba Bahrey with Other Records Concerning the Oromo*, Collegeville, Minnesota, 1995 [2003]), pp. 89–90.

hyenas, were not hunted as they were easily killed. The same was true of foxes. Hunters considered cheetahs and even leopards as lowly or second-class 'kills' because of the proximity of their habitations to the scattered hamlets and farmhouses. Ordinary farmers and even women reportedly killed leopards in courtyards and other areas of human settlements to which they were attracted by water and lambs. The wolf was taken into consideration only for its reputedly dangerous habit of hunting in packs. No significance was attached to the hippopotamus.

Boys learned hunting by using snares, spears, slings and, from about the age of ten, guns to kill culturally edible wildlife such as guinea fowl and partridge. They also killed and ate ruminants such as water buck, dikdik, gazelle, antelope and giraffe, irrespective of their sex and status in looking after their young. During periods of famine, all these edible ruminants were hunted for consumption even though the meat of old ones was tough. For target practice, travelling hunters and older boys shot duck, egret and ostrich. Ostrich eggs were collected for use as decorations for the rooftops of churches and houses, and feathers of ostrich and *sora* as decorations for hunters and warriors.

Hunting in hot, low-lying forested regions was indeed difficult, as an observer experienced:

> Alas, the lions disappeared in the twinkling of an eye ... It was impossible to follow them up through the thick bush ... In the afternoon I went back ... the impenetrable jungle so restricting my movements that it was only with difficulty that I managed to get the rifle to my shoulder at all.[44]

Significantly therefore, hunting and 'killing' games were essential in practising skills of daring and survival in regions that were considered wild:

> ዱብ ዱብ ይላል እንደበረዶ
> በልጅነቱ በረሃ አምዷ
> He springs like hail-stones
> Having been accustomed to the lowlands in his youth.

The social and political repercussions of challenging dangerous and impenetrable areas for the 'kill' were, as in most significant Ethiopian sports, reflected in sayings and songs. An Amharic couplet goes:

> ቢገድልም ገደለ ባይገድልም ገደለ
> እበርሃ ወርዶ ጥም ውሎ ካደረ
> He 'kills', if he does; he 'kills', if he doesn't.
> As long as he fasts day and night in the *beraha*!

Or:

> መናኝና አዳኝ አብረው ገሰገሱ
> አዳኝም ለግዳይ መናኝም ለነፍሱ
> The hermit and the hunter hasten together;
> The hunter to his 'kill', the hermit for his soul!

Young men and anyone else needing to go hunting were expected to play out a remarkable feat of proving their relationship with patrons in their home areas. For a young man to seek and acquire permission to

[44] Hodson, *Seven Years in Southern Abyssinia*, 1927, pp. 73–4.

join hunters going to the hunting grounds was a step towards acknowledging his patron's position as his military leader, and he showed this during his preparations for undertaking hunting expeditions, and later, when proclaiming his successes. Young men who needed to 'get over with their first-kill manoeuvres' (*mera mewetat*), adults who wanted to increase their fame, and indeed anybody interested in the sport, was expected to approach whoever was seen to be responsible for letting them go hunting. First-time hunting in particular was a social affair that had to be sanctioned both by sponsors and families. Powerful patrons extended the status of 'child' and protégé when foreigners such as Harris, Wylde and Parkyns sought their permission to hunt.[45]

In addition, youth had to seek the help of a named, experienced guide. Such men were valuable because they had understanding and familiarity with rebels and lowlanders (*qolegna*). An informant wrote:

> We would beg permission from our father or master to go on a hunt. We would wait on him (*dej entenalen*) and we would send an intermediary (*amalaj*). Meanwhile, we would prepare our provisions for the journey to depart as soon as we were given leave, or to run away, if we were forbidden to go ... We would also beg and wait on the experienced hunters and frequenters of the lowlands.[46]

In what appears to have tested the patience and loyalty of protégés, patrons took time before giving permission, but once they did, they went out of their way to give the hunters-to-be provisions, and to identify and hire for them experienced hunters as guides. Youth took the initiative of taking stock of their own provisions, which, according to the same informant, consisted of:

> *beso* [roasted barley flour], pepper, salt, *kosso* [medicinal purgative], knives, penknives, axes, water containers, drinking vessels, pans and coffee pots. We would pack our clothes and buy bullets according to our abilities, and polish our rifles.[47]

Preparing would-be-hunters' provisions was an exciting activity for mothers, sisters, wives, lovers, slaves and adopted family members. Male relatives and sponsors took the opportunity to give boys their first gifts of weapons and related items such as guns, swords, spears, knives and penknives. Food generally included two types of dried bread. By and large, this list was little different from Wylde's observations of what hunters brought with them: 'Spear, shield, sword, and knife ... he wears a tobe of Manchester cloth many yards long', and brings a few

---

[45] In 1841 Harris sought and acquired permission from *Negus* Sahle Selassie who, in the process, considered him his 'child'. Harris, *The Highlands of Æthiopia*, II, p. 5. Similar experiences are recorded by Wylde who received permission from *Dejazmach* Welde of Semien (Wylde, *Modern Abyssinia*, 1901, p. 437) and Parkyns from other sponsors. See, for instance, Parkyns, *Life in Abyssinia*, 1853, Vol. I, p. 329.
[46] My father, *Balambaras* Berhane-Selassie Yigeremu, himself a former hunter and soldier, wrote letters in reply to my queries on the subject in 1977 and 1978.
[47] From correspondence of *Balambaras* Berhane-Selassie Yigeremu.

cooking utensils.[48] An earlier list of hunting [and battle] items appears in Parkyns, who refers to them as wall 'ornaments', apparently unaware of the insult in Ethiopian thinking, which holds the first four items as ready weapons: 'shields, lances, guns, swords, skins, and other trophies of the chase'.[49] Of the owners of weapons hanging for too long on walls inside houses, a poem encourages them to join those on the march, even if they do not use them:

> ባትዋጋ እንክዋን በል እንገፍ እንገፍ
> ያባትህ ጋሻ ትሀዋኑ ደርገፍ
> Stomp around, even if you don't fight!
> Let the bug fall off your father's shield!

The social endorsement of hunting, as of other paramilitary activities, was characteristically expressed in songs known as *addo wesheba*. Significant game trophies that adult hunters brought home included elephant knees or feet as 'pillows' for their wives and the tail of the giraffe as part of their necklace or bracelet. These were most important in any man's life, as correctly pointed out in the following examples.[50] Women initiated the songs once the hunters were ready to leave. Some were encouraging, if provocative, and others were suggestive of the honours that awaited the hunters on their return:

> ተኩሼ አመለጠኝ ብሎ ከማለት
> ጠጋ ብለህ ተኩስ ወርች ነው ብልቱ
> እዚህ ሆነ ታየኝ እኔ እንክዋን ሴቲቱ
> ቀን ኩታ ሱሪ መልበስ ካማረህ
> አምጣልኝ ዷጋነዋን ቀጭኔ ገድለህ
> Instead of claiming 'I fired but missed!'
> Hit the main target, the front leg and shoulder!
> Even I, the woman, can see that from here!
> If you desire to wear thin [finely woven] toga and trousers
> Challenge the giraffe and bring me its breast bone.

The first line encourages the man to take the initiative and vie for primacy; the second, to be practical, and the last two lines to come back with a trophy, in this instance the giraffe's breast bone, which women used instead of wooden bows for refining cotton.

No limit was put on the number of men who could go together to acquire hunting kills and experience of the wilderness. Expeditions varied in size from twenty to as many as four hundred men, and the higher the military ranks joining, the larger was their number. However, the size and persons involved affected neither the value of the hunt nor the procedure and order among the hunters. The routes entailed potential dangers from hostile rebels as well as wildlife and disease. Singers, including women who often accompanied hunting and war expeditions, kept up songs about the hunters-to-be and/or their sponsors, while they responded with war-cries and stated ambitions (*fukera* and *dinfata*) of what they would achieve. In the 1840s, 'Dame Twotit, one of the king's

---

[48] Wylde, *Modern Abyssinia*, 1901, pp. 442–3.
[49] Parkyns, *Life in Abyssinia*, 1853, I, p. 360.
[50] Mahteme Selassie, *Memories of Significance*, 1962 EC, p. 445.

choristers', accompanied the hunting expedition with the traveller and diplomat Harris, and sang of the 'Gyptzis' ('Egyptians', namely the foreigners present) who 'will slay the elephant, whereof all the warriors of Amhara are afraid'.[51] Because of the 'war chorus the plain was crossed without any demonstrations on the part of the outlaws', which the party was expecting *en route*.[52]

Unaware that his expedition consisted of initiates out for orientation about the landscape, Harris thought that Ethiopians lacked a hunting-related knowledge of forests – an 'indifferent idea of woodcraft' – and were cowardly as hunters.[53] Wylde drew a sharp contrast between the daring Arab and the 'boastful Abyssinian' hunters.[54] Foreign guests seem to have been allowed to camp next to each other, guarded by experienced hunters. According to Parkyns, these lay down 'as is usual, with their weapons near their heads and their shields for pillows', when he was hunting with his sponsor Merratch: 'The people all lay in a circle, the space in the centre of which was occupied by Merratch, myself, Habto [sic] Giyorgis (his chief councillor), and my principal servant Saïd.'[55]

Normally, older, experienced guide-hunters spent time disciplining the young hunters-to-be. At this stage boys focused on hunting antelope before being taken to hunt big game.[56] The guides obliged the youth to remain humble until they decided that they had trained them enough to change their status into particular aspects of military life. This preparation is not recorded for such *mekwanent* as young Menelik, who went on an expedition to overcome the *mera*.[57] Nor is it in the available narratives of *Lij* Iyasu's and *Dejach* Tafari's hunting expeditions[58] (conducted despite the laws then prevailing against hunting).

When preparing the *chewa* youth for their military lives, the guides gave them hard work such as constructing the hut, preparing earthen platforms for sleeping and sitting, collecting firewood and water, and being in attendance day and night making the camp comfortable for everyone else.

> When we arrive at the desert, after travelling for three or four days, or a month, we choose a camp (*sefer*) at the site close to a possible hide-out for game, and where water is available. The same day, we make the hut (*gojo*).
>
> The 'kill'-seeking youth retired last at night and was up first at dawn to make fire, and prepare coffee and breakfast. With great humility and politeness, he wakes everybody up and serves them with water to wash their hands and faces.[59]

[51] Harris, *The Highlands of Æthiopia*, 1844, II, pp. 310–1.
[52] Harris, *The Highlands of Æthiopia*, 1844, II, p. 315.
[53] Harris, *The Highlands of Æthiopia*, 1844, II, pp. 321–2.
[54] Wylde, *Modern Abyssinia*, 1901, p. 437.
[55] Parkyns, *Life in Abyssinia*, 1853, I, pp. 329–30.
[56] Wylde, *Modern Abyssinia*, 1901, p. 451.
[57] Bairu Tafla, *Aşma Giyorgis and his work*, p. 593, including fn. 809.
[58] Tekle Hawaryat Tekle Maryam, *Autobiography*, 1999 EC, pp. 212–15.
[59] From correspondence of *Balambaras* Berhane-Selassie Yigeremu, cited in note 46 above.

Meanwhile, the guides also looked for omens and traces of wild animals. Among recorded ill omens were the sight of a hare, a fox barking on the left, tail of the white buzzard pointing in a certain direction, and a harsh call from the *gooramaile* (a shrike family),[60] a bird that was believed definitely to augur death or some serious disaster. Among good omens were an antelope crossing one's way, a fox barking on the right, and a hyena calling to the north of the camp.[61] Once they took note of the omens, the experienced hunters held a divination known as *aste* 'soon after sunset, when the stars begin to appear in the sky', wrote my father. The belief in *aste* prediction was quite strong: 'We have seen that not even one tenth of what they said failed to pass.' If the omens and divination augured ill, the party changed camp at once and held other divinations until the conditions showed favourable predictions.[62]

The youth were allowed to learn about the omens and watch the divination. The experienced guides reserved interpreting them as their privilege until they were satisfied that the youth had proved themselves worthy of it by their humility and capacity to observe. Then they would bless the youth, along with everybody else, just before breakfast one morning, saying: 'May there be forgiveness and forgetfulness of grudges and revenges. May we encounter the "kill" and "good luck!"' The youth took these words with paramount sincerity, not only because they believed in the efficacy of their power but also because they indicated their own worth and deserving status in the camp. Then the hunters grouped themselves into parties, with the most experienced guide placing himself with the youth (and/or the guests). Everyone was supposed to have friendly feelings towards their colleagues, and nobody would play foul during the actual hunt. When everybody went out to look for animals, the guides began teaching the novices how to identify various animals' footprints, droppings and other signs pointing to their location.

To be taken to the hunting site was a thrilling moment for the initiates, not least when, as my informant wrote, 'Sometimes the animals themselves can be seen pausing or walking towards the thickets!' If there were more than one to be initiated, the novices would cast lots to decide who could have the first shot and 'kill' of the day. The guides initiating the youth showed them where to aim on the animal's body. They also watched keenly to see that the 'killer was the right person for that day'. All the hunters respected the laws and rules of the arranged rota.[63]

Casting lots was not done when there were guests, including foreigners. Once the decisions were made, battues to confuse and trap the animals were carried out according to the nature of the ground. The aim was to drive the animals towards those who were expected to

---

[60] The northern fiscal, *Lanius humeralis*, of the shrike family. Harris, *The Highlands of Æthiopia*, 1844, II, pp. 322–3 has '*Goorameila*', a mispronunciation.
[61] Harris, *The Highlands of Æthiopia*, 1844, II, pp. 322–3.
[62] From correspondence of *Balambaras* Berhane-Selassie Yigeremu.
[63] From correspondence of *Balambaras* Berhane-Selassie Yigeremu.

'kill' that day. Thus, 'battues are then engaged, and the jungle around is driven ... making it impossible for the wretched animals to escape';[64] and 'it was arranged that parties with the gunners should station themselves in the different defiles where they [the animals] were most likely to pass, and the remainder, with the horsemen, endeavour to head them, and drive them towards us'.[65]

Perhaps not understanding that all hunters had to respect the stipulations of the rota, Parkyns recorded as cowardly that, when a herd of buffalo passed close to the hunters, 'Not a lance was thrown by any one of the spearmen; all appeared anxious to get as much out of the way as possible'.[66] Showing a similar ignorance regarding such hesitation, another commented:

> Crouching in a compact group at intervals of every few hundred yards as they advanced, [the Ethiopians] lowered their shields, bristled their spears, and 'in the language of the chase', offered up a prayer for Divine assistance, coupled with abuse and defiance to the much dread object of their quest.[67]

These imputations of cowardice do not fit with the warriors' self-perception or with Wylde's observation that whatever faults there may be in 'the Abyssinian of the higher class [politico-military power-holders] ... cowardice and fear of death are not among them'.[68]

Once the designated person hit his target, a volley of shots would be fired at the same animal. Foreigners often emphasized the greediness of hunters to claim the carcase of the animal as their 'kill' simply because they had fired: 'Two bulls fell; each of the Abyssinians who had fired rushed forward to claim his.'[69] Or the 'vulgar Abyssinian soldier with his boasting who had perhaps been one of many that has done to death some little elephant calf with a rifle volley'.[70] For Ethiopians, however, additional shots at the same animal were mainly target practice. Of course, at times the randomness of the shooting caused accidents. On one occasion, around fifty out of about four hundred hunters were killed.[71] While Menelik II and his household soldiers were hunting around Alaba, where he killed an elephant, two military leaders and about twenty men lost their lives to stray bullets.[72] In common with other sporting activities, no one was to be held responsible for such fatalities.

Foreigners' misunderstanding of the rules and order of killing in turns appears to have been compounded by their claiming the kill in hunting expeditions in which they participated. When Harris killed a

[64] Wylde, *Modern Abyssinia*, 1901, p. 437.
[65] Parkyns, *Life in Abyssinia*, 1853, I, p. 331.
[66] Parkyns, *Life in Abyssinia*, 1853, I, p. 331.
[67] Harris, *The Highlands of Æthiopia*, 1844, II, p. 329.
[68] Wylde, *Modern Abyssinia*, 1901, p. 43.
[69] Parkyns, *Life in Abyssinia*, 1853, I, p. 331.
[70] Wylde, *Modern Abyssinia*, 1901, p. 440.
[71] Vanderheyn, *Une Expédition*, 1896, p. 134.
[72] Vanderheyn, *Une Expédition*, 1896, p. 191; Guèbrè Sellassié, *Chronique*, 1930–32, Vol. I, p. 364, including fn. 12.

large bull elephant he found it difficult 'to leave the spot, from a conviction that the braggart Amhara rabble would not fail to claim the honour and credit of having slain the prize with their spears ... the very first man who made his appearance' appropriated 'the tail as a trophy'.[73]

This European sense of big game hunting was related to seeing the ivory tusks of elephants (rather than the tail) as valuable items that they collected for private display, boastful writings and commercial exchange. Professional Ethiopian hunters involved in the ivory trade shared these commercial interests, of course. In both cases, elephant hunting was perceived very differently from the Ethiopian tradition of collecting the elephant's body parts as trophies symbolizing military capacity and the rigours of holistic immersion in hunting. Done with minimal resources, hunting took the sportsmen to prestige and promotion on the military ladder. Hodson had some awareness of this difference when he permitted *Fitawrari* Ayala to shoot two elephants and two rhinoceros in the Kenya/Ethiopian border area. Hodson comments: 'He was not fired with a great passion for big game shooting; he simply wanted to qualify to wear the personal adornments with which Abyssinian custom rewards the slayer of these animals.'[74]

Amidst their confusion over hunting rules, foreigners sometimes picked on unusual incidents in the whole ritual of initiation. Parkyns, for instance, noted that an aide of his host caught a buffalo calf and brought it for his master to kill and claim victory. Unfortunately, another unsuccessful would-be-hunter 'maddened by the sight of so glorious a chance, rushed up and drove his lance into the unfortunate little victim of human vanity'.[75]

Foreigners often failed to grasp the significance of what they saw and tended to write dismissively or superficially. An otherwise polite Wylde said insolently, 'These hunting expeditions, as a semi-barbarous show, leave nothing to be desired.' The subsequent dancing, singing and relating of the day's experience had 'a charm for those semi-civilised mountaineers'.[76] Harris is merely descriptive: 'Groups of women and girls lined the hill-side, and as the hunting-party crowned the steep, raised their shrill voices in praise and welcome.'[77] Hodson felt he had to oblige when asked by his orderly if he might fire off a shot: 'as according to Abyssinian custom, it was the thing to do after a successful hunt. The shot was fired, and everyone in the camp, from cook-boy to headman, ran out to meet us, and kissed my feet. Then they all had a sing-song.'[78]

For the Ethiopians, first-time hunting incorporated a ritual-like period of transition towards adulthood. 'Killers' claiming the trophy carried out an important ritual of 'overcoming the *mera*'. Hunting an

---

[73] Harris, *The Highlands of Æthiopia*, 1844, II, p. 336.
[74] Hodson, *Seven Years in Southern Abyssinia*, 1927, p. 261.
[75] Parkyns, *Life in Abyssinia*, 1853, I, p. 334.
[76] Wylde, *Modern Abyssinia*, 1901, p. 437.
[77] Harris, *The Highlands of Æthiopia*, 1844, II, p. 339.
[78] Arnold Weinholt Hodson, *Where Lion Reign: An Account of Lion Hunting & Exploration in SW Abyssinia*, London: Skeffington, n.d. (c. 1929), p. 128.

elephant was special because it meant seeking and gaining permission from the highest authority around, if not the emperor himself. In previous centuries, the tusk on the side that the animal fell on was given to the emperor.[79] Needless to say, seeking to overcome the *mera* by appropriating the trophy (*marta*) was controlled:

> Once the animal fell it meant that the person for whom the lot had fallen was successful in [his] *beles*. He went and sat on the animal, and cut the tail which then became his *marta* (trophy). This was followed by sing-songs, games, kissing each other – with the young kissing the feet of their elders – and rejoicings.[80]

It was strongly believed that hunters needed luck (*beles*), which they held was bound to come their way during their hunt, so they remained in the wild until all kill-seekers had the chance of such luck. An Ethiopian recorder of traditions wrote that young men who were unlucky 'preferred to die roaming in the wilderness in search of *beles* rather than return home without a "kill" because it was shameful to be without it'.[81]

Despite foreigners' reports of trickery, the procedures for cutting the tail appear to have left no room for the wrong person to take the trophy. In as much as what mattered was the *beles* rather than the actual wounding or slaying of the animal, the expectation involved in the sport of hunting was considered noble. In soliciting and receiving the blessings of experienced hunters and his friends, the 'owner of the *marta*' also established witnesses to his achievements. Once the killer cut the tail, his friends gave him immediate recognition, and he was allowed to announce himself with a *fukera* saying:

> ዘራፍ! ዘራፍ! ዘራፍ!
> እኔ የአገሌ አሽከር
> የእንትን ገዳይ!
> *Zeraf! Zeraf! Zeraf!*
> So-and-So's servant!
> 'Killer' of such-and-such [an animal]!

At once declaring his political loyalty and military allegiance, he proclaimed his status as a 'killer'. His friends responded immediately by striking up the *addo wesheba* tune:

> አዶ ወሸባዬ! አዶ ወሸባ!
> አዶ ወሸባዬ! አዶ ወሸባ!
> እንዲያ እንዲያ ሲል ነው ገዳይ
> *Addo Weshebaye! Addo wesheba!*
> *Addo Weshebaye!* My So-and-So!
> That is how the 'kill' happens!

The words were punctuated by the chorus:

> ግቤ አዶ በሉለት
> ይለዩለት
> Come, say the *addo* for him!
> Let him glory in it!

---

[79] Maurice de Coppet in Guèbrè Sellassié, *Chronique*, 1930–32, Vol. I, p. 166 fn. 7; Mérab, *Impressions*, 1910, Vol. I, pp. 217–26.
[80] Information from my father, *Balambaras* Berhane-Selassie Yigeremu.
[81] Mahteme Selassie, *Memories*, 1962 EC, pp. 341–2.

The *addo* was literally the elephant's foot and any jewellery made from it. The word *addo* also applied to a spirit that supposedly inhabited low-lying areas, and *wesheba* was a term of endearment to her. The compound *addo wesheba* suggests the smooth texture of the jewellery worn by the hunters and their wives. The main body of the songs describes the age, size and type of the elephant or the other animal that was killed:[82]

> ያፈልጋል ፋን ለደጋ
> ያፈልጋል ብርቱ ለጎሽ ከረምቲ
> Evaluation is needed; for the *degaga* [a large elephant]
> A strong one is needed; for the buffalo bull!

That moment of taking the trophy was regarded as the fulfilment of the experienced hunter's blessings. The point was to kill the animal and gain victory over it. Hunting was personal in that the new 'killer' assumed the supposed characteristic of the animal that the trophy (*marta*) he had collected represented physically. Evoking that sentiment, the songs signified a lot to the immediate society of the hunters back in their homes. Appearing to confirm the identification of the elephant 'killer' with the animal were such proverbs as 'The sign of the [elephant hunter] is the dancing in his home', or 'The sign of the elephant hunter is in the blood of his finger'.[83]

Hunters distinguished themselves by their physical appearance, letting their hair grow long and making it stand out in a large shade-like mop for the duration of the hunting period; those with soft hair rubbed rancid butter into it to shape it accordingly. The style marked the hunter as the lucky 'killer', deserving to be congratulated with a large amount of butter in his hair. Significantly, only hunters and women were allowed to adorn themselves with butter. In that respect, hunting symbolized the hunter's transitory status during the ritual process – that of starting a new life for the young and asserting ongoing acclaim for the established.

As a sport, hunting went far beyond a simple matter of target practice and firing to signify political jubilation and proclaim joy. Coronations in the sixteenth and seventeenth centuries occasioned hunting expeditions,[84] with those procuring elephant tusks as a trophy being accorded prestigious positions. Hunting appears to have been more socio-political in the nineteenth century, with hunters displaying their *marta*, singing a lot and firing into the air to proclaim their joy at starting their military careers. Once they decided to return, they sent back runners to their home communities with news of their exploits. Whenever they came across groups of people, however, even those who were otherwise hostile appear to have given them a special reception reserved for hunters alone:

---

[82] Information from my father, *Balambaras* Berhane-Selassie Yigeremu.
[83] Pereira, 'O Elephante Em Ethiopia', 1868, p. 8.
[84] Pereira, 'O Elephante Em Ethiopia', 1868, p. 11.

As soon as they heard us, every inhabitant of a village would turn out to receive us. Every woman in the village – both young and old – would come out ululating, and bringing butter, grease our heads saying: 'Kill again!' The 'killer' would reply 'May man and animal increase in number for you!' We would accept any amount of butter put on our heads. There is no saying 'enough!' There is no limit to the amount of butter on our heads. Our clothes and bodies would become completely covered with butter.[85]

Depending on the type and number of animals they had just killed, the occasion was also special for everybody who received the news – sponsors and patrons, families and friends. Prepared to reward the hunters with prizes, principal female relatives received them with festivities, ululations and butter and twigs of asparagus (noteworthy for its feather-like image when growing tall in the wild) for their hair.[86]

Experienced hunters of the early twentieth century led their protégés clear of routes where they were likely to encounter hostile people on their way back home. On their arrival, they displayed their trophies first to the 'master', governor, or patron (as the case might be), who would be waiting for them with pomp and ceremony. Known as 'throwing down the "kill"' (*geday metal*), the ceremony of displaying the trophy involved throwing it down before the feet of the 'master', governor, or patron. Then the hunters would go to their parents, wives and other members of their immediate families.

It appears that historically the processes were more or less similar. In the seventeenth century, Emperor Susenyos I (r.1606–32), then staying in Danqaz, killed two of three elephants that were causing difficulties for travellers around Gemales, near Gonder. In a ritual that seems unclear, he killed a goat in honour of the third elephant that escaped. *Ras* Mikael Sehul (1740–80) reportedly ran away from his family as a child and sought out elephants in the vicinity of the monastery of Waldibba and, with a monk's help(!), killed two of them. He showed his trophy to Emperor Iyoas (r.1755–69) and his mother Mentwab (empress and regent in 1722–69) in Gonder, and was given the title *ras*.[87] In 1894, Menelik waited in full regalia in his palace when *Liqe Mekuas* Abate came to display the trophy he had collected while hunting on returning from the Welayta expedition. Already Menelik's 'impersonator' by then, Abate advanced with twenty-four of his men following him in Indian file, each carrying the tail of an elephant fixed on spears. The men danced and shouted their war-cries and fired guns all along the road until they arrived in Menelik's presence. They then threw the tails (*marta*) before his feet and prostrated themselves to the ground.[88] A similar procession was held when a local leader came to present himself before the governor of Wellega, as witnessed by an amused observer who probably did not understand the important gestures:

[85] Information from my father, *Balambaras* Berhane-Selassie Yigeremu.
[86] It seems that, as well as asparagus, feathers of the *sora* bird were used for this purpose. Griaule, *Jeux et divertissements*, 1935, p. 107 fn. 2.
[87] Pereira, 'O Elephante Em Ethiopia', 1868, p. 15.
[88] Vanderheym, *Une Expédition*, 1896, pp. 134–7.

> The ensuing dance was most interesting. The man who had killed a buffalo went through all the incidents of the hunt, and his pantomimic gestures were highly amusing. All the time the chorus of women danced and sang. This went on for hours.[89]

The order for throwing down the *marta* was determined by the number of animals of the same type that they had killed. Invariably, a luncheon followed the 'throwing down the kill' ceremony, and the hunters took their places according to a specific order that they kept, irrespective of the time lapse since their 'kill' and whether or not they were of the party that had just returned from the hunt. They also followed an ascending order of self-proclamation, which may have had historical variations. The 'wolf killer' announced himself before anyone else, and the 'leopard killer', who came next, was one up on his lowly colleague by the right to claim the choicest of the meat (*brundo*) at the luncheon. As we have seen, neither was considered a real 'kill' as no one had to go on a hunting expedition for them; they were valued differently from species hunted strictly in the wild.

The leopard 'killer' was followed by the elephant, rhinoceros, buffalo, giraffe and lion 'killers'. Two or more killers of one type of animal could announce themselves simultaneously. A 'killer' of a human enemy who had already 'overcome' his *mera* was said to have 'broken the *mateb*'.[90] This word *mateb* (as in 'tying *mateb*') expresses the exchange of marital vows. It is also the 'sign of the covenant', when referring to the red cord worn from baptism around the necks of Christians. Given these, 'breaking the *mateb*' in the hunting context suggests 'breaking the covenant' with God and the personification of big game, for which memorial services were held as we will soon see.

Indeed, various numbers of elephants, lions, rhinoceros and buffalo stood for human beings. Elephants and lions counted for one human being each, a rhinoceros for ten, and a buffalo for eight. If a hunter went on to kill still more animals before his first kill of a human enemy a quite different numerical equation was used. In that case, killing six elephants stood for one human being and each rhinoceros, buffalo or lion stood for five humans. The number differed in the case of those who had started off by killing a human enemy. In that instance, an elephant counted as forty human enemies, a rhinoceros as fifteen, a buffalo as twenty, and a lion as five. Ranked higher in the hierarchical order of hunting, this form of equivalence was known as 'breaking the *ilka*', and came above 'breaking the *mateb*'. Killing more animals before killing a human enemy on the battlefield did not increase the notional equivalent of the human enemy. Whether without having killed a human enemy there was a sufficiently large quantity of animal 'kills' that would allow a hunter to convert his score into achieving the *ilka* is difficult to confirm. In any case, killing a human enemy was not the necessary purpose of the glory of hunting. Nonetheless, a hunter who announced himself as 'killer' of forty or more was certainly

---

[89] Hodson, *Where Lion Reign*, n.d. (c. 1929), p. 38.
[90] Information from my father, *Balambaras* Berhane-Selassie Yigeremu.

understood to have killed a human enemy plus an elephant, and he would be considered a hunter of high calibre, deserving of the utmost respect and honour. Such a killing should have been on the battlefield, not off it. The numerical interpretations seem to have varied even as nineteenth-century travellers were recording them. The word *ilka*, meaning 'offence' related to *ileh*, 'adamance', in Amharic according to a dictionary published in 1841;[91] in that sense, perhaps 'breaking the *ilka*' implied overcoming the indefatigable persistence of the wild. The word was also recorded in an Oromo dictionary published about the same time as 'a bracelet of ivory, ornament of women'.[92] While this probably showed either the commonality of the practice, or more likely, borrowings between the two languages, the link with ivory is noteworthy.

Beyond their numerical equations with human beings, and the possible implication of breaking the Covenant with God, the aim of destroying unwanted wildlife through hunting also carried esoteric meanings, the origins of which are difficult to trace. After acquiring trophies, hunters were expected to hold commemoration feasts for the dead (*teskar*).[93] The ritual resembled memorials for deceased human beings, down to such detail as the fortieth-day commemorative feasts.[94] A minimum feast of forty rolls of bread and forty vessels of *tella* (beer) had to be prepared for the hunters of elephants and rhinoceros to share with their families. The successful hunt of these animals would be considered incomplete without such a memorial-like feast, which if not done, would constitute an *irm* – a term approximating to 'taboo' as used in ordinary English. Otherwise, hunters 'would become lepers', it was believed. Similarly, 'killing' and eating the meat of ruminants such as the giraffe and buffalo without holding their memorial-like feast was an *irm*. Interestingly, these esoteric attributes applied to the potentially edible herbivores, and not to the culturally inedible carnivorous cat species. If hunters were delayed more than forty days before arriving home, runners would inform their families to organize the memorial feast on their behalf.

During the luncheon that followed 'throwing down the kill', the families of the successful hunters, including the women who had been presented with *marta*, would keep up sing-songs. Making it sound as though it was all undertaken for them, the women, except those of high status, would sing solicitous and playful love songs, praising and cajoling the men to 'kill' more. Indeed, women had reason to encourage their husbands to 'kill':

> The killer's wife.... was entitled to wear the *abuqdadi* [green satin, just as her husband would] to show that there was no difference between the two of them; to show that she was her husband's equal and that she was the supporter of his heroic deeds. As of present day logic, [he said implicitly referring to arguments

[91] Isenberg, *Dictionary of the Amharic language*, 1841.
[92] Charles Tutschek, *Dictionary of the Galla Language*, Munich, 1844.
[93] Information from my father, *Balambaras* Berhane-Selassie Yigeremu.
[94] NB: This is not part of the teachings of the Ethiopian Orthodox Church.

regarding 'women's oppression], the interpretation can be made to flow in any direction.⁹⁵

Their songs reflected pride in the values of the hunters' achievements in acquiring the 'kill' of various degrees of animals. Though killing an elephant calf (*elmole*) was considered a 'kill', it was not much to be proud of, and the women would sing:

> አንጓዲህ ጀመረው ሊቀመጥ ሊነሃ
> አንድ አልሞሌ ገድሏል ያውም አሠላሳ
> Now he starts to sit and rise!
> He has killed an *elmole* – and that with the help of thirty [men]!⁹⁶

In the jocular context of such songs, a killer who had killed, even ten, could not be addressed as a hunter despite presenting the *marta*. He was said to be a 'frequenter of the desert' (*berehegna*) and a lucky one (*belesam*). A real hunter would have killed fifty to a hundred. Even in songs it was said:

> አንድ ገዳይ ነወይ አውይ ያልጅ ነገር
> ሁለት ገዳይ ነወይ አውይ ያልጅ ነገር
> አሽ ዝም በሉ ባለሃምሳው ይናገር
> Is one a kill – childish talk!
> Is two a kill – childish talk!
> Hush, keep quiet! Let the fifty-killer talk!⁹⁷

The songs also showed that the position hunters acquired reflected on their women folk. The women teased each other, and reprimanded those who returned without a 'kill', as the following random collection of couplets shows:⁹⁸

> የገዳይ ወዳጅ ታስታውቃለች
> አፋፍ ላይ ቆማ በለው ትላለች
> You can tell the killer's lover
> 'Get it!' she calls from the cliff edge.

> የገዳይ አጋዳይ ሆኖ መጥቶልሻል
> ግባ በያው አንጂ አደጀን ያምሻል
> He has come back a killer's assistant!
> Well, bid him in; is he to stay the night out!

> የገዳይ አጋዳይ ሆኖ ከመምለስ
> አልነበረህም ወይ ልግዋምና ፈረስ
> Rather than return as a killer's assistant,
> Didn't you have a horse and bridle!

> አንቺ ምን ቸገረሽ የገዳይ ውሽማ
> አንተርሶሽ ያድራል አዶ አንደ ብርኩማ
> What care do you have, killer's lover!
> He has you sleep on *addo* [the elephant's feet] for headrest.

> የገዳይ ገሬድ ታስታወቃለች
> ታልቀዳች አይቀዱ ውሃ አንኪ ብትወርድ

---

⁹⁵ From my father *Balambaras* Berhane-Selassie Yigeremu, who also provided the information that follows.
⁹⁶ Mahteme Selassie, *Memories*, 1962 EC, p. 344.
⁹⁷ Unless indicated otherwise, the information in this section is provided mostly by my father, *Balambaras* Berhane-Selassie Yigeremu.
⁹⁸ Mahteme Selassie, *Memories*, 1962 EC, p. 344–5.

One can tell a killer's maid
If she goes down to the water, they won't draw it before she does!

አስቲ አንዳሻው ባቦ አንዳለ ያርገኝ
በቀጭኔ ደጋን የሚያስነድፈኝ
Just as he likes, by Abbo! Let him do what he wills by me!
He has me using the bow of the giraffe's breast for smoothing cotton!

ምነዋ ብከራ ምነው ቢጀንኝ
ቀጭኔ ተጋዳይ ያገኘሁ እኔ ነኝ
What if I am proud! What if I feel dignified!
I am the one who has won the giraffe challenger!

ዝሆን ብትገድል በጣም ደስ አለኝ
አውራሪስ ብትገድል በጣም ደስ አለኝ
ጎሽ ኮረምቱ ገድለህ ኮልባ ላክልኝ
I am pleased you killed an elephant!
I am pleased you killed the rhinoceros!
Kill the buffalo bull and send me the *kolba* [a stylized black earring]!

The height of the ceremony after the hunters' return was their patrons' acknowledgement of the hunters' various degrees of prominence and the distribution of prizes to the 'killers'. This linked the hunters to the military establishment, entitling them to wear special clothes. Apart from the butter all hunters wore in their hair, the giraffe 'killer' could wear a fine toga, along with ivory jewellery made from elephant tusk, and he could drape the lion's skin and mane over his shoulders. Awards of special prizes of gold and silver topped the elephant killer's entitlement to wear a silver chain around his neck, a gold earring in his right ear, and, if he broke the *ilka*, a second one in his left ear. A rhinoceros 'killer' was awarded with a cross-shaped chain earring for his right ear, a gold double chain wound with silk threads (*deri*) for his neck, and a silver or gold-plated anklet (*albo*) 'like that worn by women'.[99] 'Killers' of elephant and rhinoceros who broke the *ilka* were also given swords, 'prizes fit for a *dejazmach*'. The buffalo 'killer' was awarded the *bitewa* (a silver armlet), and, if he broke the *ilka*, the title *balambaras*. Adorned with the military decorations of earrings, bracelets, *zeng* (long sticks) and swords, the hunters were now considered part of the *chewa* military hierarchy, albeit of low rank.

Singers denigrated hunters who had not achieved any kill. The following sarcasm from the 1920s indicates that the hunting grounds were no longer in the central highlands:

ምኑ ተያዞ ሸዋ ሊወጣ ነው
ለሚስቱ ቀጭኔ ለሱ ሎቲ ያለው
Go to Shewa – taking what!
He has neither [tail of] giraffe for his wife nor earring for himself!

By the turn of the twentieth century, external influences were changing the use of the landscape, especially with regard to hunting. Lions, leopards, elephants and rhinoceros were visible in places like the Kessem

---

[99] In addition to information from my father, this is partly recorded in Christian Curle (ed.), *Letters from the Horn of Africa, 1923–1942: Sandy Curle, Soldier and Diplomat Extraordinary*, Barnsley, UK: Pen & Sword Military, 1988, pp. 51–2.

River valley.[100] In the forests of the Arsi highlands, lions, elephants and kudu and other ruminants were reported; in parts of Keffa there were hartebeest, giraffe, eland, oryx, topi, leopards, zebra and civet cats. Most river valleys in Ethiopia had run out of big game, and hunters were no longer free to move about as widely as they used to because British, French, Italian and German diplomats were putting pressure on the 'modernizing' government to restrict hunting.

Those perceived as 'others' external to the region influenced rulers, administrators and courts to curtail venturing across international borders. The British, for whom hunting was closely linked to trading in ivory and other products, raised disputes over those they called 'Abyssinian poachers' on 'their' frontiers. They captured some *fanno* and handed them over to Ethiopian authorities to be tried for international 'poaching', thus putting pressure on *chewa* military and political traditions of land and people.

With such challenges, and the beginnings of a 'modern' standing army in the 1930s, the training and practising of leadership through *chewa* military skills of sportsmanship, including hunting and horsemanship, lost their social and political significance. The *fanno* were restrained from venturing across the newly imposed 'modern' borders to 'kill' wild beasts. Others looking for 'masters' to serve, or to engage in slave and cattle raids, were constrained. With such pressures the *chewa* traditions were largely discontinued until the fighters resisting the Italian invasion of 1935–41 fell back on some of them, and the 'kill' became the Italian, the enemy *par excellence*.

[100] In the reign of Haile Selassie I, and even after his overthrow in 1974, the lion remained a significant symbol of power. Lions were kept caged in a small park at the Yekatit 12 Memorial Square, near Haile Selassie's palace, which later became the Sidist Kilo campus of Addis Ababa University. There were also some in the grounds of the Jubilee Palace, near Meskel Square. Descendants of Mekuria, a mascot of the emperor's bodyguard, have been maintained by the totalitarian military regime that overthrew the monarch, and by the rebel-led, ethno-nationalist group that took power from the army by armed force in 1991. A relic of the symbolism, the image of the lion, was used on the national flag. It is still used on aeroplanes and buses, and on monuments near Addis Ababa railway station and the National Theatre.

ial activities, formal council sessions and courts of justice. Though
7

Political Authority and Military Power

The willingness of the *chewa* to pay the ultimate sacrifice was animated and facilitated by rules and strategies of conflict, backed by power relations that gave primacy to locally emerging individual warriors. In victory, as in defeat and submission, high-status warriors' mannerisms reflected their military training and ritualized symbols of manhood. Local political authorities acknowledged the same rules of conflict and, accrediting and rewarding the warriors individually, they pragmatically relied on the *chewa* to defend their local communities and to participate in national political matters. As local authorities, known as 'masters', they deployed their household and external staff strategically, and, to ease their relations with the warriors, they applied the structures and notions of such politics. 'Masters' linked with warriors through the politics of ambiguity, by narrowing the differences in military rank while upholding the warriors' homeland-rooted status of manhood and leadership qualities. This informal mediation gave them a power structure that overlapped with hierarchical military and political institutions. Until the later nineteenth century, when 'kings of kings' asserted their supremacy, such politics made the nobility (*mekwanent*) intermediaries between warriors at the grassroots and the monarchy at the top.

EASING PATRON–CLIENT RELATIONS

'Masters' used different parts of the compound, *gibbi* (literally, 'inside' or 'palace'), of their hamlets, palaces or camps as centres for their political activities, formal council sessions and courts of justice. Though presided over by judges, the courts (*chelot*), for instance, were held in the presence of their loyal elders, savants and military officers, selected for their status and experience, who expressed their opinions. Similarly selected officials and retainers also formally attended the council meetings in the reception area (*adarash*), as will be indicated below. Regulating and conducting such serious activities were of paramount importance to the 'household' staff responsible to the 'master'. It broke down the rigid, clear-cut relations of hierarchical power politically.

Photo 3 Accomplished *chewa* could choose between mules and horses
(Source: R. Pankhurst & Denis Gérard, *Ethiopia Photographed: Historic Photographs of the Country and its People Taken Between 1867 and 1935* (Kegan Paul International, 1996, p. 117); by kind permission of Richard Pankhurst's family and Denis Gérard)

The best example of how ambiguity works is household relationships between subordinates and 'masters', both as state authorities and as rebels. Subordinates (*chefra*) were under selected 'heads' (*aleqa*). Seemingly creating a degree of power sharing, the *aleqa–chefra* members of the entourage were augmented by a representative (*enderase*, literally 'like me') and his deputy (*meketel*), to whom authority was delegated. The *aleqa–chefra* structure eased how the 'masters' related to one another, and how they dispensed justice, and provided economic resources and, of course, military leadership, by obliging retainers to manage and ease power relations through their offices.

The mediation of power relations between those in authority and aspirant warriors was in evidence also in the ways in which titled officers and potential soldiers related to one another and to the public. Though seemingly trivial, paying respects to the 'master', for instance, meant bowing to show deference and catch his attention. When supplicants presented their petitions (*abetuta*) shouting '*abet! abet!*', either in groups or singly, retainers paid close attention to them, noting their mannerisms and judging for themselves, and the guards did their best to sort out who their 'master' was to see. Supplicants could be abandoned, but this might lead to collective or individual confrontations, military or otherwise, with the supposedly benevolent 'master'. The 'master', therefore, showed his benevolence by visiting his hamlet, palace or military camp to give audiences, and, significantly, to assign each supplicant an ad hoc official. Known as the *baldereba* (*dereba* meaning a double or cover), this 'companion' was chosen from the trusted and favourite officers (the *balemiwal*), to look after the specific person's affairs, including arranging audiences and appointments with the 'master'. In appointing the *baldereba*, the nobles (*mekwanent*) and the military officers (*shumament*) reciprocated the attention they were given by supplicants and others. With this contact person ensuring the supplicants' acknowledgement of his authority, the 'master' took the time needed to sort out pertinent issues appropriately, before responding. The *baldereba* was expected to keep abreast of the whereabouts and well-being of those in his charge, even visiting them in cases of serious personal crisis, studying their cases and informing their 'master' sympathetically. By creating a spirit of camaraderie, he spared soldiers and farmers alike the irritation of necessary interruptions.

The practice of appointing a *baldereba* also saved 'masters'' possible awkwardness with those in the household, the retinue or members of the public by easing military rigidity. Thus linking civilian and military personnel, the *ad hoc* officer, who was expected to promote the claims to rights and privileges of ordinary members of society, gave established authority the means to show equity towards its subordinates. The performance of a *baldereba* heightened loyalties and other ties, and raised the potential for increasing the 'master's' retinue. His disgrace, like his sudden rise to the position, reflected on the cases of those in his care.

Baldereba enabled those in high political office to employ ambiguity and to sustain their personal status and authority while relating to their retainers, and at the state level, their subjects. During mobilization, monarchs designated *baldereba* by decree. In executing such a wartime assignment, the *baldereba* imposed rigid military command, sustaining political ambiguity only among similar titleholders. This strategy has been explained as 'a useful way of summarizing' the command order and hierarchy,[1] but it also clearly laid the ground for offsetting possible disobedience.

POLITICO-MILITARY OFFICIALS

The titled functionary most important in smoothing the rigid relationships was known as the *agafari* ('master of ceremonies'). With the guards, he ensured that nobody overstepped their positions relative to his 'master', and, with an assistant, the *elfign-askelkay* (guard of reception), he protected the security of the 'master' and his family. More significantly, this officer was in charge of prisoners, acted as an usher to the *adarash* (reception hall), and was generally responsible for

---

[1] Mahteme Selassie, *Memories*, 1962 EC, p. 35.

property, household law and order, and control of communication between the outside world and domestic slaves and servants.

Without involving himself in major political matters, the *agafari* also dealt with other affairs while the 'master' was on the move. While the 'master' personally was attending to cases before breakfast, for instance, the *agafari* uttered greetings on his behalf, in that sense liaising with the public, and supervised the rest of the retinue in such a way as to impart images of his 'master's' fairness, justice and high status. It was his responsibility to impress the public with the 'master's' piety, *feriha Egziabher* or fear of God, sincerity, trustworthiness and nobility, by ensuring that the 'master's' prayer sessions, blessings at table, sacred books and father-confessor were known about.

To ensure that the 'master's' power and dignity were publicly displayed equally, the duties of the *agafari* included looking after the symbols of power, including attire, drum of authority and a large number of officials wearing high-status regalia that signified dignity and the qualities of authoritative administration of labour and property. Even the relative positions in which tents were pitched during expeditions were symbols that he regulated clearly. Thus the pitching of the red tent known as the *desta* ('pleasure'), which belonged to the *neguse negest* (and/or the *negus* as the case might be), indicated that the army was to halt, and was followed by the pitching of the white and black tents of other officials. Showing the status of their occupants in descending order, the white tents belonged to the *agafari*, *belaten geta* and *tekaken belaten geta* of the king's 'household', who received large grants of land and had equal status to other high-ranking officials. Service providers, including the *yewust-ashker aleqa* ('commander of internal servants') and his assistant, and the *azazh* (head of personal and household troops), who were entitled to receive large land grants, used the black tents. At state level, the *azazh* was specifically responsible for state prisoners.

Another significant duty of the *agafari*, overseeing the formal link between established 'masters' and emerging warriors, was processing the status of the emerging warriors. With his assistant, the *belaten geta* (chief of the pages) and the latter's deputy, the *tekaken belaten geta* (chief of minor pages), the *agafari* looked after those under training. A learned, and usually middle-aged, well-respected officer with diplomatic skills and a recipient of large grants of land, the chief of the pages was often adorned in silk robes, attended council meetings and looked after the grown up and aspiring youthful soldiers living in the 'master's' house as his 'children'. His assistant coached younger pages brought there by parents and important local supporters, training them in 'court manners'. This assistant spread them among lower-ranking household staff, such as the *azazh*, who had responsibility for servants and slaves. The pages performed a host of such menial jobs as looking after the person of the master and his immediate nobles. Under the *yewust-ashker aleqa* (head of internal servants), a still lower assistant, the trainee youth also worked as *astatabi*, bringing water for respected guests to wash their hands at meal times, and carrying the master's table-knives and prayer books. Of course, assignments for trainee youth were closely scrutinized by their relatives and other members of the public who gave them advice, including leaving their 'master', or supplicated on their behalf for better treatment. Consequently, the *agafari* and his assistants were careful to ensure that issues with the trainees did not compromise a 'master's' relationships with his supporters.

Yet another influential, powerful and trusted officer was the 'treasurer' (*bejirond*), whose role in attracting the warriors to defence activities under a 'master' was specifically significant. His major duty being to organize and administer his master's income and resources, he commanded several other officers, including the *negadras*, 'head of merchants', who was concerned with finance. In the monarch's household, the *bejirond* was actually a state treasurer. He headed the cavalry unit (*balderas*), and was thus sometimes referred to as the *balderas*. Though he was entitled to a silk shirt, the treasurer was not privy to the council meetings, but, depending on his 'master's' position, he could also undertake some military duties, including even military responsibilities like that of a *ras*.[2]

In the household, the official under the *bejirond* was the *eka-bet aleqa* (store commander) who looked after cash, honey, grain, saddles, military decorations and formal regalia, guns, ammunition and other weaponry. In lower-ranking households, this officer also looked after 'the personal fief' of the 'master', collecting from farmers and storing grain and other produce of the land as tax in kind. In the monarch's palace, he had assistants known as the *zufan-bet aleqa* (keeper of the 'throne room' and official regalia) and the *molla-bet wuzef yazh* ('debt collector'). As we will see below, these household officials were also responsible for the food and drink consumed during military festivities.

POLITICAL AUTHORITY: THE COURT OF JUSTICE

As well as military might, holding courts of justice was a mark of authority. Court sessions, *chelot*, were held by the 'master' of any rank at a public square (*adebabay*) that was well outside his compound, especially if the cases involved public issues. Expected to be rooted in the 'fear of God', a master's judgements were based on the law (of God). Invariably attended by professional lawyers and learned men who had consulted the *Fetha Negest*, the authoritative law book in the country,[3] the sessions were presided over by a judge, *wember* (literally 'chair'),

---

[2] Pankhurst, *Economic History*, 1968, pp. 545–8, discusses the subject of hierarchy. In addition to travellers' accounts and the recorders of Ethiopian tradition, almost all standard works on Ethiopia give similar lists, such as in Mahteme Selassie, *Memories*, 1962 EC, pp. 21–37, 664–70.

[3] For a relatively recent study of the *Fetha Negest* regarding its religious roots and relevance to politico-military entitlement until 1930, see Aberra Jembere, *An Introduction to the Legal History of Ethiopia*, 2000, pp. 6–7, 37–8.

usually the 'master' himself, or by someone he or a higher official appointed. At state level, the supreme *wember* was the *afenegus*, literally 'mouth of the king', i.e. 'chief justice'.

Litigants presented their cases in wager-based debates known as *eset ageba* (literally 'I give-submit'), loudly throwing bets against each other concerning the validity of their arguments, making comments about the flaws in their opponent's presentations and calling on witnesses. Officers and dignitaries in attendance, whose status varied in accordance with the level of the court, were invited to comment on each case. Depending on the number of cases and the absence of military engagement, the *chelot* could go on until midday or until three o'clock in the afternoon (calculated by the direction of shadows cast by the sun). Scribes arranged hearings of pending cases and, as necessary, guards handed over prisoners, those on bail and individuals due for detention to the *azazh* of the household for security. The nature of punishments meted out to culprits, especially if these happened to be among the 'master's' retainers, had to satisfy the local population, impressing them with his political judgement. These publicly performed justice sessions significantly built up (or ruined) a 'master's' reputation and popularity. Not infrequently, *chelot* sessions, especially around holy days, were occasions for promoting ordinary soldiers into the 'master's' personal household or his formal soldiery.

POLITICAL AUTHORITY: TAKING COUNCIL

Council meetings held for establishing the sense of justice and military control in the camp or in the hamlet were equally significant for asserting authority. Held either in the *elfign* or in the *adarash*, sensitive discussions involving promotions, appointments or demotions, and on resources and local security, were attended by elders specified as councillors and the 'master's' wife, who might be noted for her political importance and acumen. The *balemiwal*, 'favoured officials', also attended depending on their number and the political importance of the topics under discussion. In times of imminent danger, when the whole establishment of a 'master' was expected to move at a moment's notice and he had to reorganize the household, including those in the backyard, subordinates and retainers waited in the *adarash* until invited for consultation. Council meetings that considered the times for holding *gibir* and *zeraf* sessions and (depending on the 'master's' status, wealth and the time of year) mobilization were open to senior staff. Also open were discussions on current trends of opinion, assessment of officers' loyalties, and the *baldereba* presentations on supplicants' cases and interests. Discussions on executing such tasks as the often-reported, tricky imprisonment or disposal of old favourites were limited only to those close to the 'master'.

BATTLEFIELD STRATEGY

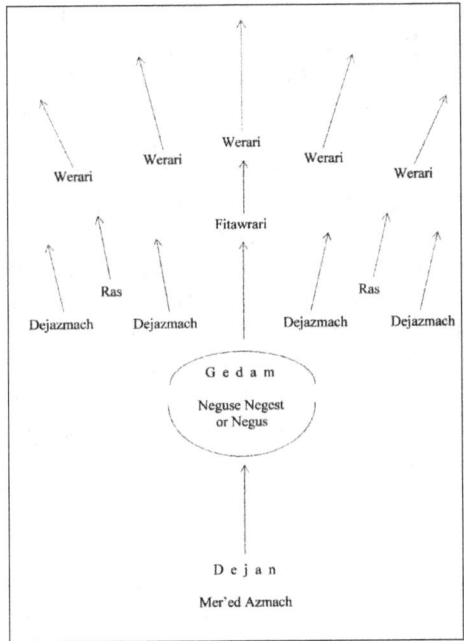

Figure 2 A *chewa* army on the attack (Adapted from a drawing by *Balambaras* Berhane-Selassie Yigeremu)

The 'master's' leadership and principles for troop mobilization, timing, the provision of rations, route selection and deployment were often personal. Mobilization messages gave instructions to the enemy, and were supplemented by sessions of *zeraf* and festivities that were held for the purpose of raising fear in the enemy and encouraging the local soldiery. Those announcing the seasonal attacks and counter-attacks initially sent verbal messages, theoretically for opening up dialogue and for peace, but in reality asking for tribute (*gibir*) and demanding submission. Placing blame on those to be attacked was inevitably concomitant on the violence and indiscriminate killings that characterized the politics of preindustrial military offensives. Where 'conciliatory' messages did not get swift responses, they were followed by marching against those who hesitated to bring tribute. To send an ameliorative message on how to avoid imminent violence, instead of mounting a sudden attack, was considered very brave. Such messages called on leaders of the proposed victims to 'avoid blood-letting', thus passing on the responsibility for damage to them. Sometimes written messages also named battlefields where the 'offenders' were to await for battle, often 'after the rains'. Though flat plains were ideal battle sites, skilled nineteenth-century 'masters' often chose hilltops or prominences from which they could observe enemy movements and bide their time before launching offensives and skirmishes.

Seasonal *chewa* attacks and counter-attacks began in the post-harvest months, October to February, and in May. With streams and rivers safer to cross and the ground drier in most parts of the country, rural people could undertake long journeys and hold weddings. Farmers were freer from farming chores, so they also delivered grain and animals from rural *meret* or 'landholdings' to the homesteads of war leaders, absent landlords and the market. Most rural men prepared to prove their manhood and claim their symbolic and real significance in society as warriors, and for the same reasons, 'masters' used this season for *zeraf* sessions. To mobilize their followers they beat their drums and announced their long-term purposes, including guarding the borders and reclaiming 'lost territories'. Significantly, to prove they were as valiant as their attackers and valuing their reputations at their communal bases, the targets of hostility often replied with defiant *zeraf* wordings or adamant refusals to submit. Ordinary people were willing to pay the ultimate price, and neither the challengers nor the challenged generally resorted to ruses. The Oromo, who reportedly attacked under cover of darkness or pretended to pay tribute before attacking, were seen as exceptions to this.

TROOP DEPLOYMENT

Formally and ideally, leaders deployed their soldiers in convex formation, literally dividing them into three: the 'invader' or *werari*, the 'main body of the army' or *gedam*, and the 'rearguard' or *dejen*. A hierarchical pattern of encampment featured in every camping site, and each contingent had 'masters' with lower titles flanking those with higher ones. Each officer would give appropriate orders in consultation with his superiors, and when joining in battle 'masters' and followers would leave their *guaz* (families, non-fighting retinue and supplies) around their respective tents with only essential staff. *Chewa* troops recognized and used *fanno* as specially organized warriors who supposedly lived in border areas as hunters. The strength of warriors to be deployed depended, of course, on the strength or weakness of the attacked party. When that was strong, even the reserve troops, *dejan tor*, at the rear would join the battle. This order of deployment would be followed until the battle was won, or until the formations fell into disarray with defeat.

Headed by the *fitawrari*, 'advance guard commander', so called irrespective of his actual title, the *werari* were made up of specially selected and trained young men from each officer's retinue. Reportedly the most lethal, their task was to mount fast and surprise attacks on horse and foot for *tor* or *teb mechar* (provoking/scratching a battle or a quarrel), to draw out the enemy before it was ready to fight. Where several officers were collaborating, the *werari* from all camps of the army would be under the command of only one *fitawrari*, whose important responsibilities included deploying the *werari* strategically. Deployed from a distance of half a day's march from the battle site, the *werari* would separate from the main force, and, moving quickly, initiate attacks, burning the first huts, trees or woods its members came across at the border, regardless of whether warriors or civilians were there. After provoking hostilities, the *werari* retreated before anyone could retaliate, if possible taking captives, their successful timing of attack and safe retreat being to the credit to the strategic capacity of the *fitawrari*. The outer flanks of the main army would repulse enemies, pursuing them during their retreat. Local people might resist having the combatants use their fields as a battle site, and might be tempted to ally with either side of the combatants. Often *werari* from either side would attack them to limit the possibility of their joining the other side.

The position of the *fitawrari* reflects best the general *chewa* strategy of direct confrontation with the enemy in warfare, and certainly the strategic location of titleholders. Irrespective of whether he acquired his authority by force or by appointment, even the humblest 'master' nominated one of his men as *fitawrari* in the generic sense, not with the formal title, of course. This leader of the vanguard engaged in face-to-face fighting when ordered to do so. His followers were proven and valiant warriors. Indispensable on any battlefield, this officer was thus in command of a key unit of any army. He was selected for his cunning, strategic thinking and capacity to launch the whole force into active engagement. As James Bruce recorded in the eighteenth century:

> On 17th [April 1770], after sunrise, the king passed the Nile, and encamped in a small village called Tsoomwa, where his Fit-Auraris had previously taken up their post. The Fit-Auraris is an officer depending immediately on the Commander-in-chief, and is always one of the bravest and most experienced men in the service.[4]

Deploying an advance guard was such a crucial strategy that the 'kings of kings' often gave the *fitawrari* position to the highest ranking and most trusted *ras* or *dejazmach*. Such deployment would not demote their rank, and indeed, in intense battles led by a 'king' or 'king of kings', the *fitawrari* and his retinue would be flanked by *ras* and *dejazmach* acting as his right and left commanders, respectively *kegnazmach* and *gerazmach*. If he died or went missing, he would be replaced automatically by the highest officer in the army.

The *gedam*, where the central command of the army was encamped, had several high-ranking leaders. At its most powerful, the army had the *neguse negest* in the centre, surrounded by *ras* and *negus*, flanked by numerous *dejazmach* and lower-ranking officers. Titleholders at either side of the *neguse negest*, including the *dejazmach* of the *ras*, were under the *fitawrari* commanding the *werari*. The *mer'ed azmach*, literally 'assistant leader', commanded the *dejan tor*, 'the rearguard'. He had troops and weapons to control rebels, marauders or enemy soldiers who might attack the army from the rear, and would normally have the title *negus*, *ras* or *dejazmach*, with some *werari* on the ready. If disaster struck the *gedam*, the *mer'ed azmach* was meant to regain whatever control of

---

[4] James Bruce, *Travels and Discoveries in Abyssinia*, Edinburgh: W. P. Nimmo, Hay, & Mitchell, 1885, p. 161. See also Plowden, *Travels in Abyssinia*, 1868, p. 56.

the situation he could. This may have occurred when Yohannes IV was killed. Though it is not easy to establish the precedence for guarding the country from there, the *mer'ed azmach* was also the title of the ruler of Shewa from the early seventeenth century.

MILITARY TITLEHOLDERS

Military symbols such as titles, feasting and using the *negarit* ('drums of authority') not only signified status and military activity but also geographical association and relative privilege, prestige and political responsibility. Titled military officials were part of a larger chain of *chewa* with increasingly higher status, and a conglomeration of such 'masters' was a category of active soldiery that stood apart from civilian society. The rigidity of the formality increased with status, and in wartime the hierarchy followed a prescribed ascending order in accordance with appropriate proximity to the camp of the 'king of kings' or another top authority. The titles of officers attending an official's council sessions and *gibir* and joining his leadership in battle indicated a 'master's' political inclination and military strength. His household staff respected the officers of his retinue. The formality of personal relationships in his military sector and in his household indicated his level of politicization, and signalled his military aspirations. From his leading position in parades, in battle sites, in *zeraf* festivities, the 'master' showed off his followers' titles, evinced by their regalia, for instance during parades, and worked to promote aspirants among them to higher positions. Followers could reciprocate by better displaying their 'master's' military status, for example by pitching their commanding officer's white tent prominently in relation to those of his superiors.

'Masters' holding the title of *fitawrari* and above required a *seyfe jagre* to carry their sword (*seyf*) and a *seyfe jagre shaleqa*, in charge of about a thousand soldiers, or a *mato aleqa* of about a hundred, some acting as their personal bodyguards. During campaigns (*zemecha*) and expeditions (*guzo*), these officers were assigned as *baldereba* to one another. Thus the *seyfe jagre shaleqa* and the *dejagafari*, for instance, were *baldereba* to the *blaten-geta* and *agafari* respectively. The duty of the *agafari* as 'companion' on the battlefield was to be 'mobilizer' (*qesqash*, literally 'alerter') to the *dejagafari*. Their roles were reversed during games associated with banquets (*gibir*). These were ritualized games when aspiring titled officers, soldiers (*wetader*) or lowly grass cutters and baggage carriers could display their sportsmanship and qualities of warriorhood to enhance their status and that of their subordinates, if they had any.

The *seyfe jagre shaleqa*, who decided who could have audiences with 'masters' on political matters, constantly assessed and recommended aspirants, while the 'outside usher' (*dejagafari*) and guards (*zebegna*) under the latter regulated the cavalry units and other warriors present

Photo 4 *Ras* Mekonnen and retinue in *chewa* military wear
(Source: R. Pankhurst & Denis Gérard, *Ethiopia Photographed: Historic Photographs of the Country and its People Taken Between 1867 and 1935* (Kegan Paul International, 1996, p. 49); by kind permission of Richard Pankhurst's family and Denis Gérard)

Table 2 Military regalia for *dejazmach*

Items of honour	Decorations for 'exterior' *dejazmach*	Decorations for 'drum' *dejazmach*
Lanka, 'chasuble'	in gold and silver thread	in gold thread
Qemis, 'shirt', mantle and trousers	in material called *mabruq*	same
Kuta, 'toga', home woven	double	better quality
Deg, 'belt', home woven	cotton sash	same
Sword	with metalwork and rhino horn	same
Shield, and horse and mule livery	silver	gold or gold plate

in the camp or in the household. Warriors sponsored younger men training in the art of war, allowing them to serve, for example, as *gasha jagre* (shield bearers) or as *dagafi*, 'supporters' for senior officers, including helping the wives and concubines to mount or dismount their riding horse or mule. Their sponsorship facilitated the promotion of emerging warriors.

The formal military titleholders from *balambaras* upwards were ranked differently from household officers and camp followers. Also charged with governing specific areas under the *neguse negest*, the titles *balambaras*, *dejazmach* and *ras* seem to indicate geographical fixedness. Indeed *balambaras* includes the words, *amba*, mountaintop and *ras* or head, hence 'commander of the mountaintop'. The *balambaras* titleholders were appointed over strategic fortresses, especially in outlying provinces. They were the lowest on the military ladder and often the youngest, though older and highly experienced men have also been known to have the title. Some *balambaras*, notable for their closeness to the 'master', were reputed to be favourites. They generally commanded the cavalry during expeditions, and, without a special camping position, they put up their tent near the top commander or anywhere in the middle of his retinue. If under the vanguard, the *balambaras* was frequently among those charged with carrying out the first raid.

Unlike the *balambaras*, the *kegnazmach*, 'leader on the right', had the duty of fighting on the right flank with his men, forming a unit distinctly separate from that of his superior's household. He appears to have been given preference over the *gerazmach*, 'leader on the left', but in all other respects these two officers had the same duty, status and privileges. Sometime in the sixteenth century, the monarch had two queens to whom they gave the title 'left queen' and 'right queen', the latter being given to the favourite.[5] The reference to right and left derived from political and religious symbolisms generally drawing on attributes of good and evil. Though decorated with a cape with silver buttons, the *kegnazmach* and *gerazmach* had no other titled holders under them, nor the authority to give any titles. They were expected to be at the forefront in campaigns like the *balambaras*, except when a higher-ranking officer was assigned to operate from their position. The *gerazmach* or even sometimes the *balambaras*, commanded the *balderas* or *yeferes zebegna shaleqa* (commander of the horse-guards), who was responsible for acquiring and maintaining horses, mules and other pack animals.

Also appearing to have geographical association, other titles reflect not only commitment to assert the 'master's' authority in the country but also to conduct battles. For instance, *dejazmach*, a word made up of *dej* and *azmach*, respectively meaning 'front part' and 'leader of campaign', was an officer designated to lead major expeditions beyond the territories under a *ras*, a king or a 'king of kings'. Accompanied by

---

[5] This arguable hypothesis is based on oral reports from my family dating from the 1920s.

a large following and titled officers from different regions, he was entitled to initiate offensives and grant titles as high as *fitawrari* without seeking permission from his superiors.

There were two types of *dejazmach: yewech* ('external') *dejazmach* and *balenegarit* ('owner of drum of authority') *dejazmach*. At the beginning of the nineteenth century, almost all *yewech dejazmach*, including Kassa who later became Tewodros II, were rebels trying to build up their personal power bases. The *balenegarit dejazmach*, with the right to beat from twelve to forty 'drums of authority', was senior to the much larger number of *yewech dejazmach* who were available for battle. He had elaborate attire, consisting of both military and civilian clothes of honour, such as lion manes decorated in silver. The 'external' *dejazmach* was less decorated. There were provinces traditionally designated as 'drum countries' where the title-holding governors had additional administrative duties. One *balenegarit dejazmach* led each wing of the army under a *negus* or a *neguse negest*, but their number on the battlefield depended on the number of *ras* they were expected to flank. Their presence, with their white tents in special positions and their beating of the symbolic *negarit*, raised the might of the fighting force.

Holders of the higher title of *ras*, literally 'head', were decorated with a gold coronet and other gold regalia. Historically held by immediate members of the royal family, this was the position from which most powerful men of the Era of Princes campaigned to be kingmakers. *Ras* Mikael Sehul, the first of these subsequently to become a kingmaker of the Era of Princes, had the title and authority to govern the provinces along the Red Sea coast in the northern parts of the Rift Valley, probably with the obligation to engage in wars of rivalry over trade routes and against invaders from the sea coast. Following his takeover of power in the centre, however, others like Wesen Seged in Shewa and Wube in Tigre assumed the title *ras* by beating 'their own' *negarit* and issuing decrees. *Ras* Wesen Seged's successors eventually assumed the title of *negus*. So did *Ras* Ali of Begemder, who, as we saw, virtually succeeded to be one by installing kings in Gonder and appointing provincial governors in their names.

Tewodros II tried to end this practice in the 1850s by giving the title *ras* only to the most able warrior among his men. In an apparently pointed move, he left a *balambaras* as his *meslene* (representative) in Gojam, lowering the local *balenegarit dejazmach* to that of 'external' *dejazmach*. In Shewa he appointed his own man as *mer'ed azmach*, 'leader of the rearguard', the position given in the early eighteenth century to Menelik's ancestor who had held the ancient title of *tsehafi lahem*, which was reserved until then to that province.[6] He also took Menelik, the heir-apparent of Shewa, and brought him up himself with only the title of *dejazmach*. Tewodros appointed *shum* in Hamasen, Agamie and elsewhere in the north; in Wag and Lasta he retained the old title of *wagshum*, 'official over Wag'.

---

[6] Guèbrè Sellassié, *Chronique*, 1930–32, Vol. I, p. 56, fn. 6.

Tewodros's reforms uncoupled the title *ras* from royalty, and transformed the system of ranking. Two types of *ras* prevailed historically: an ordinary one and a *ras-bitweded* or 'the favourite *ras*', given to the closest friend of a monarch and to only one person in their lifetime. However, Yohannes IV gave the title to Araya, his own son and heir, and to Adal Tessema, the *balambaras* whom Tewodros had left behind in Gojam. Positioned at the rear of the army during battles, the *ras-bitweded* was like a member of the household of the *neguse negest*.

When Menelik assumed the title *neguse negest*, he gave the title *ras* to Yohannes's nephew and new heir, Mengesha Yohannes, as appeasement for depriving him of the crown of 'king of kings'. Initially having given it only to his valiant warriors, such as *Ras* Gobena, over time he awarded the title *ras* also to governors of areas that qualified as 'old' provinces that he believed were deserving of it: Begemder, Tigre, Wello and Saynt, and in Northern Wello, including Yeju, Delanta, Dawent, Shedahu, Werro, Meqet, Zobel and Lasta.[7] Subsequently he also gave it to governors of 'new' areas: Hararge, Selale, Arsi, Bale, Illubabor, Keffa and Wellega.

By the mid-to-late 1890s, when Menelik was distributing titles to his officials, there were multiple *ras* and *dejazmach* with drums. However, he had stopped designating lands for military service, and appointees had to either negotiate for them with local *balabat* or allow billeted soldiers to impose on the local population – with which the soldiers of course obliged, having been removed from their own local communities and original bases, as we saw above. In historical times, the *ras* had two *dejazmach*, only one of whom he appointed himself, and the prestige and rank of his appointee depended on the current status of the province that the *ras* governed. *Ras* with the power to appoint the higher type of *dejazmach* could raise regular forces from those obliged to serve the state as recruits (*melmel*). From the late nineteenth century this changed, and these *ras* depended mainly on *weddo-geb*, volunteers who received from them wages without lands, who formed the kernel of their personal soldiery.

Above the *ras* was the *negus*, king, a generic word deriving from the ancient Ge'ez term *negasi*. Referring to any crowned head,[8] this title could be held, in theory, by any number of monarchs. The titleholders were assumed, in some cases even 'proven', to be of royal descent by real or arranged genealogy. The *ras* and *negus* under a *neguse negest* appear to have had similar privileges and camp arrangements. *Negus*

---

[7] Mahteme Selassie, *Memories*, 1962 EC, pp. 656–7.
[8] Studies of stone inscriptions show that *melek* appears to have preceded the title *negus* to refer to monarchs in the region in around the fifth and seventh centuries BC. See Sergew, *Ancient and Medieval History*, 1972, pp. 59–60. The earliest mention of *negus* appears to be in association with Ezana and Saizana (Atsbeha and Abreha), the brothers who thrived in the fourth century AD. Shack, *The Central Ethiopians*, 1974, pp. 104–5, records the usage of *negus* as referring to an overlord among nineteenth- and twentieth-century Gurage. The Oromo generic term *moti* has also been translated as 'king'.

could bestow formal titles and appoint officials of justice and administration, including *shaleqa* and *dejazmach* from their administrative areas. On battlefields or during other campaigns (*zemecha*) all, including the *negus*, were under the two *ras* flanking the camp of the 'king of kings'. In the course of the nineteenth century, conferring the title *negus* indicated the confidence of the *neguse negest*. Apart from Sahle Selassie, who assumed the title himself, Menelik and *Ras* Adal (later Tekle Haymanot) were first *negus* courtesy of Yohannes IV, and later Menelek took the *neguse negest* title himself.

Tewodros gave the status of *negus* to no one, and his three successors gave it only very carefully, deliberately controlling the title. The first *negus* of Shewa, Sahle Selassie, and his son Hayle Melekot, had no *ras*. Yohannes IV, who confidently controlled the movements of two '*negus*', for the first time since antiquity permitted each to appoint a left and right *ras*. After Yohannes's death, Menelik II as 'king of kings' renewed the crown of *negus* for Tekle Haymanot of Gojam but refrained from giving it to anyone else. Nonetheless, the precedent that there had been two *negus* facilitated the acceptance of equivalence for *kao* of Welayta, *tato* of Keffa and *sultan* of Jimma, who were considered to have the same status as *negus*. However, military privileges were not extended to these rulers, and their positions and titles (along with the *negus* of Gojam) were discontinued when the incumbents died. In this way, Menelik controlled their possible rise to the status of the *mesafint*, whose power had been gradually reduced since the time of Tewodros II.

The power of *negus* was thus limited to their provinces and was subordinated to the *neguse negest*. The *neguse negest* could assign a *dejazmach* as *baldereba* to each *negus* and place them at their rear like a *mer'ed azmach* ('leader of the reserve troops'), but without the privileges accruing to the title. Thus when the Mahdists invaded northwestern Ethiopia, for instance, Yohannes IV ordered the *negus* of Gojam and of Shewa to mobilize their forces and follow him (although they obeyed reluctantly). When Menelik headed to the Battle of Adewa in 1896, he also ordered the *negus* of Gojam and those south of the Abay River to mobilize and follow him.

Even more revealing of the prestige of the *neguse negest*, who were also known as *atse*, was the fact that they referred to themselves in the plural – as if they were the sum total of several 'masters'. A possible explanation, perhaps far-fetched, could be a wish to do justice to the aspirations of self-training warriors, all of whom were possible aspirants to the title of *negus*. The *ras masere*, who looked after the monarchs' crown and protocol and like the *liqe mekuas* impersonated them – short of wearing the crown and actual apparel – were symbolically important. They camped close by to give personal dignity and security. Besides, during battles as when travelling, the *neguse negest*'s tent was pitched in the inaccessible centre, the *gedam*, of the army from where he was expected to watch and conduct the fighting. Enemy penetration of the *gedam* caused disarray. (The word *gedam* stands for 'monastery' in Ge'ez and challenging it was analogous to the profanation of a monastery; also, analogical to its Amharic meaning, 'forest', 'undergrowth' or 'thicket', it was seen as pluckiness.)

Prohibiting the title *negus* was a symptom of the eventual demise of the *chewa* system as a whole – a move towards centralization of power. The title *negus* was briefly resuscitated when Menelik's grandson and designated heir, *Lij* Iyasu, gave it to his father, *Ras* Mikael of Wello. Later, Menelik's daughter, 'Queen of Kings' Zewditu, 'awarded' it to her maternal uncle, Welde Giyorgis, whom she named *Negusa Gonder-we-Keffa*, 'king of Gonder and Keffa', and then to the heir-designate, *Ras* Tafari as *negus*. The last titleholders, Mikael, Tafari and Welde Giyorgs, received the title *negus* as part of ameliorating intense palace rivalries among those trying to introduce state modernity. After he became *neguse negest* in 1930, Haile Selassie made the title *negus* obsolete. As we will see below, resistance fighters in 1937 popularly acclaimed their leader, Belay Zeleka, as '*atse* by his own might' in Gojam, and a boy of fifteen as symbolic *negus* in Shewa. This process glorified the social approval that warriors sought, breaking down the prescriptive assumption that the *neguse negest* title had to be based on descent and birthright.

THE *BALABAT*

Right at the bottom of the military hierarchy, but critically at the centre of relating to communities, was the *balabat*. This important person is so-called as he belonged, at least theoretically, to the local community. The administrative rights of this officer were limited to raising public support for the state, and controlling and keeping records of local land allocations. In that sense, he acted as the political link between the community and state, but other *shumament* (literally 'appointees') were his *aleqa* (superiors). Though not as high as the *mekwanent* (nobility, literally 'those that are'), the *balabat* was accountable to the state for local public attitudes.

The elevated status of some *balabat* facilitated their claims to be 'prince' (*mesfin* singular, *mesafint* plural) during the Era of Princes. Wesen Seged, a descendant of Negasi, *balabat* of Agencha in Shewa, for instance, used the title *ras* and *abetohun*[9] in the early nineteenth century, and his son Sahle Selassie eventually assumed the title *negus*. Wag, Lasta and other parts of Wello, along with Agame, Tigre, Hamasen, Begemder, Gojam and Shewa, attached the title *shum* to local *balabat*, the *wagshum* being the best known. Towards the end of the nineteenth century, the descendants of these *balabat* continued to be seen as *mesafint*, and associating with those who eventually became *neguse negest* enhanced their position.

Huge variations in the *balabat* position and title in the nineteenth century meant holding additional military titles. Thus in parts of

---

[9] In time *abetohun* became the ordinary title *Ato* (equivalent to 'mister', 'Mr').

Begemder and Tigre, *dejazmach* or *ras* titleholders were considered local *balabat*, though they had little or no association with the local community. In general, these *balabat* were expected to raise soldiers for military service, and their success in this gained them awards of titles that superseded their narrower local political responsibilities. It allowed their incorporation into the wider schemes of *chewa* titles dependent on the *negus* or *neguse negest*. Some *balabat* tried to resist the abolition of inheritance in their father's position. *Ras* Haylu Tekle Haymanot of Gojam, for instance, persisted in claiming his father's title as *negus*, and even solicited it from the Italians during the 1935–41 invasion when the colonialists saw high-ranking titles as useful for attracting the 'natives' to their side.

Similarly potent *balabat* elsewhere in the late nineteenth century continued to be referred to by with their previous titles. These included the *kao*[10] in Welayta, the *sultan* in Jimma and the *tato* in Keffa. Aba Jifar, the *sultan* of Jimma, retained his kingdom and autonomous position by making a formal submission, while *Kao* Tona, the last king of Wolayta, as we saw above, was first captured and then reinstalled as *balabat* in 1894. *Emir* Abdullahi who fled the walled city of Harar in 1887, was replaced with Menelik's cousin, *Balambaras* Mekonnen (later *ras*). When *Ras* Welde Giyorgis (later *negus*) took *Tato* Gaki Sherotcho of Keffa prisoner in 1897, the *tato* was detained and forced to stay away. The *balabat* in Wellega and Illubabor, most of whom were tribute payers by the 1880s, were incorporated within the *chewa* military system and were given high military titles. Some other local rulers were removed beyond their home bases to render military service as *de facto* leaders of further expeditions, and eventually as titled members of the *chewa* running the affairs of their original communities through proxies. This was the case of leaders in Gurage, for instance. Where similarly powerful heads did not exist, as in Sidama, Hadiya, Arsi and Bale and elsewhere in the south, the *chewa* designated notable local warriors as *balabat*. However, at the dawn of the twentieth century when the *chewa* system was being phased out, most of these local officials had become mere tax collectors under salaried governors with high titles.

Lowering the position of *balabat* and phasing out the title of *negus*, however necessary they were for sustaining the status quo of those in power, contributed to reducing the power of local communities and those emerging as warriors among them. It blocked individual soldiering through competitive hunting and other sports that used to enable men to assume political responsibility for defending their rural communal lands and people. The period coincided with powerful *neguse negest* asserting their claim to authority as prescribed in the *Kebre Negest*. Menelik's introduction of the highly centralized 'modern'

---

[10] *Kao*, 'king', was used in Wolayta and in some Sidama-speaking areas of the south. See for instance the specialized studies by Bureau, 'The "Tigre" Chronicle of Wollaita', 1990; Shack, *The Central Ethiopians*, 1974; Huntingford, *The Glorious Victories*, 1965; Ernesta Cerulli, *Peoples of South-West Ethiopia and its Borderland*, London: International African Institute, 1956.

state also meant assuming the sole right to confer any titles, especially above *fitawrari*. Over time, the absence of rivals enabled Haile Selassie I to ensure succession to the throne of the 'king of kings' theoretically to his descendants alone, as enshrined in the 1931 and 1955 constitutions.

MOBILIZATION, EXPEDITIONS AND SUPPLIES

From the Era of Princes to the late nineteenth century, annual raiding seasons, usually after the rains, were normal activities. Mobilizations (*qitet*) tested the military might of locally influential *chewa* 'masters' and the loyalty of their followers. Mobilization procedures, like announcing government orders or appointments, meant beating the drums of authority and assigning *baldereba*, a senior *qesqash* (one who alerts), and a main troop leader. As local farmers were central to troop numbers, their participation was vital to *chewa* leaders. Potential and aspiring warriors among them, who were already involved in the paramilitary games and training sessions mentioned above, voluntarily gathered around 'masters' to take part. Communal leaders and 'masters' alike encouraged each other to engage in military parades, games and collecting trophies from hunting expeditions, offering their participation through *zeraf* feasts. Existing *chewa* leaders vied with one another to report 'as soon as the ground is dry' or 'as soon as the rains stop'.

Any expedition (*zemecha*) also significantly tested the qualities of a *chewa* 'master' as a loyal supporter and a strategist. His strategies included warning and protecting those along his route, keeping up the morale and discipline of his troops and paying due deference to his commanders. His wealth and benevolence influenced his sense of responsibility to the communities he would be marching through. Problems related to supplies invariably upset communities on the route and exposed the ill-preparedness of leaders. Full-scale expeditions, even those carrying tribute, were seen as military missions because they were accompanied by a large number of followers, including families. Ideally therefore, they had to be careful not to impose heavy burdens, irrespective of the distances they travelled. Marching troops affected different local communities in a variety of ways, most frequently destroying their crops. Though often unsuccessfully, soldiers and 'masters' had to collaborate in preventing or at least mitigating unwarranted attacks on communities that were not the targets of attack.

Officers beating the drums had to be careful not to provoke hostility or incite fear of attack, depending on the local politics. To speed mobility, it was advisable to arrange safe passage through 'friendly country' by sending advance warning to seek friendship and 'permissions'. This could result in acquiring escorts, the provision of *metin* (food rations), and other items of *mestengido* 'for the guest-hood'. Advance preparation included also controlling the composition of followers. Cumbersome at the best of times, this included non-combatant household members, namely the 'master's' 'children' – domestics, slaves and other dependants. The convoys of meat on the hoof (*ye erd kebt*), extra riding horses and beasts of burden further swelled the retinue. Officers departing permanently from an administrative jurisdiction were additionally accompanied by new servants and 'friends', as well as the households of junior officers and their followers, the last often angering elders whose saw it as depleting their local human resources.

Generalized warfare that threatened to deplete resources in labour and in kind could mean raising additional tax from communities, causing resentment over providing supplies for the troops. Taxpaying communities, therefore, often offered to bring their tribute at specific times, such as 'after rains'. Sometimes, troops would appear unexpectedly to ask the leader's permission for them to pass the rains in his locality, thus deliberately passing on to him the burden of considerable socio-economic strain. The sudden appearances or extended visits of troops also brought other practical difficulties. A famous example, still reported orally, occurred when Tewodros's troops, marching in Shewa, camped in a field of grain that was about to be harvested. The soldiers refused to listen to local pleadings, and the farmers threatened to let *jibo*, hyena, loose on them during the night. Not knowing the geography of the place, the soldiers went to bed dismissing this as a vacuous threat, only to find their camp swamped in the night. The farmers had broken the banks of the local river, called Jibo.

Well-established leaders organized supplies by having and using landholdings described as 'horse-halting places' (*ye feres mekomiya*). A leader's proper use of such lands reduced aggravation, except where local people refused to let him use his *maderya* land rights and authority. Though warriors were expected to bring a month's worth of personal supplies they could run short during lengthy marches (*guzo*) far from their homes. They would pillage villages and graze their cattle, horses and pack animals on local pastures and crops. Aspiring soldiers in advance lines, especially youth looking for trophies or loot to 'throw down' before their 'master', might also provoke unexpected hostility, and their bravado in collecting booty (*zerefa*) during expeditions could have unexpected consequences. Because farmers often avoided taking sides, later looting and killing both victors and vanquished, even advance warning could not prevent clashes between local warriors and marching troops. The intervention of elders, depending on whether they felt loyal or hostile to the leader, could influence the success or failure of expeditions. In addition, an army on the move in an orderly manner could attract aspiring local youth near battlefields or halting places to bring their arms, 'present themselves' to the leader and receive a *baldereba*.

BATTLE SITE INFORMATION

It seems that troops were equipped with codes for recognizing *wegen* from *telat*, respectively friend from foe. It is not clear how widespread this practice was, but at least during the Battle of Segele in 1916, warriors in each protagonist camp had been informed of it, and one man who could not remember the code was killed by his own side.[11] Messengers known as *wof*, 'birds', also operated internally within the marching force, delivering information and taking commands back and forth on when and which way the troops were to attack or retreat. In constant touch with the *fitawrari*, *dejazmach*, and their *gerazmach* and *kegnazmach*, others ran errands of challenge and counter-challenge between the warring groups, even taking messages from the retreating *werari*, or reporting on those pursuing them. If they were in the area, *fanno* helped to provide this service, often supporting the side they judged would win, or providing the *wof* with relevant information, including offers of their armed support.

Information from the *fitawrari* was transmitted according to the hierarchy of command in the army except for urgent or confidential reports, which had to be hastily transmitted to the *dejazmach*, the *ras*, the *negus* and the *neguse negest*, even while the army was travelling. Informants busied themselves gathering news of enemy supplies and other conditions such as challenges and submission. In practice, enemy defiance would be delivered by enemy runners to the master in the presence of all his officers. As shown earlier, messengers could insist on delivering insulting messages from their 'master' in public. Submission could be initially offered to a nearby commander, in which case this officer would victoriously show off his captive. Leaders who were separated from their colleagues, for instance during actual engagements, relied mostly on their own messengers, or risked not hearing of developments until the end.

CHANGES IN *CHEWA* POLITICAL POWER

Menelik's control of high-ranking *chewa* officials deterred local people from defying his authority as 'king of kings'. He further circumscribed the principles of the emerging warriors by setting up a corps known as the *Dembegna*, 'the legals', to serve alongside provincial governors. The *Dembegna* were protégés of the state rather than qualified *chewa*. As such, the term 'the legals' implied that they were legitimate as opposed to the old, seemingly somewhat randomly generated, constantly emerging fighting forces. The *chewa* saw them as unequal, whether in terms of training or of having a well-developed socio-political base. In fact, seeing the *Dembegna* as dependent on the centralized state the *chewa*, even those settled outside their own bases, considered themselves as part of their local communities. The appointment of 'the legals' reflected the growing marginalization of both bases and local communities from politics. The *Dembegna* formed part of an administrative system of checks and balances as their leaders were directly

---

[11] Mers'e Hazen Welde Kirkos, *My memories*, 2002 EC, pp. 172–3.

responsible to the *neguse negest* or his appointee, while their duties offset the control the *chewa* exercised locally.

Instituting the *Dembegna* increased the power and authority of the *neguse negest* in the wider *hager*, 'country', and brought the farmer–military relationships under his supreme command. The *chewa* found that access to the population, which had been their reserve, was fading. In other words, Menelik's billeting of the *Dembegna* began changing the structure and principles of military authority and political administration as the *chewa* understood it. Unlike the old principles by which commanders of *chewa* troops could mobilize locally, the *Dembegna* could do so only when permitted by the *neguse negest* and his *mengest* (government) under the *tsehafe tezaz* ('state scribe', or from 1907 'minister of pen') and *afenegus* (literally 'king's mouth', i.e. 'chief justice'). Though in *chewa* ideals, *mengest* meant the institution headed by the *neguse negest*, it also referred to the provincial administrators and the autonomous authorities such as those in Welayta, Keffa, Hararge and the Oromo kingdoms of the Gibe basin, areas that powerful *chewa* leaders had incorporated within the jurisdiction of the 'king of kings', and within the *chewa* system under him. Menelik's introduction of the *Dembegna* alongside that system as a means of introducing checks and balances smoothed the transition to a 'modern', more centralized government, whose 'dead hand' curbed local initiative, eventually disrupting ordinary people's access to *mengest*. As an institution, the *Dembegna*, to whom the state gave salaries raised from local economic resources, centralized the notion of *mengest* in the state, and the *chewa* were marginal to its administration.

8

Zeraf: Symbols and Rituals of Power and Rebellion

Collecting tax and giving military banquets, both known as *gibir*, were among the duties of titled officers. Not coincidentally, the word described two aspects of military power writ large. *Chewa* officers collected tribute from land and from other taxpayers, and passed it on to the state. Even those living elsewhere regulated control of land as part of exercising their institutional politico-military power. Thus this major economic resource that officers received for their military service, and out of which they extracted tax, kept them within the community from where other socially rooted warriors emerged as *chewa* officials and soldiers. Giving *gibir* as military banquets was part of officers' duties that, as we will see here, facilitated effective communication between communities and the *chewa* and ultimately the state.

The banquets could be occasioned by appointments on the eve of campaigns or other military occurrences, such as the return of hunters or victorious troops or annual troop reviews, and the arrival of important superiors or tribute payers from some distance. 'Masters' regularly gave them for their retainers and supporters, including members of the local community. The banquets were accompanied by the *negarit*, 'drum of authority', and trumpet-like wind instruments known as *imbelta* and *meleket*. Singers feasting inside the hall enlivened the feast by rousing the guests while the drum and trumpets played. At the host's discreet prompting, the singers started *shilela*, the lyrics of which were intended to excite passions. The din increased as soldiers, hunters and aspiring politicians suddenly made their *zeraf* and *fukera* – respectively 'self-proclamation', and 'declaration of loyalty' to a cause or to a person, declaring, denouncing or celebrating issues that had occasioned the feasting.

Intrinsic to attending *gibir*, these outbursts were said to add majesty to the banquets, which would suddenly turn into venues for informal discussion of political and military opinions. They signalled the prestige of highly qualified warriors under the host, and heralded the symbols (*milikit*) of his military power and prestige. It is noteworthy here that the host had the option of entertaining only his equals and neighbours, making political points by leaving some individuals out. According to nineteenth-century *chewa*, *gibir* as *fukera* was an exercise

Photo 5 Returning from combat and hunting was cause for celebration
(Source: J. G. Vanderheym, *Une Expédition avec Le Négous Ménélik (Vingt Mois en Abyssinie)*
(Paris: Hachette, 1896), p. 169)

par excellence to communicate power relations, controlling mobility and human and material resources. Providing an occasion for communication facilitated an additional outlet for the hierarchical military system and war practices. In other words, *fukera* during *gibir* spelt out the very presence of the *chewa* warriors in the northeast African region, representing them as a power to be taken seriously.

Gibir as banquet was also a way of sharing resources the 'master' had collected as tax (*gibir*). Moreover, at military functions, the 'master' had to be ready to display his benevolence during the exchanges that occurred during the banquets. He had to impress actual or aspiring retainers and potential rivals and supporters by the display of his power. His guests knew their place in the military hierarchy, and proclaimed themselves worthy of the special cuts of meat and beverage appropriate to their status. It is not far-fetched to conclude that this distributive practice helped the *chewa* to assuage significantly the political and economic impact of land tax on society. Its absence also had consequences. Even late in the era of the practice, this was certainly reflected when many former retainers complained, saying 'Let him die alone as he ate alone', and refusing to accompany their 'masters' during the invasion of 1935–41.

The produce a 'master' shared was collected as tax in kind, *alaba-galaba* or 'surplus-cum-chaff', from lands within his jurisdiction. Often redistribution in the form of banquets and maintenance gifts was seen as expressing the prestige and privilege of those who excelled in warriorhood. As we will discuss presently, beating the drum of authority, sharing the famed cuts of raw meat and *tej* and inviting self-proclamation and the denouncement or praise of others allowed warriors and hunters to celebrate their exploits. The 'master' rewarded them with symbols of power and glory as they publicly displayed their trophies from the hunt or the battlefield.

Banquets in the master's *adarash* included some voluntary (non-tax) inputs from the local community. This contributed to the 'master's' extension of hospitality, not only to community members (including ones seeking justice), whose participation could indicate their degree of loyalty or insubordination, but also to non-locals, including travellers, traders, outsiders seeking justice, state visitors (including government agents passing through), hunters and foreigners. Foreigners, namely 'people from the country of man', as we have seen earlier, dropped by to pay their respects or came to seek help and protection. Depending on circumstances food known as *dirgo* or *metin* was given as maintenance even to local *shifta* (rebels) – gifts that ensured peaceful administration and control of the mobility of travellers. Indeed, the voluntary contribution element served the political purpose of involving the population under the 'master's' jurisdiction in controlling those who did not belong locally. Of course, rigid military command and order were not far below the surface.

Gibir feasts provided by subordinate powerholders to honour a 'master' on his first arrival in a locality[1] also signified the supposedly voluntary recognition of the power and authority of a new appointee. In this instance, *gibir* was akin to the quantified items of prestigious food and beverages given as maintenance to temporary guests.

THE DRUM OF AUTHORITY

Negarit, literally 'teller', was the indispensable drum of authority that was used for announcing *chewa* power. In the expression 'saying everything on the *negarit*', the word stood for bragging or openly telling everything, public or private, to both relevant and irrelevant people, without caring about consequences. The *negarit* was beaten to the accompaniment of *imbelta* and *meleket*, substantial trumpets often played by skilled men from the lowlands of the Ethiopia–Sudan border. Its size was comparable to the drum accompanying the sistrum (*tsinatsil*) and trumpet (*imbelta*) in churches, and probably emulated its biblical use for the Feast of the Tabernacles.[2] Its sound was distinct from the smaller drums known as *kebero*, *atamo* and *dibe* that usually accompanied sing-songs at such social occasions as weddings, or in celebrations of *zar* or other spirits.

Outside the hamlet of an officer or a rebel's camp, drumbeats proclaimed the seat of the local authority, with the number of *negarit* depending on his rank. Outside the hamlet of lower-ranking officers, such as *fitawrari* (more frequently in houses of their superiors) the drum was hit 'once or twice' to invite retainers and guests to attend meals. The strong, deep tones of the drum of authority and the blasts of the *imbelta* would indicate that the 'master' had the high rank and confi-

[1] Mahteme Selassie, *Memories*, 1962, p. 34.
[2] See, for example, Psalm 81 in the Hebrew numbering of the Bible (or Psalm 80 in the Greek and Vulgate translations).

dence assertively to display his power by engaging in public dialogue. Certain sounds announced a decree, in which case they were known as *ye awaj* (proclamation) *negarit*. High officers, especially those known as *balenegarit* ('owner of the drum of authority'), sometimes had their drums sounding continuously outside their hamlets until people gathered.

Symbolically, the multiple meanings of the drumbeats signified the potential primacy of military administration. The drums could indicate that the 'master' was at a *gibir* feast, on a tour of duty or reviewing troops. An army preparing to march was described as 'loading the drum' (*negarit mechan*), and when marching towards a battlefield the army was 'the marching drum', *ye guzo negarit*. The drums were played constantly until specific signals were given to reorder their tempo. As the players beat the drums in the corner of a camp, or from each side of the pack animal they were on when travelling, people recognized the various sounds, rhythms and beats. On battlefields and during expeditions, they indicated the deployment of titled officers or direction of the march. People knew if troops were to move fast or slow, to advance, invade an area, withdraw, pillage or follow other strategies.

During proclamations, the drummers sounded a quick note to herald the appropriate time, and functionaries relayed announcements such as mobilization or other commands by beating pieces of dry hide in marketplaces. With proclamations made on the actual drum of authority, announcers shouted or read aloud the message, with opening curses that evoked supernatural powers. By definition, those who gathered to listen to the announcement were *wegen* (insiders, friends, allies) and those who ignored it were not.

> Listen, listen! May He deprive the enemies of the *adbar* and the *awgar* of harmony![3]
> Listen, listen! May He deprive the enemies of Mary of harmony!
> Listen, listen! May He deprive the enemies of our 'master' of harmony!
> Listen, listen! May He give you harmony!

The words used for harmony also translated as the 'sense of hearing', and inviting everybody to pay attention. When the beats ceased, the 'scribe of orders' (*tsehafi te'ezaz*), accompanied by the mayor (*ligaba*) and treasurer (*bejirond*), came forward to shout or read the announcement. The start of proclamation depended on the matter at hand. In the case of a promotion, for instance, the formula would be: 'I have given this title (or appointment) to my "son" and friend! May they be cursed who do not call him by that title!' Appointments suggested that recruits follow the new appointee, often ending with 'Follow him, those of you who want to do so!' When making several appointments, the declarations of each name, position and title were accompanied by a drumbeat. The *bejirond* would give the appointees regalia appropriate to their new title and position, and lead each to kiss the 'master's' feet to show their gratitude, respect and loyalty. Entry to the banquet hall, which invariably

---

[3] *Awgar*: wooden poles in the walls of houses.

concluded appointments, followed the ranks of the appointees, primacy going to those appointed *ras* or *dejazmach* with the rank of *balenegarit*, 'drum country'. Those given the title *dejazmach* and above were also permitted to 'beat their own *negarit*' to announce the *gibir* that they then gave their families and followers to 'bless' their new regalia, titles and appointments. In fact, court musicians accompanied them to their homes initially. In the case of lower titles, the appointees would beat a piece of dry hide and also hold a substantial *gibir* feast. The appointments symbolized the rising might and purpose of new appointees, who would rally new followers and show appropriate degrees of pageantry in their hamlets. Ignoring this rule would be tantamount to rejecting both the honour and the' master' who gave it.

In the court of Menelik II, a chief drummer made the announcements, with the 'chief of scribes' adding in the case of an imminent war expedition: 'You are told to beat the *negarit* and mobilize the troops!' The announcement elaborated on the causes of the conflict and the place and date of rallying for the expedition. Invariably, the scribe concluded by spelling out future rewards for the brave and punishments for the slack. In a studied formula, leaders and their individual soldiers were addressed with a message on discipline:

ምታ ነጋሪት፡ ከተት ሰራዊት
ስንቅህን ባህያ፡ አመልክን በጉያ፡፡
Beat the *negarit*, mobilize the troops!
Bring your rations on your donkeys; your bad habits in your crotches
[this last could mean suppress your bad habits and 'be man enough']!

An army on the move was said to have 'loaded the *negarit*'. High military officials travelling on official duty, beat their *negarit* and trumpets to say onomatopoeically '*Geber*!', '*Geber*!' ('submit!', 'submit!'). The position from where the main *negarit* was beaten on a battlefield reflected the location of the 'master', and its beat reflected the success or failure of the campaign. Needless to say, the capture of that specific *negarit* led to disarray, as it did when Menelik narrowly escaped with his life during his expedition to the Arsi. His captured drum was taken to a place called Burukte, in Arsi, 'where it still is', according to a piece of oral information I recorded in 1968.

GIBIR AS 'SHARING FOOD'

Holding the politico-military feasts, *gibir*, in the hamlet with drum beats and trumpets showed the capacity of an officer, including a newly appointed 'master', to gather and sustain a large number of followers, supporters and friends (*wegen*) by distributing largesse. The celebrations were intended to convey the authority of personal military power and prowess. Retainers and hunters returning from afar considered their participation in *gibir* as greater than any gifts or rewards. It was the occasion for them, like others participating, proudly to show off the symbols of their position within the politico-military hierarchy.

The food presented during *gibir* was an integral part of the power politics of the *chewa* military establishment. As the attendees claimed the specific portions of meat to which they were entitled, they underlined their privilege by calling upon witnesses of their achievements and status.

Respect for food itself was such a deep-rooted principle that well into the twentieth century people were not to rise from their dining on any account, even if the *neguse negest* were to walk in.[4] The capacity to provide and display food was so militarily significant that it featured during the *Meskel* public holiday at the end of the rainy season. In the early part of the nineteenth century in some areas, *Meskel* feasts were used partly to rally troops before new expeditions, for instance. This was a time for reviewing the troops, announcing individual prowess and honouring deserving soldiers, warriors and officers, celebrating political appointments, land grants, titles and displaying military paraphernalia. Showing large amounts of food as bounty and asserting political power, palace banquets could last from a whole day to several days. The consumption of symbolic cuts of meat and honey mead, added to the beating of the drum of authority, concluded with paramilitary games between members of the household and the rest, or among different groups of the local community.

The performance and behaviour of the participants gave the 'master' the opportunity to pick the most alert and fit as his servants, officials and warriors, and to reward or select for special appointments and membership of councils or special corps. *Zeraf* and *fukera* were expected from participant hunters and other loyal retainers. Depending on the occasion, hunters and warriors celebrated their prizes and displayed their prisoners of war or any trophies they might have collected. The trophies (*seleba*) they brought as evidence of their valour were taken very seriously in rewarding them. They were also inspirational to the young men engaged as pages or in other tasks in the host's household.

Military leaders, including farmers and other individuals, held feasts during work association activities, religious or public holidays, births, marriages, deaths and other social occasions to relate to their wider families and the community. Joyful events such as weddings were accompanied by songs and entertainment. The type of food and drink offered, as well as the way the hostess or household retainers placed morsels of food in the mouths of guests or gave them in small containers, indicated their relative closeness or friendship. The expres-

---

[4] This custom still prevailed as late as the early 1950s. An oral tradition in the Empress Menen School lauded the practice in girls in this boarding school, which the empress sponsored. Reporting how Emperor Haile Selassie chose a wife for one of his sons, Prince Mekonnen, it is said that when he and the empress walked in during lunch, they noted one of the girls, Sara Gizaw, for her good manners: she remained seated while the other girls rose from their seats out of respect for the visitors. It is of course possible that the princess-to-be singled herself out by previous arrangement. She belonged to the *wagshum* family, presumably a status high enough to become wife to the emperor's son.

sion of social distinction around sharing food was standard among warriors, who replicated it in a way familiar to all. Seating guests by the door, by the bedside or by the pillar of the hut reflected relationships and showed relative rank in age and social status. This sense of socializing prevailed more or less intact even to the mid-twentieth century.

At the nineteenth-century military banquet, the list of invited guests signified the host's allies and foes. Some women who were 'masters' in their own right and had *chewa* duties both on the battlefield and off it followed the same practices. The number of guests at military hamlets reportedly ranged from two to three hundred at the feast of a *fitawrari*, and up to three thousand, or sometimes a lot more, at that of a *ras*. On special occasions such as *Meskel*, the guests would be in military attire, with most wearing clothes decorated in gold or silver according to their rank. Carrying at least their spears and shields signifying their status as highly qualified hunters were the wearers of lions' manes (*balegofer*), gold or silver chain earrings (*baleloti*) and silver or ivory armlets (*balebitoa*). High-ranking titled officers wore headgear of iron, silver or gold, and carried (or rather had pages carry) their swords and guns. The presence of such soldiers, collectively known as 'the decorated ones' (*shileme*), was part of the sensation of the increasing din, as Plowden observed,[5] and as the following piece by women singers[6] indicates:

> አንጎት አደራጩሁ ይላል ጎፌሬው
> አቤት ይላል ሲሃድ ጎራዼው
> አበረጃ ያለው ባለዘንገኛው
> አስራ ሁለት ነው የጎራዼው ጭዋ
> ወይ እናቴ ወልዳው ቢሆን ወንድሜ
> His hairstyle, greeting all!
> His sword, supplicating as he walks!
> That one at the door, the one with the club!
> With twelve markers on his sword handle!
> I would that he were born of my mother, as my brother!
> [Rather than as an object of my desire]

As soldiers filed in, according to their status, to eat fresh food placed on top of leftovers, they gloried in the idea of eating the *ej teragi*, 'hand wipe', of the senior ones who had eaten before them. The pieces of meat, the smell of *tej*, and leftovers, namely the points of contact between people along the chain of command, symbolized the 'master's' blessings to his servants and his 'children'. Being deprived of this privilege was resented. A ten-year-old page of *Dejazmach* Beyene, an informant, said that his 'master' punished him once by stopping him from eating with his peers, and 'My *qole* [guardian spirit] left me. I suffered from a skin condition from which I recovered only when my privileges were restored.'[7] Eating off the 'master's' table also had esoteric implications. As my maternal grandfather told us when I was a teenager,[8] as a child

---

[5] Plowden, *Travels in Abyssinia*, 1868, p. 213.
[6] Recollections of my mother, *Weyzero* Workaferahu Haile.
[7] Recollections of Alemu Mekuria, later *Basha* and then *Gerazmach*. He became malnourished, hence his skin problem.
[8] Recollections of Haile Mekuria, later *Kegnazmach* and then *Fitawrari*.

he saw soldiers returning from the palace with pieces of meat from a *gibir* that Menelik gave, saying that these had his *burake*, or blessing and approval. Speaking in a similar vein, a former *azazh* of my paternal grandfather said that when he and other attendants were pressed for time during banquets they sprayed the soldiers waiting in the front yard with *tej*. According to him, the soldiers considered the smell of the *tej* a blessing from their master even without drinking it.[9]

At formal banquets given by a *ras* or a *negus*, the host sat with his important guests towards the inner parts of the hall, sometimes even behind a curtain. The seat was well positioned for him to watch the guests sitting according to their roles – soldiers, hunters, farmers, priests, lawyers and others. He and those near him would be provided with water to wash their hands, while ordinary soldiers were expected to have washed theirs before coming in. The most senior guest would be fed directly into his or her mouth with morsels of food placed on the back of the right hand of an officer. Out of respect, the host's less-ranking guests were served their food on decorated basket-tables, the *masob*, covered with coloured material, and in the case of lower ranks, with calicoes. Distinguished titled officers were given horn-handled knives and glass drinking vessels, while the rest used wooden-handled knives and horn drinking vessels.

To please the ordinary soldiers, the 'master' and those close to him would continue to preside over the feast long after they had finished eating.[10] Ordinary soldiers, especially those planning to be recruited into the service of the feast-giver, clamoured to participate, and were expected to eat quickly and move out to make room for others. They would be seated towards the door on benches at rows of tables on either side of the *adarash*, and were expected to use their daggers or swords to cut their portions of meat. All the guests could give the attendants parcels of food directly into their mouths, and sometimes even sips of *tej*.

Invited members of the local community, including hunters and ordinary soldiers, could use the *fukera* – the emphatic and challenging prose or poetry said with gusto, including it in their ordinary speech to the attendees. The *fukera* poems of nineteenth-century warriors were normally categorical declamations or assertions of brave deeds of the past, and expressions of intended action. Soldiers in military households said them either as challenges to, or declarations of loyalty and support for, the 'master', or to express views on contemporary issues he was known to uphold. Necessarily, therefore, they were mainly political songs of self-praise and statements on strongly felt issues.

Leaders put such store in them that they initiated *fukera* sessions during *gibir* in order to gauge political attitudes or to make their views known. They even risked hosting their local rivals, who might

---

[9] Recollections of *Ato* Tsehainew Deju.
[10] Not observing this custom during banquets that he presided over was one of the allegations of rude behaviour made against *Lij* Iyasu, the uncrowned emperor (r.1913–16).

Photo 6 *Ras* Mengesha Yohannes arrives to attend a banquet in Addis Ababa, 1894; a rare image of arrival at a palace *gibir* (Source: J. G. Vanderheym, *Une Expédition avec Le Négous Ménélik (Vingt Mois en Abyssinie)* (Paris: Hachette, 1896), p. 127)

take the opportunity to raise objections to such administrative abuses as over-taxation or other injustices. Even at local community decision-making meetings, those attending would use impromptu *fukera* to throw challenges and counter-challenges at each other. Those intending to challenge the host, or his views, often bided their time until they acquired similar symbols of power, when they would host an assembly themselves. Deeply felt issues expressed in *fukera* would drown out the voices of entertainers at a local 'master's' *gibir*. If those with grievances against the 'master' challenged him in the presence of his decorated soldiery at his feast, their *zeraf* would signal either rivalry or acknowledgement of a politico-military 'master' greater than his. It could also indicate how much support or defiance he was facing from the local community.

Accommodating newcomers at a *gibir* to which they had not been invited was a way of allowing them to join a 'master's' retinue. It opened up opportunities for refugees, rebels, other supplicants and potential supporters whom the host could benevolently promote. A celebrated poem by an unknown soldier who successfully sent it to an *azmaree* entertaining the banquet shows a way of drawing a master's attention:

> አትሮጥም ይሉኛል መቻ ወፈርኩና
> ልከው ያስጠይቁኝ አበራለሁና
> They tell me I cannot run; as if I am fat!
> Send and investigate, I am at the gate!
> [Send and investigate, I can even fly!]

The first line of this poem indicates that guards had been alleging the man could not run, and the second line, inviting the 'master' to investigate this matter, threatens that this fit and suitable person will go away, in fact fly, to seek a position somewhere else. When such pleas were made, they literally signalled the large number seeking to join his soldiery. The 'master' could assign *baldereba* to them, and even provide them with *qeleb*, 'rations'. It was in the interest of the pages who carried such messages, and of the singers who echoed them, to encourage their 'master' to respond to such supplications benevolently.

CUTTING MEAT

The quality and type of beverages and food – both equally celebrated as part of the processes of military banquets, and the order of serving them at a *gibir*, reflected the military ranks of participating *chewa* warriors. In the heyday of nineteenth-century *chewa* power, brewing the beverage or killing cattle for banquets was exclusive to senior 'masters' alone. Serving specific cuts of raw meat (*qurt*) and *tej*, 'honey mead', accommodated the skilled warriors and hunters who had acquired a lion's mane (*lemid*) 'for their shoulders' and been awarded a silk shirt (*qemis*) for their military achievements. Breaking this rule had serious consequences. A story is told of a farmer, fallen on hard times, who, without a second ox for ploughing, had to sell his ox rather than kill it for badly needed food; having never bothered to become a warrior, he would have broken the law if he had killed it for the family kitchen. According to *Aleqa* Lemma Haylu, interviewed by his son Mengistu Lemma, a rich man who served *tej* at a feast he held was brought to the court of Yohannes IV accused of being a rebel (*shifta*). Judges from Tigre, Wello, Gojam, Shewa and Begemder – the provinces with areas known as *mar ager*, 'honey land' – sentenced him for treason. The judges said that, in their experience, being discovered with *tej* without being authorized to brew it was considered a serious offence punishable by the confiscation of property, even where honey was in abundance:

> It is brought from old times; it stayed from the beginning of time. It is an old custom of Ethiopia. Oh, I do not know why it was abolished later. So many people lost their property also in Shewa for defying the custom.[11]

By the turn of the twentieth century the restrictions had become looser, but as late as the 1960s people recollected 'the old days' when *tej*, *brundo* (choice lean meat) and *tchoma* (choice edible fat) were exclusive to *chewa* homes.

Given that different ranks of warriors and hunters were allocated specific parts of cattle or smaller animals, it seems that breaking the rules attached to the food and beverage offered was confrontational; it implied non-recognition of warriors' ranks. The most celebrated pertinent case is that of Kassa, the future Emperor Tewodros II, who, encouraged by his wife, rebelled against his father-in-law, *Ras* Ali II, the last

---

[11] መንግስቱ ለማ መጽሐፈ ትዝታ ዘአለቃ ለማ (Mengistu Lemma, *The Book of Reminiscences of* Aleqa *Lemma Hailu Welde Tarik*, Addis Ababa University Press, 2015), p. 54.

kingmaker of the Era of Princes, because the cut of meat that Kassa received became 'the straw that broke the camel's back'.

The parts of the animal suitable for food were identified as *tanash, limitch-ayinkash, werch, milas-ena-senber, betesaligegn talaq, yemehal-ageda, yemehal-sebrada, shint, tuntcha (nebro), gibbeta, godentedabit, shagna, firimba*.[12] Except for *gibbeta* and *firimba*, all were offered to respectable guests as raw meat, and the *shagna* was presented as an open fire roast. In descending order of their importance, the honoured parts presented to respectable guests were *tanash, betesaligegn, yemehal-sebrada* and *godentedabit*. These large pieces were never presented if parts had been cut off them, not even to passing guests. Occasional visitors could be offered the *yemehal-sebrada*, or as necessary, the *limitch-ayinkash* and the *godentedabit* (six rib bones). *Yemehal-sebrada* was presented broken into pieces and guests were expected to eat all of it, either raw or roasted on the open fire.

Tongue and tripe (*milas-ena-senber*) were the first parts to be eaten raw. A mixture of minced tripe and liver was a delicacy, eaten raw or rare, and none was to be left overnight. Cooked as *alitcha* (pepperless sauce), the tongue and tripe were also honoured at social feasts. *Talaq* and *shint* were reserved for special dishes of 'mincemeat'. They could also be eaten either as *kitfo* (pepper-spiced raw meat), or as *minchet-abish* (a hot and spicy sauce). *Shagna* had to be cut flat and square if it was to be eaten raw (*witfila*); otherwise, it had to be consumed as fried meat (*tibs*) made by male attendants inside the *adarash*. It was also prepared as *qwanta* (dried meat) for travellers. *Shint* and *talaq* were considered best as dried meat, and *werch, yemehal-ageda, tuntcha* and perhaps *gibita* were also used for that purpose. Tongue and tripe were never used for *qwanta*. A soft and tasty part of the *yemehal-sebrada*, called *tchiqena*, was served for elders and family heads. Meat parts that required a lot of cooking, for instance the *firimba* (meat off the shoulder blade) and the parts from either side of it, and the *gibbeta*, from the breast bones, were never eaten raw; nor were they ever offered to guests.

In 'masters'' banquets the strict rules on meat applied to both its preparation (cooked or raw) and its distribution. It should be emphasized that parts of small animals, though they were cut up into similar sections as the large ones, were not used for distinguishing power relations since no military symbols were attributed to them. They were, however, often offered to those at the head of the table, and to highly respected guests sitting around them, these being beyond challenge. At the *gibir*, the servants of *chewa* 'masters' brought live oxen into the banquet hall, butchered them on the spot and took the pieces to the guests. It was at this juncture that those who needed to show off their valour would recite their war cries and claim the specific parts of beef according to what or who they said they had killed. As a result, oxen killed on the spot during a banquet were the gift with which the

---

[12] The description of this topic comes from my mother who, like all in her high position before 1935, was familiar with the parts and their correct presentation to guests according to their levels of distinction.

'master' challenged his soldiers. This custom was carried out as late as 1935–41 during the invasion, when warriors challenged each other by presenting such feasts.

For the warriors, whatever their occupation – butchers, grass cutters, soldiers or nobles – the importance of sharing meat at the *gibir* by claiming the pieces strictly according to their rank as 'killer', proclaimed and asserted their achievements. There was a strict fixed rule allocating named types of meat (not the amounts) to their status and honour as 'killers'. As guests performed the *zeraf* at the *gibir* they claimed and received these cuts in that order (again, regardless of occupation). In what appears to be a deliberate blurring and reversal of status, the 'master' took only what he deserved as 'killer'. The household staff would not allow claimants to take pieces other than what was fixed by tradition. As each person asserted his claim, he had to say his *zeraf*. Ordinary soldiers entered the hall randomly, but the rank they claimed decided the duration of the *gibir* and the number of cattle butchered for them. The number of cattle killed to accommodate claimants necessarily indicated the overall number of accomplished followers a 'master' could rally.

The highest titleholder took the *shagna* (hump, and therefore with *tchoma*, edible fat), and the most valorous 'killer', the *shint* (thigh). While attendants carried around the huge pieces of raw meat, soldiers, their friends and the 'master' engaged in minimal conversation to watch who deserved this or that cut. Among other travellers, Bruce noted that the meat was so fresh that it still had life in it.[13] Rey wrote: 'As the meat comes really "hot from the cow", the animal having as a rule been only just killed, it is quite tender.'[14] According to Plowden, the correct allocation of meat was extremely detailed, and 'little indeed remains to the master'. It is crucial to understand how broadly the *gibir* involved people. It was a grave insult if a host failed to give due recognition to the achievements, for example 'kills', of ordinary camp followers, who might react by becoming *shifta*:

> All males who follow the camp are included under the term soldier. The grass-cutters and wood-cutters ... are as valorous in pursuit as the best ... Each portion of meat, which ... must be a hundred or so, has its particular claimant, such as the wood-cutter, the grass-cutter, the shield-bearer, the singer or minstrel, the butcher, the maidservants, the *gambo* [pot] carriers, the *tej* maker, and numerous others, all which are scrupulously exacted; the *negarete-match*, or head drummer, also has large rights.[15]

In the 'master's' kitchen, these strict rules also applied if animals were killed to be cooked for a military banquet. *Talaq*, for instance, was often reserved for *menchet-abish*. Household members were left with *dendes*, a part near the spine, the *werch* (cut from the *shagna*), *yemehal-ageda*, *tuntcha* and *shagna*. Ordinarily, liver, a delicacy served with tripe, was given to the 'master' and his special guests. In the

---

[13] Bruce, *Travels and Discoveries*, 1885, p. 141.
[14] C. F. Rey, *In the Country of the Blue Nile*, London: Duckworth, 1927, p. 147.
[15] Plowden, *Travels in Abyssinia*, 1868, p. 58.

context of the military *gibir*, however, liver was proverbially allocated to the buffoon.

If the animal had been killed for home consumption, family and friends ate whatever they liked. Needless to say, in 'ordinary' *chewa* homes chunks of beef (raw or cooked), lamb, mutton, goat and certain types of edible wildfowl were served randomly to all. The chicken's head, however, was strictly served only to the family head, because Emperor Yekuno Amlak took the throne in 1270 'having eaten the head of a cock' after he heard a prediction that whoever ate its head would be king. With this kitchen tale, women still serve it to the family man, or to one of his sons, with the words 'You never know; it might make him king one day!' Another esoteric explanation given in oral tradition prohibits certain parts of beef to royalty and other descendants of the 'children of Israel'. They are supposed not to eat the sinew that runs in the hollow of the thigh (*shuleda*) because God, who struggled against Jacob one night, defeated him[16] by paralysing him in that part of his body.[17]

DRINKING *TEJ*

Making and serving *tej* in one's home emphatically displayed hierarchical power. At military feasts, its potency functioned as a catalyst arousing soldiers to declare their warriorhood. A 'master' showed his esteem for his guests by the amounts and quality of *tej* he served. Depending on whether they were residing with him or travelling, guests of high significance and autonomy even received pots of *tej* and food at their quarters or at their camp outside the hamlet of the 'master'. Drinking *tej* at a master's banquet was, according to Plowden, 'the end and soul of the existence of the Abyssinian soldier, great and small'.[18] On entering the banquet hall, soldiers tried to sit as close as possible to the earthen pots containing the drink. An example of this was observed at *Dejazmach* Biru Goshu's, where gunners and men of distinguished courage were admitted first, and they clamoured to sit near the drinks pots. The frequency of serving *tej* on days other than public and religious holy days depended on the wealth of the 'master' and whether he had obligations to entertain important state prisoners, long-distance traders or other guests residing in his jurisdiction. At times of widespread trouble, 'masters' increased the size of drinking vessels to keep the soldiers happy. For example, *Negus* Tekle Haymanot of Gojam ordered vessels 'twelve times' the normal size in order to stop his soldiers deserting him for fear of lack of *tej*.[19]

[16] Genesis, Chapter 32, verses xxii–xxiii.
[17] No lungs of any animal were ever eaten. The intestines of beef or mutton were given to those who made strings out of it (for instance, Gurage of the early twentieth century) for use in stringed musical instruments or for securing skin bags.
[18] Plowden, *Travels in Abyssinia*, 1868, p. 59.
[19] Tekle Iyesus, *Aleqa: History of Ethiopia*, pp. 92–4.

Attendants chosen for their alertness were in constant touch with their 'master' over serving *tej* during the *gibir*. They discretely collaborated with him in controlling its consumption, as witnessed by Plowden at a private party in the house of a *dejazmach*:

> The attendants regulate their drinking by that of their master; so that by the time he is entirely drunk, they might be three parts so, or thereabouts; and this being a social little party, even the human candlesticks[20] are not omitted.[21]

As mentioned, the symbolic significance of *tej* also extended to receiving the 'master's blessing'. For instance, a 'master' would free his heroic warrior slave by spraying *tej* on him from his mouths just as elders blessed their protégés by spraying spittle from their mouths. Also involving honey was the ritual use made of it when adopting non-related persons as kin – as we have seen: the adopted fictive kin suckled honey from the thumb of the 'parent'. In many parts of the south, where beekeeping is associated with the despised specialist potter or blacksmith communities, honey is still widely used for ritual purposes.

Providing and receiving food and drink, especially meat and *tej*, for symbolic use was perhaps the ultimate expression of *chewa* exercise of privileged power. Made rare commodities by law, the political use of *tej* and beef ritually reclassified their potency, even in rituals of belongingness. Putting them beyond the reach of non-soldiers distinguished the warriors from the rest, and made their privileges equivalent to associating their identity with the land they were expected to defend to the death. Engaging in these idealized privileges was tantamount to socializing the hunter-warrior ritually into soldier and defender – a process of transforming ordinary men. Lamentations for the deaths of 'masters' usually had refrains that recalled the *tej* and *tchoma* (choice edible fat) that they used to provide. Thus, an unknown poet lamenting the death of *Lij* Iyasu, one of whose horse-names was *Aba* Gragn, ran:

ግራኝ ወዳጄ ግራኝ ወዳጄ
የሚያበላኝ ጮማ የሚያጠጣኝ ጠጁ
ግራኝ ወዳጄ
Gragn, my friend! Gragn, my friend!
The *tchoma* he fed me with, the *tej* he got me to drink!
Gragn, my friend![22]

ZERAF WAR-CRIES AND SONGS: EXPRESSING POLITICO-MILITARY OPINIONS

The custom of allowing ordinary people to express themselves, especially on political matters, was yet another nineteenth-century

---

[20] A reference to pages, some of whose duties included holding wax candles. They also shielded their 'master' on the battlefield with their togas when privacy was called for, e.g. when he relieved himself or changed his clothes.
[21] Plowden, *Travels in Abyssinia*, 1868, p. 210.
[22] From recorded music made around the 1950s.

practice. It was expressed especially in *fukera* during *gibir*. The use of war-cries aroused by the strength of feeling on issues was widespread in all linguistic areas, including the formerly autonomous entities of Keffa, Wolayta and the smaller ones along the Gibe River. Shepherds, traders, hermits and other travellers spread popular *fukera*, thereby transmitting messages between the highlands and the associated lowlands. The most outstanding recording in the Oromo language was made by Cerulli.[23] A standard version in Amharic started with:

> የማንን አገር ማን ይወስዳታል
> የማንን እናት ማን ይነካታል
> የማንንስ ሚስት ማን ያንገላታል
> ወንድ ልጅ አላት ይሞትላታል
> Whose country, who will take!
> Whose mother, who will touch!
> Whose wife, who will manhandle!
> She has a man who will die for her!

Valorous and established warriors and hunters known to the attendants used the occasion of banquets to make their points. The challenges and counter-challenges would start when a claimant of a special cut of meat suddenly said his *zeraf* and *fukera* as follows:

> ዘራፍ የአገሌ አሽከር
> የእንትን ላይ ገዳይ
> የእንትን ገዳይ
> ይህን ያህል ገዳይ
> ካይናችሁ ያውጣኝ ጌቶቼ
> Zeraf, so-and-so's servant!
> Killer at such-and-such a place!
> Killer of such-and-such an animal!
> Killer of such-and-such a number!
> May He spare me from your eyes, my masters!

In this typical studied start (*qinkena*) to *zeraf* recitations, the first line declared loyalty to a particular named master, and the rest enumerated the speaker's exploits – of animal and human kills or prisoners taken. His peers and witnesses would punctuate his words with 'it's true' or 'it's a lie!', thus acknowledging or challenging his claims. The standard *zeraf* ending – 'May He spare me from your eyes, masters' (*Kaynachihu yawtagn getoche*) – also challenged all at the banquet.

The provocative plea was with God to spare him – the precious, fresh and valorous killer – from the jealous and evil watchful 'eyes'. It also challenged those who had not done as well. It is said that warriors used to foam at the mouth from the speed and sensation of their own gusto (*dinfata*), and their listeners would be aroused to the point of restlessness. All being well, the rest at the banquet would show their support, approval and appreciation by saying *Nor! Nor!* (at *gibir* this meant 'hail!'; normally it welcomes someone respectfully into a room), and attendants would assist by offering *tej* to the *fokari* (the one saying the *fukera*,

---

[23] See, for example, song 24 in Enrico Cerulli, *The Folk Literature of the Galla of Southern Abyssinia* (Harvard Africa Studies, Vol. 3), Cambridge, MA: African Department of the Peabody Museum of Harvard University, 1922, pp. 45–51.

here meaning the presentation in general) if the host approved. This was in acknowledgement of the status, real or potential, of the *fokari* as a warrior. The words of the *fukera* were considered inspirational to the young, who reportedly begged and clamoured to go on hunting expeditions every time they were exposed to *gibir* sessions.[24] In that sense, the *zeraf* was similar to presenting trophies (*geday metal*) to a 'master', a father, or whoever had sponsored a hunter's expeditions.

Declamations during *fukera* implicated the individual person's social circle, *wegen*, the local community or *hager*, all of whom were expected to take responsibility for the announced theme, including defending local land and its extended meaning of 'country'. Once they made their intentions known, therefore, individuals would carry them out without resorting to murder (which would incur capital punishment, payment of blood money, or confiscation of property). As their intended message and action implicated their community, everybody would also suffer the consequences of blood money payment, confiscation of communal land or revenge in case of murder. A 'master' not agreeing to popular demands made during his banquet, even if only stated by an individual, could show his political skill by political manoeuvrings. Not doing so would lose him local communal and military support. His followers might even refuse to respond to his mobilization, or disobey him in other ways, and, if necessary, might battle against him.

A *gibir* held when declaring war following a political event would occasion exchanges between challenger and challenged. Known as *mefwaker* (a word suggesting not only throwing words at each other, but also a serious display of courage and competition to supersede others) the exchanges would focus on the purpose at hand. Formally, *mefwaker* could be through runners bringing the messages back and forth, or informally, through singers at *gibir*. Disgraced and pardoned former retainers might be admitted to the banquets too, and even allowed to express their opinion. Important prisoners would be seated where their humiliation relative to their former status would show, and their soldiers would be barred from participation unless they had changed sides. More often than not, humiliated leaders would only 'throw' couplets of sadness and sorrow at the harp/lyre (*begena*) players. A man of high status, wrongly condemned for treason and punished with losing his eyes but later declared innocent, was invited to the banquet of his 'master' where he said to the *begena* player:

> ሁለት ዜዬ በላሁ እዚህ ቤት ገብቼ
> ፊትም በነጋሪት ኋላም ተመርቼ
> I ate twice, in this hall!
> With *negarit* before, and with a guide later!

[24] Although *gibir* accompanied with *fukera* is no longer practised, soldiers are still held in the highest esteem because of their identity as soldiers; at least, their tales of heroism are listened to with admiration. Such ways of thinking continue to be apparent, for example when children take up the 'whipping' game (*jeraf*) during the rainy season, and when Ethiopians resorted to military ways of sorting out their political difficulties as in 1974 and 1991.

Controversial points too can be raised, even concerning those attending the banquet. In the following example a message is sung out by supporters of *Dejazmach* Zewde who had rebelled against his father-in-law and overlord *Dejach* Goshu. Zewde had tricked his father-in-law into allowing him to see his wife while he was in prison, and she had given birth as a consequence:

> ቤተስኪያን አትግባ ዘውዴ አለ ብይን
> ሚስትህ ተወለደች አንተማራስ ሁን
> Do not go to church, Zewde, there is a law!
> Now that your wife has given birth, be a *ras* yourself!²⁵

In this verse with a double meaning the surface 'wax' meaning indicated that it was a good thing that his wife had given birth, but it also advised that, like the new mother who should refrain from going to church until the completion of her purification ritual, Zewde should stay away from public view until the appropriate time. The 'gold' (deeper meaning) was telling this *shifta* not to ring the church bell seeking amnesty. Now that his wife has a child, the relationship with the 'master', who happens to be his father-in-law, would be close in any case. It would be worth his while to bide his time and seek the position of *ras*.

Once the political purpose was established and underscored at a *gibir*, all could voice their opinion, however uncomfortable it was to the 'master'. Warriors claiming portions of meat could highlight divided loyalties, expecting a 'master' to tolerate them benevolently. As a whole, the 'master', his followers and the rest attending the banquet were seen as distinguished and worthy soldiers who could defy and control their enemies. Depending on the circumstances, the warriors were considered capable of excluding unwanted high authority, including the 'master' himself or significant rebels (*shifta*). The session allowed the host to gauge the trend of opinion in his jurisdiction and, of course, the level of support or insubordination he faced on specific matters such as prisoners of war or tax increments.

Zeraf was also a social display by individual *fokari*. For instance, during a political meeting it would be used to mention the people or objectives they 'would die for' in appropriate songs and poems. Except when holding guns with the barrel facing down, *fokari* would hold their weapons with pantomimic gestures of a fighting man. The 'master' or another promoter of an issue would provide support by raising an *aqrari*, a specialist in arousing emotions by singing the *shilela* (*qererto*, or *gerara* in Oromo). These professional men and women singers would be known for their good voices at weddings, funerals, political gatherings and during mobilization. Having them sing when opinion was divided was a usual tactic for influencing people at military or political meetings. An established 'master' would have more than one *shelay* in his permanent pay, and during an expedition several were spaced at equal distance in the marching army to keep up the warriors' spirits.

---

²⁵ Mahteme Selassie, *Memories*, 1962 EC, 1958, p. 332.

Sung slowly and loudly in long drawn-out tunes, *shilela* were audible beyond the immediate surroundings. Unlike *fokari* (those who perform *fukera*), *shelay* (those who perform songs to arouse challenges and counter-challenges) were said to be audible from mountaintop to mountaintop. It will be recalled that similar poems helped Menelik's acceptance in Shewa after his escape from the prison of Magdala in 1868. As the singers tried to arouse feelings, often by using standard beginnings, soldiers or would-be soldiers were expected to respond with *fukera*. If the *shelay* (the performer) started to sing after someone declaimed his *fukera*, their theme would be from that source, at least at the beginning. They could be prompted by others, as *Dejach* Germame did, in order to attract people from afar. The social contexts of *shilela* and *fukera* provided the themes for Germame, who used the services of Enat Awaj to criticize Menelik for billeting his personal retainers on Shewa.

In local historiography, a warrior's *shilela* and/or *fukera* were reported as 'the statement' that the 'master' made before taking up arms. Most such songs found in late nineteenth-century writings expressed the opinions of established soldiers and interested politicians addressing leaders or influential people. A common beginning (*qinkena*), punctuated with themes that were given eventually, was:

> እረ ጎራው እረ ደኑ
> እረ ጎራው እረ ደኑ
> እረ ጎበዝ እረ ጀግና
> እረ ገዳይ እረ ገዳይ እረ ገዳይ እረ ገዳይ
> Come, the *gora* [valley!]! Come, the *denn* [forest]!
> Come, the *gora*! Come, the *denn*!
> Come, *gobez* [young and brave]! Come, *jegna* [hero]!
> Come, 'killer'! Come, 'killer'! Come, 'killer'!

The following was considered appropriate if the meeting was about a war that had been declared by someone the protagonists regarded with low esteem:

> የፍየል መጣጤ ልቡ የጎበረበት
> እንዋጋ ብሎ አነብር ላከበት
> የፍየል መጣጤ ዘጠኝ ተመልጻለች
> ስምንቱን ጨርሳ ባንዱ ታለቅሳለች
> The young goat with the swollen heart
> Declared war against the leopard!
> This she-goat calves nine,
> Finishes eight, and is left with only one to cry over!

In these examples, the names of those declaring war would be mentioned instead of 'goat'. The names of local leaders would be inserted in the place of the generalized *denn* (forest), *gora* (valley) or *gobez* (brave). Such *fukera* beginnings, as with hunter's songs, were understood as addressing the whole community or the brave young individual warriors, or generally proclaiming the importance of fighting. In the following Amharic standard *shilela*, the repetitive words and phrases were meant to attract attention. Every second line of the poem followed from the spirit of the time, some from historically famous incidents:

ገለሌ ደሞም ገለሌ ደሞም ገለሌ
ይቀነጠለማል ከነዝናሩ ከነፈረሱ
ገለል በሉት አንድዜ ለሱ
ግልግል ያውቃል ከነፈረሱ
በለው! በለው በለው
በለው! በለው በለው
ወንዶች አሉበት ሜዳው ምቹ ነው
ጦር አወራወሩ እንዳባቱ ነው
ከዋሽ ማዶ በቀልቀለቱ
ደፋው በንጉቱ
ወይ እናቱ አይደለሁ ሚስቱም አይደለሁም
ወይ በሆንኩኝ እቱ
ሳየው ሽነጠኝ እኔ ሴቲቱ
በለው! በለው! ሲል ነው የጋሜ ኩራቱ
ሴትም ትዋጋለች ከረጋ መሬቱ
ኽረ ነ ጎበዝ ኽረ ነ ጀግና ኽረ ነ ጉብል
እምቢ አሻፈረኝ እምቢ አሻፈረኝ እምቢ አሻፈረኝ
ለቆላ ለደጋው እዳን አለብኝ

The lone one,[26] again the lone one, and again the lone one!
Restless, with his cartridge belt and his horse!
Make room for him.
He knows what to do.
Do it! Do it! Do it!
Do it! Do it! Do it!
There are men in it, and the plain is convenient!
His spear throwing is like his father!
Beyond the Awash, at the precipice,
He strangled and threw him face down!
I'm neither his mother nor his wife!
Wish I were his sister!
The sight of him has stirred me, the woman!
The pride of youth [*game*] is when it heats up!
Even woman can fight when the land is peaceful!
Come, the brave! Come, the hero! Come, the youth!
No, I refuse! No, I refuse! No, I refuse!
I owe it to the lowlands and to the highlands!

The reference to the Awash in the above poem recalls the annual raids and counter-raids between the populations on either side of the river from at least the late eighteenth century. When troops of Gojam and Shewa fought each other 'to reclaim' the western lands in 1882, Menelik's troops were reported to have said in advance:[27]

ኽረ ለምን ይሆን ውሉ የፈረስ
የሚሞት ሰው አለ ቀኑ የደረስ
ሴቶች ተሰብስቡ እንርገጥ ዳንኪራ
ክርክር አይቀርም ከከሰው ጋራ

Oh, why could it be the agreement is broken!
Someone's days are numbered!
Come, women! Let us step the *dankira* [dance]!
Disputing that man is inevitable!

In the courts of established 'masters', as in ordinary countryside meetings, *shilela* were known to have convinced people to consider the period's political issues and even resort to coercive action. Individuals who

---

[26] This refrain is attributed to Sahle Selassie, *negus* of Shewa. The set of poems are oral recollections.
[27] Recollections of my mother, *Weyzero* Workaferahu Haile.

initiated *shilela* at local decision-making meetings of their communities might achieve spontaneous applause and support for a military uprising. They could attract sympathetic responses, even if temporarily, that might lead to the formation of a band of soldiers whose *fukera* and *zeraf* affirmed agreement. As late as the Italian invasion of 1935–41 it was common for such sessions at community meetings to be followed by military offensives.

In the nineteenth century, 'masters' used the drinking occasions to instigate *fukera* in ways that suited their purposes. Hosts prolonged *gibir* sessions, after providing the soldiers with *tej* and raw meat, and inviting them to recite their *zeraf* and *fukera*. Discreet communication between the 'master' and his domestics facilitated and controlled the candour, openness and sincerity of the atmosphere. Meanwhile, domestics and others transmitted military repartee on themes that the 'master' wanted conveyed and spread far and wide. In other words, *tej*-instigated *fukera* could lead to aggression and even rebellion. That is, the sessions could usefully arouse the desired spirit in all, especially on the eve of declaring war. No one would be allowed to be so drunk as to be disorderly. The 'master' would have set the theme for war-cries and boasting via the pages who took his verbal messages to the singers (*azmaree*). The latter would start only when he signalled them to do so. High-ranking officers would respond loudly with repartee couplets, and ordinary soldiers would join in with their *fukera*. Prompting by the singers might, for example, compare the guests with inanimate objects, for instance with widely known refrains such as:

> በልቶ ዝም የድስት ወንድም
> ውጦ ዝም የጋን ወንድም
> Eat-quiet, brother of the cooking pot!
> Swallow-quiet, brother of the brewing pot!

Indeed a joyous and complete military banquet had to include the energetic reciting of *dinfata* – war-cries and threats after eating and drinking. Plowden, among others, observed while the entertainment progressed:

> Meanwhile the mead is not idle; a buffoon, or rather a fool, enters and makes the chief laugh; *Asmarees* at the farther end, with one-stringed fiddles, begin their praise of the entertainer; outside the *negarete* [drum of authority] and *umbilta* [trumpet] are heard through the increasing din; and presently as all get warmed, horsemen, dressed in the most splendid array, are seen galloping up to the tent, shouting their war-cry, and brandishing their spears.[28]

However, a famous example of an *azmaree*-provoked session from the early twentieth century involved *Lij* Iyasu (r.1913–16). Finding himself under the strict tutelage of a regent, the prince used the process to provoke insulting comments on the exploits of the senior warriors of his grandfather, Menelik II. This eventually gained him some independence from the old palace guards and government authorities, but made him unpopular. The misplaced challenge he threw at them during

---

[28] Plowden, *Travels in Abyssinia*, 1868, p. 213.

a state banquet aroused such resentment that the highly qualified senior soldiers engaged in *fukera* on the spot, undertaking to work hard to remove him from office.

With the privilege of brewing *tej* or killing cattle for meat, collecting these animals and honey as tax gave high-ranking *chewa* officers a monopoly in distributing these products as gifts locally. Their superiors would do the same in the wider areas they controlled. As well as using the symbolic value of *tej* for liberating slaves, honey for adopting dependent 'children', or meat for the rituals that symbolized warriorhood, they could enhance their centrality as 'masters' by displaying largesse. In addition, cattle, honey and other resources received as tribute enriched the treasury of the state and empowered it to run its defence through the *chewa* system, as well as its judiciary and other state institutions beyond the scope of this book.

BATTLEFIELD SYMBOLS AND TROPHIES

Organizing the declarations of warriorhood and its practices had a historical impact on Ethiopian society. Aside from displaying personal involvement, the feasts and military paraphernalia identified *chewa* warriors' place in the politico-military system. In the early nineteenth century, when *chewa* engaged in fighting during the annual cycles of wars to control the Ethiopian region by claiming the areas frequented by trophy hunters, the trophies manifested the symbolic values and privileges of territorial power. A trophy from a human body symbolized the power to deprive the enemy (*dina*) of essential masculinity. When collected on the battlefield, the trophy distinguished friend from 'blood enemy' (*dina*) symbolically. Acquiring the *seleba* was considered a great feat of manhood, and, in a wider sense, signified victory over the 'wild' environment that the enemy posed. The banquet at which successful warriors were honoured showed off the growth of the fighting force with which to control the enemy, subjugate possible local dissent, and of course overcome ecological challenges.

The practice of taking human trophies was found among the Amhara, the Oromo, the Sidama and all the lowlanders in the Rift Valley and the eastern escarpments, including the Somali. The more such *seleba* a man acquired, the more valorous he was considered to be. Soldiers brought such trophies from the battlefield, and rural people glorified themselves by taking them during and after battles when provoked by advance troops (*werari*). The aspiration to take trophies was so widespread, and so frequent, that, in practice, establishing who was liable for emasculation was difficult. In general terms, and theoretically, Christians did not emasculate other Christians and Muslims did not emasculate co-religionists. Highlanders believed that lowlanders would emasculate them if they travelled on their own in their midst, and vice versa. Outside of warfare, that is, emasculation appears to have followed perceptual classification of 'local' and 'outsider', determined perhaps according to topographical divisions.

The word *seleba* denoted 'spiriting away' anything – from human relationships to material objects. In everyday language, to be *selabi* was 'to acquire' magical or supernatural powers. Warriors were known to justify the booty, *zerefa*, of crops and goods from farmers near the site of battle, by claiming that they captured them from the enemy. On the battlefield, *seleba*, reported also by travellers,[29] had a different meaning. Referring to cutting the male genitalia as a trophy, it had similar importance to the hunter obtaining a 'tail' (*marta*) from his 'first kill' (*mera*). Tales exist of desperate men even murdering their friends, companions or relatives who trusted them to get the *seleba*, and then being brought to court by suspicious relatives. Officially, therefore, claims of acquiring *seleba* were allowed to stand only with additional evidence from eyewitnesses.

Warriors presented *seleba* to their 'master' in a ritual that was spoken of as 'throwing the *geday* ("kill")'. In the same sense that the *seleba* was 'spiriting away' the essence of anything by supernatural powers, acquiring a trophy from the enemy implied taking away the victim's identity, and perhaps personality. It meant that the trophy hunter or warrior deprived someone else of their social standing and (including animals representing human beings) their physical and spiritual identity and well-being. Saying *zeraf* while 'throwing down' the trophy, the valiant warrior declared his invincibility. Performed in the same spirit, a hunter 'throwing down' *marta* showed the number and types of kills he had achieved, while the *seleba* from the battlefield symbolized a warrior's intention to be established as a soldier. Indeed, the *seleba* could even be seen as the highest achievement of an individual on the battlefield. This conclusion is made on the basis of what individual soldiers were supposed to learn from their military training while growing up, a fact that has not been included in the search for a universal meaning of emasculation, including its occurrence at the Battle of Adewa in 1896, as we will see below.[30]

'Masters' receiving such *geday* from soldiers had the obligation to organize a session for their social recognition. This was done through the *gibir*, banquet, provided after warriors had thrown down their *seleba* and other booty to the 'master', singing out: '*Zeraf*, killer of such-and-such a number!' After the *fukera*, the 'master' would determine what the warrior could keep. The soldier with the most trophies from the human enemies killed would be given a place near the 'master'. The rewards that trophy collectors achieved could increase in the course of their politico-military lives. The presentation of

[29] See for instance Hotten, *Abyssinia and its People*, 1969 [1868], p. 45, referring to what Henry Salt witnessed in 1809/10, and quoting De Bry writing in 1599.
[30] Raymond Jonas has discussed such possibilities as the practice being punishment, or of biblical origin, or a sign of victory over the vanquished. See his *The Battle of Adwa: African victory in the age of empire*, Cambridge, MA: Belknap Press of Harvard University Press, 2011, pp. 221–8.

trophies and booty guaranteed the 'master' an increased following, and by the *gibir* he gained in his status. In receiving and throwing down *geday* (kill), *gibir* and *seleba* combined the various meanings and symbolisms of displaying collective power. Ideally, one *seleba* was supposed to be enough.[31] The symbolisms of *seleba* and *gibir* intertwined to strengthen the *chewa*'s socio-political significance: *gibir* by including more supporters (*wegen*), and *seleba* by excluding the enemy (*dina*).

By showing their visible achievements – *seleba* and/or booty – warriors could attract followers. Their claims in *fukera* at the banquets, if positively acknowledged, might be seen as a form of legitimate certification as soldiers. While collecting first-time *seleba* from a human enemy or *marta* from wild game was conceptually a once-in-a-lifetime exercise for a warrior, his performance at *gibir* represented his transition from one stage of social life to the next. A young trainee became an accomplished soldier ready for expeditions.

It is difficult to put a date on when the practice of emasculation by the emergent *chewa* warriors started. Warriors in general practised such mutilation in the late nineteenth century, and, as we saw above, Menelik issued an edict to stop the practice in 1882. As we will see below, however, it was in evidence at the Battle of Adewa against the Italians in 1896 as well as during the second Italian invasion of 1935–41. At the start of the second invasion, warriors in some localities reportedly showed the Italians, on whose side they were fighting, *seleba* that included women's breasts or heads,[32] and similarly ripped open pregnant women in eastern Shewa to emasculate their unborn male foetuses. The practice of *seleba* was still in evidence in the late 1950s, and the fear of it continues.

GIBIR AS MAINTENANCE

In practical terms, a *chewa* 'master's' redistribution of resources was extended to gifts he made to visitors in areas under his jurisdiction. Known as *mestengido*, 'guest-hood', these were often 'quality gifts' for maintenance (*dirgo*), and some were *metin* (a specified 'quantity' for a limited period). In official cases, *dirgo* recipient guests would be known as *dirgogna*, and, depending on their status, would receive fixed amounts of uncooked food and *tej* at regular intervals. Government-sponsored guests, including foreign travellers, received

---

[31] *Chewa* progress along a social and military hierarchy was as rigid as it was in the Oromo *gada* cycle, where age-based engagements brought men into an eight-year cycle of wars of migration. Between the sixteenth and eighteenth centuries, on their trek from the south to the west and the north, such Oromo warriors practised *seleba* and glorified themselves by it.

[32] They presented these trophies to those they assumed to be their new 'masters', the Italians, who, having no knowledge of the ethnography, had no idea what to do with them.

amounts quantified by the state. In the case of local visitors, for instance marriage negotiators, the amount of *metin* would depend entirely on the 'master's' personal treasury. The local community would contribute officially only if they felt he deserved their additional input for this personal occasion.

It is worth noting here that giving *dirgo* was an honour, but receiving it, particularly over a long period of time, was an embarrassment. Occasionally a 'master' would use such gifts to show off his wealth and status so that his visitors' retainers would defect to his camp. In other words, such rations were ways of attracting potential soldiers who would swell the retinue, and the local 'master' would accommodate their requests at his discretion. Recipients were expected either to go away, prove their valour and be independent, or to bring themselves and their followers under the service of the local 'master', conveying their intention through the *baldereba* that the 'master' would have assigned to them. Earlier in the nineteenth century, when foreigners were considered threats to the safety and security of the territories through which they were expected to pass, high officials frequently used delays and lapses in allocating *dirgo* to control and regulate their movements. Foreign travellers reported that the *baldereba* subjected them to considerable humiliation in order to hasten them into deciding their next move.

Similarly, controlled allocation of *dirgo* was made to *shifta* and potential upstarts who might challenge local authority. The 'master' could assign a *baldereba* to *shifta* with a considerable following from elsewhere, but without appropriate income. The *baldereba* would do all in his power to impress them with his master's benevolence, wealth and power, and might even get them invited to occasional banquets so that the 'master' could judge their temper and military capacity. As we saw earlier, *shifta* were an anomalous group in the military and political order, and helping them often led to accommodating them as supportive warriors. In their own setting *shifta* followed the same processes, and, like those who chose to be independent of local powerholders, they might shelter others aspiring to challenge authority. The degree to which *shifta* were accommodated in the local community might even encourage them to beat the *negarit*, sound trumpets, collect *gibir* as tax in kind and even give feasts for their followers. As evinced in the case of *Dejazmach* Kassa Haylu (later Tewodros II), challenging their activities would incur their hostility and that of the local community sheltering them.

A local community's support for *gibir* feasting and for the provision of *dirgo* and *metin* showed the level of power a 'master' exercised. Nineteenth-century titled officials and other 'masters' imposed taxes for specific purposes on behalf of their superiors. Some even recovered for themselves from the local community the equivalent of the gifts they had made to guests. The local community might consider their 'master' as 'father', patron and defender, and would comply, allowing guests to travel through its lands without molestation, and responding positively when the 'master' sent his 'servants' to collect taxes or additional supplies.

Taking such additional gifts without the use of force could cause problems for the non-military sector supporting the 'master'. The community could be defiant and rebellious and try to exclude the 'master' or his guests from their midst, and he could engage in punishing them, for instance, by expelling the defiant from their lands. As we have seen, the occurrence of such irregularities was reduced by Menelik's system of checks and balances that he set up alongside the *chewa*. Placing the *Dembegna* alongside corps of *chewa* warriors left the non-military sector of the administration to operate through the underlying principle of the fear of God (*feriha Egziabher*).

The *chewa*, whose power was thus reduced, evaluated the weakness of governments after Menelik in their own terms – the idiom of *gibir*. Menelik's reign, which saw relative peace after 1896, was implicitly felt as the *zemene tsigab* ('era of plenty'). Probably dating from the 1920s, the following three lines rhymed the rulers' names with pithily expressed dire conditions of *gibir* under *Lij* Iyasu, Empress Zewditu (r.1916–30) and *Ras* Tafari (later Haile Selassie I (r.1930–74)):

> በኢያሱ ዳቦ ነው ትራሱ
> በዘውዲቱ ተደፋ ሌማቱ
> በተፈሪ ጤፉ ፍርፋሪ
> In the days of Iyasu, bread is for pillow;
> In the days of Zewditu, the table[33] is overturned;
> In the days of Tafari, even leftovers don't exist!

The ditty encapsulates the continued relative prosperity in the days of *Lij* Iyasu (r.1913–16), who gave way to the powerless Zewditu, and the totally different atmosphere engendered by her regent, Tafari. In general, the ditty expresses regrets about the diminishing importance and continuing marginalization of the *chewa* in the first few decades of the twentieth century. Referring first to plenty, followed by greed and lastly shortages, the attitudes in these lines focuses on the changing function of feasting as a *chewa* military tradition of relating to the public.

The transition to salaried state office holders in the first three decades of the twentieth century was characterized by two different ways of seeing the use of resources and the exercise of power – one newly imposed and one long-established – that added to the marginalization of the *chewa*. In the early days of Empress Zewditu, when *Ras* Biru replaced *Dejazmach* Balcha Safo (horse-name: *Abba* Nefso) as governor of Sidamo, one of the difficulties was paying tax in cash to the *ras*, who was salaried. The following couplet reflects this, and

---

[33] The table is made of basketwork, including its lid, which normally 'honours' the presence of food underneath while keeping away prying eyes and flies. The lid is overturned when the table is empty; a ready metaphor for poverty. This and the following poem are from the recollections of my mother, *Weyzero* Workaferahu Haile.

implies a lack of input from him in the form of the banquets that the *dajazmach* used to give:

ብሬን ብሩ በላው እህሌን አምበጣ
እባክህ አምላኬ አባ ነፍሶን አምጣ

Biru has eaten my *birr* (cash) and the locust my crop;
Please, God, bring back *Abba* Nefso.

The *ras* was famed for laughing off such comments, but later composers who initiated such ditties were seen as hostile to *mengest* (government) and began to get into trouble with the authorities. The subsequent silence, apart from a brief resurgence during *ye telat werera zemen* ('period of enemy invasion') of 1935–41 when the state had collapsed, indicates both the end of *chewa* predominance and the start of despotism. The end of the banquets and *fukera*, which had represented *chewa* political parlance, was also the end of a two-way means of communication between state and people at the grassroots.

9

First Italian Invasion, 1896

In the second half of the nineteenth century, British and French rivalry for colonial domination of the Red Sea posed a threat to Ethiopia greater than historical Egyptian and Turkish hostilities. In growing control of Egypt and promoting its interests in the Suez Canal, Britain was encouraging Italy to occupy parts of Ethiopia. Though Italy had emerged as a unified country only in 1861, an Italian company had bought the coastal town of Assab from its local ruler in 1869, thus providing it with a foothold in the region, and Britain was intending to use this to stop the French making overland links between Fashoda on the White Nile and Djibouti on the Red Sea.[1] At the same time, the British, French and Italians were divisively calling the northern parts of the country 'Abyssinia', using the country's proper name, Ethiopia, only in their diplomatic communications with its rulers. From about 1875, Emperor Yohannes IV had been repulsing attacks from Egyptians, who were coming under the hold of the British. He was insisting on the restoration of Senhit and Massawa, and had his governors collecting taxes and politically relating to the local population along the Red Sea coast.[2] His ruler of Hamasien, *Ras* Alula, encountered five hundred Italian soldiers marching treacherously from the Red Sea coast in January 1887 (having promised not to march inland) and duly wiped them out at Dogali, near Massawa. In 1889 Yohannes routed an Egyptian-supported attack on Metemma, but he lost his life to a stray wing of the retreating Mahdist army.

Such European hostility could not have come at a worse time for Ethiopia. Famine, pestilence and drought (1888–92) made internal conditions difficult. The emergent warrior leaders were unable to provide feasts, encourage their followers and threaten their potential competitors as they could neither put together supplies for large forces nor distribute firearms for ambitious would-be followers. Ecological disaster and rinderpest, probably introduced from India around 1880, wiped out 90 per cent of the cattle. Cholera devastated Akele Guzay and the north during 1889 and 1890, and locusts were persistent in Tigre

[1] Marcus, *Life and Times*, 1975, pp. 118–19.
[2] Zewde Gabre-Sellassie, *Yohannes IV of Ethiopia*, 1975, pp. 78, 153.

from 1888. Lack of rain and smallpox hit Harar and Shewa (1888–90), with food shortages in Begemder and the highlands of Hamasen. People migrated to Massawa, while others in Shewa, Gojam, Begemder, Wello, and Tigre migrated to the south, and (to Menelik's chagrin) some were apostatizing in Jimma.[3] The state was impoverished, depleted of human population and agricultural products. The newly crowned *neguse negest* Menelik II (r.1889–1913) issued a proclamation (*awaj*) asking people to pray for reduction of ecological difficulties and for improvements in the economy.

In a direct imitation of British colonial divide-and-rule policy, the Italians bribed the coastal rulers even after their disaster at Dogali, and promised help to *Ras* Mengesha, heir of Yohannes IV, to take the crown of *neguse negest*. Taking advantage of *Ras* Alula's absence, some Italians, taking relief from the heat of Massawa in a quarter of Asmara, garrisoned the town he had founded in the highlands of Hamasen in 1890, and overrunning the area adjacent to Massawa, called it 'Eritrea'.[4] Similar deceit had already enabled the Italians to claim a protectorate over Ethiopia.[5] This was discovered only after Menelik had signed the Treaty of Wichale on 2 May 1889. The Italians used different wording in the Amharic and Italian versions of Article 19 of the treaty. The Italian version said that Ethiopia *should* use Italy as its European mouthpiece whereas the Amharic stated that Ethiopia *could*, if it wanted to. This difference, the history of which forms the most commonly narrated preamble to the first Italian invasion, highlighted that the Italians intended to undermine Ethiopia's relations with the rest of the world.[6] Menelik sent a circular to European nations not only protesting against the Italian claims but also revoking the treaty by declaring it would become null and void from 1 May 1894.

CAUTIOUS PREPARATIONS

Menelik had been preparing against possible invasions, following the strategies of emperors since Tewodros II. He had been rallying *chewa* leaders to unite for the defence of Ethiopia, making sure that dissenters were neutralized. Starting by coordinating his local resources for the effort, he sent warriors to reclaim what had been lost in the south, west, east and southeast within the expanse of northeast Africa, as we have

---

[3] Richard Pankhurst, 'The Great Famine of 1888–1892: A New Assessment', *Journal of the History of Medicine and Allied Sciences*, Vol. XXI, No. 2, 1966, pp. 95–124.
[4] For a list of vacillating local allies of the Egyptians against Yohannes IV, see Zawde Gabre-Sellassie, *Yohannes IV of Ethiopia*, p. 66; on wavering local allies of the Italians against Menelik at this stage, see Marcus, *Life and Times*, 1975, pp. 120–1.
[5] Caulk, *Between the Jaws*, 2002, pp. 157–8; Rubenson, *The Survival of Ethiopian Independence*, 1976, p. 385.
[6] Rubenson, *The Survival of Ethiopian Independence*, 1976, p. 386.

seen. He actively reorganized land and society to raise state resources by increasing commercial tax, by ending an old practice of confiscating property for crimes, and by reorganizing agricultural land tax on the basis of farm size, fertility and productivity.[7]

Early in his reign his land policy resulted in protests, at least in the north. These were used by the Italians to claim that northern Ethiopians resented Menelik of Shewa, that there was rivalry for the throne of Yohannes IV, that the Ethiopian political system was tribal,[8] that its nobles were keen on self-aggrandisement, and that the population preferred Italians over local rulers. Indeed, an Italian general, Baldassare Orero, even believed that the presence of the white man alone was sufficient to establish colonial rule over Ethiopia. Undeterred by the advice of Antonneli, the architect and negotiator of the failed Treaty of Wichale, Orero crossed the Mereb River and entered Adewa on 26 January 1890.[9] He supported his official excuse – that of pacifying Tigre, where *Ras* Mengesha, his nephew *Dejazmach* Seyoum and *Ras* Sebhat of Agamie were in rebellion against Menelik – by entering a pact with *Ras* Mengesha in early 1891. Notable in his list of rebellious dignitaries of the Mereb Melash were *Ras* Welde Selassie and his son *Dejach* Negash. Orero also believed that *Negus* Tekle Haymanot of Gojam would follow suit.

It seems that Orero did not comprehend Ethiopian perspectives towards foreigners in the early 1890s – the period of the transition of power – an opportune moment for warriors to assert local superiority. He misread why *Ras* Mengesha and *Ras* Alula rivalled others over accessing resources and attacked *Dejach* Wele of Yeju on 31 October 1892. Similarly misunderstood was their need for weapons acquisition from foreigners, most of whom were posing as commercial agents, even though they had earlier tried and failed to take advantage of Menelik's signing of the Treaty of Wichale, which he had done in order to acquire weapons.

As we will see, these leaders were not going to allow foreigners whom they considered external enemies to control them. Before strategizing for an effective military expedition against the Italian invasion in the north, Menelik led his troops north to discipline those fighting each other there, having left behind *Dejazmach* Tessema Nadew to guard the capital, to run the rest of his realm and to engage in a show of force were Gojam to make a move. He cautiously deployed loyal troops elsewhere and engaged local leaders in dialogue about sparing the already devastated countryside from possible raids. Menelik worked out with *Ras* Mikael, for instance, ways of avoiding putting pressure on Lasta, Yeju and Wello. When he came across two bishops, *Abune* Petros and *Abune*

---

[7] Mahteme Selassie, *Memories*, 1962 EC, pp. 104–11.
[8] Their records to this effect became the template for linguistic-based administrative divisions in 1991.
[9] On rumours, propaganda and Italian assessments see, for instance Jonas, *The Battle of Adwa: African victory*, 2011, pp. 122–3, 124 *et passim*; Marcus, *Life and Times*, 1975, pp. 143–8.

Luqas, who had returned from Metemma, where they had accompanied Yohannes IV, he quartered them in places far apart from each other so that their followers could access supplies, thus reducing the impact on any one place. Continuing carefully to lessen the effects of supplies acquisition by his troops, he sent one branch ahead directly towards Begemder and led the rest personally towards Mekele, leaving Empress Taytu in Dessie to secure supplies from her lands in Yeju. *Ras* Mengesha and *Ras* Alula submitted so as to spare Tigre. *Dejazmach* Tessema Nadew's show of force, accompanied by a reminder from Menelik of the importance of a sense of responsibility for the countryside, also convinced *Negus* Tekle Haymanot to accept Menelik's rule. The two *ras* and the *negus* were conscious of the dire economic consequences of additional troops passing through the countryside under their control. More significantly, at a time of confrontation with an external foe, challenging or contesting the position of the *neguse negest* for their personal aggrandisement was not an option for most.

GIBIR BEFORE DEFENCE

Nearly two years later, in June 1894, Menelik put on a military display that showed his full control of Ethiopia. Also, on 1 May 1894 the Treaty of Wichale had become null and void. The banquet (*gibir*) involved a historically dramatic and symbolic pageant of power. *Ras* Mengesha Yohannes came to the capital to engage in a ritual of reconciliation with Menelik, involving priests and elders. Menelik concluded his peace with Mengesha by introducing him to the empress. Also reporting at Addis Ababa was *Wagshum* Biru of Wag, brother of Emperor Tekle Giyorgis, who asked permission to beat his drum right into the palace grounds, a request that was granted. Similarly in attendance were *Negus* Tekle Haymanot of Gojam, *Ras* Mikael of Wello and *Ras* Wele Bitul of Semien.

By no mere coincidence, the symbolism of allowing *Wagshum* Biru to beat his *negarit* right up to the *adarash* showed the relatively higher position of the descendant of the Zagwe. However, Menelik sat *Wagshum* Biru and *Ras* Mengesha side by side, but though the *wagshum* had a higher status, he ritually washed his hands in a silver basin, while the *ras* washed his in a gold basin into which he threw gold pieces.[10] This asserted the fact that this dynasty had given up its position to the 'Solomonic' one in 1270 and that its last occupant of the throne of *neguse negest* had been defeated by Yohannes IV, Mengesha's 'father' (actually his uncle). This particular part of the pageantry indicated the consolidation of Menelik's internal position, confirming his overlordship and sole right to designate Biru's and Mengesha's respective ranks. Besides, Menelik effectively asserted the ultimate primacy of the *Kebre Negest* as the formal source of power for the title of *neguse negest*. The pageantry also rendered ineffective the systemic and multi-

---

[10] Guèbrè Sellassié, *Chronique*, 1930–32, Vol. I, pp. 356–7.

farious challenge that the *chewa* leaders would otherwise pose to his power.

After the *gibir*, Menelik shared with the nobles his plan to campaign in Welayta after the rains, so many stayed on in the capital to join him. As noted before, this expedition partly replenished the state treasury, which had been depleted since the great famine of 1888–92. On his successful return from it he placed loyal warriors in the south to continue reclaiming historical territories.

The *gibir*, and this expedition were part of Menelik's preparations against the Italian invasion. European observers in his court were left in no doubt that Menelik was fully in control of the country. Having put his house in order and confident that his former rivals were now loyal, Menelik also ordered *Ras* Mengesha Yohannes to move to Debre Haylat, less than 150 kilometres from the Italian fortress in Adigrat. The *ras* reached Debre Haylat on 9 October 1894. In December, Menelik also encouraged a former friend of the Italians, Bahta Hagos of Akele Guzay, to stage an uprising against them in the name of Ethiopia,[11] but the Italians crushed it, and gaining confidence, strengthened their alliance with others such as the *Sultan* of Awsa and *Dejazmach* Guangul Zegeye, a *shifta* hiding among the Azebo.

Aiming to invade the rest of Ethiopia from this time onwards, Italian soldiers continued to make incursions, strongly believing in the superiority of the white man against supposedly inferior, barbaric, primitive and weak Ethiopians.[12] In January 1895, they crossed the Mereb, strengthening the fort at Adigrat on 25 March. This threatened to encircle *Ras* Mengesha at Qoatit, but, before they could trap him, the *ras* retreated south. This only encouraged the Italians to fortify and occupy Amba Alage and release a prisoner, *Ras* Sebhat, who promised to help them take Mekele and Adewa. Their rapid march south has since been attributed to their ill-preparedness, inadequate number and arrogant assumption of innate superiority.

On his retreat from Debre Haylat, *Ras* Mengesha issued the following seemingly facile *zeraf*:

እሪ በሉ ለሸዋ ንገሩ
እሪ በሉ ለወሎ ንገሩ
እሪ በሉ ለጎጃም ንገሩ
መንገሻ ለቀቀ ተከፈበት በሩ
Shout, tell Shewa!
Shout, tell Wello!
Shout, tell Gojam!
Mengesha has let go; the door is open!

In fact this was taken as a clarion call, but Menelik still lacked the scale of weaponry and other resources required to resist the European foe. Before he mobilized some months later, he tried to lobby for the support of other Europeans, for example by taking out membership of the Inter-

---

[11] Jonas, *The Battle of Adwa: African victory*, pp. 101–4.
[12] Jonas, *The Battle of Adwa: African victory*, pp. 5, 82, 100, 153–4, 334–5; Rubenson, *The Survival of Ethiopian Independence*, 1976, pp. 75, 166.

Photo 7 Menelik II in coronation garb (Source: R. Pankhurst & Denis Gérard, *Ethiopia Photographed: Historic Photographs of the Country and its People Taken Between 1867 and 1935* (Kegan Paul International, 1996, p. 45); by kind permission of Richard Pankhurst's family and Denis Gérard)

national Postal Union. However, neither his lobbying of the powers nor membership of that union was enough to change the desire of Europeans to see Italy succeed in its colonial drive. The British in Aden flatly refused to sell rifles to *Ras* Mekonnen. The Germans banned the export of arms to Ethiopia, and the Austrians followed suit. The French, who were initially amenable to allowing weapons traffic to Ethiopia from January 1895, changed their minds in return for the Italians allowing them a protectorate over Tunisia. The French blocked weapons that Ethiopia had already paid for.[13] Even distant Russia would not trade in arms with Menelik. Not for the last time, the promised European collaboration was held back for lack of acceptance of Ethiopia's right to defend its sovereignty. Menelik was limited to a cartridge-producing machine (that he got serviced over the rainy season),[14] and to storing some weapons and grain supplies at Were Illu.

MOBILIZATION AGAINST THE ITALIANS

When Menelik issued a mobilization decree (*qitet*) on 17 September 1895, most of his soldiers had only old rifles, and his cavalry and infantry only lances. Reflecting the core *chewa* defence principles, the wordings of the decree read, according to his *Chronicle*:

> God in his grace has so far kept me without any enemy and has increased my state. So far, I have ruled with God's grace. Since we all die, I will not regret if I die now. God has never failed me, and I am confident that he will not abandon me in the future.
>
> Here an enemy has come across the waters that God made our frontier to destroy the country and change the religion. I have only kept my peace taking into account the deaths of cattle and the weakened conditions of the people in my country; but the enemy has advanced, digging the earth like moles.
>
> With God's help I will not pass my country on to him now. I do not think I have ever offended you my countrymen, and you have not offended me. You who are strong, help me with your strength; and you who are weak, with your prayers for your child, wife and religion. If you fail to help for any reason, you will quarrel with me. I will not forgive you, in the name of Mary! I will not accept any negotiations on this. I start my campaign in *Teqemt*. So, those of you in Shewa [gather your supplies and] meet me at Were Illu by the middle of *Teqemt*.[15]

Invoking the full spectrum of *chewa* traditions, Menelik spoke, in this *kitet* ('call to the people to mobilize'), of his personal courage in the face of death, referred to the 'natural frontier' of his territory by the sea, and called on the loyalty of the warriors to him personally. A historian who accuses Menelik of making false statements in the decree, misun-

---

[13] Marcus, 1975, *Life and Times*, pp. 154–60.
[14] Chris Prouty, *Empress Taytu and Menelik II: Ethiopia 1883–1910*, London: Ravens Educational and Development Services; Trenton, NJ: Red Sea Press, 1986, p. 133.
[15] My translation from Guèbrè Sellassié, *Chronique*, 1930–32, Vol. I, pp. 373–4.

derstands them,[16] while some foreign observers used the word *fanno* to describe the *chewa* troops he was calling up, not understanding the socio-politics of the time.[17] He commended the strong to help him in the war, and urged the weak to pray for the safety of family and religion. The perennial individual sense of responsibility for country, religion and monarch were also mentioned as he called directly on each person to respond to the enemy's threat to the country, and recalled the historical attitude towards Turkish–Egyptian hostilities. The religious theme reflected policies that Yohannes IV had followed not long before.

Read out to drumbeats in the palace and widely in the country, Menelik's decree resonated strongly with the warriors, to whom he also specified where and when to meet. His chronicler indicates that he deployed those in Gojam, Dembiya, Qwara, Begemder and 'to the north of Checheho' to Ashengie; those in Semien, Welqayt and Tegedie to Mekele; and those from Shewa to meet him at Were Illu, about two hundred kilometres north of the capital.

RESPONDING TO MOBILIZATION

The message was immediately followed by rapid preparations in most places. Irrespective of the multiplicity of groupings, the mobilization brought together the self-assertive warriors, highly conscious of their defensive role, and even some *shifta*. Those from Shewa headed towards Were Illu to serve directly under Menelik. Many regional leaders arrived late. Having waited to avoid impassable torrents, they delayed troop movements until the rains stopped (in many areas, at the end of August or early September). Most brought with them *tabot* (representing the Ark of the Covenant), and priests and other religious personnel, including Muslims, to ensure prayers of intercession. *Ras* Mekonnen, the first to arrive in the capital in September, brought a thousand head of cattle he had raided recently in the Ogaden. He received personal supplies from his kinsmen waiting for him in Shewa Meda, just outside the capital. Those closer to the route of invasion, namely *Ras* Wele from Semien and *Dejazmach* Hayle Maryam from Welqayt and Tsegedie, marched rapidly towards Ashngie and Mekele.

The legacy of the cattle disease posed serious difficulties on the way. Horses and mules of the cavalry under *Ras* Mikael, for instance, were badly infected as they passed through Begemder, and a segment of troops with Menelik passing that way had to divert because of the stink. Similarly, *Fitawrari* Tekle, who arrived from Wellega in the west, and *Negus* Tekle Haymanot from Gojam and Dembya were hesitant, conscious of the devastating after-effects of the ecological disasters. Caution required *Dejazmach* Beshah Aboye, at the head of the troops from Sidamo, to leave *Dejazmach* Lulseged to guard

---

[16] Prouty, *Empress Taytu*, 1986, p. 134.
[17] De Coppet in Guèbrè Sellassié, *Chronique*, 1930–32, Vol. I, p. 374 fn 3.

the southern regions. *Ras* Mekonnen left some of his forces to guard Hararge.

Dejazmach Guangul, who was a *shifta* in the north, asked pardon and made a ceremonious submission, seeking permission to participate in 'the defence of his country and master'. Menelik deployed him to operate under *Ras* Mengesha, and sent *Bejirond* Balcha to punish a neighbourhood that had been harbouring another *shifta* on an *amba* ('plateau on top of a mountain') called Arara. A more serious dissident was Mohammed Anfari, then *sultan* of Awsa, whose predecessors had been known for their close commercial and political relationship with the rulers of Shewa while guarding trade to and from the Red Sea coast. He was reported to be in liaison with the Italians, probably since 1888 when they had been luring him with promises of power. Menelik diverted troops that arrived late due to heavy rains to stop possible threats from the *sultan*. These were under *Dejazmach* Tessema of Illubabor, *Ras* Welde Giyorgis of Kullo, Konta, Limu and Keffa, and *Wehni Azazh* Welde Tsadik of Addis Alem. A significant religious fact of local warfare on the battlefield showed during their subsequent confrontation with the *sultan*. When *Ras* Welde Giyorgis sent the characteristic message asking the *sultan* to submit peacefully, the latter warned him of destruction if he advanced, saying that his 'savants and magicians' would not allow bullets to touch him past their prayers.[18] As proof, the *sultan* yoked and chained the savants to one another at their request, and left them in the front lines while he fled his town of Awsa.[19]

Menelik's deployment showed that Ethiopia now had fewer and weaker dissidents, and that the *neguse negest* was essentially in full control for the first time since the sixteenth century. Regional 'masters', like ordinary soldiers, actually went on the expedition with the single purpose of repelling an external attack, looking to Menelik for leadership. They were keen to show their warriorhood and leadership qualities of networking, coordination and command of social support. Individual warriors were ready to show off their skills in horsemanship and daring actions, and their grooms and pages looking after their war materials, tents and pack animals hoped to attract attention as fighters as well.

It seems, however, that due to the shortage of weapons, Menelik could not accommodate everyone who had come from all over the country, some more poorly equipped than others. So, while camping at Were Illu, eighteen days after he started from his capital, Menelik sent back *Kao* Tona of Welayta, *Sultan* Aba Jifar of Jimma, *Dejazmach* Gebre Egziabher of Leqa Lekemt and *Dejazmach* Jote of the borderland 'Shanqela and Arab' to safeguard 'his country'.

---

[18] Guèbrè Sellassié, *Chronique*, 1930–32, Vol. II, pp. 404–5.
[19] An oral story from my family seems to corroborate this: According to my mother, her grandfather, *Basha* Mekuria Dinku, then enrolled under *Wehni Azazh* Welde Tsadik, was blinded when blood got into his eyes when he 'raised his sword and hit one of these men at the front, while the man pleaded "Don't! Don't! I have Wekabi (a spirit) on me!"'

ON THE MARCH TO ADEWA

The warriors followed the tradition of sharing the burden of supplies. As usual, each warrior brought at least a ten-day ration. They came with their wives, concubines and domestic servants to prepare food and give personal service, and, depending on their status, shield bearers and grooms. Almost all had mules and pack horses to carry flour, tents and other requirements. Thousands of women, most of them slaves, carried containers with food and drink 'fermenting or maturing on their backs', as the expression goes. Empress Taytu had commissioned weavers in the palace to make clothes suitable as rewards, potters to prepare kitchenware, and the kitchen to prepare dry food and beverages. Her personal staff of women carried high quality *tej* in fifty or so containers decorated with horn and silver. Having sent messages to her lands in Yeju and Lasta to prepare supplies, including for *gibir*, she had people waiting for the royal household at different places. Menelik also had to allow the soldiers to raid farmers, planning to have the troops arrive in Tigre 'before the farmers had collected their harvests'.

Youth in various officers' households also marched with their 'masters'. In his autobiography, Tekle Hawaryat (later *Fitawrari*), gives an account of himself as a thirteen-year-old page in *Ras* Mekonnen's retinue. He was struck by the urgent preparations that started the moment rumours were heard of the pending Italian invasion. Tents furtively made from canvas were to look fresh, later distinguishing *Ras* Mekonnen's camp from the rest. He also reports that the *Gondere* and *Werwari* between them had five *fitawrari*, nine *kegnazmach*, one *gerazmach* and one *balambaras*. They had come to accompany *Ras* Mekonnen from Werehume Werebello in the mountain chain of Chercher, in western Hararge. When *Ras* Mekonnen's troops reached Shewa, Tekle Hawaryat and his elder brother (then serving as a soldier) found that their relatives had brought them dry food supplies, along with a female slave to cook for them during the expedition.

The training that Tekle Hawaryat and other children had so far received included hunting small animals and birds.[20] He pleaded to join shooting competitions and won an award of a gun of his own from the *ras*. He incurred the envy of the other boys when Mekonnen permitted him to join the expedition. Eager to prepare for battle, the child decided to fill up his empty cartridge belt. He first begged the arsenal keeper of the *ras*, who discreetly gave him bullets. He then asked Mekonnen directly for bullets with which 'to kill the Italians', and the amused *ras* allowed him to take fifty. With this, he declares: 'At once, I became *chewa*'! Of course, the *ras* confiscated the bullets from his cartridge belt during the march, and gave strict orders to restrain Tekle Hawaryat within the camp during the battle. As was to be expected, however, the child stole out and tried to shoot, only to find that his gun, which was probably for shooting small birds and animals, did not shoot far! Not

---

[20] Tekle Hawaryat, *Autobiography*, 1999 EC, pp. 54–6.

surprisingly, he also turned the battlefield into a game when he realized that standing up meant drawing enemy fire in his direction. He encouraged this by raising a pole with a piece of cloth tied to it, but though he entertained a slightly older friend, the other warriors had to teach him not to attract enemy fire.

Menelik started his march only on 11 October 1895, travelling at a leisurely pace, 'following a custom' that, according to his *Chronicle*, had been 'known from the days of *Atse* Libne Dingil and Zera Yaqob',[21] of the sixteenth and fifteenth centuries respectively. The *Destoch*, a special corps of mostly captives from Welayta, carried, pitched and packed the tent equipment for the monarch's household: eighteen tents, nine of them for food preparation. At every new camp, they positioned and put up the red tent first; the rest of the warriors would then know where to erect theirs. The tent of *Bejirond* Balcha, commander of the treasury, was close by for easy access, on the right side of the emperor's red tent, while those for the horses and mules of the emperor and the empress were on the left.

Among the other seven to eight thousand personal retainers accompanying Menelik were the *Gendebel* from Shewa, who brought what they had in their care – namely cattle, household effects and regalia for official rewards to notable warriors. These were to join the *werari* from the emperor's household. Other corps included the *Weregenu*, those who looked after the cattle for feeding the troops, and two hundred 'tribute payers' (*gebbar*), bringing 250 to 260 mules and pack horses from Shewa, and assisted by the 'box loaders' looking after cooked bread and *enjera*. Pot bearers carried huge pots in which beverages and dough continued fermenting while on their backs. Household waiters (*qwami*), carrying the ready-to-eat food and drink for the emperor and his immediate entourage, replenished their loads by making sure that cooks took turns in baking *enjera* during the night.

After each day's journey, mealtimes in the form of *gibir* supplied food for the soldiers who proclaimed their bravery and claimed raw meat from freshly butchered cattle. According to his chronicler, Menelik's travelling kitchen fed thousands of soldiers from various regions – 'without opening their personal supplies'.[22] Soldiers added to their reserves at Ergibo, where Empress Taytu had made previous arrangements, and at Azebo, where Menelik allowed them to raid defiant farmers for grain.

FIRST ENCOUNTER

Menelik's advance troops reached Amba Alagi in Tigre in early December. Under *Ras* Mekonnen, these included *Ras* Mikael at the head of the Wello cavalry, *Dejach* Wele Betul leading the warriors of Yeju and nearby Begemder, *Ras* Mengesha Yohannes and *Ras* Alula

---

[21] *Chronique du Regne de Menelik II*, p. 365.
[22] *Chronique du Regne de Menelik II*, p. 407.

of Tigre. *Ras* Mekonnen sent a terse message asking Major Toselli to withdraw peacefully and warned him that a bigger force under Menelik was coming up behind. Though Toselli saw the large size of the army ranged against him, he considered himself on a defensible height, and firmly believed, with false information, that his superiors were sending him reinforcements. Probably knowing that the *ras* had once expressed admiration of European civilization, and hoping that he would prefer an alliance with the Italians, Toselli tried to discourage Mekonnen, pointing out the advantages of allying with them – parties with whom Mekonnen had become acquainted over the previous seven years.

An unexpected attack mounted on 7 December 1895 by *Fitawrari* Gebeyehu – the first skirmish of the Battle of Adewa – interrupted any rapport between the two. The *fitawrari* had been surprised by a scouting unit from the Italian side while he was on his way to *Ras* Alula's camp. *Ras* Mekonnen joined by attacking two flanks manned by collaborators, *Ras* Sebhat and *Sheik* Talha, and a group of *askari* ('locally recruited soldiers') from Eritrea. The attack blocked Toselli's route of retreat and killed him. The local population then disarmed and disrobed the survivors, who barely managed to clamber down from the heights they had been occupying. Only a handful reached the Italian camp at Mekele. The battle lasted just four hours, but loss of life was heavy. *Fitawrari* Gebeyehu was disciplined for attacking without authorization, but ordinary warriors sang in rhymes in his praise:

> ገቢየሁ ገቢየሁ
> ጎበዝ አየሁ
> Gebeyehu, Gebeyehu!
> I have seen a warrior.

SECOND CONFRONTATION

Ras Mekonnen and his troops arrived on 19 December at Mekele, thirty-five miles north of Amba Alagi, where the Italians had their flag flying on a formidable fort on a precipice that was difficult to scale. The Italians meant to defend it for its symbolic importance as a former capital of Yohannes IV, according to a historian.[23] The senior commander, General Arimondi, had only a skeletal force of 1,200 remaining there, but Major Galliano, who commanded it, made some preparations, hauling up water into pits lined with tarpaulins.[24] The foraging parties he had sent out on 9 December found that the farmers as far as six miles from the fort refused to let them buy or forage for supplies. *Ras* Mekonnen encircled the route of escape from this fort, sent a letter asking Major Galliano to withdraw, and, on 3 January, despatched soldiers to scale the fort during the night – only to find them gunned down by heavy weapons assisted by flares.

[23] Jonas, *The Battle of Adwa: African victory*, 2011, p. 134.
[24] Jonas, *The Battle of Adwa: African victory*, 2011, pp. 135–6.

Meanwhile, Menelik, reviewing his troops at Wefla near Ashngie on 15 December, received news of the victory at Amba Alagi, and arrived at Mekele on 6 January 1896, nearly three months after he started out from his capital. *Negus* Tekle Haymanot of Gojam, who had joined him on 23 December, and *Dejazmach* Gessese of Semien (Taytu's nephew) arrived the same day as Menelik. Gessese brought butter and other items, including sheep and other meat on the hoof, to the delight of those in Tigre where meat had been scarce for some time.

At this first stop Menelik had gathered an estimated 73,000 to 120,000 warriors. *Ras* Mekonnen's men, who had repeatedly tried to scale the fortress, even using ladders between 9 and 11 January, had incurred heavy loss of life, with six hundred dying in one night alone. The newly arrived courtiers took Mekonnen to task for causing so many casualties without result. Menelik called off the attack, and reportedly on the suggestion of the empress, allowed her men to encircle the two springs below the fort, forcing Major Galliano to ask for an end to the siege. Not surprisingly, when Felter, the merchant who had negotiated for this, tried to present Galliano to Menelik, the emperor sent the major away angrily, but giving him a mount and other animals for transporting his personnel and wares. On 21 January, when the major and his men were escorted out of the fort, the Ethiopians dismantled it within hours, and took vital armaments. Interestingly, Italy and the rest of Europe celebrated news of this escape.

ADEWA, THE FINAL BATTLE

Menelik then led his force towards Adewa and deployed it on the hills overlooking the Adewa valley. He placed *Ras* Mekonnen, *Ras* Mengesha and *Ras* Mikael as *werari* in the middle, put himself and the empress at the centre, *Negus* Tekle Haymanot on his right and *Ras* Alula on his left. General Baratieri had taken up positions nearby, but he had been running short of supplies, reportedly within only a month of forcing Mengesha to evacuate Debre Haylat. In late February 1896, therefore he had advised his government to consider delaying attacking Menelik's troops so that they too might run short and disperse. Irrespective of any advantage he might get from such delay, however, the Italian government ordered him to act, and, at a meeting he called on 29 February, this command was supported by his immediate subordinates.

Planning, therefore, to attack the following morning of 1 March, at 9 a.m., Baratieri advanced three brigades at night to occupy the crests of three mountains in three parallel formations. General Albertone on the left was to set the pace, with General Dabormida to follow on the right and General Arimondi in the centre. General Ellena led the reserve force immediately to their rear. Albertone intended to position himself on the summit known as Kidane Mehret, theoretically to command a view of Ethiopian movements along the narrow tracks to Adewa. Contrary to the plan, however, the advancing brigades spread across a wide terrain and Albertone marched directly into the position of *Ras* Alula, on guard duty for the Ethiopian camp that night.

Runners brought Menelik news of the Italian advance before dawn. The guards were already fighting and, with the additional force of 25,000 men he sent them, they dislodged Arimondi from his position. At 6 a.m., an artillery force[25] repulsed Albertone and his *askari* towards Arimondi's brigade, and captured Albertone himself. Dabormida's brigade, which was meant to relieve Albertone, perished when it marched into *Ras* Mikael's cavalry troops. The forces of *Negus* Tekle Haymanot outflanked and destroyed Baratieri's remaining troops, and by noon, all the contingents that had rallied to Menelik's mobilization had participated in the defence. The surviving Italians, in full retreat from their camp, fled towards Eritrea, barely escaping further attacks by local farmers.

The Battle of Adewa was over, having cost the lives of four to five thousand Ethiopians, and leaving eight thousand wounded. Subsequent reports showed that innumerable domestics also sacrificed their lives. General Albertone was taken prisoner with three thousand others. Two hundred of these later died of their wounds, and around 800 *askari* suffered amputation of their left legs and right arms as punishment for joining the enemy. The Italians reportedly lost about seven thousand, had fifteen hundred wounded and left behind artillery, eleven thousand rifles and most of their transport.

Some Italians and their local *askari* also suffered emasculation, *seleba*, removal of the male genitalia, a practice forbidden by Menelik as discussed above. The warriors who collected such trophies 'threw down the *seleba*', as 'kill' in front of their commanding officers. Foreigners reported that, at the Battle of Adewa, the Wello cavalry in particular shouted what sounded to them like '*Ebalgumè! Ebalgumè!*'[26] It appears to me that the war-cry *Aha bel gume!* ('Say blood money!') was misheard as *Ebalgumè*. Though the word does not exist,[27] its rendering by some foreigners as 'Reap! Reap!' has been perpetuated over the years.[28] This interpretation of the misheard word decontextualizes sympathy for the victims and reduces the action of trophy-taking to numbers. It ignores the warriors' expressed intention of seeking retribution. It is worth noting that the word *guma*, a word loaned from Agew and used in Amharic and in Oromiffa, means 'blood money'. This is normally payment of money in settlement of disputes, almost invariably after

[25] Some describe this as consisting of Russian mountain guns, others as Hotchkiss and Maxim pieces captured from the Egyptians or bought from the French.
[26] George Fitz-Hardinge Berkeley, *The Campaign of Adowa and the Rise of Menelik*, New York: Negro Universities Press, 1969, pp. 326, 344.
[27] The word for 'reap' in Amharic is *etched*, and in Oromiffa it is *haamuu*. (By then the Wello cavalrymen were Amharic speakers, though they may also have spoken Oromiffa.)
[28] For example David L. Lewis, *The Race to Fashoda: European Colonialism and African Resistance in the Scramble for Africa*, New York: Weidenfeld and Nicolson, 1987, p. 118; Johanna Maula, *The Jasmine Years: From my African Notebooks*, Bloomington, IN: iUniverse, 2012, p. 175.

homicide. The warriors were mutilating the enemy while defending their country and its people at the Battle of Adewa, and the correct version of the war-cry that the enemy heard was, from the warriors' perspective, proclamation of the right to retribution. Further, the cry at that battlefield was accompanied by the refrain '*guma may guma; lale guma*', literally 'retribution, retribution, sweet retribution' – *guma* actually means blood money. In the context of the Battle of Adewa, the enemy had to pay retribution for invading: in the warriors' thinking he was justly suffering the consequences. Of course, such mutilation is unacceptable nowadays; we think in terms of material or financial compensation, not blood money retribution through cutting off parts of the body.

Menelik returned to his capital on 22 May with his surviving troops, and, as a direct result, signed the Treaty of Addis Ababa with Italy, which abrogated any claims that Italy had on Ethiopia. Two themes have dominated discussions on the history of the battle. One concerns the Treaty of Wichale, which played a role in helping Italians gain a colonial foothold.[29] A biographer of Yohannes cites Menelik's note of protest to the Italian king, in which he said that Italy should have at least 'come to an accord' with the emperor before occupying Massawa.[30] It is noteworthy too that, with or without a treaty, the Italians were encroaching on Ethiopian soil, bribing local leaders and even murdering them. Their activities in the highlands of Hamasen and the Afar lowlands were intended to undermine the Ethiopian sense of unity.

The perceived failure of Menelik and his warriors to pursue their victory by dislodging the Italians from the highlands of Hamasen and the Red Sea coast of Massawa is a false reading of their capacity at that moment in history. It takes little account of the ecological disasters and the well-coordinated European refusal to sell Ethiopia the necessary arsenal of weapons. Besides, whether Menelik had pushed forward or had delayed joining battle at Adewa, his troops would have run short of supplies. Forging ahead beyond Adewa with completely inadequate supplies and limited weaponry would have given the advantage to the Italians who would have regrouped effectively to use a large amount of weaponry and fresh troops that had recently arrived in Massawa, though too late to be deployed at Adewa.

THE *CHEWA* AFTER ADEWA

After the victory of March 1896, ordinary Ethiopians, especially the warriors who participated in the battle, were convinced of the invin-

---

[29] Zewde Gabre-Sellassie, *Yohannes IV of Ethiopia*, 1975, pp. 203, 263–9; a long-time traveller to the northern regions of Ethiopia, Wylde, *Modern Abyssinia*, 1901, pp. 38–9; Jonas, *The Battle of Adwa: African victory*, 2011, pp. 47–8; Rubenson, *The Survival of Ethiopian Independence*, 1976, pp. 384–6.
[30] Marcus, *Life and Times*, 1975, pp. 83–4.

Photo 8 Ethiopia in Europe: Ethiopian ambassadors at the Elysée, Paris, 1898
(Source: *Le Petit Journal, Supplement Illustré*, 24 July 1898, No. 401)

cibility of their country. They had made a successful response to the Italian armed incursions of January 1895. Despite the deaths, depletion of supplies and other losses, the battle was an example *par excellence* of *chewa* politico-military readiness to defend the country against *dina*, the external enemy. Indeed, the victory is still seen as a historic achievement that left 'Italy' synonymous with that word. Menelik held a public memorial feast on the seventh anniversary to remember the souls of Ethiopians who had sacrificed themselves at Adewa.

He had been changing how the army worked, essentially by bringing the warriors under the sole command of the *neguse negest*. He achieved this in the first place by controlling the availability of weapons for transmitting the practices of warriorhood,[31] and second by constricting local communities' control of access to rural lands.

Expressly for collecting tribute in kind (and later in cash) for the central state treasury, Menelik reassessed land holdings, taking into account their size, fertility and agricultural productivity. Making 'masters' the functionaries of labour and other resource extraction for the state, he constrained their relationships with socially sanctioned and self-trained emergent warriors. As we have seen, he also placed new regiments known as *Dembegna* alongside the named *chewa* corps of soldiers. The *Dembegna* and the *chewa* shared the task of raising economic resources. However, they differed in the way they related to the state, in that the chain of command for the *Dembegna* passed directly from the governor to the monarch while the *chewa* still felt tied to the local population and its lands. The measures forced the *chewa* to refrain

[31] Pankhurst, *A Social History*, 1990, pp. 277–95.

from engaging in the politics of local communal lands, and in time also took away their capacity to rebel openly on account of those lands.

It took the collapse of the central power in 1935–41 before *chewa* warriorhood could re-engage in its role of defence of land and people. Edicts accompanied by the beating of drums had circulated rules and regulations on land in the rural areas with the land-based population getting little say. The prohibitive land laws blocked individuals' acquisition of political space, and discouraged the emergence of socially responsible political power seekers. It stymied the involvement of ordinary individuals in local and national politics and distanced the public from the state. The bureaucracy appointed by the head of state was patrimonial at best. Those seeking justice against burdensome taxation, or on the procedures of land assessment or other administrative demands, no longer had any local recourse. Often supplicants had to appeal to the monarch in the capital. The *chewa*, and probably others, saw this as a loss of the two-way communication between state and farmers that they had facilitated. The new land measures curtailed the population's capacity to use land as a counterweight whenever it deemed the administration was unjust, and the land tax measures effectively undermined the self-training of emergent warriors.

This was part of the wider project of 'modernity' with which Menelik capped the changes. The bureaucracy of salaried and titled administrators, including in the regions, owed loyalty to the 'modern' state ruled by an energetic monarchical absolutism.[32] In defence matters, the disconnection between traditional warriorhood and the new highly centralized system of administration was achieved by undermining the various ways of seeking social approval for engaging in local politics. Legal restrictions on hunting, for instance, first in 1909 and then in 1930[33] directly affected the transmission and spirit of *chewa* warriorhood. When anti-hunting laws came in, *chewa* warriors encouraged their family members and would-be warriors to continue self-training. They sent their youth clandestinely to accompany professional hunters or to join either *fanno* or *shifta*. Nonetheless, the modernizing central government had no use for the celebratory singing that accompanied such hunting expeditions. The old *chewa* charged with implementing the prohibitions closed their eyes, but salaried officials sometimes took participants to court. Hunting, horsemanship and other martial sports for defending the local community and its rural lands were eventually detached from seeking and acquiring social approval. Coupled with diversion of commodities previously available for the associated feasting, those who fought against the second Italian invasion of 1935–41 were left with only the memories of the famed autonomous individual warriors – their forebears who fought at the Battle of Adewa.

[32] On the 1931 and 1955 constitutions, see Bahru Zewde, *A History of Modern Ethiopia*, 2001 pp. 140, 206.
[33] Edicts were issued in, for example, Teqmt 1901 EC and Hamle 1923 EC. See Mahteme Selassie, *Memories*, 1962 EC, pp. 347–58. The restrictions on hunting were said specifically to have the purpose of preserving wildlife.

Yet the changing system of administration and related tax affecting the organization of defence was still not detached from the past. The officials responsible for implementing the new laws governing land rights were both familiar with and loyal to the traditional politico-military practices.

Using 'modernity' as an excuse, the monarchy and its officials chose to promote the sense of prestige and internal cohesion that the Adewa victory had brought about. They enhanced the monarch's role in involving individuals in politics and defence. When faced with the need to sort out the rules of succession to the throne at the middle of the second decade, the new administrators, in the form of a council, crowned Menelik's daughter, Zewditu, in 1916, ousting, as we saw above, Menelik's designated heir *Lij* Iyasu. This contradicted the prescribed rules of the *Kebre Negest*, which prohibited women's enthronement.[34] More than that, it set a new precedent for manipulating the position of *neguse negest*. When Zewditu's successor, Haile Selassie I, restricted succession to the throne only to his male heirs and descendants in the 1931 constitution, the parliament that ratified it became a rubber stamp that manipulated even the *Kebre Negest*.

The failure to have an adequate transitional institution plagued the departure from the old practices to new working methods. Most of the first ministers Menelik appointed seem to have missed the notion of impersonal working methods in the 'modern' offices they held. They understood neither the need to separate the use of personal salaries from state resources, nor the difference between delivering state services and ruling over subjects of the state. Foreign-educated officials and even foreigners were sought to set up and help create workable institutions. Even before Menelik's death in 1913, a minister of finance and two consecutive ministers of war were accused of failing in their duties. Later, in the early 1920s, younger political activists actually accused all the ministers in a similar vein. Most of the foreign-educated men and women lost their lives during 1935–41, and the few who survived were handicapped because decisions continued to be made by the monarch alone both during and after 1941.

The educated elite recruited in the post-1941 period inherited their predecessors' patriotism, but they too lacked the institutional means to make their duties reflect the interests of society. Part of the fundamental deficiency came from the failure to develop the spirit of a civil service, in the full sense of those words. The emergence of that spirit was precluded by the autocratic tendencies in the state under a monarchy that was fixed on its overwhelming course. It generated a political environment – engrossed in manipulating the political community – in which state authorities continued to exercise abnormal power, even by later pretending to share power in multi-party arrangements.

---

[34] E. A. Wallis Budge (trans.), *The Queen of Sheba and her only son Menyelek (I) being the 'Book of the Glory of Kings' (Kebra Nagast)* (2nd edn), Oxford: Oxford University Press, 1932, p. 39.

10

Guerrilla Warfare, 1935–1941

Undeterred by Ethiopia's victory against its invasion in 1896, Italy joined Britain and France in reasserting European hegemony regarding Ethiopian sovereignty. Colonialist French and British interests over Fashoda had nearly caused a clash in 1898, but in 1904 France and Britain signed an *Entente Cordiale*, and in 1906 the Tripartite Treaty on Ethiopia. The latter was infamous for specifying European spheres of economic influence over Ethiopia without its knowledge.[1] It provided for the French to construct the railway line in eastern Ethiopia, the British to control Ethiopian waters feeding the Nile and the Italians to feel included in European power politics. Each was to enjoy its colonial interest without the others' involvement, while subjecting Ethiopia, practically though not formally, to British, French and Italian colonial intervention.

With this in the background and for many other good reasons, Italy's inimical status enhanced Ethiopian suspicion of Europeans. International conditions in the years leading up to the 1930s were similar to those on the eve of the 1896 Italian invasion.[2] The regent (the future Haile Selassie I) took steps to sustain international connectedness just as Menelik had done. He secured Ethiopia's membership of the League of Nations (founded in 1919) on 28 September 1923, despite protests by Italy, a founding member. The emperor and his officials also saw the Covenant of the League of Nations as a panacea of security against Italian aggression. They were reassured by the 'collective security' clause enshrined in Article X of the Covenant, forbidding members from attacking each other. Haile Selassie even signed a twenty-year treaty of friendship with Italy in August 1928. Aptly described as one side of Italian 'double policy of diplomatic public collaboration and secret subversion',[3] this failed to placate Italy's persistent hostility.

Though Ethiopians treated them with a degree of trust, Italian diplomats and merchants shamelessly engaged in treacherous and hostile

---

[1] Edward C. Keefer, 'Great Britain, France, and the Ethiopian Tripartite Treaty of 1906', *Albion: A Quarterly Journal Concerned with British Studies*, Vol. 13, No. 4, Winter, 1981, pp. 364–80.
[2] Bahru Zewde, *A History of Modern Ethiopia*, 2001, p. 152.
[3] Sbacchi, *Legacy of Bitterness*, 1997, p. 328.

Photo 9 Haile Selassie in modern military uniform in October 1935, just before the second Italian invasion (Source: R. Pankhurst & Denis Gérard, *Ethiopia Photographed: Historic Photographs of the Country and its People Taken Between 1867 and 1935* (Kegan Paul International, 1996, p. 77); by kind permission of Richard Pankhurst's family and Denis Gérard)

activities inside Ethiopia. Its consuls accumulated weapons on Ethiopian soil, gathered intelligence, and bribed and recruited ethnic leaders whom they assumed not to belong in what they conceived of as a state and society dominated by 'Amhara'. To promote Italian understanding of Ethiopia as a barbaric and primitive society and to inculcate Mussolini's purported championship of Islam, they successfully bribed dissident nobles, whom Ethiopians later derogatively called *banda*, an Italian word for 'group or mercenary troops' (subsequently meaning 'traitor' in Amharic).

The duplicity of the Treaty of Friendship (1928) came to a head when the Italians built a fort at Welwel, 120 kilometres inside Ethiopia.[4]

---

[4] G. L. Steer, *Cæsar in Abyssinia*. London: Hodder and Stoughton, 1936, p. 18. Steer's detailed scaled map inside the back cover of his book shows Welwel as 250 miles from the nearest coast and 85 miles from the Somali border. Mockler's *Haile Selassie's War*, 1987, p. 38, says that Ethiopians on the spot pointed out that the Italians were 'well over 180 miles from the Somali coast'. This apparently refers to the Italians having come far over the border they had accepted in 1897, i.e. the line 180 miles parallel to the coast (Baer, *The Coming of the Italian-Ethiopian War*, p. 45, including fn. 2, and p. 47, fn. 5). The Treaty of Friendship (1928) apparently placed the border less than half the distance from the coast, but, given Italy's underlying purpose, this was mere subterfuge. Indeed, Italy apparently occupied Welwel the same year (Marcus, *Haile Selassie I*, 1995, p. 164). According to Spencer, by November

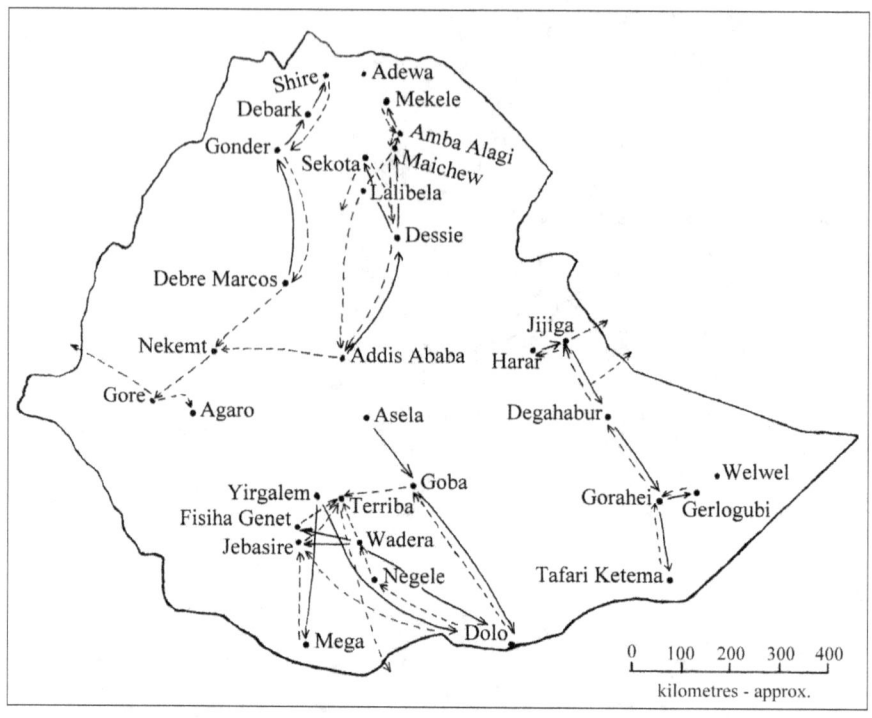

Map 3 Some defensive movements (⟶) and retreats (- - -➢) in the early phase of the 1935–41 invasion (drawn by Peter Esmonde)

Ethiopian border guards commanded by *Gerazmach* Afework Welde Semayat (posthumously, *Dejazmach*), recognized this as an invasion, and opened fire on the fort on 5 December 1934. An international border commission came, but the guards considered its arbitration as intervention on their border issue. A treacherous French lawyer whom Ethiopia had employed to pursue arbitration at the League conceded too much and failed to insist on the issue of sovereignty. Therefore, the Italian leader, Mussolini, followed this up with a brazen and haughty demand for apology and reparations from Ethiopia. That is, emboldened by the delay in condemning the invasion of Ethiopia's eastern borders, on 5 February 1935 Mussolini decided on a full-scale invasion without declaring war formally, ignoring the question of Ethiopian sovereignty.[5] The League's instrumentality in its outright betrayal of Ethiopia in support of the Italians was the second time that Ethiopian deference to international opinion influenced its fate, the first being its conduct of internal affairs during World War I.

(contd) 1932 General Graziani had been appointed military governor of the Italian colony of Somaliland. The Italian plan to use their bases in Eritrea and Somalia against Ethiopia were well developed, and Italian troops had already reached Welwel and nearby Warder by 1932. John H. Spencer, *Ethiopia at Bay: a personal acount of the Haile Sellasie Years*, Algonac, MI: Reference Publications 1984, pp. 32–3.

[5] Spencer, *Ethiopia at Bay*, 1984, pp. 39–40.

Unfortunately, the hostility Ethiopia faced was complicated in 1935 by international conditions within the League of Nations, where deliberate prolongation of discussions on the border conflict gained Italy time to amass further weapons and troops.[6] Mussolini's High Commissioner for East Africa, General De Bono, had ordered massive shipments of weapons and placed them in the Italian colonies of Eritrea and Italian Somaliland. On the morning of 3 October 1935, he led his highly equipped force over the Mereb River from Eritrea into Tigre. Simultaneously, General Graziani moved from Italian Somaliland to the Ogaden, aiming to take Jijiga and Harar in the east. He sent General Geloso a few months later to advance through Dolo to take Bale and Sidamo in the south. Leaving the full history of 1935–41 to a volume following the present one, a few selected accounts illustrate how the *chewa* traditions helped Ethiopians assert their sovereignty against all odds.

'COLLECTIVE SECURITY' AND MOBILIZATION IN 1935

The same day that De Bono crossed the Mereb, Emperor Haile Selassie issued a mobilization decree (*kitet*) at the old palace, accompanied by Menelik's drum, announcing in familiar wording that the enemy had come to attack religion and take away the land.[7] He enjoined the warriors not to wear white, a tip they followed seriously by immersing the white cotton clothes in brown earth. Galvanized, the warriors assembled in front of the palace in Addis Ababa and outside the compounds of provincial governors. Those in Addis Ababa rallied on 17 October to pledge their loyalty to the leader and the country in the traditional manner.

The emperor deployed his governors in Tigre, *Ras* Seyoum and *Dajazmach* Haile Selassie Gugsa, and *Ras* Kassa in Begemder. *Ras* Imru, coming from Gojam, was to flank them at Shire. *Ras* Mulugeta, the Minister of War, coming directly from Addis Ababa, was to supplement their forces from the rear. The troops under *Dejazmach* Nesibu Ze'amanuel of Hararge were to resist Graziani's advance from the east, while *Ras* Desta Damtew, commanding *Dejazmach* Beyene Merid of Bale, and *Dejazmach* Amde Mikael Yinadu of Arsi, were to resist Italian advances directly from the south through Dolo. As commander-in-chief, the emperor arrived in Dessie on 30 November, accompanied by spirited troops supplemented by the small 'modern' army that he had been training.

WEAPONS EMBARGO AND WAR DRUMS OF UNEQUALS

With a coordinated strategy, Nazi Germany and Fascist Italy succeeded in threatening the League of Nations over peace in Europe. As a result, the key powers barely hid their willingness to sacrifice Ethiopia's

---

[6] Spencer, *Ethiopia at Bay*, 1984, pp. 40–3.
[7] Marcus, *Haile Selassie I*, 1995, p. 166.

Photo 10 Mobilization with Menelik's drum, 1935 (Source: R. Pankhurst & Denis Gérard, *Ethiopia Photographed: Historic Photographs of the Country and its People Taken Between 1867 and 1935* (Kegan Paul International, 1996, p. 158); by kind permission of Richard Pankhurst's family and Denis Gérard)

Photo 11 Marching through the capital on the way to the northern front of Italian invasion, 1935
(Source: R. Pankhurst & Denis Gérard, *Ethiopia Photographed: Historic Photographs of the Country and its People Taken Between 1867 and 1935* (Kegan Paul International, 1996, p. 162); by kind permission of Richard Pankhurst's family and Denis Gérard)

rights. To placate the Italians, the international community blocked Haile Selassie's attempt to get a loan from the League for buying weapons.[8] In control of the Suez Canal, Britain was especially aware of the contrasting preparedness of Italy and Ethiopia, and in March 1936 stated that Italy had shipped 259 tons of war chemicals to its colonies in east Africa.[9] The massive arsenals of weapons and equipment that De Bono stockpiled in Eritrea and Italian Somaliland included planes, tanks, lorries, shells, bombs, guns and poison gas. Having prevented Ethiopia from importing weapons for which (as in 1896) it had already paid, the French allowed the importation of Italian weapons via Djibouti to Addis Ababa. To avoid risking their stake in the railway by breaking the terms of the concession agreement in the event of Ethiopia not losing the war, they called these weapons 'agricultural machinery'.[10]

Ethiopian weapons and supplies could not even begin to match those of the invader. In 1934–5, prior to the embargo that lost the country access to its weapons dealers, Ethiopia had only imported 659 light machine gun rifles and 125 machine guns. Its other weapons included an estimated fifty to sixty thousand modern rifles, thirteen poorly supplied Oerlikon anti-aircraft guns (which had to be smuggled in), and two or three batteries of light mountain artillery. Out of eleven aircraft, only eight were usable, all unarmed, slow and bereft of spare parts. One of these was assigned to the Red Cross.[11] The emperor spread the machine guns between his southern and northern forces, but reportedly *Ras* Seyoum, for instance, never distributed them to the warriors and later allowed them to be captured. Of the rifles, the Schneider, Gras and Lebel were 'all more than forty year old'.[12] The elderly survivors of the Battle of Adewa were proudly carrying such weapons, cherishing them so much that they vowed to jettison or hide them rather than allow their capture. The few with such heirlooms were perhaps better armed than the majority of their compatriots, who only carried swords, spears and truly antique guns from as far back as the sixteenth century.

Ethiopia also suffered serious supply shortages. As indicated above, changes in the politico-military land-based relations had undermined the traditional means of arranging military provision, and alternative means of accumulating supplies were not in place. The old *chewa* 'masters' had lost the resources with which to provide *gibir* festivities, and faced with several difficulties following the land policies of the late 1890s and later, were confronted by former retainers retorting with 'let him die alone [on the battlefield] as he ate alone' (*endebela yimut*). Their problems were compounded by the distance they had to travel and their unwarranted assumption that they could raise popular support and supplies *en route*. Each warrior brought their initial supplies, some expecting to utilize traditional government supplements, but

[8] Sbacchi, *Legacy of Bitterness*, 1997, p. 57.
[9] Sbacchi, *Legacy of Bitterness*, 1997, p. 57.
[10] Spencer, *Ethiopia at Bay*, 1984, p. 46.
[11] Steer, *Cæsar in Abyssinia*, 1936, pp. 51–6, 173.
[12] Spencer, *Ethiopia at Bay*, 1984, p. 43.

their resources were insufficient for the large numbers of dependants. These included personal service providers and drivers of pack animals carrying personal supplies and, in the case of the wealthy, their horse and mule mounts. Wives, concubines, domestic servants and slaves accompanying the fighters brought very little. During the 1930s ordinary *chewa* soldiers and 'masters' had not been bothering with *gibir*, and for that reason, the luggage train accompanying the warriors was not as cumbersome as in the past.

THE FIGHTING SPIRIT IN 1935

When the invasion came, the ill-prepared warriors, including the Minister of War, *Ras* Mulugeta, wanted to fight the invaders face to face. Many lacked information on the large-scale, strong and mighty force that was arrayed against them in 1935. They thought that they would repeat the victory of the Battle of Adewa in 1896. According to John Spencer, a trusted American advisor of the emperor, offsetting the pressures of such enthusiasm made Haile Selassie seek a solution under the Covenant of the League of Nations even after the invasion.[13]

Few warriors knew anything about the League and its principles. In August 1935, Haile Selassie informed the Ethiopian parliament about the peace efforts his government was making with the League, but mainly highlighting the principle of 'collective security'.[14] Those who knew, some postmen among them, could only share their views with like-minded friends.[15] The majority who had heard of the League of Nations – translated as *yalem mahiber* (strictly 'World Association') – assumed it was similar to the Ethiopian neighbourhood associations (*mahiber*) discussed above. This raised Ethiopian's expectations of what membership of a world association would bring. They thought that Emperor Haile Selassie I was a 'master' among nations of status equal to his. Some believed, therefore, that the League would assist the monarch, and even send an army that would match the enemy force. As we will see below, women joined the campaign, some in order to assert their right of access to the military lands they had inherited, and others as slaves and domestics in the supply sections of the troops.

Ras Imru, then governor of Gojam, appears to have been among the few with the wisdom to try to warn people about Italian weaponry.[16] He recruited a school teacher and writer, Haddis Alemayehu, to stage a play that he had put on in Addis Ababa. It was about Ethiopians beating a foreign invasion.[17] The author delivered an address at the end, asserting

[13] Spencer, *Ethiopia at Bay*, 1984, p. 42, fn. 1.
[14] Mahteme Selassie, *Memories*, 1962 EC, pp. 261–6.
[15] Haddis Alemayehu, *Memories*, n.d., pp. 16–18.
[16] Accounts of *Ras* Imru's camp and his mobilization are from Haddis Alemayehu, *Memories*, n.d., pp. 37–43.
[17] His play, expressing patriotism, was entitled የሃበሻና የወዴህዋላ ጋብቻ ('The Wedding of *Habesha* and *Wedehwala*). See Haddis Alemayehu, *Memories*, n.d.

that Ethiopian history was one of indefatigable warriorhood. Talking of the impending Italian attack, he made light of the Italians' weapons, including planes and tanks, hardly what Imru had in mind as a way of warning people. Obviously carried away by the invitation to show his play, he added that tanks, planes and other modern weapons were mere toys that were going to be 'ineffective' in the illustrious, rugged landscape of Ethiopia. At a later time, Haddis admitted, almost laughing at himself in hindsight: 'I knew very little' of Ethiopian history of warriorhood and had no notion of 'what I was talking about', having seen an aeroplane only once when the country's first plane landed in a field near his school in the capital.

Prompted by his speech, warriors started *zeraf* sessions there and then, 'to the alarm of some Europeans in the audience'. They promised to take personal responsibility for asserting the ideals that were threatened by the invasion. At least one elder swore 'to Heaven and to Earth' in his *zeraf* before *Ras* Imru 'to make his land his burial ground before the enemy took it'.[18] All the warriors in Gojam followed the *ras*, marching enthusiastically to Shire. Of course, when the troops saw the speed with which Italian aeroplanes attacked, and even more, how they were departing unscathed by the shots fired at them, Haddis had difficulty explaining his earlier optimism. At least one young warrior marched back to Gojam when elders intervened to stop him from over-reacting in challenging Haddis right in the battlefield.

Ras Imru had also attempted to secure finances for use during the campaign. However, such planning was complicated by the Italian strategies, and frustration was felt when *Ras* Imru tried to procure the reserves he had entrusted to key people at critical locations. *Dejazmach* Ayalew Biru, for instance, took time to hand over the money to a messenger whom the *ras* sent. This *dejazmach*, who had been harbouring resentment over *Ras* Gugsa Wele's death at the Battle of Anchem on 31 March 1930, was reportedly exasperated at the time by the emperor's order to retreat. He subsequently submitted to the Italians, but he did send back the money later. Another trustee, *Abune* Abraham of Gonder, preferred to hand over the money to the Italians. As the *ras* learned later, the bishop had been bribed by the Italians before the invasion.[19]

Though poorly armed, the highly spirited warriors, governors and administrators who had said their *zeraf* in the *chewa* tradition were determined to uphold their deep commitments and personal responsibilities for country, society and state. They saw the invasion as revenge for Italian defeat in the Battle of Adewa, and unfortunately took it for granted that they could similarly stop the enemy. In fact, Haddis Alemayehu heard an elder adamantly saying that brave warriors did not attack in secret and from behind like brigands or thieves.[20]

(contd) Haddis became a famed writer and diplomat after the war.
[18] Haddis Alemayehu, *Memories*, n.d., p. 42.
[19] Haddis Alemayehu, *Memories*, n.d., p. 53.
[20] Haddis Alemayehu, *Memories*, n.d., pp. 94–5.

In Gojam there was a popular song, *ashereshere* ('he is sliding back'), for challenging those who hesitated to join the campaign.²¹ Elsewhere too, most who went to the provincial capitals to express their loyalties and willingness to fight were joined by new categories of warriors such as priests and school teachers. Their enthusiasm was expressed by a son of *Memre* Zena, the main priest of Kidane Meheret church in Agere Selam, Sidamo. He showed his feelings of personal responsibility in the following poem he wrote before leaving the house of his ageing father before departing to join the troops of *Ras* Desta at Dolo, where he died:

> ተማሪ ቤት ግቢ ተመለሺ ቅኔ
> ወንዶች አዋሉበት አውላለሁ እኔ
> Go back to school, *qene* [a double-entendre on 'education']
> I am going to spend time where the men are!²²

Members of the small standing army, also known as the 'bodyguard', showed exemplary discipline, military camaraderie and loyalty to their divisions and commanders. They had been recipients of a pittance in pocket money for salary. Those in Sidamo, for instance, received only twelve *birr* per annum. They also had to bring their own supplies, but expected this would be only for initial use. Their writings show that later their inexperience inhibited their cooperation with the rural-based traditional warriors; they were also openly reserved about mixing with women fighters. It took them a while to work out ways of negotiating with country people to supplement their meagre resources with bare necessities.

Overall, most provincial governors and their subordinate men and women, including domestics and slaves, intended to fight the enemy face to face without appropriate weapons. The paucity of their information on modern artillery, motorized military vehicles and the havoc that modern war equipment could inflict led to unexpected antics. Not a few warriors died while trying to climb onto tanks to attack the occupants with only their swords. To stop Graziani advancing through the flat country were barefoot soldiers under *Dejazmach* Nessibu Zamanuel; some indefatigable warriors reportedly dug holes in the sand and at least one tank sank driving over camouflage. Others, ranging in age from youth to middle age and beyond, simply perished in the desert: the mule of a seventy-year-old, *Gerazmach* Gessese Fanta, found its way back to the village, but his own fate remains unknown.²³ Not even that much information could be associated with *Balambaras* Welde Yohannes.²⁴ *Ras* Desta, heading towards Dolo,²⁵ prompted the emperor

---

²¹ Haddis Alemayehu, *Memories*, n.d., pp. 16–18.
²² Often repeated by my mother, *Weyzero* Workaferahu Haile.
²³ Information obtained February 2018 from *Ato* Kidane Alemayehu, a participant in the action.
²⁴ Information obtained February 2018 from Professor Getatchew Haile, whose grandfather was among those who perished without trace.
²⁵ The best account of this front is the dedicated history by ሰይፈ አባ ወሎ፡ የታሪክ ቅርስ፡ 1935 (Seyfe Aba Wello, *Legacy of History*, Addis Ababa, 1935 EC); see also the autobiography, ብርሃነ ሥላሴ ድገለሙ (ባላምባራስ)፡ ነገር አለስታሪኩ ተውልደ ሀያው

Photo 12 The Imperial Guard, part of an army training since 1930, with its 2.8m-high band leader (Source: Ladislas Farago, *Abyssinia on the Eve* (London: Putman, 1935, p. 75); by kind permission of John Farago, the author's son)

to send him supplementary forces from Hararge, Wellega and Wolayta, and as we will see below, a member of the new army he had trained was able to throw petrol bombs with which he burned two tanks.

FORMAL RESISTANCE ON THREE FRONTS

The emperor left Addis Ababa on 28 November 1935 for Dessie, from where he conducted the war. By then, of the Ethiopian forces under four *ras*, *Ras* Seyoum was around Abiy Addi (with three thousand men), and *Ras* Kassa was leading forty thousand men to support *Ras* Seyoum. Also advancing to take up positions on the steep-sided hill of Amba Aradam was *Ras* Mulugeta Yigezu with eighty thousand men. *Ras* Imru and his forty thousand men, heading towards Mai Timket, were to support the left of *Ras* Seyoum. Only the emperor's camp was equipped with a small radio communication system. A degree of troop coordination of leaders in the south and southeast from the centre was possible as Haile Selassie received information on a daily basis.

De Bono, who had advanced from Adewa to Mekele on 8 November, was removed in December and replaced by Pietro Badoglio (entitled Marshal of Italy). The emperor planned to split this army by isolating it in Mekele, while it was advancing towards Eritrea. He therefore positioned *Ras* Seyoum and *Ras* Kassa in the Ethiopian centre, charging them with splitting the Italian forces. *Ras* Mulugeta, commanding the *mehal sefari*, was to their right with the purpose of crushing the Italian

(contd) ቀርስ ነው፡ 1996 (Berhane-Selassie Yigeremu (*Balambaras*), *The Past is a Living Heritage for the Descendants of Those Who Were in It*, Addis Ababa, 1996 EC).

left, while *Ras* Imru and his troops from Gojam were on their left in order to take back Eritrea. Indeed, a thousand-strong force of Ethiopians crossed the Tekeze River and pushed back Major Crinitti from the Dembeguina Pass, cutting his route of retreat and encircling him. They overwhelmed much of his force, partly by rolling down boulders from the heights of the pass and setting two tanks on fire, before the major made a break for his life.

However, the emperor had given orders not to shoot until the enemy fired first, and even commanded *Ras* Seyoum to pull back a day's march. This was claimed to have given De Bono the chance to advance rapidly from the Eritrean border. The warriors saw the order straightaway as procrastination. It thus spawned an unexpected leadership crisis, with many defying the order to hold fire and others leaving the field to disperse in anger. Haddis Alemayehu saw at least one retainer of *Ras* Seyoum who had withdrawn in anger and come to the camp of *Dejazmach* Ayalew Biru who was camping by the road to Gonder. As we will see below, another who retreated hastily to Shewa was later to engage in guerrilla attacks against the Italians. The warriors' reaction against the emperor's order to retreat was caused by their lack of proper information on the international situation, especially the imbalance in weapons and supplies. The emperor's strong belief in the singularly foreign maxim, namely 'collective security', was blamed for inhibiting his defences.

De Bono, having taken Adigrat on 5 October, entered Adewa on a white horse the following day, no doubt savouring its symbolic significance for himself. Badoglio, having succeeded De Bono, 'sprayed villages, herds, pastures, rivers, and lakes with yperite', in November 1935 alone. From 1935 to 1936, Italian planes dropped 1,600 'C 500T' yperite bombs.[26] Though *Ras* Mulugeta and *Ras* Kassa had arranged with *Ras* Seyoum to coordinate their efforts, Badoglio sprayed the troops in Temben with poison gas on 20 December and *Ras* Imru's troops at Adi Kwala on 22–23 December.[27] Similarly *Ras* Desta's army, which had dug in near Dolo on both banks of the Genale River, was attacked in January 1936 by heavy air and ground forces, including using poison gas.[28]

In search of easy and rapid victories, Italy used artillery shelling and aerial spraying to deliver poison gas indiscriminately, with horrifying results on man and beast. Sbacchi's analysis of the records indicates that Italy used at least five hundred tons of poison gas against Ethiopians in the course of the invasion of 1935–41.[29] In addition to the huge air power that they utilized to its fullest extent, the Italians outnumbered the Ethiopians four to one. Many perished under the overwhelming firepower of Italian tanks and aerial bombing, or died from or were left severely affected by poison gas.[30] Graphically depicting some of the

[26] Sbacchi, *Legacy of Bitterness*, 1997, p. 60
[27] Marcus, *Haile Selassie*, 1987, p. 172.
[28] Sbacchi, *Legacy of Bitterness*, 1997, pp. 59–61.
[29] Sbacchi, *Legacy of Bitterness*, 1997, p. 60.
[30] For an extensive account of the stockpiling and use of poison gas, see Sbacchi, *Legacy of Bitterness*, 1997, pp. 55–77. Alex ('Sandy') Curle wrote from

atrocities committed during the initial attacks in the north, the famous writer Haddis Alemayehu reported how his sixteen-year-old cousin was burned by a canister of poison gas, which he touched without knowing, and was then killed when another was dropped on the shelter to which he had been moved. Haddis also saw a woman whose warrior companion had charged her with delivering his luggage back to his home. Refusing to hear those shouting for her to take shelter, she was struggling to pull a mule carrying these effects out of the water when a bomb pulverized both woman and animal.

The scattered hamlets provided entertainment for Mussolini's son-in-law, who recorded 'the beauty' of the conflagrations and burning of the houses he bombed. Italian planes bombed twelve Red Cross camps, five of them Ethiopian. At Korem, south of Maichew, the massive air raids hitting troops and others over large areas were described by a member of the Swiss Red Cross, Dr Marcel Junod. He wanted to:

> ... [get] away from this exploding hell... I became aware of a strange chant-like plaint in the distance, an uncanny sound which made me shudder. It was a heart-rending chant which came and went in a slow but persistent rhythm 'Abiet... Abiet... Abiet...' Men were stretched out everywhere... I could see horrible suppurating burns on their feet and on their emaciated limbs. Life was already leaving bodies burned with mustard gas. 'Abiet... Abiet...' There were no doctors available and our ambulances had been destroyed...[31]

In the particular circumstances of that plain of death 'Abiet!' was a word of supplication to God. Taking it in the usual sense of a supplication to draw attention to a government agent or an emperor, Junod translated it as 'have pity', and, perhaps not surprisingly, he misinterpreted it as pleading with the emperor, who was camped in a cave just above the field.

THE DEPARTING EMPEROR

Despite the massive air raids, the troops continued fighting, making crucial stands in Temben in January and February 1936, at Amba Aradom in February and finally at Maichew on 31 March 1936.[32] Maichew – the emperor's position on 31 March 1936 – has subsequently come to designate all the battles fought under various warrior leaders on the northern front. The emperor ordered a retreat on 2 April, starting his own on 3 April. Combined with the shortage of weapons and supplies, his retreat to his capital lost him much prestige. Local people attacked the retreating troops partly because of this and partly

---

(contd) Yabello in March 1941, 'We found a dump of Mustard Gas bombs the Italians had blown up and left all ready to fill in and hide when they retreated.' Curle, *Letters from the Horn*, 2008, p. 245.

[31] Junod, *Warrior without Weapons*, trans. Edward Fitzgerald, London: Jonathan Cape, 1951, pp. 60–1.

[32] Bahru Zewde, *A History of Modern Ethiopia*, 2001, pp. 153–7.

following the usual custom of looting vulnerable soldiers, and reportedly also recalling the loss inflicted on *Negus* Mikael in 1916.[33]

The emperor tried to make the best of his personal retreat by planning to plead, yet again, with the international community and the League of Nations. After conferring about this with some government officials and his immediate family in Addis Ababa on 30 April, he departed to appeal in person at the League. Before he left on 5 May he collected his family, sending an aeroplane twice in one day to Yirgalem for his daughter, Princess Tenagnework.[34] The princess left with her children, but her half-sister, Princess Romanework, and his sons-in-law stayed behind.

Complaining about the emperor's sudden departure, at least one foreign journalist who was known only to some ardent supporters and a few other officials, claimed that his decision was influenced by news of Italian bombing of Harar on 8 April,[35] but of course, there had been also regular bombing of Addis Ababa for months prior to that.[36] As the emperor's train passed through Hararge, Graziani wanted to bomb it but was refused permission by Mussolini, who hoped to compromise the emperor on his arrival in Europe.[37] Indeed, though the war was still in progress, the Italians capitalized on the emperor's flight into exile to lobby the world to recognize their takeover of Ethiopia; only a few countries had not recognized this claim within a year and a half.

Haile Selassie's departure was the first time in Ethiopian history for an emperor to leave the country. Some saw his absence as the 'falling apart of the country', while others were satisfied with contrasting him with Tewodros II who committed suicide when faced with defeat in 1868, to Yohannes IV who sacrificed himself in 1889, and to Menelik II who won a resounding victory in 1896. Some would refuse to accept his legitimacy after his return from exile on 20 January 1941.[38] In a well-known story, the emperor's personal appeal at the League of Nations on 30 June 1936 was rejected. Once in Britain he gave an interview in London in which he spoke of the arrangements for setting up a new government headed by *Ras* Imru.

A member of the 'modern' army later observed that rumours that '*getochu* [the 'master'] had left' had a devastating effect.[39] Another member wrote:

---

[33] Mockler, *Haile Selassie's War*, 1987, pp. 116, 121.
[34] In Yirgalem at the time, *Weyzero* Workaferahu Haile witnessed the plane landing twice.
[35] Steer, *Cæsar in Abyssinia*, 1936, p. 365.
[36] Spencer, *Ethiopia at Bay*, 1984, p. 19.
[37] For details of the attempted negotiation over this, see Spencer, *Ethiopia at Bay*, 1984 p. 82–5.
[38] Haile Selassie flew to Um Idla near the Ethiopia–Sudan border, after flying from Khartoum to Roseires on 18 January. Mockler, *Haile Selassie's War*, 1987, p. 316; Duncan McNab, *Mission 101: The Untold Story of the SOE and the Second World War in Ethiopia*, Stroud: The History Press, 2012, p. 134.
[39] *Dejazmach* Bizuwerk Gebre, in notes he kindly wrote for my reference in 1972.

First news of the defeat of Maichew was heard... Then came the news that the enemy was in Harar... The greatest blow was yet to come: the rumour that His Majesty had left to appeal at the League of Nations... We later discovered that he had left a message, just as Elias left his scarf... he had told us to wait for him fighting in various places...[40]

Those who realistically attributed the retreat to the Italian's superior weapons and cowardly aerial activities lamented:[41]

> ተሃብሽ ጠሎት ጥልያኖች በለጡ
> በአርባ ዘመናቸው ክንፍ አው ጥተው መጡ
> Italian prayers got better than Ethiopians?
> They developed wings in forty years and returned?
>
> በትግሬ ቢመጣ መች ይገባ ነበር
> በጎንደር ቢመጣ መች ይገባ ነበር
> በጎጃም ቢመጣ መች ይገባ ነበር
> በሐረር ቢመጣ መች ይገባ ነበር
> በሰማይ ላይ መጣ በማናውቀው አገር
> Would it have entered, if it had come through Tigre?
> Would it have entered, if it had come through Gonder?
> Would it have entered, if it had come through Gojam?
> Would it have entered, if it had come through Harar?
> It came through the skies, the lands we did not know!

At the start of the summer rains of 1936, anger against those who had submitted to the Italians spread from one part of the country to another:

> ንኬሉም ያልቅና አርከይ ይሄድና
> ያስተዛዝበናል ይሄ ቀን ያልፍና
> With the nickel [Italian currency] finished, the *arkey* [Agew for friend] gone,
> And these days over; we may reflect back on [the mischiefs of] each other!

Interestingly, this warning that the present period of mischief would pass was changed by the end of the same rainy season to:

> በቅዳሜው ባቡር የሄድከው ንጉሥ
> ንኬሉም አለቀ ችሎ ተመለስ
> The king who left on the Saturday train!
> The nickel is finished, come back soon![42]

A PROXY GOVERNMENT

Ras Imru and his substantial following retreating from Shire, in Tigre, were, like others, harassed by those who resented the retreat. Delegated by Haile Selassie to transfer the seat of government from Addis Ababa to Gore, the *ras* was travelling to the western province of Illubabor. He had expected support from old *chewa* leaders such as *Negadras* Welde Semayat and *Bitweded* Welde Tsadik. Indeed, he found that the emperor had actually sent a letter to the *bitweded* in July, asking him to be deputy head of state and prime minister in the alternative govern-

---

[40] My translation from Sahle Tekalegn, in Demiss Welde Amanuel collection, folios 5–6.
[41] The following two pieces are from Memhir Abdu Mohamed, *Miyazia 27 Ken*, accessed on Ethiomedia on 23 May 2016.
[42] Both poems appear in Gerima Tafere, *The Gondere*, 1948/1949), pp. 22–3.

ment. Initially too, *Fitawrari* Yohannes Jote Tulu and *Dejazmach* Habte Maryam Gebre Egziabher, *balabat* in Leqa and Wellega respectively, welcomed the *ras*[43] and even joined him in collecting tax and administering the area.

Imru also found that members of the 'modern' army had come from the Maichew front seeking shelter in the west and setting up the Black Lion Association. Having vowed to work with others in harassing the Italians, they had already burned one of three Italian reconnaissance planes that landed on the night of 26 June 1936, killing almost all its occupants. *Dejazmach* Habte Maryam, the local *balabat*, fled to Gimbi, leaving the soldiers to their fate. Lieutenant Kifle Nesibu and Dr Alemework Beyene defused an unexploded bomb and impressed the local people, who had also become hostile to them. The soldiers then spread the rumour that *Dejazmach* Fikre Maryam and *Dejazmach* Balcha had managed to recapture the capital. This ruse frightened *Dejazmach* Habte Maryam and *Fitawrari* Mosa into inviting them to pass the rest of the rainy season in the local capital, Lekemt (also pronounced Nekemt). It is said that these locally rooted *balabat*, who had held grudges for losing their privileges or for being imprisoned or under house arrest for various reasons, were pro-Italian and *Dejazmach* Habte Maryam again became hostile to the soldiers following reports of further Italian incursions.[44] When *Ras* Imru appeared, these soldiers asked him to help them move the resistance to Shewa.

Though they and the *ras* lacked means of assessing the local situation, on receiving their proposal *Ras* Imru circulated a scheme. He would head towards Ambo with the 'modern' soldiers, while *Bitweded* Welde Tsadik and *Negadras* Welde Semayat would link up with *Kentiba* Tena Gashaw from Jimma, and follow later. He was to find that, resentful of the emperor's departure, *Bitweded* Welde Tsadik was reserved about the scheme. The *ras* also encountered a symbol: someone had killed two goats, one white and one black, and hung them from a tree. Being local, *Belata* Deressa Amante explained to the *ras* that this signalled hostility.[45]

Things looked temporarily brighter for the *ras* when a messenger returned from Sudan, bringing a cache of arms bought with the money the *ras* had entrusted to *Dejazmach* Ayalew Biru of Begemder. Rearming his followers with these arms, he resumed his move east, only to be attacked at Guye and forced back southwestwards. When he arrived

---

[43] ታደሰ ሜጫ፣ ጥቁር አንበሳ፣ አዲስ አበባ፣ 1934 (Tadesse Mecha, *Black Lion*, 1934 EC), p. 78.

[44] Information from *Kegnazmach* Bitewa Meshesha, Gojam, July 1971; Kebede Tessema, *History Notes*, pp. 135–6; ገብረ ወልድ እንገዳ ወርቅ የማይጨው ዘመቻ፣ አዲስ አበባ፣ 1941 (Gebre Wold Engeda Work, *The Battle of Maichew*, Addis Ababa, 1941 EC), pp. 118–20.

[45] Richard Pankhurst, 'The Ethiopian Patriots: the Lone Struggle', *Ethiopian Observer*, Vol. 13, No. 1, 1970, p. 216; የቀዳማዊ ኃይለ ሥላሴ ጦር ተምህርት ቤት ብር-ኢ-ዩ መታሰቢያ፣ 1952 (*Silver Jubilee of the Haile Selassie I Military School*, 1952 EC), p. 104.

in Gore in mid-October, he found *Sheik* Hojelie Al Hassan, *balabat* of Assosa, had been attacked by *Fitawrari* Yohannes Jote of Jimma. Not realizing that Yohannes had declared support for the invaders, the *ras* delegated *Dejazmach* Taye Gulelate and *Belata* Daressa to effect a reconciliation. *Sheik* Hojelie quickly had to facilitate the escape of *Belata* Daressa and some of the 'modern' troops to Sudan. He was murdered by the Italians for doing so.

Perhaps too trusting, *Ras* Imru advanced towards Jimma to meet up with *Dejazmach* Taye Gulelate. However, on arriving at Agaro in Limu on 18 November 1936, he learned that *Sultan* Aba Jobir, whom the Italians had released from prison and armed, was calling for the massacre of Christians. Men, women and children fleeing the town sought shelter with *Ras* Imru, unexpectedly encumbering him. In addition, his erstwhile deputy, *Bitweded* Welde Tsadik, had secretly submitted to the Italians who had executed him on the spot. Disappointed, but lacking alternatives, *Ras* Imru headed towards Gera, still expecting help from *Dejazmach* Taye Gulelate in Jimma. Some forty-four kilometres from his destination the *ras* met *Belata* Takele Welde Hawaryat, who informed him that *Dejazmach* Taye was also pro-Italian. By then, however, it was too late to change his direction yet again.

On 12 December 1936, *Sultan* Aba Jobir's men pushed *Ras* Imru into a trap where Italian forces were awaiting him on the other side of the Gojeb River. Two Italian officers came with some of the attackers and asked him to surrender. He promised to submit the following day and negotiated for the safe passage of the civilians. Taking advantage of the lull, Eritreans who had joined his camp escaped during the night, some to the border areas and others to Shewa, and the rest of his followers threw their rifles and ammunition into the river. Adding insult to injury, *Dejazmach* Taye Gulelate came with *Negadras* Tessema Eshete to see *Ras* Imru off at the aerodrome when he was flown out of Bonga to his imprisonment on the Mediterranean island of Asinara.

PATRIOTIC GUERRILLA FIGHTERS

Very few survived the frontal attacks. On the southern front, some slaves stayed with their 'masters' until Italian troops declared them free in February 1937. The majority of survivors, whether former slaves or not, joined the guerrilla groups. The bedraggled retreating warriors carried news of the defeat at the northern front and the emperor's departure. A few of them trekked to Sudan, Kenya and British Somaliland, subsequently communicating with the emperor to link him with those fighting inside Ethiopia, especially after Italy declared war on Britain in 1940. Guerrilla groups started harassing Italian columns to stop them going to Addis Ababa or to keep them away from the countryside. In different places they had structures ranging from loosely organized bodies to formalized kingship. The Italian disarmament policy and local people's demand for leadership brought together *shifta*, previous administrators and individual fighters. Though some groups collaborated with one another to a limited extent, it took a while for most to identify each other's existence. For the rural people, the war was far from over.

Seeing the Italian presence as only a temporary military setback, young and old came forward to train and work their way up the traditional politico-military ladder. A most famous example comes from youth of Janifakara in Armacheho, Begemder, who were challenged by elders about their entitlement to sing *zeraf* songs at weddings. Thus shamed, the young men left the wedding celebrations to kill, and acquire social approval for their warrior status. Departing to the lowlands, they massacred two lorries full of enemy soldiers, including, to their shame, their own neighbours who had joined Italian service, for which reason they had to remain in the wild.[46] As we will see, they found shelter with a former *shifta* who had turned to guerrilla warfare against the Italians. In Yifat, Shewa, a group of men attacked an Italian convoy on 11 May 1936, killing an Italian soldier, and two of them 'buttered' themselves as killers.[47]

ATTEMPTS TO RECAPTURE THE CAPITAL

A major guerrilla action that actually unnerved the Italians arose from a secret plan to reclaim the capital, Addis Ababa. The aim was to attack it from the surrounding hills, simultaneously descending from east, north and west to meet in the centre. Having retreated from the northern front, many of the plotters had come to realize the scale of Italian military power and left the capital after looting it, just as the Italians arrived there in May 1936. The capital became the seat of the Italian viceroy, the centre of his administration, and his military headquarters, air force and weapons depot. The motivator of the plan was the chief of police, *Balambaras* Abebe Aregay, who had first gone to nearby Jirru to recruit his father, *Afenegus* Aregay. To his dismay, the *afenegus* and his friend *Dejazmach* Meshesha Tewend Belay, refused to join him, but his mother, Askale Maryam, daughter of *Ras* Gobena Dachi, immediately left her husband and engaged in raising local support for her son.[48]

Another plotter, *Lij* Haile Maryam Mammo, who rallied people in Suke Sarabe, Chacha and Selale, had been harassing Italian trucks in the Entoto hills just to the north of the city since May 1936.[49] With him were other Oromo, such as the locally elected leader, Hunde Bulto.

---

[46] ጉርማ ታፈሪ ዘብሂረ ጎንደር፤ ትስፋ በጋሼው፣ አዲስ አበባ፤ ተስፋ ገብር ሥላሴ ማተሚያ ቤት (Gerima Tafere, *The Gondere*, Tesfa Gebre Silassie Printing Press, 1948/1949), p. 187.

[47] Demiss Welde Amanuel, folios 8 and 11.

[48] Salome Gabre Egziabher, 'The Ethiopian Patriots: 1936–1941, *Ethiopia Observer*, 12, no. 2. 1969, pp. 73–4.

[49] Salome Gabre Egziabher, 'Ethiopian Patriots', 1969, p. 76; Tadesse Zewelde, *Surprise to Survivors*, 1960 EC, p. 19.

Fitawrari Bantyirgu Welde Kidan, a leader whom other local farmers had elected, operated in adjacent territory further to the east. The Italians captured and beheaded this man and took his head around the capital as an example of what their opponents should expect. Other leaders, Major Mesfin Seleshi in Badidda, in the Entoto hills, had some 'modern' troops with him.[50] To the west was *Dejazmach* Balcha of Adewa fame, but he had been under house arrest in Becho in Adabarga for more than a decade. He overcame the limitations of his social and political isolation by attacking and snatching firearms from the retreating forces.[51] Though he could not convince his kinsmen in Agemja to join him, he drew support from farmers around Becho who had seen him ambushing and disarming the retreating soldiers.[52]

Dejazmach Fikre Maryam had also developed fame after distributing the weapons he had looted in the capital to the local population in Bulga, directly to the east. Starting on 6 July1936, he frequently attacked the railway line between Akaki and Mojo.[53] This gave him a reputation in the area covering Mojo, Ziqwala, Yerer, Minjar and the area around the railway bridge on the Awash River. His name was used in *fukera* among the followers of *Dejazmach* Bahriyaw (a retainer of *Ras* Seyoum of Tigre until the *ras* went over to the Italians), *Agafari* Yaregal from Lasta, *Fitawrari* Zewdu Abba Koran and *Ato* Haile Maryam Gezimu, all of whom had retreated from the north. Fikre Maryam's camp had a marginal advantage because of support from two local prophets, *Abba* Welde Maryam, a monk who was locally called Marami, and *Fitawrari* Kidda, a medicine man known as the 'king of Yerer' (after the mountain on which he lived). These were preaching that the Italians would be thrown out after the summer rains of 1936 or stay for five years. Until he died in battle on 21 October 1937, Fikre Maryam also enhanced his reputation by giving titles.

The attack on Addis Ababa was to be mounted on the night of 27/28 July. The planners elected two *dejazmach* brothers, Aberra Kassa and Asfa Wesen Kassa, to coordinate efforts. These were grandsons of Menelik's uncle, *Ras* Darge. Their father, *Ras* Kassa, had departed with the emperor, but as members of a well-known family then residing at Fiche in Selale, north of the capital, the choice seemed well made. Unfortunately the Italians got wind of the plan. So not only did they negotiate with the fighters individually but they also spread false information regarding a change of scheme and date. They posted sentries along the various routes into the city and sent a cordon of troops to the rear of the Kassa brothers' position. In the confusion, the brothers

---

[50] *Silver Jubilee of the Haile Selassie I Military School*, 1952 EC, p. 82.
[51] Information from *Dejazmach* Abderahman Hojale and Mezemir Haylu (October 1972).
[52] መዝጋቢ ኃይሉ የባልቻ ደጃዝማች ባልቻ አብነፍስ አጭር የሕይወት ታሪክ፣ 1956 (Mezemir Haylu, *A Short Biography of His Excellency Dejazmach Balcha*, Addis Ababa, 1956 EC), pp. 23–5.
[53] ደምስ ወልደአማኑኤል (ደጃዝማች)፣ መታሰቢያ :: (Demiss Welde Amanuel (*Dejazmach*), *Memories*, n.d.), p. 21.

ordered an early mobilization on 24 July (three days prior to the plan). They brought with them the farmer warriors of Selale, some cadets from Holeta, *Abune* Petros, a bishop who was staying with them, and *Lij* Haile Maryam Mammo – 'who did not know what else to do' about it. Needless to say, the Italians repulsed them, and capturing the prelate, they executed him on the spot, near St George's Cathedral where his statue now stands.[54]

This debacle severely reduced the prestige and following of the two brothers, setting in motion recriminations and competition among the rest of the warriors involved in the scheme. Desertions from *Dejazmach* Aberra's camp increased after the population came to hear about a letter of apology he wrote to Graziani, the Italian viceroy. In December 1936 the brothers began discouraging attacks against Italian positions and even made their negotiations with the invaders open.[55] Later that month they submitted to the Italians who rewarded them with summary execution.[56]

The population in the brothers' area then chose Major Mesfin and *Lij* Haile Maryam Mammo as their joint leaders. The major mounted an attack on the capital on 28 July, but barely made it into the city. *Dejazmach* Balcha, who at first had difficulty crossing the Akaki River but tried again a few days later, was immediately repulsed by Italian reinforcements led by the infantry of Abba Jobir of Jimma. The *sultan* had support from Italian air force planes flown from Dire Dawa,[57] and pursued the *dejazmach* to isolate him from his men. The *dejazmach* continued shooting from a hideout, but tried to gallop away when his servant mistakenly handed him a gun loaded with the wrong cartridge. His mount was shot from under him, injuring his leg, and, caught and brought before an Italian officer, he shouted his *fukera*. The Italian cut him short with a fatal shot. Balcha was buried the following day at a nearby church by his servants. Thus ended the life of the great *chewa* warrior of Adewa fame.[58]

The only leader who struck according to the scheduled night of 27/28 July was *Dejazmach* Fikre Maryam, who attacked before dawn.[59] He and his men advanced as far as the vicinity of Menelik's palace, where they fought for three days before withdrawing to continue a guerrilla resistance from the outskirts. The audacity of the attempt to recapture the capital inflicted severe shock and nervousness on the Italians, and their ruthless reprisals pushed many more to join the guerrillas in the countryside surrounding the towns and roads that they controlled.

[54] ታደስ ዘወልደ፡ ቀን ዘመው፡ 1960 (Tadesse Zewelde, *Surprise to Survivors*, 1960 EC), pp. 22, 305.
[55] Pankhurst, 'The Ethiopian Patriots', 1970, p. 41.
[56] Tadesse Zewelde, *Surprise to Survivors*, p. 311.
[57] Mezemir Haylu, *A Short Biography*, 1956 EC, pp. 23–5.
[58] Mezemir Haylu, *A Short Biography*, 1956 EC, pp. 23–5.
[59] *Dejazmach* Bizuwerk Gebre, *Notes*; Demiss Welde Amanuel (*Memories*, n.d.), folio 45.

Photo 13 *Dejazmach* Balcha Safo, a hero at both Italian invasions (Source: R. Pankhurst & Denis Gérard, *Ethiopia Photographed: Historic Photographs of the Country and its People Taken Between 1867 and 1935* (Kegan Paul International, 1996, p. 54); by kind permission of Richard Pankhurst's family and Denis Gérard)

ATTACK ON GRAZIANI

The guerrilla activities included a further attack in Addis Ababa, and two others on Italian soil in Europe. One of four young men who expressed their anger at the impudent Italian invasion was an Eritrean, Zeray Deress. On 15 July 1937 he lashed out at Italians in a square in Rome because someone interrupted his prayer in front of a lion of Judah statue that had been stolen from Addis Ababa and placed under a memorial commemorating the Dogali massacre of 1887. He was studying in Italy and was already irritated by other experiences with Fascists. He hit back against anybody around, hurting several people until he was shot. He subsequently ended up in a mental hospital, and though some memorials, for instance, the first ship of the former Ethiopian navy carrying his heroic name, have not survived, his name continues to conjure admiration and pride both in Eritrea and Ethiopia.[60]

[60] See መርስዔ ሃዘን አበበ፤ አብዲሳ አጋ በኢጣልያ በረሃዎች፤ አዲስ አበባ 1959 (Mers'e Hazen Abebe, *Abdisa Aga in the Italian Deserts*, Addis Ababa, 1959 EC);

Abdissa Aga, another young man, found himself in Italy having been captured and deported after brief imprisonment in Addis Ababa. He was a former fighter from Wellega, but he broke out of a high security prison and, walking for miles, joined other guerrilla fighters in a mountain hideout in Yugoslavia. They let him hoist an Ethiopian flag from a pole in their camp, join them in blowing up bridges and burning ammunition depots in Italy and even become their second in command. However, after the Allies had reached Italy, his colour attracted hostility while he was relaxing in a bar with these friends. In the scuffle that followed a racist slur, they beat the provocateurs, and Abdissa was condemned to be court marshalled, but escaped with only a prison sentence. He was later ransomed by other Ethiopians. On his return to Ethiopia, the Ministry of War ordered him to join the Holeta Military Academy. He refused, thus risking falling out of favour, and disappeared from the limelight. He had to be searched out and brought forward during Joseph Broz Tito's state visit in 1956 because one of his former comrades-in-arms, a high-ranking general in the entourage from Yugoslavia, happened to ask for him. Embarrassed, the Ethiopian authorities searched him out and presented Abdissa in the uniform of a lieutenant; subsequently he became commander of a unit in the Imperial Bodyguard.[61]

Moges Asgedom and Abraha Deboch, two other Eritreans who had grown up in Addis Ababa, threw two grenades at the Italian viceroy. Moges and Abraha knew Amharic, having attended Tafari Mekonnen School, and spoken Italian since childhood. Moges was employed in the Fascist political bureau in the capital, and (unemployed) Abraha was staying with another friend who worked at the German Legation. Intending to throw grenades at Marshal Graziani during celebrations to mark the birth of a prince of Milan on 19 February 1937, they planned to join the crowd that the Italians were assembling in the palace, now the *Sidist Kilo* campus of Addis Ababa University. The festival was scheduled to start with an alms-giving event, followed two days later by another function.[62] Officiating at the ceremony of speeches and fly-past of planes, Graziani was standing above the steps between the pillars of the portico. Moges and Abraha placed themselves near enough to him without raising any suspicions. The ceremony being over at 11 a.m., soldiers began to distribute alms to the city's beggars and priests. It was then that Moges and Abraha hurled the grenades at Graziani. Running

(contd) Alessandro Triulzi, 'Across the Mediterranean: Acknowledging Voices and Silences of (Post)Colonial Italy', in Paolo Bertella Farnetti and Cecilia Dau Novelli (eds), *Colonialism and National Identity*, Cambridge Scholars Publishing, 2015, pp. 161–76.

[61] A talk about his own recollections given at a public meeting in Canada and posted by Robele Ababya, 28 June 2006, as: 'Col. Abdissa Aga's heroic feat in Italy: WWII'; accessed on 19 March, 2018: www.ethiomedia.com/carepress/col_abdissa_aga.html. See also Mers'e Hazen Abebe, *Abdisa Aga in the Italian Deserts*, 1959 EC.

[62] Salome Gabre Egziabher, 'The Ethiopian Patriots', 1969, p. 81; Tadesse Mecha, *Black Lion*, 1934 EC, p. 320.

out of the compound, they headed first for the guerrilla camp of *Balambaras* Abebe Aregay and then for the Sudanese border where unknown people killed them.

Graziani, it is claimed, had 365 fragments in his body, and several others standing around were also hurt. The Italians' sense of confidence, already damaged by the persistent guerrilla activities, was deeply shaken. They issued a *carte blanche*, empowering their men to massacre all Ethiopians on sight – starting with guests and beggars who had been lured to the palace with offers of alms. Guards identified the perpetrators, Moges having been missed from his work area, by searching their house where they found an Italian flag stuck to the floor with nails and a dagger. They traced Moges's wife, it was said, at Debre Libanos, a monastery north of the capital, where she had sought shelter. They massacred monks and all others they found there. In three days alone they murdered thirty thousand Ethiopians. For months afterwards Italian soldiers continued to engage in cold-blooded genocidal murders of civilians going about their daily lives, of captured guerrilla leaders, of monks, nuns and priests in various monasteries and churches, and of soldiers and other prisoners who had survived the invasion fronts or were captured from among the guerrilla warriors. They hunted down and killed youth educated before the invasion, believing that they were the originators of nationalist feeling.

THE LAST *CHEWA* CORPS IN THE SOUTH

In 1935, *Ras* Desta, commanding troops from Sidamo, Arsi and Bale, had with him 260 'modern' young soldiers whom he had recruited and trained in Yirgalem with the help of a Belgian, Lieutenant Armand Ferere.[63] His main force was made up of named corps, the *Gondere* and the *Barud Bet*. They had been in the provinces since about the mid-1870s, and, of course, had been affected by the changes faced by the *chewa* since the late 1890s. However, at the time of the invasion they collaborated with the *Dembegna* or *kuter tor* – the soldiers who had come as a restraining force. The only difficulty the *Barud Bet* and *Gondere* faced arose from their non-provision of banquets (*gibir*) resulting from their lack of *gebbar* or other formal income. This had created a layer of discontented potential retainers who even jeered at the mobilization. The combined force under *Ras* Desta was said to be fifteen thousand, about seven thousand of them from Sidamo. This was a much smaller number than on the northern front. As we will soon see, many were killed at Dolo by bombs and poison gas delivered by the Italian air force. The thirty-two *fitawrari* of the *Barud Bet* from Sidamo and many of their retainers survived and went on trying to halt the Italian northward advance until the end of January 1937.

[63] Seyfe Abba Wello, *Legacy of History*, 1935 EC, p. 45; Sbacchi, *Legacy of Bitterness*, 1997, p. 64.

On 3 October 1935, Italian planes attacked the *Gondere* troops of Bale and Arsi, frightening *Fitawrari* Ademe Anbesso, *Ras* Desta's advance column commander, who therefore surrendered to the Italians on 13 October 1935. To the surprise of the *Barud Bet* who felt the *ras* was wrongly accusing them, the *ras* telegraphed the emperor that 'the people of Sidamo' had deserted him. Perhaps unaware that they thought sending Ademe was ill judged on the *ras*'s part, the literature on the war echoed Desta's telegram for decades afterwards.[64] Those who escaped the attack on Dolo fled either towards Kenya or retreated to British Somaliland via Hararge. Separated from their troops, *Dejazmach* Beyene Merid and *Dejazmach* Amde Mikael Yinadu retreated north towards the Arsi highlands where they were eventually to meet *Ras* Desta. The emperor's response to *Ras* Desta's telegram was to send him reinforcements from Hararge under *Dejazmach* Gebre Maryam, from Welayta under *Dejazmach* Mekonnen Wesene, and the *Werwari* from Wellega under *Dejazmach* Debay.[65]

Those in Yirgalem at the time recalled for a long time afterwards the heroic *Werwari* men singing their *fukera* of '*Wellega belew!*' ('show them, Wellega!') all night long before they left town.[66] The townspeople came out to see the 'modern' soldiers leaving the provincial capital, Yirgalem, marching with a spectacular show under the command of Major (also *Kegnazmach*) Bezabih Seleshi. Three days later they arrived at Agere Selam and 'met up with the *neftegna*, the *yebet lij* [the 'household' retainers] and the *Barud Bet*' who had been told to rally there. *Ras* Desta reviewed the troops and reorganized them, placing some of the thirty-two *fitawrari* of the *Barud Bet* under his command, and others under *Fitawrari* Yigeremu Gebre Tsadik. The troops were accompanied by a remarkable female singer the soldiers endearingly named Kurta (to indicate her inspiring determination). Twenty-five days later most of the soldiers arrived near Dolo, and the *ras*, who had brought priests and a Kidist Maryam *tabot* in the three lorries at his disposal, made his headquarters at Malka Dida, and reviewed the troops at Borana Amino.[67]

The planes machine-gunned the properly marked Swedish Red Cross tents on 22 December. On the 30 December, ten of them bombed and destroyed the same target. Some twenty-seven planes followed this by showering the troops with mustard gas and bombs from 17 to 19 January 1936. On 19 May, the *Barud Bet* contingent downed two planes they had nicknamed *shanko* and *shasho*, respectively black and white, for their colour. Despite their flash of success, most of the *Werwari*, *Gondere* and *Barud Bet* perished within a few days of the start of their new attack, along with most members of the 'modern' army.[68] At one stage, Major Bezabih Seleshi showed two volunteers of the 'modern' corps how to throw petrol bombs at the vehicles, and the men managed to burn a tank

---

[64] See for instance, Spencer, *Ethiopia at Bay*, 1984, p. 46.
[65] Seyfe Aba Wello, *Legacy of History*, 1935 EC, p. 187.
[66] *Weyzero* Workaferahu Haile.
[67] Berhane-Selassie Yigeremu, *The Past is a Living Heritage*, 1996 EC, p. 27.
[68] Seyfe Aba Wello, *Legacy of History*, 1935 EC, p. 94.

and inflict other damage on the enemy.[69] The defection of about two hundred Eritreans from the Italian side crowned their success, and it was then that the warriors and *Ras* Desta came to know the commander of their adversaries, General Geloso. The renewed air raids decimated the defenders, enabling Italian tanks and lorries to push northwards.

Dr Junod (the Swiss doctor mentioned above), who came to see the conditions of the destroyed Swedish ambulance unit, also saw those of the Ethiopian camp. On 6 January 1936, a Belgian officer attached to the general staff informed Junod that the Sidamo force 'had never been more than 15,000... [and was now down to between] 4,000 and 5,000', despite Junod being told in Addis Ababa that *Ras* Desta's force was half a million. In his search, he saw that 'The half-starved soldiery offered little or no resistance to the scourges which decimated their ranks: malaria, dysentery'.[70] From such a scene, he found himself invited to *Ras* Desta's tent:

> ... [for] an excellent... [lunch]... with most savoury dishes and a variety of wines... [and the *ras*] opened two bottles of champagne and ceremoniously raised his glass to the health of his guests... [Then] he led me to the bank of the river... [where] crocodiles were sunning themselves... [The entertainment was]... the relaxation of a prince in the ante-room of hell...

Recalling his experience of similar bombing at Dessie, in December 1935, he noted that there had been 'at least... the assistance of the army in sorting ourselves [the Red Cross] out again and all the resources of an accessible area was at our disposal. Here there was nothing.'[71]

Ras Desta rewarded the few surviving officers, in the name of Haile Selassie, with titles ranging from *balambaras* for the younger ones, and *kegnazmach* and *gerazmach* for the older ones.[72] He then redeployed his remaining force. He sent the few surviving *Werwari* under *Dejazmach* Debay and the *Barud Bet* under *Fitawrari* Yigeremu to hold out against Italian advances along the road from Negele to Agere Maryam. He instructed the trained soldiers and officers to follow the Dawa River to meet up with him for deployment later, giving each officer a handful of *dabokolo* (crouton-like travel food) from his personal supplies as a gesture of bidding them well. He then left the field in the only remaining lorry, retreating north to the Jemjem highlands, taking with him *Dejazmach* Gebre Maryam, Major Bezabih Seleshi, and the priests and *tabot*.

The survivors of the 'modern' army trekked northwest along the Dawa River, without rations, and, except for a few bullets in their cartridge holders, without ammunition. It was three days before they spotted a giraffe, which they killed and ate. In the highlands, they found hospitable Uraga, who gave them a goat and a bullock to eat, and further

---

[69] Berhane-Selassie Yigeremu, *The Past is a Living Heritage*, 1996 EC, p. 20.
[70] Junod, *Warrior without Weapons*, 1951, pp. 43–8.
[71] Junod, *Warrior without Weapons*, 1951, pp. 48–50.
[72] Among these were my father, *Balambaras* Berhane-Selassie Yigeremu, and his elder brother, *Balambaras* Gebre Maryam Yigeremu, both members of the newly trained 'modern' army.

respite at Kibre Mengist in the house of the erstwhile sub-governor, *Fitawrari* Welde Tsadik. A fortnight later the *ras* summoned them to his camp and accorded their young leader, the newly entitled *Balambaras* Berhane-Selassie Yigeremu, a special reception. Drawing up a list of the large number of Eritreans who had deserted from the Italians, the *ras* then asked the *balambaras* to take them to Yirgalem for rest. To the chagrin of his exhausted men at arms, the young man refused to leave the battlefield, and the *ras* had to send the Eritreans with someone else.

After the retreat from Dolo, *Fitawrari* Yigeremu with the *Barud Bet* engaged in face-to-face fighting at Malka Dida for a week. Having barely escaped, they joined *Ras* Desta at his fort in Wadera. The *ras* reassessed his troop movements on 8 June 1936,[73] and, receiving information that the Italians were heading towards his headquarters, he deployed *Dejazmach* Gebre Maryam to Fisiha Genet. He also deployed, under *Fitawrari* Yigeremu, the ageing *Dejazmach* Debay and the *kuter tor* under his *aide-de-camp*, *Fitawrari* Kassa Yagilew. Yigeremu was told to win back his governorate, as the people of the Awata River had reportedly been receiving bribes from the Italians. Besides Debay, two of this group were close family: Kassa, Yigeremu's son-in-law, and Berhane-Selassie, his son. After Yigeremu managed to win back the specified population, the *ras* redirected him to fortify Jebasire, near the town of Agere Maryam. Notwithstanding planes and tanks, the group managed to repulse the Italian mechanized force back to its camp along the Gololcha River in Bale after a one-day fight.

The group was aware that nature was bogging down the Italians in their camp, and as the weather began to dry in September 1936, seventy-eight youth from Jebasire mounted a surprise attack, taking shelter in the forest of wild olives. They heard and saw three open vehicles with white soldiers emerging from the camp very early in the morning. They fired at the first lorry, killing all the soldiers in it, but unfortunately, some of the youth started looting before the others could stop them, and reinforcements arriving from the Italian camp killed six of them. The rest escaped, taking booty back to their camp at Jebasire, and presented *geday* to the *fitawrari*, *Dejazmach* Debay and others.

Within two weeks, however, relentless air and ground attacks harassed the group for a full day. By 4 p.m., *Dejazmach* Debay and many more were dead and *Fitawrari* Yigeremu was wounded. His son wrote:

> I ordered the operator of the mountain gun to destroy it, and, abandoning our fortress, followed my father for about two kilometres before he looked back and seeing me weeping, collapsed in a pool of blood... I sat him up under a tree until a few of our household members found us... We made a stretcher... In the night we found a mule and managed to reach our house in Annole in the morning.[74]

Dejazmach Gebre Maryam at Fisiha Genet was pushed back after heavy fighting.[75] These failures meant that most of the force under the *ras* lost ground. *Balambaras* Berhane-Selassie arrived with the information

[73] Seyfe Aba Wello, *Legacy of History*, 1935 EC, pp. 124–36.
[74] Berhane-Selassie Yigeremu, *The Past is a Living Heritage*, 1996 EC, pp. 42–3.
[75] Seyfe Aba Wello, *Legacy of History*, 1935 EC, pp. 114–18.

on Jebasire to find that the *ras* had moved to Watadera. Major Bezabih Seleshi took the young messenger and Major Bekele Weya (later *dejazmach*) to a mountaintop at dawn on 12 November 1936. Using a mountain gun they fired at an Italian camp below them until 9 a.m., Major Bekele operating the gun while Berhane-Selassie passed him the shells. Berhane-Selassie continues:

> ... after which we quickly retreated dragging our gun, but the enemy bombed and shelled the mountain top all day long thinking that we were camped there. At 4 p.m., the *Ras* called me and said: 'You have now fulfilled your duty and you should return to your father.' When I refused, Major Bezabih Seleshi and *Dejazmach* Gebre Maryam joined in, and one of them called me '*ajire yajire lij*' (meaning 'You, son of your father!') and *Ras* Desta told 'me to return to my father's camp'.

The phrase 'You, son of your father!' was a mixture of praise, admiration and no doubt, exasperation. Shortly after Yigeremu recovered from his wounds *Ras* Desta ordered him to 'fortify and defend Yirba'. The Italians had bombed Yirgalem on 9 November 1936, but did not bring troops into it until 8 January 1937.

The resistance to them obliged the Italians to attack Watadera and the surroundings of Tafari Kela.[76] This forced *Ras* Desta to move to Arbegona, and 'From there he summoned us to abandon our fortress too, and report to him', writes Berhane-Selassie. On their way to meet up with the *ras*, Yigeremu and Tessema Abdi, both *fitawrari* of the *Barud Bet*, fought off a group of Italian *askari*, who attacked them at Melka Karaba. They captured much Italian currency and weaponry before escaping. When they met *Ras* Desta in Arbegona, they found that *Dejazmach* Beyene Meri'd and *Dejazmach* Amde Mikael had come from Arsi on 20 January and joined him.

This meant that the Italians had cornered the surviving leaders of the Dolo front at one spot, and they soon sent a peace offer through a resident Italian called Castagna[77] ('Qestegna' to Ethiopians), reportedly a 'godson' of *Ras* Desta. At a meeting to consider this proposal many advocated slipping through the lowlands to the Kenyan border. Along with the Eritreans, *Kegnazmach* Haile Mekuria (a former *yenetsa dagna* – so called for his position before the invasion as an anti-slavery court judge), who had been responsible for constructing the fortress at Tafari Kela, proposed to lead the *ras* along a route Haile knew from his long-distance trading days. The *ras* rejected the proposal on the advice of the thirty-two *fitawrari* of the *Barud Bet*. He even went so far as to put the *kegnazmach* in chains and place him under the guard of the *kegnazmach*'s daughter's father-in-law, *Fitawrari* Yigeremu.[78] The pressures were beginning to create demoralizing situations.

[76] Seyfe Aba Wello, *Legacy of History*, 1935 EC, pp. 124–36 and p. 187.
[77] Another resistance leader, Geressu Duki, hanged Castagna when he approached him with a similar mission.
[78] This is my mother, *Weyzero* Workaferahu Haile, and the source of my information.

Ras Desta, *Dejazmach* Gebre Maryam and *Dejazmach* Beyene Merid met with the leaders of the *Barud Bet* for further discussion near the Kebena stream in Terriba. By the end of the meeting, they resolved to resume fighting the following day, all agreeing to stand and fight to the end. It has been widely reported that they actually made their vow while walking between two rows of guns, pointing at each weapon and saying: 'If I desert, may I be caught by this if not by that!' The *fitawrari* of the *Barud Bet*, Yigeremu Gebre Tsadik, Tessema Abdi and thirty others left the leaders at Ḳebena for the night and returned to their camp a couple of kilometres away.

On reaching their camp, however, the thirty-two *fitawrari* and their retainers found their tents had been surrounded while they were at the meeting with *Ras* Desta. The Italians had brought additional troops from Addis Ababa via Shashemene, and, with others advancing from Arsi, Agere Maryam and Jebasire, they had put the warriors in a pincer grip. Surprised, *Fitawrari* Tessema Abdi and *Fitawrari* Yigeremu Gebre Tsadik sent runners to inform headquarters. The messengers returned with the information that *Ras* Desta, *Dejazmach* Gebre Maryam, *Dejazmach* Beyene and Major Bezabih Seleshi had abandoned camp soon after the *fitawrari* departed, setting fire to the guns and ammunition in their care. The *ras* had already been informed by his personal scouts of the whereabouts of the enemy positions.

Later, people expressed surprise and resentment that the leaders had neither informed the *fitawrari* about the Italians nor left them the weapons. Subsequently, some saw *Ras* Desta's deployment of *chewa* troops at the forefront as symptomatic of his desire to be rid of them. Faced with certain capture, the *ras* had left the surviving 'modern soldiers' and the *Barud Bet* to their fate. *Kegnazmach* Haile Mekuria, who was still in chains, was freed later by the Italians. The Eritreans, along with others who had favoured Haile's plan, made their escape to Kenya during the night.

Relatively unencumbered by troops, *Ras* Desta, his sister-in-law, Princess Romanework, her husband *Dejazmach* Beyene, *Dejazmach* Gebre Maryam and Majors Bezabih Seleshi and Bekele Weya fled towards the Gurage in the centre of the country. Pursuing this force of relatives and friends, the Italians engaged them in a skirmish around Shashemene where *Dejazmach* Beyene was killed and the two majors escaped to join the resistance in eastern Shewa. Left with only about ten men, *Ras* Desta and *Dejazmach* Gebre Maryam tried to escort Princess Romanework to safety among their relatives in Gurage country. On 23 February, however, some local men at Gogot pretended to lead them to safety but opened fire, killing *Dejazmach* Gebre Maryam and most of the others. The *ras* 'fired on his own until he ran out of ammunition', and was captured and handed over to Italian officers in Butajira, who executed him on the spot on 24 February 1937.[79] They subsequently deported the princess to a prison on Asinara, an island off Sardinia in the Mediterranean (where she died).

---

[79] Seyfe Aba Wello, *Legacy of History*, 1935 EC, pp. 104–18.

In Terriba, *Fitawrari* Yigeremu Gebre Tsadik and *Fitawrari* Tessema Abdi looked out of their tents at dawn to find that almost all of their *Barud Bet* colleagues had posted white flags outside theirs. The muzzles of Italian guns, some poking through the openings, were trained only against their tents. As usual, the Italians executed on the spot the *fitawrari* who had submitted, and took *Fitawrari* Yigeremu and *Fitawrari* Tessema to prison, first at Tafari Kela, the temporary fortress taken from the *ras*, and then at Qaliti in Addis Ababa. Yigeremu was accompanied by his household *azazh* and a secretary, both of whom were later imprisoned at Danane near Mogadishu. The *azazh*, who survived the harsh prison conditions there, later returned to the family and reported how the Italians treated both *fitawrari*. The captors questioned them for several days 'meaning to release them', but one day *Fitawrari* Yigeremu lost patience and got up to strangle his interviewer. Soldiers shot him dead along with his friend Tessema Abdi. Like *Ras* Desta's, these executions coincided with the continuing murders following the attempted assassination of Graziani on 19 February.

Some fifty kilometres away from Terriba some young members of the *kuter tor*, the *Barud Bet* and the 'modern army' kept fighting. They were unaware that their headquarters had capitulated, and *Ras* Desta and the remaining *fitawrari* had gone. Messengers from *Fitawrari* Yigeremu's wife to her son *Balambaras* Berhane-Selassie sent them the information, and they dispersed in different directions, some to Keffa and from there to Kenya. Many survivors of the southern front considered *Ras* Desta's withdrawal from Terriba as the end of the first phase of the invasion, and took pride in pointing out that it took only until May 1936 for the Italians to break through and reach the capital, but it took them till February 1937 to take Sidamo. They later joined and assisted British forces that came to clear the Italians from the south in 1941.[80]

ARBEGNA GUERRILLA WARRIORS

Unlike the forces under *Ras* Imru and *Ras* Desta, the new warriors that arose in many parts of rural Ethiopia as early as the summer of 1936 relied entirely on support from local farmers for supplies and leadership. Elected leaders (*ye gobez aleqa*) and their followers set up local administrative units. They saw the whole country as a large *fanno*

---

[80] See for example Curle, *Letters from the Horn*, 2008, pp. 234–51, on the highly effective 2nd Ethiopian Irregulars under her father's command. He had known some of them when they escorted the Border Commission at the time of Welwel in 1934. He also had known more of them in British Somaliland and during their evacuation from there to Kenya, where later he recruited his Irregulars. From British Somaliland he wrote in July 1940: 'We also have many... who fought... against the Italians and all they ask for is to fight again – pay is no object to them and all they want is rations. They say "We fought for two years without pay for our country and that is all we want to do".' Curle, *Letters from the Horn*, 2008, p. 225.

territory, in which various similar groups could operate. Their disparate locations reconfigured the country into what had prevailed prior to the rise of Tewodros II. Some promoted qualified warriors to high status, including as monarchs, crowned or uncrowned, and saw them as a controlling power beyond their immediate localities. After the first few months, such groups of men and women began systematically to attack Italian troops and disturb their peace. Groups in their home bases expanded their networks by linking, depending on their performance, with other new leaders. Mobile *fanno* groups who went to fight from difficult terrain – forests, mountains and river valleys away from their home bases – also managed to keep links with those staying within neighbourhoods maintaining local law and order. Their persistence in sacrificing their lives in defence of country and people in accordance with their *chewa* politico-military traditions is still remembered in oral tradition for making the country ungovernable by the Italians during the lengthy 'period of the invasion'.

Many were convinced spiritually that the Italians would be there only for a limited duration. A prophecy had also been circulating, saying that the emperor would either return within the three months of the rainy season, or would stay away for five years.[81] Reportedly originating in the monasteries of Ziqwala (to the southeast of Addis Ababa), Itissa in Bulga, Mahibere Selassie in Begemder, and in other religious centres,[82] this had helped to offset the disappointments following the defeat of the troops at the invasion fronts. Their guerrilla strategies, which included surprise attacks from hideouts, and retreating as

---

[81] Demiss Welde Amanuel collection, folio 8; Gerima Tafere, *The Gondere*, 1948/1949, p. 187; ታደስ ዘወልዴ፡ ያለፈኝ ዘመን (Tadesse Zewelde, *Era of Discord*, n.d.), p. 54; Steer, *Cæsar in Abyssinia*, 1936, pp. 362–3, speaks of the *wooha boha*, an expert in the occult and 'oracular Scotland Yard' who 'seeks out thefts and petty misdemeanours', who had prophesied the failure of the Ethiopian army. The emperor's departure abroad was reportedly influenced by his prophecies, which were also given a respected spiritual angle by the priests of the Ethiopian Orthodox Church. I have found it impossible to establish what or who Steer's *wooha boha* was. Then, as in 1991, 1974, and similar periods of change in the nineteenth century, uncertain situations were accompanied by prophecies expressing what people were hoping to see and were working to achieve. 'Prophecies' reflecting political projections often 'originated' in monasteries and other religious centres where holy men were supposed to have made them. Sometimes shrewd political priests and hermits seem to have influenced opinion by messages alleged to come from such monasteries. An instance of this was when Yohannes IV decided to mobilize against the Dervishes in northern Ethiopia before he had consolidated his internal hold. Messages said to have been organized in Menelik's camp, which feared being attacked by Yohannes, predicted death and reward in the kingdom of heaven for Yohannes if he fought the Dervishes, but only victorious life on earth if he fought against Menelik. This, more than the pressure at the border, was said to have influenced Yohannes's priority to fight the Dervishes.
[82] The *Dersane Raguel* offers the best example of prophecies that record the sensitive hopes, aspirations of rulers and their past. For belief in prophecies in the life of Menelik, see Guèbrè Sellassié, *Chronique*, pp. 74–5.

quickly as they appeared, were different from traditional battlefield practices.

By the beginning of 1937, the rural population was led by groups that were promoting or demoting leaders, and, out of such processes, arose leaders like Belay Zeleke in Gojam, who achieved the nickname 'emperor by his might', and Abebe Aregay in Shewa who gained the title *ras*. Such developments enhanced the perception that the Italians were never in control of government in the countryside. The worst time for the population came in September 1937 when the Italians issued a disarmament order, expecting to rule over them as though they were all female, as was said in Gojam. Even many who had initially backed the Italians withdrew their support and increasing numbers fled the cities to join the guerrilla camps. Popular leaders in Shewa, Semien and Armacheho in Begemder, Gojam and Wello developed significant connections, popularity and ability, and, on that basis, increased their standing by distributing titles in their own names. *Chewa* symbols, images and practices relating to power and authority were adopted in places that competed to hold the highest seat of power. For example, we have seen the story from rural Begemder of young men who found themselves 'in debt of blood' with their own community for mistakenly killing neighbours in Italian pay. They then vowed never to 'butter themselves' unless their 'kill' was a white man so long as the Italians were in the country.[83] The place where they found protection was the camp of Wibneh Tessema, a self-made leader who was popularly acclaimed *ras*.

As mentioned earlier, the individual resistance fighters were *wetader*, 'those who live out', from the words *wato ader* 'one who lives by roaming', but the most enduring term for the guerrilla fighters became *arbegna* ('patriot').[84] The *arbegna* distinguished themselves physically by wearing cartridges around their belts, guns across their shoulders, and, to give the impression that they were wild, letting their hair grow into a disorderly mass, with tangled and matted strands deliberately greased and twisted between the palms of their hands. All walked barefoot and wore khaki trousers if available, and long shirts with *dig* – a long 'toga' (*netela*) wrapped around the waist like a belt – for support. Women fighters turned themselves out similarly, growing their hair in the same way. Demiss Welde Amanuel (selected to talk to the Italians when they later sued for peace) emphasized: 'It was very important that we did not wash; it was our distinguishing mark.' The *fanno*, as the leaderless bands were called, were accepted by the warriors as *arbegna* and legitimate to work with as they later raided hostile villages for crops, attacked trade caravans, and, significantly, looted Italian camps for

---

[83] Gerima Tafere, *The Gondere*, 1948/1949, p. 187.
[84] A fourteenth-century song described Emperor Amde Tsion as an *arbegna* for his military achievements. Later documents applied the same term to religious fanatics who, banished to the lowlands during religious controversies, died for their beliefs. Modified as *Ye Kristos arbegna*, 'defender of Christ', preachers in recent years going from one place to another without church authorization have been using it in reference to themselves.

ammunition, weapons and other goods. *Fanno* and other *arbegna* rarely attacked towns, and almost always stayed in the countryside, often camping near farms and settled villages in forests, and sometimes in caves. They left their wounded or sick in rural peoples' huts. All over the country, fighters had secret collaborators known as *ye west arbegna*, literally 'internal patriot', some of whom worked in Italian political offices.[85] In true *chewa* tradition, over and above their attempts to maintain law and order they undertook to fulfil the personal responsibilities expected of individuals regarding the relationship between land and society and their defence.

THE CROWNED HEAD

Falling back on *chewa* traditions appears to have been facilitated by also creating links with the monarchic tradition. *Kegnazmach* Hailu Welde Medhin, the trusted follower of *Dejazmach* Fikre Maryam (mentioned already in association with trying to recapture the capital), was the first to articulate setting up a viable monarchy in eastern Shewa.[86] *Kegnazmach* Hailu crowned a boy-king, Melake Tsehai, who was reportedly one of the sons of *Lij* Iyasu. *Lij* Girma, a half-brother of Melake Tsehai, was reportedly murdered on the Kenya–Ethiopia border by some people who saw him as an 'embarrassment' to Haile Selassie. Another son, *Gerazmach* Feleke Iyasu, who had been under house arrest in Sidamo, left his wife and family in the care of the *Barud Bet*, and lived incognito in Addis Ababa after 1941. *Lij* Yohannes, the eldest son of *Lij* Iyasu, was considered a near-king in Begemder and Semien, as we will see below. In general the ideal person they wanted to have as leader was to be known either for bravery or for connections with the prescribed dynasty. An example of this was Belay Zeleke in Gojam, where the former *shifta*-leader-turned-valiant-resistance-warrior developed a large following of fighters, and was nicknamed 'emperor through his own might' (*atse begulbetu*).

The boy-king in Shewa, called Engdashet, was promoted and crowned by *Kegnazmach* Hailu who himself owed his title to *Dejazmach* Fikre Maryam whom he had succeeded as leader. Hailu had the support of *Dejazmach* Mengesha Wesene, who had wide family ties in Bulga, Shenkora and, to some extent, Menz. Mengesha had retreated from the northern front with a seriously depleted soldiery, but he used his lofty title and his local connections, first to support Fikre Maryam and then Hailu. He enabled them to collect tax, provide effective leadership, and make Hailu's idea of a monarchy acceptable. They had found Engdashet in a nearby monastery where his 'aunt', Tsehai Work Darge, had reportedly left him in the care of the monks. She was a daughter of

---

[85] Tadesse Mecha, *Black Lion*, 1934 EC, p. 22.
[86] The story of Hailu and his candidate for the crown is based on information collected in the course of 1972 and from the notes of *Dejazmach* Demiss Welde Amanuel, folios 87–9.

Menelik's uncle, *Ras* Darge, and therefore an aunt of the Kassa brothers in Selale, and first cousin twice removed of *Lij* Iyasu. She had gained notoriety for attempts on the life of Haile Selassie before the invasion.[87]

The boy's coronation ceremony in July 1937 left out none of the traditional paraphernalia. 'They gave him ceremonial clothes, including a mantle and other things they could lay their hands on', and crowned him in the presence of the 'whole population', according to 'ancient rites', in the church in the monastery of Itissa Tekle Haymanot, which brought him up recognizing his descent from Menelik II.[88] They gave him the throne name of Melake Tsehai, which is also a title normally given to a church official and probably suggested institutional support for accepting him as king. Among several other reasons cited for the choice of name was the fulfilment of a prophecy that a great monarch with that name would rule the country.

The occasion was marked by the distribution of titles ranging from *balambaras* to *dejazmach*, but no higher. Hailu was the only new *dejazmach* created in this first round of appointments. In a second set on Ethiopian New Year's Day, 1 Meskerem 1930 EC [12 September 1937], he was also 'elected' by the people as regent. This placed Hailu in a stronger position to reorganize the fighters. Unquestionably an elected leader sanctioned by a sense of respect for traditional hierarchy, Hailu expressed his prestige and strong warrior principles in the Ge'ez words on his own seal: ዘይለብስ ልብስ ዘንተሁ በደም: ወስይሞ ደጃዝማች ኃይሉ ('Clothed in mantles sprayed with blood, he called him *Dejazmach* Hailu').

On 13 September 1937 the abbot of the church and monastery of Itissa was given the position of *echege*, a title held by a historical prelate, *Abune* Tekle Haymanot (c. 1215–1313), who founded the monastery of Itissa. Whether this was also meant to evoke *Abune* Tekle Haymanot's role as a restorer of the Solomonic dynasty is a moot point. The historic associations were intended to impress people regarding the legitimacy of Melake Tsehai Iyasu's coronation. Kidane Weld, a friend and associate of the regent, received the title of the most trusted and responsible person of government, the chief secretary of the king's court (*tsehafi tezaz*). His current duty was writing letters in the name of the king and circulating information on the existence of the kingdom – pointing out that the *arbegna* 'had crowned the son of *Lij* Iyasu, called Melake Tsehai'. The regent signed the proclamations, and made announcements in markets and other open places. People of eastern Shewa took the ceremony and pageantry seriously, accepting the titles and open air proclamations as coming from a king of royal blood. This added to the fighters' confidence, and many came to join the king's camp at Debre Beg'e in Bulga.

When one of the circulars reached the former chief of police, *Balambaras* Abebe Aregay, in his home region of Jirru, he asked for a list of

---

[87] Kebede Tessema, *History Notes*, p. 67.
[88] *Dejazmach* Demiss Welde Amanuel, folios 87–9.

'patriots on that side' of the country without mentioning king or regent.[89] The regent replied briefly, specifying that they had crowned a son of *Lij* Iyasu, but excluding any listing of patriots. The *balambaras* and his party came and approached the king's camp. In the tradition of a guest of equal stature joining his hosts, he sent a messenger to say that they were arriving. The cavalry scouts of Bulga came out from the king's camp to receive them. According to an eyewitness, their entry into the presence of the king was accompanied by dramatic pageantry:

> He [the king] was sitting on a throne properly laid out. *Negarit* [ceremonial drums] were being beaten and the Ethiopian flag was flying in the open plains. On either side of the camp, machine guns were mounted and the patriots of Bulga, Berehet, Terra and Kembibit were lined up. Priests in ceremonial robes were also in place. When the newcomers saw this pageant, some of them wept in pleasure. On our entrance to the camp, the army was reviewed. Then *Abba* Yerdaw made a speech saying that the boy was put in his care by *Woyzero* Tsehai Work Darge. When the boy grew up [somewhat], he said, he took him to His Majesty [Haile Selassie] who said that he did not have the features of his father, and told him, therefore, to bring him up himself. Then, he said the patriots found him. He concluded by saying that he was now handing over [responsibility for] his care to them.[90]

Neither the regent nor the priest came forward to identify the king as a royal person, and the newcomers also showed little interest in the explanations about his parentage or about those who brought him up. In fact, the spokesman made no secret of the doubts expressed about the boy's parentage and his connections with Tsehai Work, the lady nemesis of Emperor Haile Selassie. A member of this group, Lekelesh Beyan, said later that many, including her, had doubts about his looks.[91]

Nonetheless, they used him as a source of legitimacy, and the leaders responsible for his coronation were devoted to the boy-king, as the circumstances of his death in the summer of 1939 illustrate. In fact, they soon handed over the monarch to *Balambaras* Abebe and his group. By then *Balambaras* Abebe had received the title *ras*, and he took over as regent when Hailu Welde Medhin died. On 7 June 1939, the Italians attacked Abebe's camp from the air, and used a pincer movement of Adal and Karayu lowlanders from the eastern escarpment. The guerrilla warriors and their followers suffered heavy casualties, and Haile Maryam Mammo was killed. Fighters and non-combatants had to be on the move constantly, and many died of fever and exhaustion. The symbolic king, Melake Tsehai, who had to be transported on a stretcher, according to Lekelesh Beyan, due to 'fatigue and nose-bleeding', died after a week of illness.

This attack was part of continuing Italian efforts to control the countryside three years after they had claimed to have conquered Ethiopia, just as exiles, returning secretly from neighbouring countries, were bringing letters from Haile Selassie. As others had done elsewhere, *Ras* Abebe declared support for the emperor, after discussions on whether

---

[89] Demiss Welde Amanuel, folios 88–9.
[90] Demiss Welde Amanuel, folios 88–9.
[91] Interview with Lekelesh in 1972.

or not to accept the rights of Haile Selassie. This clouded the narratives on the death of Melake Tsehai, generating secret suspicions of murder, some implicating *Ras* Abebe.[92] In what an informant called propaganda, a Muslim cobbler brought by the *ras* to make shoes for Melake Tsehai was claimed to have administered poison to the body of the king while measuring his feet, thus causing his nose-bleeding and death. This, of course, ignores the ravaging fever that killed many, including, it seems safe to assume, the boy-king.

POPULARLY ACCLAIMED *RAS*

The guerrilla activities of *Balambaras* Abebe illustrate how warriors achieved leadership by working with local people. Abebe was elected to lead a substantial number of survivors of the attempt to recapture the capital. In September 1937 he led these from Gendeberet and northern Shewa to Bulga where, as we have seen he met with *Dejazmach* Hailu Welde Medhin and his protégé, Melake Tsehai Iyasu. The movement of such a large force obliged the Italians to deploy the Muslim lowlanders of Adal against it in October, causing havoc to the fighters and the surrounding population and forcing the guerrilla to evacuate their camp.

It was on 30 October 1937 that *Balambaras* Abebe, *Fitawrari* Zewdu Aba Koran and Haile Maryam Mammo took over personal responsibility for the king and the fighters of Bulga. The fighters found respite in November to hold the meeting at which they offered Abebe the overall leadership of the forces around the boy-king and the position of regent and leader. After accepting this new position, Abebe mounted an attack on an Adal town, Babbi, which increased his popularity further. In April 1938 he undertook a tour to popularize the kingdom beyond eastern Shewa. On his arrival at Chafe Maryam the warriors acclaimed Abebe as *ras*, and his deputy, Zewdu Aba Koran, as *dejazmach*. This made Abebe just one of three popularly appointed *ras* in the country at the time. Hayle Maryam Mammo, who refused a title for himself, continued to look after the titular king, while Demiss Welde Amanuel and others set up an association acknowledging only Haile Selassie's authority.

While *Ras* Abebe was at Debre Beg'e, Bulga, the Italians sent him a letter offering peace. This he rejected. They then sent a large force that spread across a huge area in eastern Shewa, namely Minjar, Yifat, the lowlands of the Awash River, and over the highlands of Feres Tifir, Terra, Kembibit, Bulga and Shenkora. Aeroplanes dropped supplies to their troops but some fell in guerrilla camps. Locally recruited *banda* deliberately abandoned their weapons to the guerrilla, and 'the forests were filled with boxes of ammunition so that bullets that used to be less than ten to the *birr* now reached one hundred to the *birr*'.[93] After

[92] Salome Gabre Egziabher, 'The Ethiopian Patriots', 1969, p. 81.
[93] Demiss Welde Amanuel, folios 111–12.

thirty-seven days the Italians withdrew this large-scale offensive, taking more than four hundred country people to a prison in Mojo.

The rest of the warriors fanned out in separate groups, and *Ras* Abebe retreated to Wayu. *Dejazmach* Hailu Welde Medhin decided to stay in Bulga, where he mounted an attack on 26 July 1938 and was wounded. Slipping away from enemy pressure, *Ras* Abebe began another tour in July to rally other fighters. In late January 1939 he arrived at Merhabete planning to meet with those operating locally, especially under the leadership of Teshome Shenkut (later *dejazmach*).

Teshome was in hiding with the vulnerable local population, in Ametegna Washa, a cave capable of holding three thousand. On Easter Sunday he and his group were gassed in it:

> Seven cylinders containing poison gas were heard rolling down the precipice, and they were stopped at the mouth of the cave by fixed wires. Soon these were shot at by the enemy with all sorts of guns. The barrels exploded and gas escaped, some of it yellow, some green and some purple. The force of the shots drove the fumes into the cave. Around nine o'clock, everybody's eyes in the cave were affected; some even went mad, and began to shoot at one another.

By the evening, only 260 were normal, and over the following three days, the majority in the cave had died, among them the parents and siblings of Teshome. When the survivors emerged on 12 April 1939, some who had washed their eyes with their urine had escaped blindness. The stragglers were shot at as they left the cave, and of 1,262 souls, 930 of them non-combatant civilians, only 175 made it to another cave in Menz.[94]

Ras Abebe abandoned northern Shewa, unable to connect with any guerrilla force in the area. When he returned to Bulga, he found that an Italian garrison close by had surrounded Hailu Welde Medhin and three hundred other fighters who had lost their lives while attempting to escape through an apparent gap. The disruption pushed the *ras* and a small number of followers to camp along the Kebena River on the outskirts of Addis Ababa. Apparently threatened by reports of the presence of this 'invincible leader', the Italians sent another peace mission to him in May 1939.[95] The emissaries included *Negadras* Afework Gebre Iyesus, *Negadras* Tessema Eshete, *Dejazmach* Aba Wekaw, and Castagna.[96] Suspecting that this elderly Italian had come to spy on him, the *ras* hid the symbolic king, Melake Tsehai, in Gelila, and sent back conditions, including recognition of their jurisdiction as an independent area. The Italians also sent *Ras* Abebe's young son, Daniel, with a letter saying that his presence was required as a witness about the Ethiopian monastery in the Holy Land. After a series of other attempts, the Italians dropped leaflets from the air warning the rural population against

---

[94] Ministry of Justice, *Documents on Italian War Crimes: Affidavits and published documents*, Addis Ababa: Ministry of Justice, 1950, p. 20.
[95] Demiss Welde Amanuel, folios 128–65.
[96] This was the same man who had tried to negotiate with *Ras* Desta in Sidamo. He was killed by Geressu Duki, a guerrilla fighter to whom he had tried to bring Italian peace offers.

supporting 'the *shifta*'. By then the *ras* had received a letter from Haile Selassie. He had also formed serious contacts with other groups of warriors, and even written to *Lij* Yohannes Iyasu advising him to stall any communication with the Italians.

At one time during the negotiations, *Negadras* Tessema Eshete suggested that Zewdu Aba Koran meet some Italians in the capital. This led the fighters to try and murder the *negadras* and curtail the rapport, but upon other advice they sent Demiss Welde Amanuel and a colleague. Colonel Lorenzini, governor of Debre Birhan, saw this as a success and took them to meet General Nasi, the governor of Shewa, who told Demiss: 'You have not lost the battle and we have not won you.' This being the eve of *Meskel*, the Italians bought military clothes and shoes for the delegates and took them to witness an Italian emulation of a *chewa* military title-giving ceremony on the *Meskel* Day celebrations. At a luncheon at the grand palace, the patriots noticed they had been placed between the mayor of Addis Ababa and Lorenzini and they realized that they had been given a 'place higher than the Ethiopian grandees' in Italian service.

After showing off his prizes, General Nasi took them to see the viceroy, Duca d'Aosta, who gave them a pistol each. He then returned the patriots to the countryside, entrusting Demiss with a message for the *ras* to come in person. As Demiss had warned Nasi that such a meeting would be entirely up to all the fighters in his camp, an Italian police chief, Major Luchetti, accompanied them to *Ras* Abebe. Finding that individual warriors were firmly loyal to the *ras*, who was unflinching, they were forced to reduce their presence around the camp of the *ras*. Also seeing that they had to rely on Demiss alone, they began treating him like an official delegate, and even assigned him a residence, located of course in what they called the indigenous quarter of Addis Ababa. They took him and his friend on a tour to visit and speak with other leaders, such as *Balambaras* Geressu Duki, and Demiss used the opportunity secretly to deliver letters and messages to this leader. However, the Italians were alerted to this and, breaking the vows they had made, they attacked the guerrilla camps, and sent another delegate to the *ras* without telling Demiss and his colleague.

At the end of 1939, General Nasi reported that the camp of *Ras* Abebe was much more solid than expected. To appease Abebe the Italians tried and sentenced some of their soldiers who had reportedly killed or captured guerrilla fighters. They also offered compensation money. Angered, the fighters postponed the date for making the vows yet again. Nonetheless, Nasi also asked Demiss to prepare the *ras* for a promise of cooperation before the Minister for Italian East Africa's visit in February 1940. By February the *ras* was still asking Nasi to postpone any meetings for making vows of friendship. Finally on 6 March, Nasi launched fresh attacks on the camp of the *ras* without giving a hint either to Demiss or to the resistance. He had brought eleven thousand troops led by *Ras* Hailu Tekle Haymanot, and the 'white shirts' under General Gazera and the *Sultan* of Jimma. As these tried to find *Ras* Abebe's camp in August 1940, the marauders dropped poison gas and other bombs from the air, unleashing terror attacks against the guerrillas. In June 1940, Mussolini had declared war on the Allies in Europe. In Ethiopia, Italian offensives were focused on eliminating the resistance.

LIJ YOHANNES IYASU

An equally intensive resistance in Begemder, Gojam and elsewhere had also established leaders with local legitimacy. *Lij* Yohannes, one of the sons of *Lij* Iyasu, had been in prison before the invasion as he was seen as a threat to Haile Selassie. The Italians had freed him and appointed him governor of Gishen, a small province in Wello. Under the disarmament policy of September 1937 he was reported for owning a machine gun that he had not declared to the invaders, and fearing its possible confiscation, he joined the local guerrilla fighters under *Gerazmach* Gobena Amede. Gobena saw Yohannes off to Begemder, another area of strong resistance, where he was received by two leaders, Tadesse Yimam and Gebre Kristos Desta. His new hosts lost no time in offering to make him a rallying figurehead over a wider group of fighters.

Unlike his young half-brother, the crowned king in Shewa, *Lij* Yohannes accepted the warriors' offer on condition that his position would not be that of a fully-fledged king.[97] Agreeing to this, they introduced him as a son of *Lij* Iyasu. He received an acclamation by a large network of fighters from Semien, Begemder and Lasta. The local people expressly allowed them to live off their lands, and keeping a strict control over the symbolic value Yohannes represented, it was soon arranged for him to marry the daughter of Shewanesh Abraha, the lady who had led her fighters from Lasta in Wello when her husband, *Wagshum* Hailu Kebede, was killed by decapitation. Yohannes's marriage and the local people's grant of resources established a most prestigious alliance for the warriors.

By February 1938 *Lij* Yohannes had become so popular that all groups in the area looked to him for military manoeuvres and justice to prisoners. In May all the fighters, including those from the westernmost parts of the province, elected him as an overall leader and made appointments and distributed titles in his name. Expressly saying that the emperor was still alive, he rejected the inevitably compromising idea of associating his name with titles loftier than *dejazmach*. Only a few, including *Gerazmach* Gobena Amede, who refused to accept any titles or appointments, supported this argument. The majority protested because his refusal inhibited awarding titles to those they saw as deserving heroes.

The immediate difficulty came from two major figures. One of these, Wibneh Tessema, had, as we have seen, already been made *ras* by

---

[97] Mostly from interviews with former resistance fighters, Addis Ababa, March 1972; Gerima Tafere, *The Gondere*, 1948/1949, p. 187.

popular acclamation[98] for his heroism and also for reducing the tax that local people paid him. Wibneh, according to his own account, was a local farmer who assumed leadership in Begemder when he became a *shifta* after killing his brother's assassin before the war. He was known to slip frequently back and forth over the border with Sudan from his home base in Wegera, thereby having the reputation of being in contact with the emperor in the 'English country'. Comfortable with local support, this *ras* had looked for Yohannes's confirmation of his title. On being refused, the *ras* challenged Yohannes to battle but lost to Yohannes's well-armed supporters.

The other major figure who was troubled by Yohannes was Tadesse Yimam of Lasta, the very man who had first introduced him to the resistance fighters. Wanting to head his whole army, he demanded the title *dejazmach* and invited all the fighters to his home base on his uncle's estate in Sade Muja. During a week-long stay, he provided a *gibir* of lavish entertainment accompanied by great festivities and pomp, which reportedly prompted several weddings on the spot. The title that Tadesse demanded was within the limit Yohannes had set himself, but the latter deferred the choice of overall leadership to the patriots. When refused, Tadesse tried to assert himself by throwing Yohannes into a private prison. He refused to disclose its location, even pretending to have killed him, and had Yohannes's wife kidnapped and returned to her mother (who had not been invited to the festivities). In a move tantamount to war, he held the guests hostage to get his demands. Gobena and the rest of the warriors had to mount an attack before Tadesse finally produced Yohannes, but he absolutely refused to return the guns he had confiscated. He also withdrew the warriors of Lasta from the resistance group led by Yohannes.

Exasperated by the infighting, farmers of Wegera decided to keep Wibneh and Tadesse out of their area for the rest of the invasion period, preferring to continue fighting the Italians without them. Retreating to isolation in Semien, Yohannes remained with Shewanesh Abraha, who contributed guns and ammunition to rearm him and his reduced number of fighters. Their restricted movements in the Simien highlands lost them access to the Sudanese border, and though they had expressed their adherence to the authority of the emperor, whom they believed was still alive, Wibneh and others gained the emperor's ear first. They accused Yohannes of ignoring, if not challenging, the emperor's authority during 1940/41. Yohannes had to spend decades under house arrest afterwards.

THE SELF-MADE EMPEROR BELAY ZELEKE AND HIS RIVALS

Several elected leaders emerged in Gojam by harassing Italian convoys and settlements. In Mecha and Achafar, the rural people elected *Dejaz-*

---

[98] Gerima Tafere, *The Gondere*, 1948/1949, pp. 46–7.

mach Mengesha Jembere,[99] a grandson of Menelik's general of the previous century, *Ras-Bitweded* Mengesha Atikem. This man collaborated with the Italians until their disarmament policy came in. Reluctant to accept personal titles or relinquish his own, he tolerated his retainers accepting titles from *Lij* Yohannes Iyasu, and attracted to his camp other fighters from Begemder. One of these, Aberre Yimam, wanted to take Mengesha's leadership position for himself. He fought unsuccessfully for it for a week, and, when defeated, went over to the Italian side.

Local farmers also asked *Dejazmach* Negash Bezabeh, a grandson of Tekle Haymanot,[100] to abandon his post as Italian governor of Burye and lead them in the resistance in Damot. This also coincided with the Italian disarmament policy; he did not need much convincing. They saw him as a good choice because of his family connection with the locality. Besides, he was known to have provided shelter to resistance fighters, Major Mesfin, commander of the bodyguard, and *Belata* Takele Welde Hawaryat, as they passed through his area on their way to the Sudanese border in the summer of 1937. These politically astute survivors of the attempted recapture of the capital had advised Negash to style himself መስፍነ ጎጃም መግዮን ('Prince of Gojam and Ghion'). The *dejazmach* readily accepted this and used it on his seal in his activities with the local farmers he led.

Of other resistance fighters in Gojam, Belay Zeleke in Bichena earned popular acclamation and near-monarch status. His pre-war activities were similar to *Ras* Wibneh's.[101] He grew up in a rebel's camp because his father, Zeleke Lakew, was a *shifta* leader sheltering in the Blue Nile gorge. Zeleke had killed a man in protest against taxation by *Ras* Hailu Tekle Haymanot, and sought protection from his mother's relatives in the lowlands of Bichena, but was killed when Belay was twelve. When the government gave amnesty to all rebels on the eve of the invasion, Belay came to the highlands and killed his father's killer. He re-emerged while Italian sympathizers were attacking the retreating troops of *Ras* Imru, and killed two more members of the same family. These killings made Belay a rebel in his own right, and he continued to attract Italian attention by suddenly appearing and departing from towns, and taking blame for acts of outlawry. The Italians sent a *banda*, Sammu Nagawo, to attack his camp in Bichena, but Belay caught and hanged Sammu in the marketplace. This gained him yet more popularity, as expressed in the following couplet:

> ያበላይ ዘለቀ ይሄ ነው ወይ ለካ
> ግንባር ሚተረከክ በአውቶማቲክ
> So this is Belay Zeleke,
> He fractures the skull with an automatic gun.

---

[99] Interviews with *Dejazmach* Deress Shiferaw, *Kegnazmach* Damte Shibeshi, *Fitawrari* Belay, July 1972.

[100] Interviews in Gojam with *Kegnazmach* Damte Shibeshi and *Fitawrari* Kelkay Abesha, July 1972.

[101] Interviews with *Kegnazmach* Negatu Aycheh, July 1972, *Dejazmach* Deress Shiferaw, October 1972.

In summer 1937 his maternal uncle from Amhara Saynt, across the Abay, joined him, bringing other family members. Local farmers also elected Belay as their commander and leader, and he duly rewarded them with titles. He gave appointments to newcomers loyal to himself alone, intending to 'enrol them efficiently' in following his leadership. He gave the highest and most respected posts to elders among his kinsmen, making two of them, including an uncle, *ras*, several others *dejazmach*, and many more *fitawrari*, and appointed one of his kinsmen *afenegus*, chief justice. A story is told of his younger brother asking him: 'You have given away all the titles; what are you reserving for yourself?' His response, playing on the meaning of his name, was that his mother had called him Belay ('superior') and that was enough, and he preferred his horse-name, *Abba Kostir*, 'father of fire-lighter'. This self-respect, detached from seeking prestigious accretions, endeared him to fighters everywhere.

For all practical purposes, however, Belay behaved as a king. Everyone near and far called him *atse begulbetu*, 'emperor by his own might', and although he resisted the term, those in his own camp addressed him as *leul hoy* (Your Highness). Belay, like many leaders, was illiterate and used his father-confessor as his secretary.[102] A priest made him another seal, probably designed to his order, which significantly indicated his lofty intentions and aspirations: በላይ ዘለቀ የኢትዮጵያ ደም መላሽ ('Belay Zeleke, Avenger of the blood of Ethiopia'). Using the word *Ethiopia* on his seal reflected his thinking behind the high titles he gave, and showed a *chewa* sense of responsibility for regions beyond his local jurisdiction. Belay deliberately began to make his presence felt by Italians and Ethiopians alike in the few months following his election. Former governors were keen to collaborate with him and, especially between 1937 and 1939, their active cooperation contributed to restricting Italian presence to roads and forts.

Hailu Belew, a grandson of *Negus* Tekle Haymanot in neighbouring Mota, was elected by local farmers for his prestigious birth, even though he was restricted by his well-known pursuit of praying piously in a local monastery. Without expecting him to demonstrate any quality of either leadership or warriorhood, they referred to him with the title *lij*. Hailu reluctantly accepted this symbolic leadership, and, with the added excuse of recognizing only Haile Selassie's authority, he left it to the population to fight off any Italian attacks without rewarding them with titles.

At one stage, Belay invited *Lij* Hailu to take the leadership of Bichena as well, but seeing his reluctance to harass the Italians, Belay made forays into his jurisdiction, and tried to lure local people to his own camp, offering titles and appointments. Belay also organized skirmishes so that the warriors could claim to have killed, but these angered Hailu who in turn provided shelter to some of Belay's followers, especially those protesting at the disciplines he imposed. In fury, Belay said he

---

[102] This man had made an seal for Belay before the invasion depicting an effigy of his patron saint with the words 'Belay Zeleke Berhane Gebre Giyorgis', which can only have been a religious expression.

would make Hailu 'come out and fight'. He installed his own governor over two districts of Mota, but in a classic demonstration that even a heroic warrior needs local approval, the farmers came out in large numbers and forced Belay to retreat; he barely escaped with his life.

LEKELESH BEYAN, AN EXEMPLARY WOMAN FIGHTER

Just before the invasion, women's legal access to *gult* and other military lands was challenged, and their enrolment in the *demb* (referring to the *dembegna*) was rejected, though their regency of male minors was allowed. The following decree about accessing the old military lands, promulgated at the time, threatened women. It intended to keep women off the battlefield and promoted using them only as proxies, or having their rights transferred to grown-up sons. It read:[103]

> May it reach His Excellency *Ras* Biru, Minister of War,
>
> As of the wordings in Article 34 of the Constitution concerning daughters of deceased officers and soldiers, and as of the discussion in the Chamber of Lords, and of that on *Miyazia* 9 current, in the presence of the Presidents of Parliament, ministers, and other dignitaries and yourself, and considering Article 46 of the Constitution, a daughter is no longer to enlist in the *demb* and is no longer to 'hold the rifle'; but should be eligible to receive as of nos. 9 and 10 of the law issued on *Tahesas* 21, the security towards the upbringing of deceased officers' or soldiers' sons who are not yet of age to enlist in the *demb* and to 'hold the rifle', until the boys are fifteen years of age. It has been said, in the event that an officer's or soldier's daughter has a son who is old enough to enlist in the *demb* and also if the deceased or aged officer or soldier has a grandson, he should not be prohibited from enlisting in the *demb* as of the law issued on *Tahesas* 21.
>
> *Miyazia* 26, 1927. [May 4, 1935.]
>
> T. T. [*Tsehafi Te'zaz*] Welde Meskel.
>
> Minister of Pen.

For practical reasons, implementing the decree proved unworkable. Provincial officers who were expected to oversee its implementation were accused of abusing their power, and a circular had to be passed deferring its application:

> May it reach His Excellency the Minister of War.
>
> Article 34 of the Constitution passed by both chambers of Parliament, decrees that a daughter should not enrol in the *demb* and 'hold the rifle'; but now it is reported that the *shaleqa* are appointing their favourites and disinheriting their enemies. Therefore let what happened since the decree stand as it is; but for what had been happening before that, examine the evidence any woman produces regarding her long proprietorship and let her perform her duties by proxy. The new decree shall be put to work later. Inform this to the *shaleqa*.
>
> *Pagume* 5, 1927. [September 10, 1935.]
>
> T. Haile. [*Tsehafi Te'zaz* Haile Welde Rufe]
>
> Minister of Pen.

---

[103] This and the following decree appear in Mahteme Selassie, *Memories of Significance*, 1962 EC, pp. 248–9.

Women came to fight against the invasion, but their involvement differed among various troops. Most *chewa* fighters on the northern front had brought their whole family trailing behind them. Those on the Dolo front had personal retainers, but the *Barud Bet* in Sidamo, the *Werwari* in Wellega and the *Gondere* in Arsi and Bale were not encumbered with their families until the Italians reached the areas where they had left them. The *Barud Bet*, for instance, brought their women and children after the Italians reached Agere Maryam and Yirgalem. After the *Barud Bet* was defeated at Jebasire, the women became involved in raiding for food and finding appropriate shelter. However, when the leaders of the *Barud Bet* were killed, their women-folk were taken prisoner, and their slaves and other household service people were freed. Some families of *Barud Bet* leaders were kept under surveillance, but most managed to avoid any contact with the invaders. Most *chewa* widows and wives of prisoners remained in the countryside in protest at the invasion, making a point of wearing traditional clothing and keeping away from the 'civilization' of the Italians.

Among the few women fighters who went to the northern front, some joined other warriors returning to the towns but many such women rearmed to join the resistance. Lekelesh Beyan, who had been to Maichew with her own rifles to assert her land rights, became a fighter. Shewanesh Abraha allowed her social position and connections to encourage the resistance in Semien right from its early stages, as we saw above. Shewarreged Gedle campaigned against the invaders, most powerfully in the last two years of the invasion. Lekelesh Beyan said:[104]

> I would not let down the memory of my father. When the emperor said that an enemy that would take our lands and defile our churches was invading the country, I took up my father's gun, put my four-month-old daughter on my back and joined the *Kambata Tor* [troops from Kambata] under the command of *Dejazmach* Meshesha Wende. I wore men's clothes.

Her 'father' was her maternal grandfather, Shibiru Tena, who had passed on some army land in Kambata to his daughter, who passed it to his granddaughter. Lekelesh, who had a little brother, could not use her husband as proxy because he had to stand for his own piece of army land. So she took up her responsibility as if a man. The couple had no horses or mules, but they walked as far north as Maichew in Tigre, taking with them attendants and slaves to carry their supplies. Reputedly, Lekelesh fought with valour equal to the men, killing several enemy soldiers in the battles of Temben. Though she got separated from her husband in the hasty retreat to Shewa, they met afterwards. They stayed in Addis Ababa until, on 5 May 1936, they left the city with a group of friends, Lekelesh carrying their baby girl on her back. She said:

[104] The following quotations are from interviews I conducted with women patriots in Addis Ababa, November to December 1972. See also Tsehai Berhane Selassie, 'Women Guerrilla Fighters', *Northeast African Studies*, Vol. 1, No. 3, Winter 1979–80, pp. 73–83.

> My house in Addis Ababa was in Arat Kilo, in the vicinity of the palace. I left it open and went to Jirru. I had to leave it open so that people would not suspect that I had gone away indefinitely.

Lekelesh and her husband joined a group of about forty fighters, who engaged in forming a wandering guerrilla band. Within a fortnight, they were harassing small Italian patrols outside the capital. 'I also went into battle. I fired many shots and killed many of the enemy, but I was not even wounded', Lekelesh recalled. At one stage, her small group was forced to withdraw towards the gorge of the Abay River, north of the capital, and live off the country people for food and shelter. They eventually joined the camp of Haile Maryam Mammo, when, as we saw above, the Kassa brothers disappointed the warriors. Subsequently they found themselves in the camp of *Balambaras* Abebe, and later, still with him, in the camp of boy-king Melake Tsehai Iyasu. Lekelesh had five women domestics, including one to look after her baby, and undertook some household tasks on top of her guerrilla activities.

> I always fought, but in the spare time we had, I did domestic work as well. I used to spin, and had it woven to give clothes to *Ras* Abebe, *Fitawrari* Zewdu and such people. There were times when we had a long respite of a fortnight at a stretch. I spun at such moments ... I always operated the *baleweha metreyes* (full automatic machine gun). I was also responsible for the light mountain Hotchkiss. He [her husband] did not know how to operate the latter.

She lost her husband in a battle on 10 August 1937. She said she saw him firing behind tall grass. Suddenly he waved to her and when she got there he had dropped down dead. She pulled away his body and his gun, and buried him the following day. Her group was disrupted for a while, but the main body of warriors continued fighting day and night. Her skill in warfare appears to have been considerable. On one heroic occasion, in the midst of a fight, she rescued a dying man.

> It was a night battle, and men were finding it difficult to remove the dying. Someone called out for me and I saw it was Mammo Badane. He was severely wounded. I picked him up and took him to Mugerie Zala and gave him to his superior. One of the machine gun bearers was rescued by Tedla Mekonnen. Later on the same night, with two of my men we outflanked an enemy group and snatched a machine gun that I gave to *Fitawrari* Abebe Weldu, who I met later in the morning.

Each new acquisition was a godsend, and such snatches were the only way the fighters could increase their supply of machine guns. Collaborators in Italian camps used to sell light guns, but never such heavy ones. In the above rescue operation she also saved an old flag from falling to the enemy.

> It was on the day of Debre Zeyt [mid-Lent] and we had to travel a long distance in the night. There was light rain, and we wanted to pitch camp. But a surprise attack obliged us to fight. We had fourteen machine guns, and although we lost many people, the men saved these. Many of our number were taken captive from the camp.

On 7 June 1939, Lekelesh came across the dying Haile Maryam Mammo (whose group she had joined in 1937):

> I was shocked and frightened, but he told me to take the flag and get on with the battle. The flag-bearer was dead. I found the flag as we were about to go away. Tekle (one of the men responsible for it) refused to take it, but I took it and put it around my neck. As I turned to leave, I saw that the man was dead. I said: 'You are dead!' By then I was left alone. I crossed a river and found myself surrounded by enemy soldiers on all sides. I climbed a tree before they spotted me. I stayed in that tree for five days. I was so hungry. I had no food to eat. I had a field glass, and one day I saw two men approaching with a sack of something and an *enchet mauzer*. I made them drop that and ate what they had been carrying. On the fifth day, the enemy went to Ankober. I was then able to join my group.

That summer, the Italians had given up hope of convincing *Ras* Abebe and other famed warriors to collaborate with them. They persecuted the country people so much that they refused to give the fighters food and shelter so that the latter had to loot for food. 'I was not considered a woman who should stay behind in the camp', Lekelesh said. 'I was even responsible for the battle at Erret Meda', one of the last offensives by the guerrillas in eastern Shewa, and 'our most bitter battle' against Italian patrols. From August the Italian air force bombarded all the countryside areas to flush out the resistance fighters. This forced the guerrilla to the brink of famine in the arid and barren lowlands. Like the boy-king and many others, Lekelesh and her child were affected by an epidemic characterized by dysentery, nose-bleeding and death. She was unable to move:

> I got the disease and was taken so ill that I did not distinguish day from night. *Shaleqa* [later *Dejazmatch*] Feleke Dagne, *Fitawrari* Bekele Lanagatu and *Ato* Demiss Beyene used to care for me, taking me around with them. *Kegnazmach* Niguse and eighteen other men were also affected by starvation and disease.

Feleke Dagne, the scout for the day, had too few fit men to remove the sick. It was only three months before liberation. Lekelesh found that Feleke was only able to visit her at the eleventh hour during an encounter with an enemy troop that had found them in their hideout. She then gave him her gun and asked him to leave.

> They left me in an old hut and went away. The attackers threw grenades, burned the door open and entered. One of them hit me with the butt of his gun because he thought I was feigning sleep. I was thus taken prisoner with my child.

She remained in prison until liberation, and at the time I interviewed her, decades later, she still had the bump from that blow on her shoulder blade. The Italians used to punish their local mercenaries if they killed women guerrilla. Partly due to that attitude, but reportedly also because she was well known to them as a fighter, the Italians gave Lekelesh medical attention and generally treated her well, while they executed all the men they had captured with her. In the post-1941 period, she was rewarded with a medal for her heroism, and was among the *arbegna* who always participated in the annual memorial parades.

'MY EXCELLENCY'

While infighting among individual leaders provoked the anger of local populations, their failure to create a political structure supported by a local community was unacceptable, as shown by the experience of *Gerazmach* Zewde Asfaw, son of *Dejazmach* Asfaw Darge. After retreating from Maichew in 1935, Zewde came to Selale with a Tigre troop of two hundred. He had hoped for support from the local community on the strength of his family connections. However, the plan to attack the capital was already under way under the coordination of his cousins Aberra and Asfa Wesen Kassa. So, Zewde and his men joined the camp of Hayle Maryam Mammo, then better known for his valour. When Hayle Maryam died in 1939, Zewde trekked to Gojam and tried to join the camp of Negash Bezabeh, but, disappointed at the lack of enthusiasm for his family fame, Zewde returned to Selale in the summer of 1940. By then almost all guerrilla groups had heard from the emperor, which encouraged new groups to mushroom almost everywhere.

Zewde did not think he had enough men to form his own group, but, expecting to take up leadership, he wrote to Kebede Bezunesh (later *dejazmach*), a leader of one of the new groups. He signed his letter simply with his name, but it was framed in a picture of an Ethiopian flag on a flag post, with his name written from top to bottom on horizontal strips around the pole: 'My excellency, *Gerazmach* Zewde Asfaw'.[105] The letter did not elicit an invitation from the farmers, and he became frustrated when no response came. He handed himself over to the Italians who immediately executed him for having fought against them since their invasion began.[106] Apart from showing that there was never a time for submitting to the frustrated invaders, his sad case also shows that taking up leadership depended on convincing the community.

CHANGES IN *CHEWA* REWARDS

Help came to the guerrilla fighters after Mussolini declared war against Britain in June 1940, and the British expanded the theatre of war to northeast Africa in what they called 'mopping up' operations. British Prime Minister Winston Churchill allowed Haile Selassie to return to Ethiopia in the company of British troops. The emperor contacted the guerrilla fighters and exiles. While most were ready to accommodate him as their commander and *neguse negest*, some, for instance *Ras* Wibneh, needed convincing. This *ras*, however, became the earliest to meet the emperor on his return and the first whom the emperor honoured, acknowledging his popularly acclaimed title of *ras*. Belay

---

[105] The letter was in the possession of *Dejazmach* Kebede Bizunesh, who kindly showed it to me in October 1972.

[106] This information is from one of his followers, the Honourable Ayele Gessese, who, when I interviewed him in November 1972, was a parliamentary deputy for Shire, Tigre.

Zeleqe was said to have refused to shake hands or even meet with members of Colonel Orde Wingate's Gideon Force, but he eventually accepted them too.

By the time the British and the emperor walked into the country, the Italians 'had at least 300,000 men, 400 guns [presumably artillery] and 200 aircraft at their disposal'.[107] Once in the capital, Haile Selassie rewarded the majority of resistance leaders, including women. Some did not get what they deserved. Yohannes Iyasu, for instance, could not repair the damage of failing to rush from the Semien Mountains to meet the emperor then passing through Gojam. Belay Zeleke suffered too, being implicated in a protest against an overtaxing governor of Gojam, though he was said to have deliberately kept aloof from it. He was thrown into prison, and shot dead trying to escape. It fell to the revolutionaries of 1974 to honour him too by naming a street in Addis Ababa after him. Others, like Negash Bezabeh, were implicated in the attempted palace coup of 1960 and imprisoned by the emperor; Negash Bezabeh was subsequently released.

Annual speeches and discussions to mark Haile Selassie's return to the capital on 5 May 1941 – formally called Liberation Day – continued to express trust in the United Nations after it replaced the League of Nations. The British who came to his help insisted on treating Ethiopia as an occupied enemy territory, alleging the absence of a government. If Britain had also had local support its priorities might have been different. Ethiopian diplomats fought against what they saw as an unjustifiable continuation of the invasion, and worked for years to dislodge the British.[108] Wrenching from them the country's sovereignty and territorial integrity included trying to limit their looting of material left behind by the Italians, and convincing them to accept Ethiopia's right to reclaim Eritrea as part of Ethiopia. Among those who tried to challenge their domination, *Dejazmach* Kebedde Tessema, *Ras* Imru and Aklilu Habte Wold have shared their experiences. Their decision to be less dependent on one power proved useful in reasserting Ethiopian sovereignty. Eventually, obtaining the friendship of the United States counterbalanced the British economic and political stranglehold.[109] Those involved in this struggle saw themselves as successors to the guerrilla fighters of the five-year period, and later adamantly claimed metaphorically to have 'fought and died' against the serious British threat to Ethiopia's sovereignty. During the annual celebratory memorials, therefore, fighting British claims became part of proud tales of bravery and responsibility for the country and its people.

---

[107] W. E. D. Allen, *Guerilla War in Abysinnia*, Harmondsworth and New York: Penguin Books, 1943, p. 30, quoting the official British account.
[108] See for instance Aklilu Habte Weld in Aberra Jembere, *Agony in the Grand Palace, 1974–1982* (2nd edn), trans. Hailu Araaya, Addis Ababa: Shama Books, 2005, pp. 84–109; Spencer, *Ethiopia at Bay*, 1984, pp. 139–57.
[109] Aberra Jembere, *Agony in the Grand Palace*, p. 144.

Conclusion

Tracing the multi-faceted traditions and history of the *chewa* defence force since ancient times, the foregoing pages have highlighted that nineteenth-century sports such as hunting game appear particularly similar to practices in ancient Axum, which traded in forest products. Hunting in various regions brought the *chewa* to know land and people, and with other aspects of martial training, helped them to define and redefine the identity of local people and, by extension, Ethiopia and its borderlands. They encountered valorous resistance (which is not discussed for lack of space) and, following historical precedents dating back to antiquity, the monarchs perpetuated Ethiopian territorial holdings. As the medieval kings promoted the settlement of troops, the *chewa* raised inclusive support from home bases among the increasing population of the northeast African region. In the process, self-trained warriors in their rural societies actively participated in local politics, influencing the country's national and international policies. Warriors and monarchs alike saw land as part of their cherished identity of being Ethiopian, not just an economic resource. The tradition still survives as historical consciousness of personal and ancestral places within the country's frontiers.

Investigating the history and structure of this relationship with land has led to an exploration of the fascinating history of heroes, as the guerrilla warriors were considered, who, like their predecessors, sustained the country's independence, which they never lost. The *chewa* developed an alertness to external enemies during the transition of the monarchy to a peripatetic existence. In the changes occurring over centuries, a legacy of martial reputations was inculcated. Now known about notably in association with nineteenth-century monarchs who were basically *chewa*, these are: Tewodros's defiance of the Turks in his *zeraf*, and his later suicide to avoid capture at Magdala in 1868; Yohannes IV's victory (and death) at the Battle of Metemma in 1889; and Menelik II's victory at the Battle of Adewa in 1896. The tradition of self-identification with land, country and society enabled Menelik to rally the whole country to repulse the first Italian invasion at the Battle of Adewa in 1896. It endured and resurfaced during the resistance to the second invasion of 1935–41. Depictions of the resistance of 1935–41 promoted by the Patriotic Association, which was set up by former guerrilla fighters, continue to enjoy both popular and official support. The *chewa* legacy of ideals continues to acknowledge the possibility of internal hostilities, but in its view the Italians are external enemies who have sustained their status as *dina* by never having paid indemnity for invading Ethiopia. This view partly explains why people were upset when the UN proposed to send an Italian-headed peacekeeping force in 2002 after the war between Ethiopia and Eritrea. Thus the campaign literature that succeeded in changing the UN proposal pointed out that the blood spilt during the Italian invasion had not yet dried.

This argument necessarily begs questions about traditions that militarized the whole of society. It should be noted however, that the militarization was reduced by the introduction of 'modernity' in the centralized state during the early decades of the twentieth century. This was accompanied by government control and regulation of tax and access to land. 'Modernity' generally, and specifically the changes it brought concerning land, discouraged pretenders and successors of formerly autonomous regions. There was certainly a reduction in the exploitation of the rural population. However, the transformation also caused the loss of the role of land as the significant leverage that rural people had with the government and its local agents. Added to limitations on hunting and other training of warriors, it also stymied the nuanced practices of *chewa*-based politics, especially local level politico-military initiatives. The changes prevented the population from organizing its local economy and politics, thereby also preventing the usual policy inputs at the national level.

The break in tradition, which had enabled the political environment to perpetuate a two-way political communication between state and society, changed the state administration by encouraging the appointment of political leaders who had neither military training nor political experience with rural people. Between the battles of Adewa and Segele, the 'modern' state recruited young courtiers and claimants to inherited positions to hold political office simply because they were hanging around core leaders in the centre. This was followed by urban-based *chewa* establishing their descendants in power to the exclusion of others. Already in the 1920s, those in government positions lacked connectedness with rural people. Only a few provincial leaders benefited from clandestine hunting or local communication with rural people at the time. After the 'modernizing' politics of Haile Selassie excluded the population as a whole from engaging in political matters, those in political power used their 'modern' status to become 'aristocrats'. Their salaried and bureaucratized political positions excluded the *chewa*, their retainers and local communities. In the persistent confusion, those who attempted to take initiatives or engage in participatory politics had to become *shifta*, while others chose to side with the 1935–41 invaders. Disappointingly, the result was that the 'modern' state became patrimonial, even dictatorial, and those who were in office came to be seen as aristocrats.

Most telling in phasing out the last vestiges of *chewa* tradition was the distribution of ancient titles and the holding of a semblance of some of its old practices. Emperor Haile Selassie honoured elderly members of the judiciary, provincial administrators, members of parliament and favourite courtiers with traditional politico-military titles. He also gave banquets (*gibir*) on ceremonial occasions such as *Meskel*, New Year and other anniversaries, and allowed his bodyguard to play *genna* games at their leisure. These occasions were essentially private and exclusive in the sense that they no longer had the old-style bantering and teasing in which anyone could engage. The disappearance of the old nuances that eased power relations left the public distanced, and thereby further reduced two-way dialogue. A slightly different but significant *gibir* that the emperor gave in 1955 merely celebrated his twenty-fifth anniversary as *neguse negest*. Officials down to *balabat* level from all over the country participated and were expected only to glorify his personal existence in power. The titles conferred and the entertainments given were mere shadows of meritorious participatory politics. The titles were neither distributed to the younger generation nor served anything like the old purpose of evaluating the personalities involved in politico-military leadership.

In *chewa* tradition, troops carried out their commitment to regain and reassert a unitary nation state while owing personal loyalty and sense of responsibility to their local communal origins. In any of the rural areas, whether their place of origin or newly 'regained' territories where they held politico-military positions, neither the *chewa* nor even the monarchs were an aristocracy in the sense of claiming exclusive and inheritable privileges. As we have seen, one of the purposes of their *gibir* was to distribute the tribute they collected and increase their numbers. That is, they used their access to the traditional political economy to sustain a committed sense of inclusive nationhood. This tradition was far removed from the 'modern' professional, bureaucratically run and salaried army.

The last monarch's ambivalent attachment to the traditional state structure widened the distance between the state and the rural population after 1941. Consequent rebellions, at least in Gojam and Bale, were articulated as protests against tax rather than ownership. Even parliamentary elections were highly constricted, making representation just a rubber stamp for those in power. The ongoing differences between the 'modern' and the *chewa* systems is best illustrated in the simple but practical aspect of the people–state relationship – the freedom to circulate and discuss political information. Of course, some people still recall the conscious use of information by the guerrilla leaders and their supporters during the 1935–41 resistance, when they handled such matters as whom to recognize as a new leader, including women, rivalry among groups of warriors, and supporting or opposing the emperor's return from exile. Apart from this resort to *chewa* traditions, 'modernity' failed to bring about genuine principles of dialogue between state and society. On his return in 1941, Haile Selassie allowed a degree of space to their honoured history of warriorhood by allowing the resistance fighters to form the 'Territorial Army' (*Beherawi Tor*), and the rest of the population to retain their personal, outdated guns and ammunition. This 'army' proved useful while the monarchy was setting up a standing army. When a military council known as the Derg removed Haile Selassie in 1974, it picked out and massacred members of the patrimonial bureaucracy that it had inherited, but it also mobilized the veteran warriors of the 'territorial army', calling them the *Abat Tor* or 'Father Soldiery', as an additional force that fought against the irredentist Somali invasion of Ethiopia in 1977.

The absence of a socially rooted traditional force following the fall of the monarchy left the way open first for the Derg and then the EPRDF (Ethiopian People's Revolutionary Democratic Front). These used their military power to turn themselves into exclusively privileged economic and political powerholding rulers, as if that was the purpose of accessing political power. Of course they rhetorically promised to improve the economic and political lives of the population. They also took initiatives on state political matters: the Derg to sustain a unitary state at all costs, and the EPRDF to organize federalism by creating exclusive ethnic territories, even drawing up a constitution allowing for the breaking away of ethnic groups from the rest of the federation. Despite their rhetoric on improving the economic and political lives of the population, the exclusivist and oppressive conditions of their governance have made such goals unobtainable.

Land issues remained in the background during this transition from a monarchic state to military rule by salaried soldiers. With the passage of time and continuing disengagement between the state and ordinary people, young ideologues in the early 1970s were already speaking about the state bureaucrats who had distanced themselves from what they assumed to have been historically a passive rural population. This myth also portrayed rural people as landless peasants serving a 'feudalist' monarchy and 'aristocratic class'. The Derg used the idea of removing feudalism and creating a classless society to justify its taking over the state in 1974. A plan to resolve the ill-defined rural problems accruing to 'feudalism' also featured in the setting up of an exclusive ethno-national federation when the equally militaristic group of soldiers, under the Tigre People's Liberation Front (TPLF) which coordinated the EPRDF, overthrew the Derg in 1991. TPLF's land policy has since allowed it to extend its power and coordinate the language-based states, while enlarging its home base of Tigre. Also attributing rural poverty to inherited socio-political practices and ecological deficits, and supported by international financial and commercial partners and an increasing series of loans and foreign aid, it has lately been relying heavily on the lease of rural land for 'development'. With the Derg having nationalized land, and the EPRDF, steered by the TPLF, keeping it nationalized and leasing swathes of it to international and local entrepreneurs, both have sacrificed the interests of local people.

Of course both the *chewa* and members of the military regimes wear distinguishing regalia and cherish the heroism of 'our ancestors', but the similarity ends there. The *chewa* derived their political and military power from people in communal lands, engaged them in dialogue and thereby influenced state politics with them. The Derg trained its army in military camps, and the EPRDF claims to have done so 'in the bush'. Unlike the system featuring *chewa* warriors, the command structure of these armies has been beholden to no one. The salaried soldiers, therefore, have neither connection with the public nor toleration of its opinion. The political elite lack consciousness of traditions that allow people to challenge their access to power. A small core group in both regimes has ruthlessly suppressed public scrutiny and accountability in relation to land. Both the Derg and the EPRDF have been particularly sensitive to the use of information collection and dissemination, and their handling of their privileged official positions does nothing to change this attitude.

Further examples illustrate inhibiting factors in the relationships between salaried soldiers and rural people. Since the 'modern' state is bereft of grassroots-generated criteria, rural people consider bureaucrats as mysteriously salaried, wealthy and powerful citizens of officialdom. Despite the official criterion for promoting bureaucrats – educational merit for instance – the officials in the regime reject educated elites. The TPLF has deliberately used language for the purposes of discouraging national commonality, establishing federal state divisions and undermining a *lingua franca*. There is no structure that eases communication between bureaucrats and the public. Though ordinary people still know the meaning and spirit of the word *baldereba*, for instance, even secretaries, infamous as gatekeepers for those in power, lack understanding that 'modern' neutral service provision is a function of civil servants' relationships with the public.

Popularly, singers evoke themes of protection of society and nation, and even emulate some aspects of *chewa* traditions such as *zeraf* and *fukera* that they use in social gatherings. The Derg broadcast *fukera* performances over the radio and television, but mainly when it announced punishments or executions of real or imagined opponents. The EPRDF has a similar propagandist approach in several languages. Singers' performances of *zevat* are now restricted to stage plays, perhaps because recently some of its tunes have been reduced to sing-songs devoid of verve. Their lyrics, however, are analytical when addressing the politics of the ethnocentric government, the consequences of its mistaken labelling of *chewa* as *neftegna* ('wanton gunmen'), its claims of exclusive ethnic categories such as Amhara, or its suppression of the rights of rural people and their local lands.

The popularity of such performances has immediate precedence (other than the patriotic performances in the early 1940s) in revolutionary students' use of protest songs against the monarchy in the late 1960s. While promoting armed insurrection they referred to themselves as *fanno* and associated their movement with international socialist solidarity:

ፋኖ ተሰማራ
ፋኖ ተሰማራ
እንደ ሆቺሚን እንደ ቼጉዌቤራ
Get out and about, *fanno*!
Get out and about, *fanno*!
Like Ho Chi Minh and like Che Guevara.

In everyday life there is a legacy of joyfully expressing an inherited passionate love of familial history and moral standards. The word *chewa* persists widely, commonly evoking nobility in personal character, especially trustworthiness, sincerity, reserve and unselfish consideration of others. It features during weddings as part of enjoyable horseplay and family repartee. Though the bridegroom and his best men are no longer expected to go through the warrior's rites of passage, the bride is still serenaded in most of rural Ethiopia as 'of *chewa* origin' and deserving of gifts of gold jewellery:

ድሪ ጣሉባት በደረቷ
ጣሉባት በደረቷ
የጨዋ ልጅ ናት መሠረቷ
ጣሉባት በደረቷ
Throw gold jewellery on her chest!
Throw [it] on her chest.
She is of *chewa* origin!
Throw [it] on her chest.

Bibliography

NOTES ON BIBLIOGRAPHY AND REFERENCES

Ethiopian names are given in full if possible (own name followed usually by father's name). EC stands for Ethiopian Calendar (and GC for Gregorian Calendar). Until 1979, I spelt my name variously as Tsehay Brhane Selassie (1969), Tsehai Berhane Selassie (1971), Tsehai Brhaneselassie (also 1971), Tsehai Brhane Selassie (1975), Tsehai Berhane Selassie (1979) and Tsehai Berhane-Selassie thereafter.

The present work on Ethiopian traditions of warriorhood is primarily from Ethiopian resources. Many of my oral informants were fighters in the historical campaigns, and include former slaves and domestic or personal service providers. Former slaves had long abandoned their names in preference to their 'horse-names', and though these have not survived, the *chewa* tradition prohibits pointing out their actual names (even if known) and their old status (their name and status being explicitly linked); so it has been necessary to avoid using their personal names.

Most of the unpublished documentation on the 1935–41 war in the Bibliography is accommodated in the Institute of Ethiopian Studies, which very kindly facilitated my access to it. This is supplemented by my father's autobiography and similar useful brief notes others wrote for my benefit. Apart from references to travellers' accounts, most information about children's and other traditional games is taken from the work of the French anthropologist, Marcel Griaule, who seems to be the only one who has published on the subject.

INFORMANTS

In addition to my father, *Balambaras* Berhane-Selassie Yigeremu, and my mother, *Weyzero* Werkaferahu Haile, the following have usefully and generously shared their information. *Abba* Bora, *Weyzevo* Aleke'akalate, *Ato* Mekonnen Yigletu, *Ato* Tsehainew Deju, *Ade* Okoto, *Ato* Jigsa Habte Maryam, *Dejazmach* Bezuwork Gebre, Addis Ababa, 1969–73; *Dejazmach* Abderahman Hojele, 1971; *Weyzero* Lekelesh Beyan, 1973–4; *Kegnazmach* Bitewa Meshesha, Gojam, 1971; *Kegnazmach* Mezemir Haylu, Addis Ababa, 1969–71; *Dejazmach* Demiss Welde Amanuel (DWA), Addis Ababa, 1972–3; *Dejazmach* Kebede Tessema, Addis Ababa, 1970–1, *Dejazmach* Deress Shiferaw 1972; *Kegnazmach* Damte Shibeshi, 1972; *Fitawrari* Belay, 1972; *Gerazmach* Alemu Mekuria; *Fitawrari* Haile Mekuria; the Honourable Ayele Gessese.

PRIMARY SOURCES

ደምስ ወልደአማኑኤል (ደጃዝማች) የኢትዮጵያ ጀግኖች አገራቸውን ከወራሪው ከፋሺስታዊ ኢጣሊያ ሰራዊት ጋራ ያፈጸሙት ተጋድሎ (Demiss Welde Amanuel (*Dejazmach*). *The struggle accomplished by Ethiopian Patriots against the fascist Italian army that invaded their country* (n.d.)). This collection includes untitled manuscripts by ዘውዴ ተሰማ (Zewde Tessema) and ሳህሌ ተክልኝ (Sahle Tekalegn).

ደምስ ወልደአማኑኤል (ደጃዝማች)፤ *መታሰቢያ*:: (Demiss Welde Amanuel (*Dejazmach*), *Memories*, n.d.).
ብዙወርቅ ገብሬ (ደጃዝማች)፤ *ማስታወሻ*:: (Bizuwerk Gebre (*Dejazmach*), *Notes*).
ነገደ፤ የራስ ጎበና ዳጭ *ታሪክ* (Negede, biography of *Ras* Gobena Dachi, n.d.).
ሐዲስ አለማየሁ *ትዝታ* (Haddis Alemayehu, *Memories*, n.d.), Institute of Ethiopian Studies, Addis Ababa University: Digital Collection of Ethiopian Manuscripts, No. 286_IES03387.

UNPUBLISHED SOURCES IN ENGLISH

Tsehay Brhane Selassie, 'Menelik II: Conquest and Consolidation of the Southern Provinces', senior dissertation, Haile Selassie I University, Addis Ababa, 1969.
Tsehai Berhane-Selassie, 'The Balabat and the Coffee Disease', unpublished conference paper, 1978.

PUBLISHED WORKS IN AMHARIC

ኃይለ ሥላሴ *ሕይወቴና የኢትዮጵያ እርምጃ* (Haile Selassie, *My Life and the Progress of Ethiopia*, 1929 EC).
መርስዔ ሃዘን ወልደ ቂርቆስ፤ *የዛያኛ ክፍለ ዘመን መባቻ የዘመን ታሪክ ትዝታዬ፤* ካየሁተና ከሰማሁት፤ አዲስ አበባ፤ ዩኒቨርሲቲ ፕሬስ፤ 2002 (Mers'e Hazen Welde Kirkos, *My memories of what I saw and heard of the history of the beginning of the twentieth century*, Addis Ababa University Press, 2002 EC).
መርስዔ ሃዘን አበበ፤ *አብዲሳ አጋ በኢጣልያ በርሃዎች፤* አዲስ አበባ 1959 (Mers'e Hazen Abebe, *Abdisa Aga in the Italian Deserts*, Addis Ababa, 1959 EC).
መንግስቱ ለማ፤ *መጽሐፈ ትዝታ - ዘአለቃ ለማ ኃይሉ ወልደ ታሪክ፤* አዲስ አበባ ዩኒቨርሲቲ ፕሬሥ:: 2015 (Mengistu Lemma, *The Book of Reminiscences of Aleqa Lemma Hailu Welde Tarik*, Addis Ababa University Press, 2015 GC).
መኮንን እንዳልካቸው፤ ቢቶደድ፤ *መልካም ቤተ ሰቦች፤* አዲስ አበባ 1949:: አሥመራ የኩሪዬሬ ኤሌትሬዎ ማህበር ማተሚያ ቤት:: (Mekonnen Endalkachew (*Bitoded*), *Fine Families*, Addis Ababa: Asmara Corriere Eritreo Association Printing House, 1949 EC).
መዘምር ኃይሉ *የክቡር ደጃዝማች ባልቻ አባነፍሶ አጭር የሕይወት ታሪክ፤* 1956 (Mezemir Haylu, *A Short Biography of His Excellency Dejazmach Balcha*, Addis Ababa, 1956 EC).
ማህተመ ሥላሴ ወልደ መስቀል (ባላምባራስ)፤ *ዝክረ ነገር፤* አዲስ አበባ፤ 1962 (Mahteme Selassie Welde Meskel (*Blaten Geta*), *Memories of Significance*, Addis Ababa, 1962 EC).
ማህተመ ሥላሴ ወልደ መስቀል *(ባላምባራስ)፤የቀድሞው ዘመን ጨዋ ኢትዮጵያዊ ጠባይና ባሕል፤*መጋቢት ፳፭ ቀን ፲፱፻፶፰ ዓ.ም 1958 (Mahteme Selassie Welde Meskel (*Balambaras*), *Ethiopian Chewa Character and Culture of Former Times*, Megabit 25, 1958 EC).
ሰይፈ አባ ወሎ፡ *የታሪክ ቅርስ፤*1935 (Seyfe Aba Wello, *Legacy of History*, Addis Ababa, 1935 EC).
ብርሃነ ሥላሴ ይገረሙ (ባላምባራስ)፤ *ነባር ለባለታሪኩ ተውልድ ህያው ቅርስ ነው፤* 1996 (Berhane-Selassie Yigeremu (*Balambaras*), *The Past is a Living Heritage for the Descendants of Those Who Were in It*, Addis Ababa, 1996 EC).
ተክለ ሐዋርያት ተክለ ማርያም ሌታውራሪ፤ *አቶባዮግራፊ* 1999 (Tekle Hawaryat Tekle Maryam, (*Fitawrari*), *Autobiography*. Addis Ababa: Addis Ababa University Press, 1999 EC).
ተክለ ኢየሱስ [ዋቅጂራ] አለቃ፤ *የኢትዮጵያ ታሪክ፤*ሕተታ በስርገው ገላው 2002 (Tekle Iyesus [Waqjera], *Aleqa: History of Ethiopia*, perhaps 1917 EC, introduction and annotation by Sergew Gelaw, Addis Ababa: Berhanena Salem Printing Press, 2002 EC).
ተክለ ጻድቅ መኩሪያ፤ *ዐፄ ቴዎድሮስ እና የኢትዮጵያ አንድነት* ኩራዝ አሳታሚ ድርጅት 1981 (Tekle Tsadik Mekuria, *Emperor Tewodros and Ethiopian Unity*, Addis Ababa: Kuraz Publishing Agency, 1981 EC).
ታደሰ ሜጫ፤ *ጥቁር አንበሳ፤*አዲስ አበባ፤ 1934 (Tadesse Mecha, *Black Lion*, 1934 EC).
ታደሰ ዘወልዴ፤ *ያለሽኝ ዘመን* (Tadesse Zewelde, *Era of Discord*, n.d.).
ታደሰ ዘወልዴ፤ *ቀሪን ገረመው፤*1960 (Tadesse Zewelde, *Surprise to Survivors*, 1960 EC).

እምሩ ኃይለ ሥላሴ (ልዑ-ል ራ-ስ) ካየሁተና ከማስታውሰው 2002 (Imru Haile Selassie (Li'ul Ras), *From What I Saw and Recollect*, 2nd edn, Addis Ababa: Addis Ababa University Press, 2002 EC).

ከበደ ተሰማ (ደጃዝማች) የታሪክ ማስታወሻ፡ አዲስ አበባ፡ አርቲስቲክ ማተሚያ ቤት፡ ኢትዮጵያ 1962፡፡ (Kebede Tessema (*Dejazmach*), *History Notes*, Addis Ababa: Artistic Printing Press, 1962 EC).

ኪዳነ ወልድ ክፍሌ መጽሐፈ ሰዋሰው ወግስ ወመዝገበ ቃላት ሐዲስ፡ ዲሬዳዋ አርቲስቲክ ማተሚያ ቤት፡፡ 1948 (Kidane Weld Kifle, (*Aleqa*), *Book of Grammar, Verbs and Dictionary of New Words*, Dire Dawa: Artistic Matämiya Bet, 1948 EC).

የቀዳማዊ ኃይለ ሥላሴ ጦር ትምህርት ቤት ብሩራዊ መታሰቢያ፡ 1952 (*Silver Jubilee of the Haile Selassie I Military School*, 1952 EC).

ገብረ ወልድ እንግዳ ወርቅ የማይጨው ዘመቻ፡ አዲስ አበባ፡ 1941 (Gebre Weld Engeda Work, *The Battle of Maichew*, Addis Ababa, 1941 EC).

ገሪማ ታፈረ ዘብሃረ ጎንደር፡ ጎንደሬ በጋሻው፡ አዲስ አበባ፡ ተስፋ ገብረ ሥላሴ ማተሚያ ቤት 1949 (Gerima Tafere of Gonder, *The Gondere with his Shield*, Tesfa Gebre Silassie Printing Press, 1949 EC).

ጌታቸው ኃይሌ፡ የአባ ባሕርይ ድርሰቶች ኦሮሞን ከሚመለከቱ ሰነዶች ጋር፡ ኮሌጅቪል ሚኒሶታ፡፡አዲስ አበባ 1995 [2003] (Getatchew Haile, *The Works of Aba Bahrey with Other Records Concerning the Oromo*, Collegeville, MI, 1995 [2003]).

PUBLISHED ARTICLES

Aschalew Bililigne, 'Female Disempowerment: some expressions in Amharic', Addis Ababa University, 2012, MA thesis linguistics, accessed on 12 February 2018: http://etd.aau.edu.et/bitstream/123456789/6475/1/7.Desalegn%20Leshyibelu.pdf.

Ayele Tekle-Haymanot, 'Le antiche gerarchie dell'Impero Etiopico', *Sestante*, 1965, Vol. 1, No. 2, pp. 61–7.

Bairu Tafla, 'The 'Awāǧ: An Institution of Political Culture in Traditional Ethiopia', in Sven Rubenson (ed.), *Proceedings of the Seventh International Conference of Ethiopian Studies*, Institute of Ethiopian Studies, Addis Ababa; Scandinavian Institute of African Studies, Uppsala; African Studies Center, Michigan State University, East Lansing, 1984, pp. 365–72.

Bairu Tafla, 'Three Portraits: Ato Asmä Giyorgis, Ras Gobäna Dači and Ṣähafé Tezaz Gäbrä Selassé', *Journal of Ethiopian Studies*, Vol. 5, No. 2, 1967, pp. 133–50.

Bureau, Jacques, 'The "Tigre" Chronicle of Wollaita; A Pattern of Kingship', in Richard Pankhurst, Ahmed Zekaria and Taddese Beyene (eds), *Proceedings of the First National Conference of Ethiopian Studies*, Addis Ababa: Institute of Ethiopian Studies, Addis Ababa University, 11–12 April 1990, pp. 49–64.

Caulk, Richard, 'Bad Men of the Borders: Shum and Shefta in Northern Ethiopia in the Nineteenth Century', *International Journal of African Historical Studies*, Vol. 17, No. 2, 1984, pp. 201–27.

Guidi, Ignazio, 'Documenti amarina', *Rendiconti della Reale Accademia dei Lincei*, Vol. VII, 1891.

Haberland, Eike, 'The influence of the Christian Ethiopian Empire on southern Ethiopia', *Journal of Semitic Studies*, Vol. 9, No. 1, 1964, pp. 235–8.

Horvath, Ronald J., 'The Wandering Capitals of Ethiopia', *Journal of African History*, No. 2, 1969, pp. 205–19.

Keefer, Edward C., 'Great Britain, France, and the Ethiopian Tripartite Treaty of 1906', *Albion: A Quarterly Journal Concerned with British Studies*, Vol. 13, No. 4, Winter 1981.

Kramer, Ruth, 'Gender in Amharic: A Morphosyntactic Approach to Natural and Grammatical Gender', July 2012. Accessed on 12 February 2018: http://ling.auf.net/lingbuzz/001844.

Merid W. Aregay, 'Military Elites in Medieval Ethiopia', *Journal of Ethiopian Studies*, Institute of Ethiopian Studies, Vol. 30, No. 1, June 1997, pp. 31–7.

Pankhurst, Richard, 'The Great Famine of 1888–1892: A New Assessment', *Journal of the History of Medicine and Allied Sciences*, Vol. XXI, No. 2, 1966, pp. 95–124. Accessed 12 April 2018: https://doi.org/10.1093/jhmas/XXI.2.95.

Pankhurst, Richard, 'The Ethiopian Patriots: the Lone Struggle', *Ethiopian Observer*, Vol. 13, No. 1, 1970.
Pankhurst, Richard, 'Linguistic and Cultural Data on the Penetration of Fire-Arms into Ethiopia', *Journal of Ethiopian Studies*, Vol. IX, No. 1, January 1971, pp. 47–8.
Pereira, Fransisco Maria Esteves, 'O Elephante Em Ethiopia', 1868. Accessed in the library of the Hiob Ludolf Centre for Ethiopian Studies, University of Hamburg, Germany.
Perruchon, Jules, 'Histoire des guerres de Amde Seyon, roi d'Ethiopie', *Journal Asiatiques*, Series 8, XIV (1889).
Robele Ababya, 28 June 2006, 'Col. Abdissa Aga's heroic feat in Italy: WWII', accessed April 2018: www.ethiomedia.com/carepress/col_abdissa_aga.html.
Salome Gabre Egziabher, 'The Ethiopian Patriots: 1936–1941', *Ethiopian Observer*, Vol. 12, No. 2, 1969.
Taddia, Irma, 'Land Politics in the Ethiopian-Eritrean Border Area between Emperor Yohannes IV and Menelik II', *Aethiopica: International Journal of Ethiopian Studies*, Vol. 12, 2009, pp. 58–82.
Tarafa Walda Sadiq, 'The Unification of Ethiopia (1800–1935): Wallega', *Journal of Ethiopian Studies*, Vol. 6, No. 1, 1968.
Triulzi, Alessandro, 'The Background to Ras Gobana's Expeditions to Western Wallage in 1886–1888: A Review of the Evidence', in *Proceedings of the First United States Conference on Ethiopian Studies 1973*, 1975, pp. 143–56.
Tsehai Berhane Selassie, 'An Ethiopian Medical Text-Book Written by Gerazmach Gäbräwäld Arägahañ Däga Damot', *Journal of Ethiopian Studies*. Vol. 9, No. 1, January 1971, pp. 95–180.
Tsehai Berhane Selassie, 'Women Guerrilla Fighters', *Northeast African Studies*, Vol. 1, No. 3, Winter 1979–80, pp. 73–83.
Tsehai Berhane-Selassie, 'Where or what is "Abyssinia"? – An investigation', 15 August 2016, accessed 2 April 2018: www.ethiomedia.com/1016notes/6037.html.
Tsehai Brhane Selassie, 'The question of Damot and Wälamo', *Journal of Ethiopian Studies*, Vol. 13, No. 1, January 1975, pp. 37–46.

PUBLISHED BOOKS IN ENGLISH

Aberra Jembere, *An Introduction to the Legal History of Ethiopia, 1434–1974*, Hamburg: Lit Verlag Münster, 2000.
Aberra Jembere, *Agony in the Grand Palace, 1974–1982* (2nd edn), trans. Hailu Araaya, Addis Ababa: Shama Books, 2005.
Abir, Mordechai, *Ethiopia: The Era of the Princes: The Challenge of Islam and the Re-unification of the Christian Empire, 1769–1855*, London: Longmans Green, 1968.
Allen, W. E. D., *Guerrilla War in Abyssinia*, Harmondsworth and New York: Penguin Books, 1943.
[Annesley] George, Viscount Valentia, *Voyages and Travels to India, Ceylon, the Red Sea, Abyssinia, and Egypt, in the years 1802, 1803, 1804, 1805, and 1806* (three volumes), London: William Miller, 1809.
Asmarom Legesse, *Gada: Three Approaches to the Study of African Society*, New York: Free Press, 1973.
Azaïs, R. P. and R. Chambard, *Cinq Années de Recherches Archéologique en Éthiopie*, Paris: Geuthner, 1931.
Bahru Zewde, *A History of Modern Ethiopia, 1855–1991* (2nd edn), Oxford: James Currey, 2001.
Bairu Tafla (ed.), *Aṣma Giyorgis and his work: History of the Gāllā and the Kingdom of Šawā* (Äthiopistische Forschungen, Band 108), Stuttgart: Franz Steiner Verlag Wiesbaden GMBH, 1987.
Baer, George W., *The Coming of the Italian-Ethiopian War*, Cambridge, MA: Harvard University Press, 1967.
Baxter, P. T. W., Jan Hultin and Alessandro Triulzi (eds), *Being and Becoming Oromo: Historical and Anthropological Enquiries*, Lawrenceville, NJ: Red Sea Press, 1996.

Beckingham, C. F. and G. W. Huntingford, *The Prester John of the Indies: being the narrative of the Portuguese Embassy in Ethiopia in 1520, written by Father Francisco Alvares*, London: Hakluyt Society, 1961.

Belaynesh Michael, S. Chojnacki and Richard Pankhurst (eds), *The Dictionary of Ethiopian Biography. Volume I: From Early Times to the End of the Zagwé Dynasty c. 1270 AD*, Addis Ababa: Institute of Ethiopian Studies, Addis Ababa University, 1975.

Berkeley, George Fitz-Hardinge, *The Campaign of Adowa and the Rise of Menelik*, New York: Negro Universities Press, 1969 (reprint of 1st edition, London: Constable, 1902).

Bertella Farnetti, Paolo and Cecilia Dau Novelli (eds), *Colonialism and National Identity*, Cambridge Scholars Publishing, 2015.

Borelli, J., *Éthiopie Méridionale: Journal de mon Voyage aux Pays Amhara, Galla et Sidama, Septembre 1885 à Novembre 1888*, Paris: Ancienne Maison Quantin Librairies-Imprimeries Réunies, 1890.

Bruce, James, *Travels and Discoveries in Abyssinia*. Edinburgh: W. P. Nimmo, Hay, & Mitchell, 1885 (abridged from Bruce's five-volume work, *Travels to Discover the Source of the Nile*, Edinburgh, 1790).

Budge, E. A. Wallis (trans.), *The Queen of Sheba and her only son Menyelek (I) being the 'Book of the Glory of Kings' (Kebre Negest)* (2nd edn), Oxford: Oxford University Press, 1932.

Bulatovich, Alexander, *Ethiopia through Russian Eyes: Country in Transition, 1896–1898*, trans. and ed. Richard Seltzer, Lawrenceville, NJ; Asmara: Red Sea Press, 2000.

Caulk, Richard, *'Between the Jaws of the Hyenas': A Diplomatic History of Ethiopia (1876–1896)* (Äthiopistische Forschungen, Band 60), ed. Bahru Zewde, Wiesbaden: Harrassowitz Verlag, 2002.

Cerulli, Enrico, *The Folk Literature of the Galla of Southern Abyssinia* (Harvard Africa Studies, Vol. 3), Cambridge, MA: African Department of the Peabody Museum of Harvard University, 1922.

Cerulli, Ernesta, *Peoples of South-West Ethiopia and its Borderland*, London: International African Institute, 1956.

Combes, E. and M. Tamisier, *Voyage en Abyssinie, dans le pays des Galla de Choa et d'Ifat*, Paris: Louis Desessart, 1838.

Crummey, Donald. *Land and Society in the Christian Kingdom of Ethiopia: From the Thirteenth to the Twentieth Century*, Oxford: James Currey, 2000.

Crummey, Donald, *Priests and Politicians: Protestant and Catholic Missions in Orthodox Ethiopia 1830–1868*, Oxford: Clarendon Press, 1972.

Curle, Christian (ed.), *Letters from the Horn of Africa, 1923–1942: Sandy Curle, Soldier and Diplomat Extraordinary*, Barnsley, UK: Pen & Sword Military, 1988.

D'Abbadie, Arnauld, *Douze Ans dans le Haute-Éthiopie (Abyssinie)*, Paris: Librairie de L. Hachette, 1868.

D'Abbadie, Antoine, *Dictionnaire de la Langue Amariñña*, Paris: F. Vieweg, 1881.

Daniel W. Ambaye, *Land Rights in Ethiopia*, Springer International Publishing Switzerland, 2015. e-book ISBN 978-3-319-14639-3.

Darkwah, R. H. Kofi, *Shewa, Menilek and the Ethiopian Empire 1813–1889*, London: Heinemann, 1975.

De Castro, Lincoln, *Nella terra dei Negus, pagine raccolte in Abissinia*, Milan: Fratelli Treves, 1915.

Denti di Pirajno, Alberto, *A Cure for Serpents: A Doctor in Africa*, trans. Kathleen Naylor, London: Andre Deutsch, 1955.

Doresse, J., *La Vie Quotidienne des Éthiopiens Chrétiens aux XVIIe et XVIIIe Siècles*, Paris: Hachette, 1972.

Erlich, Haggai, *Ethiopia and the Middle East*, Boulder, CO: Lynne Reinner, 1994.

Ficquet, Éloi and Wolbert G. C. Smidt (eds), *The Life and Times of* Lïj *Iyasu of Ethiopia: New Insights*, Zurich and Berlin: LIT, n.d. [2014].

Forbes, Rosita, *From Red Sea to Blue Nile: Abyssinian Adventure*, New York: Macauley, 1925.

Franzoj, Augusto, *Continente nero: note di viaggio*, Turin: Roux e Favale, 1885.

Gibbon, Edward, *The History of the Decline and Fall of the Roman Empire*, Vol. 4,

Chapter XLVII, 'Ecclesiastical Discord', Part VI, 1782, revised 1845.
Griaule, Marcel, *Jeux et divertissements abyssins* (Bibliothèque de l'École des Hautes Études, Sciences religieuses, Vol. 49), Paris: Ernest Leroux, 1935.
Guèbrè Sellassié (*Tsehafi Tezaz*), *Chronique du Règne de Ménélik II Roi des Rois d'Éthiopie*, trans. Tèsfa Sellassié, Paris: Librairie Orientale et Américaine, Vol. I, 1930, Vol. II, 1932.
Guidi, Ignazio, *Vocabulario amarico-italiano*, Rome: Casa editrice italiana, 1901.
Habtamu Mengistie Tegegne, *Land Tenure and Agrarian Structure in Ethiopia, 1636–1900*, PhD dissertation, University of Illinois at Urbana-Champaign, 2011, accessed 12 April 2018: https://www.ideals.illinois.edu/handle/2142/26337.
Harris, William Cornwallis, *The Highlands of Æthiopia, described, during eighteen months' residence of a British embassy at the Christian court of Shoa* (3 volumes, 2nd edn), London: Longman, Brown, Green and Longmans, 1844.
Hodson, Arnold Weinholt, *Seven Years in Southern Abyssinia* (Ed. C. Leonard Leese), London: T. Fisher Unwin, 1927.
Hodson, Arnold Weinholt, *Where Lion Reign: An Account of Lion Hunting & Exploration in SW Abyssinia*, London: Skeffington, n.d. (c. 1929).
Hotten, John Camden (ed.), *Abyssinia and its People; or, Life in the Land of Prester John*, New York: Negro Universities Press, 1969 [1868].
Huntingford, G. W. B. (trans. and ed.), *The Glorious Victories of Amda Seyon, King of Ethiopia*, Oxford: Oxford University Press, 1965.
Isenberg, Charles William, *Dictionary of the Amharic language in two parts: Amharic and English, and English and Amharic*, London: Richard Watts, 1841.
Isenberg, Charles William and J. L. Krapf, *Journals of the Rev. Messrs. Isenberg and Krapf, Missionaries of the Church Missionary Society, Detailing their Proceedings in the Kingdom of Shoa, and Journeys in Other Parts of Abyssinia in the Years 1839, 1840, 1841, and 1842*, London: Seeley, Burnside, and Seeley, 1843.
Junod, Marcel, *Warrior without Weapons*, trans. Edward Fitzgerald, London: Jonathan Cape, 1951.
Johnston, Charles, *Travels in Southern Abyssinia, through the Country of Adal to the Kingdom of Shoa, during the years 1842–1843*, London: J. Madden, 1844.
Jonas, Raymond, *The Battle of Adwa: African victory in the age of empire*, Cambridge, MA: Belknap Press of Harvard University Press, 2011.
Katsuyoshi Fukui, Eisei Kurimoto and Masayoshi Shigeta (eds), *Ethiopia in Broader Perspectives: Papers of the XIIIth International Conference of Ethiopian Studies, Kyoto, 12–17 December 1997*, Kyoto: Shokado Book Sellers, 1997.
Lefebvre, Théophile, *et al.*, *Voyage en Abyssinie exécuté pendant les années 1839, 1840, 1841, 1842, 1843* (Vol. 3), Paris: Arthus Bertrand, Libraire de la Société de Géographie, 1845–1851.
Levine, Donald N., *Wax and Gold: Tradition and Innovation in Ethiopian Culture*, Chicago: University of Chicago Press, 1972 (1965).
Lewis, David L., *The Race to Fashoda: European Colonialism and African Resistance in the Scramble for Africa*, New York: Weidenfeld and Nicolson, 1987.
Lienhardt, Godfrey, *Divinity and Experience: The Religion of the Dinka*, Oxford: Clarendon Press, 1961.
Lipsky, G. A., *Ethiopia, its People, its Society, its Culture*, New Haven, CT: Human Relations Area Files, 1962.
McNab, Duncan, *Mission 101: The Untold Story of the SOE and the Second World War in Ethiopia*, Stroud: The History Press, 2012.
Marcus, Harold G., *The Life and Times of Menelik II: Ethiopia 1844–1913* (Oxford Studies in African Affairs), Oxford: Clarendon Press, 1975.
Marcus, Harold G., *Haile Selassie I: The Formative Years, 1892–1936*, Lawrenceville, NJ: Red Sea Press, 1995.
Markakis, John, *Ethiopia: Anatomy of a Traditional Polity* (Oxford Studies in African Affairs), Oxford: Clarendon Press, 1974.
Maula, Johanna, *The Jasmine Years: From my African Notebooks*. Bloomington, IN: iUniverse, 2012.
Mérab, Paul, *Impressions d'Éthiopie*, Paris: Ernest Leroux, 1921–9.
Mesfin Welde-Mariam, *An Introductory Geography of Ethiopia*, Addis Ababa: Berhanena Selam, 1972.

Messay Kebede, *Survival and Modernization, Ethiopia's Enigmatic Present: A Philosophical Discourse*, Lawrenceville, NJ: Red Sea Press, 1999.
Ministry of Justice, *Documents on Italian War Crimes: Affidavits and published documents*, Addis Ababa: Ministry of Justice, 1950.
Mockler, Anthony, *Haile Selassie's War*, London: Grafton, 1987.
Mohammed Hassen, *The Oromo of Ethiopia: A History, 1570–1860*, Trenton, NJ: Red Sea Press, 1994 (Cambridge University Press, 1990).
Murphy, Dervla, *In Ethiopia with a Mule*, London: John Murray, 1968.
Pankhurst, Richard, *Economic History of Ethiopia: 1800–1935*, Addis Ababa: Haile Sellassie I University Press, 1968.
Pankhurst, Richard, *History of Ethiopian Towns: From the Middle Ages to the Early Nineteenth Century* (Vol. 8), Wiesbaden: Steiner, 1982.
Pankhurst, Richard, *A Social History of Ethiopia: The Northern and Central Highlands from Early Medieval Times to the Rise of Téwodros II*, Addis Ababa: Institute of Ethiopian Studies, Addis Ababa University, 1990.
Pankhurst, Richard, *The Ethiopian Borderlands: Essays in Regional History from Ancient Times to the End of the 18th Century*, Lawrenceville, NJ: Red Sea Press, 1997.
Pankhurst, Richard, *State and Land in Ethiopian History* (2nd edn), Hollywood, CA: Tsehai Publishers, 2006.
Parkyns, Mansfield, *Life in Abyssinia: Being Notes Collected During Three Years' Residence and Travels in that Country*, London: John Murray, 1853 (New York: D. Appleton, 1854).
Pearson, Hugh Drummond, *Letters from Abyssinia: 1916 and 1917, With Supplemental Foreign Office Documents*, ed. Frederic A. Sharf, Hollywood, CA: Tsehai Publishers, 2004.
Plowden, Walter Chichele, *Travels in Abyssinia and the Galla Country: With an Account of a Mission to Ras Ali in 1848*, ed. Trevor Chichele Plowden, London: Longmans, Green, 1868.
Prouty, Chris and Eugene Rosenfeld, *Historical Dictionary of Ethiopia*, African Historical Dictionaries, No. 32, Metuchen, NJ: Scarecrow Press, 1981.
Prouty, Chris, *Empress Taytu and Menelik II: Ethiopia 1883–1910*, London: Ravens Educational and Development Services; Trenton, NJ: Red Sea Press, 1986.
Reid, Richard J., *Frontiers of Violence in North-East Africa: Genealogies of Conflict since 1800*, Oxford: Oxford University Press, 2011.
Rey, C. F., *In the Country of the Blue Nile*, London: Duckworth, 1927.
Rubenson, Sven, *King of Kings Tēwodros of Ethiopia*, Addis Ababa: Haile Selassie I University Press in association with Oxford University Press, Nairobi, 1966.
Rubenson, Sven, *The Survival of Ethiopian Independence*, Lund Studies in International History, 7, London: Heinemann in Association with Esselte Studium and Addis Ababa University, 1976.
Rubenson, Sven (ed.), *Correspondence and Treaties 1800–1854*, with Getatchew Haile and John Hunwick, Acta Æthiopica, Vol. 1, Evanston, IL: Northwestern University Press; Addis Ababa: Addis Ababa University Press, 1987.
Salt, Henry, *A Voyage to Abyssinia, and Travels into the Interior of that Country, Executed Under the Orders of the British Government, in the Years 1809 and 1810*, London: F. C. and J. Rivington, 1814.
Sbacchi, Alberto, *Legacy of Bitterness: Ethiopia and Fascist Italy, 1935–1941*, Lawrenceville, NJ and Asmara: Red Sea Press, 1997.
Sergew Hable Sellassie, *Ancient and Medieval Ethiopian History to 1270*, Addis Ababa: United Printers, 1972.
Shack, W. A., *The Central Ethiopians: Amhara, Tigriña [sic] and Related Peoples* (Ethnographic Survey of Africa, ed. Daryll Forde, North-Eastern Africa, Part IV), London: International African Institute, 1974.
Shack, William and Habte-Mariam Marcos, *Gods and Heroes: Oral Traditions of the Gurage of Ethiopia*, Oxford University Press, 1974.
Sheridan, Michael J. and Celia Nyamweru (eds), *African Sacred Groves: Ecological Dynamics and Social Change*, Oxford: James Currey, 2008.
Simoons, Frederick J., *Northwest Ethiopia: Peoples and Economy*, Madison, WI: University of Wisconsin Press, 1960.

Spencer, John H., *Ethiopia at Bay: a personal account of the Haile Sellasie Years*, Algonac, MI: Reference Publications, 1984.
Steer, G. L., *Cæsar in Abyssinia*, London: Hodder and Stoughton, 1936.
Stern, Henry A., *Wanderings among the Falashas of Abyssinia: Together with a Description of the Country and its Various Inhabitants*, London: Wertheim, Macintosh, and Hunt, 1862.
Taddesse Tamrat, *Church and State in Ethiopia, 1270–1527* (Oxford Studies in African Affairs), Oxford: Clarendon Press, 1972.
Trimingham, J. Spencer, *Islam in Ethiopia*, London: Oxford University Press, 1952.
Tutschek, Charles, *Dictionary of the Galla Language*, Munich, 1844, accessed 24 February 2017: http://trove.nla.gov.au/work/11537100.
Vanderheym, J. G., *Une Expédition avec Le Négous Ménélik (Vingt Mois en Abyssinie)*, Paris: Hachette, 1896.
Walker, C. H., *The Abyssinian At Home*, London: Sheldon Press, 1933.
Welby, M. S. *'Twixt Sirdar and Menelik: An Account of a Year's Expedition from Zeila to Cairo through Unknown Abyssinia*, New York and London: Harper & Brothers, 1901.
Winstanley, William, *A Visit to Abyssinia: an account of travel in modern Abyssinia*, London: Hurst and Blackett, 1881.
Wylde, Augustus B., *Modern Abyssinia*, London: Methuen, 1901.
Yirga Gelaw Weldeyes, *Native Colonialism: Education and the Economy of Violence against Tradition in Ethiopia*, Trenton, NJ: Red Sea Press, 2017.
Zewde Gabre-Sellassie, *Yohannes IV of Ethiopia: A Political Biography* (Oxford Studies in African Affairs), Oxford: Clarendon Press, 1975.

Index

Abasha Garba, 81
Abate Bwayalew, *Abba Yitref, Liqe Mekuas,* 91, 92, 93, 169; *Dejazmach,* 95; *Ras,* 95, 95 n.94
Abay (river), 47–8, 56–7, 79, 82–4, 87, 112, 114, 189, 279, 282; Map 2, 106
Abdallah al-Sadiq, 98
'Abd al-Malik, 42
Abdisa Aga, Colonel, 260
Abdullahi, *Emir* of Harar, 191
Abe Lahm (Abe-Lam), 36; *meret,* 73
Abebe Aregay, *Balambaras,* 7, 256, 261, 271, 282; *Ras,* 269, 272–6, 283; Abebe Weldu, *Fitawrari,* 282
abegaz, 'governor over billeted lands', 73–4, 93; Gurage ruler, 73 n.31
Aberra, 34; Map 1, 26
Aberra Jembere, 19 n.1, 179, 285, 297
Aberra Kassa, *Dejazmach,* 257–8, 284
abeto, 'prince', 79, 98–9
Abiye, *Mer'ed Azmatch,* 41 n.62
Abraham, *Abune,* 247
Abraham Ar'aya, 102
Abreha (Arabia), 29
Abreha Deboch, 260–61
Abubeker Ibrahim, *Negadras,* 98
Abyssinia, 8 n.1, 46, 69, 99, 108–9, 114, 152, 163, 165–6, 174, 208, 222
Abyssinian horse, 154 n.28
Achefer, 38
Adabay (river), 114
Adal (region), 33, 36, 43, 113, 272–3
Adal Tessema, *Balambaras,* 45, 54, 56–7, 79–81, 84, 88; *Ras* 188–9; as Tekle Haymanot, *Negus,* 57, 75–6, 78, 80 n.56, 81–6, 88–9 inc. n.74, 224–5, 229, 234
adarash, 'hall', 124–7, 175, 177, 180, 198, 203, 206, 225; *elfign adarash,* 126
adbar, 'important person', 127; 'physical focus', 118–21, 119 n.1, 127, 142, 199; *teleq sew,* 68, 119, 121–2
Addis Ababa (formerly Berera), 33, 79, 91, 95, 98, 101–3, 109, 111, 204, 225, 236, 243–6, 252–3, 255–60, 263, 266–70, 274–5, 281–2, 285; Map 1, 26
Aden, Gulf of, 42, 228
Adewa (town), 33, 53, 249–50; Map 1, 26
Adewa, Battle of (1896), 7, 36, 46 inc. n.80; 75, 93, 189, 217–18; cautious preparation for, 223–5; *chewa* after, 236–9; final battle, 234–6; first encounter, 232–3; *gibir* before defence, 225–8; mobilization, 228–30; on the march to, 231–2; second confrontation, 233–4
Adigrat, 226, 250
Adulis, 27–8, 30, 158
Afework Welde Semayat, *Gerazmach, Dejazmach* (posthumously), 242
Afro Aygeba, 15, 35
agafari, 6,123, 149; *dejagafari,* 184; duties and status, 177–9; as title, 257
Agere Maryam, 263–4, 266, 281; Map 1, 26
Agere Selam, 34, 248, 262; Map 1, 26
Agew (kingdom of Axum), 28–30; words in, 31, 158, 235, 253
Agew Meder (Gojam), 79, 88
Agraroha, 33
Ahmed Ibn Ghazi (fl.1529–43) of Adal, *Imam,* 36, 43, 56; mythology of, 113
ahzab, 'nations', 30
Albertone, Mateo, General, 234–5
Ali, *Ras-Bitweded,* 10
Ali Alula II, *Ras,* 40, 47–50, 52, 68, 187, 205
Alula Qubi, *Abba Nega, Shaleqa,* later *Ras,* 34 (founds Asmara 1890), 44–5, 88, 222–3; Battle of Adewa, 224–5, 233–5
Amara (regiment), 35
Amba Alagi, 232–4; Map 1, 26
amba-gennen, 69
Amde Mikael Yinadu, *Dejazmach,* 243, 262, 265
Amde Tsion (r.1314–44), 31–2, 42, 159, 269

Amede Liben, *Abba Wattew*, 53
Ametegna Washa (cave), 274
Amha Iyesus, *Mer'ed Azmatch*, 41
Amhara, claimed as origin, 17, 111; government service providers, 113; regiment, 35; region 31; stereotypes, 36, 76, 90, 112
Anbesa Wedm, King, 31
Ankober, 34, 79–80
Antonnneli, Pietro, 224
Aosta, Duke of (Di Savoia-Aosta, Amedeo, Prince), 275
Aphilas, 29
Aqetzer (regiment), 35
Arabia, 28–9, 41–2
Araya Selassie, *Ras,* 57
Arbegona, 265, Map 1, 26
Aregay, *Afenegus,* 256
Arimondi, Francesco, General, 233–5
Arsi, 24, 56, 76–7, 79–83, 91, 99, 174, 188, 191, 200, 243, 261–2, 265–6, 281
asash, 'surveyor', 72
Asfa Wesen, *Dejazmach,* 257, 284
Asfa Wesen, *Mer'ed Azmatch,* 41, 61
ashker, retainer, 12; head of household retainers, 178
Askale Maryam Gobena Dachi, *Weyzero,* 256
Asmara, 34 inc. n.34, 89, 95 n.94, 223; Map 1, 26
Ashngie, 229, 234
assertions: (regarding) boundaries, 63–7, 112–15; coordinated, 223–7, 243; foreign invaders, 222–35, 240–84; territory, 116–18; wandering monarchs, 18–21, 30–32
associations, 120, 122, 128–32; *debo* and *jigi*, 'work associations', 134, 136; League of Nations, as 'World Association', 246, 250–3, 285; social networks, 134–8 inc. n.34; United Nations, 285
Assosa, 48
Aster Mengesha, *Weyzero,* 105
Aswan, 42
atrocities, 77; fascist, 2, 236, 251
Augustus Caesar, 28
authority, 5, 7, 12; *awaj,* 'edict', 21–2, 79–80, 103, 199, 213, 223; changes in grassroots, 194–5; communal, 18, 22, 47, 68–9, 71, 115–16, 134–6, 138, 167, 194, 212, 277; declaring (*zeraf*), 212–16; deputized, 176–7, 219; *dergo,* 'maintenance', 218; *gebbar,* 'tribute payer', 71, 74, 77, 148, 232, 261; *gibir,* banquets as symbols of, 200, 215, 279–80; government, 5, 7, 12, 15–16, 32–42, 47–61, 71, 95, 97, 175, 273, 277, 279; grassroots, 5, 12,
15–17, 22; 68–70, 115–16, 134, 212, 219–21; justice, and, 180–2, 273; *qitet,* 'military mobilization', 192, 228; *mestengido,* 'guesthood', 192, 218; *meten,* 'food rations', 192, 198, 218–19; military, 12, 68, 72, 186–7, 195, 200–5; political rivalry during war, and, 273–7
Awash (river), 56, 101, 214, 257, 273; Map 2, 106
Axum/Axumite, 5, 27–32, 35, 39, 42, 53, 70, 158–9; Map 1, 26; Map 3, 242
Ayalew Biru, *Dejazmach,* 247, 250, 254
Azebo, 226, 232
azmari, 'singer', 62, 79

Badel Tsehai, 35
Badoglio, Pietro, Marshal of Italy, 249–50
Bafena, queen of Menelik II, 34
Bagibo (r.1825–61), *Abba,* 19, 41
baher negash, 43, 55
Bahrey, *Abba,* 33, 36, 159 inc. n.43
Bahriyaw, *Dejazmach,* 257
Bahru Zewde, 100
Bahta Hagos, 226
balabat, 21, 25; as communal landowners, 65, 120; as office holder, 70–6, 92–3, 116, 136, 188, 190–2, 254–5, 288
balager, 9, 33; rural person, 70–1, 71 n.22, 93
Balcha Safo, *Abba Nefso, Bejirond,* 91–2, 157, 230, 232; *Dejazmach,* 99, 103, 220, 254, 257–8
Bale, 32, 35, 56–7, 76–7, 80, 99, 188, 191, 243, 261–2, 264, 281, 288; Map 1, 26
bale meret, 'landowner', 98
Bantyirgu Welde Kidan, *Fitawrari,* 257
Baratieri, Oresto, General, 234
Barud Bet, 36 n.1; 57, 76, 80, 102–3, 123, 261–7, 270, 281
Bashbiziq (regiment), 67
battles, see *zemecha*
Be Adal Mebreq (regiment), 35
Begemder, 7, 33, 35, 47, 49, 53, 57, 61, 70, 77, 97, 104; social categories, 111–14, 187–8, 190–1, 205, 223, 225, 229, 232, 243, 254, 256, 268–70, 276–8; Map 1, 26
Beguna, 31
Be'ide Maryam (r.1468–78), 33
Bekaffa (r.1721–30), 39
Bekele Weya, *Dejazmach,* 265–6
Belay Zeleke, *Atse-Begulbetu,* 'emperor through his might', *Dejazmach,* 7, 269–70, 277–80, 279 n.102; 285
Beni-Amer, 48
Beni Shangul, 48, 80
Berence, 28

Berhane-Selassie Yigeremu, *Balambaras*, 122, 161 n.46, 181, 264–5, 267
Beshah Aboye, *Dejazmach*, 24, 57, 91, 229
Bete Isra'el (Felasha), 111
beteseb, 'family circle', 181
Beyene Mered, *Dejazmach*, 243, 262, 265–6
Beyene Wendim-Agegnehu, *Ligaba, Dejazmach*, 93, 202
Bezabeh, *Ato*, 79
Bezabeh Seleshi, Major, *Kegnazmach, Dejazmach*, 262–3, 265–6
Bezabeh Tekle Haymanot, *Dejazmach, Ras*, 82
Bichena, 278, 279
Biru, *Wagshum*, 225
Biru Aligaz, *Dejazmach*, 47, 50
Biru Goshu, *Dejazmach*, 34, 47, 50–2, 79, 208
Biru Welde Gebrel, *Dejazmach, Ras*, 104, 220–1, 280
Bizet, King of Agabo, 30 inc. n.16
Blue Nile, 75; Map 2, 106
Bofu, 41
Bogos, 44
Boko, *Abba* (r.1859–62), 19, 41
Borana, 57, 262
border lands, 11, 13–17, 19, 20, 32, 36 n.42, 48, 110, 112–15
Boru Meda, 54
Boyna-Tigre, 'farmer-Tigre' in Welayta, 17, 90
British military power, 77
Buko, *Dejazmach*, 38
Bulga, a patriot kingdom, 7; resistance in, 257, 268, 270–4

Castagna ('Qestegna'), 265, 265 n.77
Chafe Maryam, 273
Cheleya, 84
Chercher, 231
cheqa 'boundary markers', 63, 66 (forest), 108, 116
chewa, 'emergent warriors'; aspiration to leadership, 12–13; camaraderie, 150, 153–4, 156, 162, 193–4; changes in, 36–9, 71–3, 77–8, 244–6; defence, 19–25, 211–16; definition, 8; history and, 28–31, 35; importance of, 1–2, 114–15; land, attachment to, 11–12, 64–5; last *chewa* corps, 261–7; loss of power, 174, 237–9; new fighters, 246–9, 255–61; object of warfare, 67; patriots, 267–85; rivalry with monarchs, 17–18, 74–7; self-trained, 8–9, 20, 229–31; ; slavery, 132–34; social support, 63, 119–21, 143–4; territory of, 115–18; *zega* (landless),

61–2, 61 n.4, 77
Chilga, 33, 52
civilian titles: *afenegus* 'chief justice', 196; *bejirond*, 'treasurer', 91–2; *lij*, 'young noble', 190; *kentiba*, 'mayor', 254, *liqe mekuas*, 'impersonator', 91–2 ,189; *tsehafi te'ezaz* 'scribe of orders', 199
conflict with Egyptians, 6, 34, 42–50, 54, 57, 222, 229
conflict with Europeans, 44–6
conflict with Italy, 1, 5, 6–7, 18–19, 65, 87, 89, 98, 105, 114, 174, 182–4; 191, 215, 218, 222–39, 240–84
conflict with Ottoman Turks, 41–4, 48
country, 2–8, 10; as personal identity, 150; monarch's authority in, 194–5, 226; significance of ecology and earth, 97, 139, 186–7, 276–7; socializing view of, 116–19, 140; strategic use of, 181–4, 192–3, 224–5, 236, 270, 282; as 'unutilized land' (*taff*),109
Crinitti, Major, 250

Dabormida, Vittorio Emanuelo, General, 234
Dahlak (islands), 42, 43; Map 2, 106
Damot, 27, 31–2, 35 inc. n.41, 37, 90, 92, 148, 278
Daressa Amente, *Belata*, 255
Dawa (river), 263; Map 3, 242
Dawaro, 32–3, 35, 56, 76
Dawit I (r.1380–1412), 33, 42
Dawit III (r.1716–21), 39
De Bono, Emilio, General, 243, 245, 249–50
Debay, *Dejazmach*, 263–4
Deboroa, 43
Debre Haylat, 226, 234
Debre Libanos, 261
Debre Markos (Debre Marcos), 246; Map 1, 26; Map 3, 242
Debre Tabor, 33, 47, 53
defence notions, 10–11; on the battlefield, 182–4; of borders, 112; commitment to land 66, 231–2; 'dying in defence', 66, 68,70; ecological dangers, overcoming of, 8, 107, 109–12, 131; gendered social base, 138, 140; responsibility for, 1–2, 7, 69, 279, 281, 285; self-sacrifice, 66–7; taking captives, 119; *wof*, 'messengers', 194
defence practices: annual cycles, 37, 80, 90, 116; at the battlefield, 234; *dejen*, 'rear guard', 182; deployment, 182–4; garrison towns, 31–4; history of, 26–9; internal rivalry, 39–44; military review at *Meskel*, 'Feast of

the Cross', 153, 201–2; mobilization, 192–3, 227–30; *qeleb*, 'rations', 205; strategies, 68–9, 78, 115–16, 120, 127, 175–6, 180, 183, 193, 223–4; supplies, 192–3, 218–19, 231–2; territorial assertions, 16, 18–21, 63–7, 112–15,116–18, 224–5, 226, 243; vigilance, 12, 20–5, 43–6, 106–9, 193–4, 246–8

defence landscape, 11, 15, 17–21, 32, 41, 43, 46, 49–50, 53, 55, 59, 63–5, 66–7, 66 n.13, 70, 72, 75, 83–4, 92–3, 99, 103–5, 107–10, 111–12, 115, 210–16, 226, 228–30, 247–8, 253, 267–8

defence training: *berehegna*, 'frequenter of the desert', 172; competitive sports, *guks* and *genna*, 80, 96, 151–5, 288; during childhood games, 145–54; on ecological familiarity of *kola/bereha*, 'lowland / desert', 108; in horsemanship, 154–6; in hunting, 156–74; in leadership, 146, 152; in wits and leadership, 10, 11, 12, 29, 66, 231–2; restrictions, 194–5, 220–21

Dembya, 37, 48, 49, 50, 229
Demiss Beyene, 283
Demiss Wolde Amanual, *Lij, Dejazmach,* 269, 270 n.86, 273 –5
Dengel Ber, 50
Deqe Mehari, 28
Dereso, *Dejazmach, Ras,* 81–3, 85, 86
Dessie, 105, 225, 243, 249, 263; Map 1, 26; Map 3, 242
Desta Damtew, *Ras,* 7, 57, 79, 178, 243, 248, 250, 261–7, 274 n.96
Dil Nead, 31
DMT dynasty, 27
Dogali, 222, 223, 259; Map 1, 26
Dolo, 243, 248, 250, 261–2, 264–5, 281; Map 1, 26; Map 3, 242
Dori, *Ras*, 40

Egypt, 45–6, 48, 52–4, 56, 72; along Red Sea coast, 57; appeal to, 47 n.4, 222; church of, 42–4; in Harar, 48; hostility of, 6, 34, 42, 44; Ottoman Turks and, 43–44, 45–6; and Yohannes IV, 89, 222
Eleni, Empress, 104
Ellena, Guiseppe, General, 234
Embabo, 57, 78–98, 78–79 n.33, 89, 214
Enat Awaj, singer, 79, 80, 213
Enda Ceros, 27
Endybis, 30
enemy: *dina*, 'external enemy', 12, 20–1, 23, 32, 42–3, 45–6, 48, 55, 63, 66, 120, 216, 218, 237; exclusion of, 109–10; *felfeltu*, 'spiritual enemy', 20; *folle*, 'warfare', 24; friends and foes, 19–21, historical friends and foes, 41–4; submission, 76, 80, 88–9, 93, 175, 181, 191, 194, 230; *telat*, 'enemy', 20, 216
Ennarya, 35, 37–8, 41, 90
Entoto, 33, 82, 87, 256
Eritrea, 28, 30 n.17, 35, 61, 159, 223, 233, 235, 242–3, 245, 249–50, 259, 285, 287; Map 1 (26); Map 2, 106
Eritreans, 255, 259–60, 263–6
Erlich, Haggai, 42, 97, 100
Erret Meda, 283
Europe, hostility of, 45, 55, 222
Ezana, King, 29, 30, 46, 188 n.8

fanno, 9, 13–17, 19, 20, 55–6, 76, 174, 182, 194, 229, 238, 267–70, 291
Fasil (Fasildes) (r.1632–67), 39, 52
Feleke Dagne, Major, *Dejazmach,* 283
Feleke Iyasu, *Gerazmach,* 270
Felter, Pietro, 234
Fikre Maryam, *Dejazmach,* 254, 257, 270
Fisiha Genet, 264; Map 1, 26
foes: 19–21; *dina,* 'external enemy', 12, 20–1, 23, 32, 42–3, 45–6, 48, 55, 63, 66, 120, 216, 218, 237; exclusion of, 109–10; *felfeltu*, 'spiritual enemy', 20; *folle,* 'warfare', 24; *telat*, 'enemy', 20, 216
friends and allies: 5, 19–20, 41–6, 107; inclusivity, 128–32, 134–8, 197–8; social boundary, 110–11; *wegen,* 'insiders', 12, 20, 62–3, 66, 67–8, 81, 120, 122, 129–33, 193, 199, 200, 211, 218; *bae'd,* 'non-related', 120; *yesew ager sew,* 'foreigner', 120
Fulas, *Negadras,* 93

Gadar, King, 28
Gadarat, King, 28
Gaki Sherocho, *Tato,* 93, 191
Galliano, Guiseppe, Major, 233–4
Gambella, 28
Gazera, General, 275
Gebeyehu, *Fitawrari,* 91–2, 233
Gebre Egziabher, Kumsa Moroda, *Moti, Dejazmach,* 74, 230
Gebre Hiywot Baykedagn, 100
Gebre Krestos, Emperor, 40
Gebre Krestos Desta, 276
Gebre Maryam Gari, *Dejazmach,* 262–6
gedam, 'camp centre', 84–5, 182–3, 189; red tent, 178
Gelawdewos (r.1540–59), 33, 37
Geloso Carlo, General, 243, 263
Gemu Gofa, 33, 76; Map 1, 26
Genale (river), 250; Map 2, 106
Germame, *Dejazmach,* 213
Gessese, *Dejazmach,* 234
Gessese Fanta, *Gerazmach,* 248
gewaro (back yard), 126

Gibe (river), 33, 35, 39, 41, 80,195; Map 2, 106
gibir, 6, 71, 76, 121, 125, 127, 180–1, 184, 196–8; as sharing food, 200–8, 210–12, 215, 217; before defence, 225–8; 231, 232, 245–6, 261, 277; maintenance, 218–21; 219–20
Gigar, Emperor, 40
Gishen (mountain), 276
Gobena Amede, *Gerazmach*, 276, 277
Gobena Dachi, *Aba Tegu, Ras*, 57, 78 n.33, 80–3, 85, 86, 87, 89, 153, 157, 188, 256
Gojam (Gojame), 23, 34, 37–8, 40, 47–53, 56–7, 61, 68, 70, 75, 77–88, 97, 113–14, 147, 187–91, 205, 208, 219, 223–6, 229, 234, 243, 246–8, 250, 253, 269–70, 276–8, 284–5
Gololcha (river), 264
Gonder, 31, 33, 35, 38–40, 43, 49–50, 52, 61, 77, 113, 157, 169, 187, 190, 247, 250, 253; Map 1, 26; Map 3, 242
Gordon, Charles, General, 45
Gore, 253, 255; Map 3, 242
Goshu Zewde (fl.1835–52), *Dejazmach*, 40, 49–50, 52, 212
Graziani, Rudolfo, General, 241–2 n.4, 243, 248, 252, 258, 259–61, 267
Guangul Zegeye, *Dejazmach*, 226, 230
Guba, 48
guerrilla warfare,1935–41: *arbegna*, 'patriot', 1–2, 7, 19, 255–6, 269; attack on the capital, 256–9; attack on Italian Viceroy, Graziani, 259–61; Italians sue for peace, 273–6; kings of resistance, 270–3; the last *chewa*, 261–7; patriots, 267–70, 273–84; *shanqo* and *shasho*, 'black and white' labels for enemy planes, 262
Gugsa Aliye, *Dejazmach*, 101
Gugsa Merso, *Ras*, 40
Gugsa Wele, *Ras*, 104, 247
gult, administrative land, 6, 16, 32, 37; changes in, 60–2, 77, 280; *gulte-gez*, 'official of *gult*', 70
guma, 'blood money', 81, 235–6
Gundet, 44–5
Gura', 35, 44
Gurage, 31, 35–6, 56–7, 72, 73 n.31, 76–7, 80, 91, 111, 113, 191, 208 n.17, 266

Habesha, 112–15
Habte Giyorgis Dinagde, *Abba Mechal, Fitawrari*, 57, 94–5, 103–4, 157
Habte Maryam Gebre Egziabher, *Dejazmach*, 254
Haddis Alemayehu, 247, 250–1
Hadya, 31–2, 35, 56, 76
hager (*ager*), 4, 6, 66, 93, 107, 112–14, 116–17, 195, 211

Harar, Hararge, 22, 44, 48, 56–7, 76–7, 97–9, 100–4, 191, 195, 223, 230–1, 243, 249, 252–3, 262; Map 1, 26; Map 3, 242
Haile Maryam Gezimu, 257
Haile Maryam Mammo, 256–8, 272–3, 282
Haile Mekuria, *Kegnazmach, Fitawrari*, 202 n.8, 265–6
Haile Melekot, *Negus*, 41, 189
Haile Selassie I, *Abba Tekil* (r.1930–75), 7, 20, 105, 157, 174 n.100, 190, 192, 201 n.4, 239–41, 243, 245–6, 249, 252–3, 263, 270–3, 275–6, 279; as Tafari Mekonnen, *Dejazmach, Ras, Negus*, 98–9, 102–5, 163, 190, 220
Haile Yosadiq, *Ras*, 39
Hailu Welde Medhin, *Kegnazmach, Dejazmach*, 270, 272–4
Hamasen, 34, 44–5, 187, 190, 223, 236
Hijaz, 42, 98
Hojelie Al Hassan, *Sheik*, 255
hunting, 6, 11–15, 18, 30, 64, 97, 100, 117, 133, 138, 140, 142–3, 145, 147, 156–74

Illubabor, 48, 57, 76–7, 80, 188, 191, 230, 253
Imru Haile Selassie, *Ras*, 7, 243, 246–7, 249–50, 252–3, 267, 278
information generation, dissemination and reaction, 21–6
Ismael, Khedive, 42 n.67, 44 n.76
Italian invasions, *yetelat werere zemen*, 1, 2, 5–7, 11–12, 18, 87, 105, 174, 215, 218, 221; Battle of Adewa (1896), 222–39; second invasion (1935–45) and guerrilla resistance to, 240–85
Italy, as *dina*, 48; with European stranglehold, 45–6; 163; Wichale, 224
Iyasu, *Aba Tena, Lij, Abeto* (1895–1935), 94–103, 95 n.94, 96–8, 101 n.111; accusations against, 98–9, 98 n. 102; at banquet, 203 n.10; hunting by, 163; ousting of, 102–4, 239; reputation, 209, 215, 220; sons of, 109, 270–3, 275–8, 282, 285
Iyasu I (r.1682–1706), 33, 39, 40, 55
Iyasu II (r.1730–55), 39
Iyasu IV, 40
Iyoas (r.1755–89), 39 inc. n.60, 169

Jebasire, 264–6, 281; Map 1, 26
Jibat, 76
Jibela (fortress), 34, 51–2
Jifar I (Sana), of Jimma (r.1830–55), *Abba*, 41
Jifar II, *Sultan* of Jimma, *Abba*, 57, 74, 91–3, 191, 230

Jijiga, 99, 121, 243; Map 3, 242
Jimma, 22, 41, 57, 71, 74, 90–1, 97, 189, 191, 218, 254–5, 258, 275; Map 1, 26
Jimma-Kakka, 41, 81
Jirru, 256, 271, 282
Jobir of Jimma, *Abba*, 258
Junod, Marcel, 251, 263

Kaleb (r. *c*.514–30), 29
Kambata, 56, 72, 76, 90–1, 281
Kaskase, 27
Kassa Hailu Darge, *Ras*, 243, 249, 257
Kassa Yagilew, *Fitawrari*, 264
Kebedde Bizunesh, *Dejazmach*, 284
Kebedde Mengesha, *Dejazmach*, 98
Kebre Negest, 'Glory of Kings', 5, 15, 17, 47, 52–3, 56, 191, 225, 239
Kedida, 81, 83
Keffa, 7, 35, 56–7, 68, 76–7, 81, 86, 88, 90, 93, 99, 113, 174, 188–9, 190–1, 195, 210, 230, 267; Map 1, 26
Kenfu Adam, *Dejazmach*, 39, 48–9
ketema, 'garrison town', 6, 12, 32–4, 83
Khedive Ismail, 42 n.67, 44–5
Kidane Meheret, 234
Kidda, 'King of Yerer', *Fitawrari*, 257
Konso, 56
Korem, 31, 251
Kurfa, *Fitawrari*, 93

Lalibela, 32; Map 3, 242
Lalibela, King (*c*.1185–1225?), 42 inc. n. 70
land, 3, 7, 8, 60–1, 64; communal ownership, 6, 9, 15–16; functions of, 73–5; grants, 11 n.7, 12, 73–5; inalienable right (*atseme rest*), 9, 11, 37, 61, 63–5; inheritance (*rest*), 63–5, 71–5, 83; landowner (*bale meret*), 7, 98; landlessness (*zega*), 61–2; military, 6, 9–10, 59–60, 64; *milmil meret*, 'recruits' land', 73; as organizing principle, 16, 54–5, 252–5; as personal identity (*atint ena gultmit*), 64; prescriptive rights to, 18, 56–7, 89–94; reform, 4, 54; *ye-feres makomeya*, 'horse-grazing land',154
Lay Armacheho, 38
leba shay, 'thief seeker', 100, 101 n.111
Leche, 54, 102, 270, 274
Lekelesh Beyan, *Weyzero*, 280–3
Lekemt, also Nekemt, 74, 254; Map 3, 242
Leqa (Lekemt, Qellem), 41, 74, 230
Libne Dingil (r.1508–40), 33, 41, 43, 232
Limmu, 82
Limmu-Ennarya, 41
Lorenzini, Colonel, 275
'lost territories', reclaiming of, 19, 56, 60, 75–6, 78–94
Luchetti, Major, 275
Lulseged Atnafseged, *Dejazmach, Ras,* 91–2, 98, 103, 105, 229
Luqas, *Abune,* 225

Machakal, 38
Magal, *Abba*, 41
Mahbre Selassie, 268
Maichew, 250–51, 253, 281, 284; Map 1, 26
Makeda, Queen of Sheba, 47
Malazo, 27
Marye, *Ras*, 40
Massawa (Mitsewa), 25, 32, 42–4, 46, 48, 222–3, 236; Map 1, 26
Matara, 27
Mattewos, *Abune,* 96
Mazhar, Ahmed, 97–8,100
Mecha, 38, 76, 79, 80–1, 277
Megal, *Abba*, 41
Mekdela (Magdala), 52–3, 79; Map 1, 26
Mekele, 225–6, 229, 233–4; Map 3, 242
Mekonnen Endalkachew, *Bitweded*, 95 n.94
Mekonnen Haile Selassie, Prince, 201 n.4
Mekonnen Tewendbelay, *Fitawrari,* 98
Mekonnen Welde Mikael, *Aba Kagnew, Balambaras, Ras*, 157, 191, 228–34
Mekonnen Wesene, 262
Mekonnen Yigletu, 292
mekwanent (plural of *mekonnen*), 'officers and nobles', 6, 9, 13–16, 31–8, 47, 57, 69–72, 76–8, 87, 93–105, 104, 163, 175, 177–9, 182–90; administrative, 38, 40, 71, 74–5, 102; *chelot*, 'high court', 175, 179–80; military, 72–3, 76, 81, 86, 152; modern, 12, 65; as nobles, 54–5
Melake Tsehai Iyasu, Engdashet, *Negus* (r.1937–39), 269–74, 282
Melka Dida, 262, 264
Melkakeraba, 265
Menelik I, 35
Menelik II (r.1889–1913): banquet of, 203–4, 225–6; in battle, 214; Battle of Adewa, 18, 222–26, 232–6; billeting, 195; consolidation of, 189–90, 194–5, 220; exercise, 165; government reforms, 236–9; land reforms, 11 n.7; marching to Adewa, 231–2; marginalizing the *chewa*, 4; mobilization, 200; mobilization edict, 227–8; modernization by, 191; power increase of, 75; popularity, 213; reclaiming lands, 75–8, 113, 191; recruitment, 153; rivalling the grassroots, 17; secular orientation, 46; socializing, 138 n.34;

trophy collection, 218; unifying the warriors, 45, 53–4; weapons acquisition, 18
Menen Ali Liben, Empress (1831–55), 40, 49, 51, 104
Menen Asfaw, Empress, 105 n.4, 201
Mengesha Atikem, *Ras Bitweded,* 86, 278
Mengesha Jembere, *Dejazmach,* 278
Mengesha Wesene, *Dejazmach,* 270
Mengesha Yohannes, *Ras,* 188, 223, 225–6, 230, 232, 234
Mentwab, Empress (regent 1722–69), 104, 169
Mereb (river), 43, 44, 224, 226, 243; Map 2, 106
Mered W. Aregay, 30, 31
Mers'e Hazen Welde Kirkos, *Belaten Geta,* 97
Mersha Nahusennay, 98
Mesfin Seleshi, Major, *Ras,* 257, 259, 278
Mestayit, Queen, 82, 84–6
Metemma, 44, 54, 222, 225
Mikael (Mohammed Ali), *Abba Shanko, Ras, Negus,* 54, 88, 91–2, 96–7, 101–5, 190, 224–5, 229, 234, 252
Mikael Sehul, *Ras* (1740–80), 39, 40, 48, 61, 169, 187
military: categories, 13–15, 25, 27, 37, 50, 54–5, 78, 165, 174, 228, 243, 268, 270, 286–8, 290, 292; confrontation, 7; contingent lands, 3, 5, 6, 16, 18, 33–4, 37, 59; definition and traditions,10–11; deputizing, 199–201; feasts, 121, 200–16; *feriha Egziabher,* 'fear of God', 220; histories of, 27, 139, 236, 247, 252, 286, 289, 291; integration, 38, 56–7; land and power, 6; political roles, 4, 5; power politics, 59–62, 175–7; principles, 5, 253; reforms, 4, 19, 34, 49–55, 236–9; 258, 287; settlements 34–9; symbolism, 6; training, 6; views of, 1, 2, 3; vigilance, 12
military *baldereba,* 'power mediator', 6, 87; on battlefield, 184, 189, 193; duties of, 177–80, 205, 219, 290; at mobilization, 192
military hamlet-cum-camp, 119–20, 122–8, 202, 208; *fit ber, yegwaro-ber, serkosh ber,* 'front', 'back' and 'secret' gates, 123–4; *dej,* 'outside or public place', 126, 159, 161, 186; household, 10; houses, 123; house 'reception' (*elfign, elfign-adarash*), 126, 159, 161, 186; house *medeb,* 'divan', 124; house *zufan,* 'throne', 127, 179
Military land administration: *chisegna,* 'tenant farmers', 74; *madbet,* 'officer's personal fief', 74–5, 93; *Maderya,* 'military land grant', 59, 72–5

military merits: *beles,* 'luck', 167; divination, *aste,* 164; *geday,* 'achieving a kill', 12, 158, 169, 211, 217–18, 284; *geday metal,* 'displaying a trophy', 169, 211; *gobez* or *jegna,* 'brave', 100; hunting animals, 163, 166–9, 217; omens, 164; personifying wildlife, *erm, 'taboo',* 171; *teskar,* 'commemoration feast' for wildlife, 171; trophies from animals, 144, 158 161, 163, 166–7, 170–1, 173 217; trophies from battlefield, 79, 86–7, 117, 146, 216–18, 235
military operations: *kitet,* 'mobilization', 228, 243; *zemecha,* 'expedition', 184, 189, 192; *zerefa,* 'looting', 193, 217
military *qesqash,* 'alerter', 184, 192
Mofer Weha (river), 114
Moges Asgedom, 260–1
Mohammed Anfari, *Sultan,* 230
Mohammed ibn Ghazi, *Imam (Gragn),* 5, 33, 43
monarchs, 1, 3–7, 9–10, 12–13, 15–17, 27, 31–2; and *chewa,* 19–21, 34–41; *janhoy,* 'your majesty', 31, 34–8, 69–72, 76–8, 93–105, 158, 177–9; and society, 17–18; regional monarchs' titles: *emir,* 191; *kao,* 90; *sultan,* 191; *tato,* 191; symbolic value of, 18, 276
Mota, 279–80
Mulugeta Yigezu, *Ras,* 243, 246, 249
Munzinger, *Pasha,* 45, 46
Mussolini, Benito, 1–2, 241–3, 251–2, 276, 284

Napier, Robert, Lieutenant-General, 53
Nasi, Guglielmo, General, 275
neftegna, 'gunman', 1, 262, 290
negade, 'trader', 25
Negash Bezabeh, *Dejazmach,* 278, 284–5
negasi, 'crowned head', 40, 188
Negasi, *Mer'edazmatch,* 40, 40–41 n.62, 190
Negele, 263, Map 3, 242
negus, 5, 16; history of, 27–9, 41,54, 57, 73 n.31, 75, 79, 82, 84, 89, 96, 102, 133, 178, 183, 187–94, 188 n.8, 203, 225
neguse negest, 5, 9, 13–18, 20, 27, 35–6, 38, 40–1, 43, 47, 53–8, 61–2, 66, 70, 74, 76–8, 84, 86, 89, 94, 96–7, 104, 178, 183, 186–91, 194–5, 201, 223, 225, 230, 237, 239, 284, 288
Nero, 28
Nesibu Ze'amanuel, *Dejazmach,* 243

Ogaden, 98, 229, 243
Orero, Baldasare, General, 223, 224
Ozdemir Pasha, 43

patrimonial relationships of *aleqa-chefra*, 'heads–subordinates', 176–7
Petros, *Abune*, 224, 258
politico-military officers: *balderas*, 'cavalry', 179; *dej qalbas*, medieval officer, 159; *enderase*, representative, 176; *ligaba*, 'mayor', 199; *negadras*, 'head of merchants', 179; power mediators, 175–7; *seyfe jagre*, 'sword carrier', 184; *shumament* (in 19th century), 177–8, 189–92
politico-military titles: *balambaras*, 185–7; *dejazmach*, 183–4, 186–7, 193; *fitawrari*, 182–4, 192–94; *gerazmach*, 186, 194; *kegnaznach*, 186, 194; *negus*, 188–93; *neguse negest*, 184–93; *ras*, 186, 188, 191; *ras-bitweded*, 188

Qwara, 16, 49–51, 229

Raya, 68
Reba, *Abba* (r.1855–59), 41
Red Sea, 10, 20, 28, 30, 32, 36, 42–6, 48, 56–7, 112–13, 118, 159, 187, 222, 230, 236
regiments, ancient (*serawit* or *serwe*): *Dakwen*, 31, 158; *Damawa*, 31, 158; *Damot*, 31, 158; *Falha*, 29; *Hadar*, 31, 158; *Halen*, 29; *Hara*, 29; *Harab Gonda*, 29, 31; *Jan Amora*, 29; *Jan Qantaffa*, 29; *Laken*, 29; *Maggaro*, 29; *Mattin*, 29; *Mhaza*, 29; *Sabarat Sena*, 29; *Tekula*, 31; *Qeste Nihib*, 31
regiments, medieval: *Afro Aygeba*, 35; *Amhara*, 35; *Aqetzer*, 35; *Badel Tsehai*, 35; *Bashbiziq*, 35; *Be Adal Mebreq*, 35; *Gane-Geb*, 74–75; *Giyorgis Hayle*, 37; *Ilmegwazit Boran*, 37; *Kokeb*, *Legewon*, 35; *Qurban*, 35; *Sellus Hayle*, 35; *Senan* (*Seqeyat*), 35; *Wenbedie*, *Yehabeta*, 35
regiments, 19th-century: *Balderas*, 73, 152, 155, 179, 186; *Barud Bet*, 36, 57, 76, 80, 102–3, 123, 261–7, 270, 281; *Dembegna*, 78, 194–5, 220, 237, 261, 280; *Gendebel* (Amharic), *Weregenu* (Oromo), *Abe Lahm* (Ge'ez), 35–6, 73 n.29, 232; *Gondere*, 35–3, 76, 80, 101, 114, 231, 253, 256, 261–2, 281; *Milmil*, 73, 102, 188; *Seyfejagre*, 184; *Wedo-geb*, 188; *Werwari*, 76, 80, 90, 92, 101, 182–3, 194, 216, 231–2, 262–3, 281; *Wiha Senqu*, 73; *Ye bet lij*, 128
retainers: 12, 15, 18, 20, 25, 61, 68–71, 73–4, 76, 78, 87, 125–8; *degafi*, 186; *dejagafari*, 184; *zebegna shaleqa*, 186; symbols of *shileme*, 'decorated ones', 202, 206

retainers, household, *yebet lij*, 132–4, 152–3, 155–6, 175–7, 180; *ashker*, 'servant', 12, as head of household retainers, 178; aspiring youth, 69–70, 231–5; *azazh*, 'commanding officer', 125, 178, 180, 203, 267; *guaz*, 'retinue', 176–7, 180, 182; *negarit mechi*, 'drummer', 187, 196–8, 201, 211, 213, 219, 232, 245, 261, 263, 266, 278, 281; retainers and slaves, 132–3
retainers' rewards: *addo wesheba*, 'laudatory hunters' sing-songs', 162, 167–8, 172; *brundo* or *qurt*, 'choice meat', 170, 205–8; *dri*, 'gold chain', *albo*, 'anklet' and *kolba*, 'earring', 173; *marta*, 'tail', 167, 169–72, 217–18; *tej*, 'honey mead', 7, 73, 125, 197, 202, 205, 208–10, 215–16, 218, 231; *zeng*, 'stick', 173
Roha (later Lalibela), 31–3
Romanework Haile Selassie, Princess, 252, 266

Sahle Dingil, Emperor, 40, 52
Sahle Selassie, *Neguse Shewa*, *Abba Dina* (r.1813–47), 41, 48, 56, 80, 103, 157, 161 n.45, 189–90
sanga dagna, administrators in Welayta, 93
Saynt, 35, 70, 88, 114, 188, 279
Sbacchi, Alberto, 122 n.2, 250
Sebestyanos, *Mer'edazmatch*, 41
Sebhat, *Ras*, 224, 226
Seble Wengel, Empress, 104
Se'ela Krestos, *Ras*, 38
Segele, Battle of (1916), 16, 66, 78, 94–105, 194, 287
Selale, 77, 79, 188, 256, 257–8, 271, 284
Selama III, *Abune*, 47, 52,
selay (*wof*),'scout', 84, 233, 266, 272, 283
Sembrouthes 'the Great', 28
Semien, 35, 50, 52, 161 n.45, 225, 229, 234, 285
Sergew Hable Selassie, 28, 29, 30
Sertse Dingil (r.1563–97), 33, 43, 159
Seyoum Mengesha, *Dejazmach*, *Ras*, 224, 245, 249–50, 257
Seyoum Tekle Haymanot, *Dejazmach*, 85–6
Shewanesh Abraha, 276–7, 281
Shewarreged Gedle, 281
Shiferaw Bekele, 98
shifta, 'rebel', 9, 13–15, 19–20, 23, 48–9, 70, 76, 79, 82, 88 n.74, 108, 198, 205, 207, 212, 219, 226, 229–30, 238, 255–6, 270, 275, 277–8
Shire, 243, 247, 253; Map 3, 242
Sidamo (Sidama), 21, 24, 35, 57, 68, 76–7, 91, 93,102, 111, 113, 129–30 n.26, 139, 191, 216; Map 1, 26

Shirka, 32
Shewa, 31, 33–4, 36, 40–1, 51–3, 55–7, 61, 64, 69, 73, 75–6, 78–80, 82–3, 85–7, 89, 98–9, 105, 113–14, 150, 157, 173, 184, 187, 189–90, 193, 205, 213–14, 218, 223–4, 226, 228–32, 250, 254–6, 266, 269–71, 273–6, 281, 283; Map 1, 26
Solomonic dynasty, 225, 271
Somaliland, 45, 80, 101, 241, 242 n.4, 243, 245, 255, 262, 267
Sulayman, Caliph, 42
symbols: of adulthood, 89, 139–44, 256; *bale-negarit* 73, 187, 199–200; of battlefield, 216–18, 269; consuming *tej*, 7, 73, 197, 202–3, 205, 207–10, 215–16, 218, 231; feasting on meat, 7, 50, 125, 150, 160, 171, 178, 193; of hunting, 216–18; of land (*meret, meder*), 11; of political power, 174 n.100, 198–200, 204–9, 218, 225–6; of warriorhood, 6, 7, 185, 196–8, 215–18
symbols of authority, 11–12, 21, 18, 68, 178, 184–7, 196–8, 198–200; symbol of *embilta*, 196, 198; symbol of *negarit*, 'teller', drum of, 21, 40, 184, 187, 196, 198–201, 211, 219, 225, 272; symbol (political): 31–7, 40, 59 n.2, 57, 61, 68, 72, 93, 95, 97, 175–9; symbol (prescribed), 5, 15, 17, 19, 47–55, 57, 191–2, 269–70; symbol (prescriptive), 17

tabote Tsion; Ark of the Covenant, 84
Tadesse Tamirat, 42
Tadesse Yimam, 276–7
Takele Welde Hawaryat, *Belata*, 255, 278
Talha, *Sheik*, 233
Tamo (fortress), 34; Map 1, 26
Tana (lake), 28, 113; Map 2, 106
tax, 6, 71 n.22, 72; in cash, 220; in childhood games 147–8; in kind 179, 216, 219–20; popular view of, 62; protest over, 10, 55, 68, 77, 204, 238, 278, 285, 288; as resource redistribution, 196–7, 212, 219; in service, 77; in war, 193, 239, 254, 270
tax collectors, 68, 71, 74, 116, 179, 222
tax (land), 42, 200, 216, 233, 236
tax reform, 37, 60, 75, 224, 277, 287
Taye Gulelate, *Dejazmach*, 255
Taytu Betul, Empress, 94, 104, 153, 225; and Battle of Adewa, 231–2, 234
Teferi Kela, 265–67; Map 1, 26
Tekeze (river), 250; Map 2, 106
Tekle Giyorgis II, *Abba Jihad* (*Wagshum Gobeze*), Emperor (r.1868–72), 18, 45, 53, 57, 61, 79–80, 225
Tekle Haymanot, *Abune* (c.1215–1313), 36, 39, 91–2; Itissa monastery of, 271

Tekle Haymanot, *Negus,* 57, 75–6, 78, 80 n.56, 81–6, 88–9, 88 n.74, 224–5, 229, 234; as Adal Tessema, *Balambaras,* 45, 54, 56–7, 79–81, 84, 88; as *Ras,* 188–9
Tekle Haymanot II (r.1706–08), 39, 48
Tekle Iyesus, *Aleqa,* 69, 85–6, 88
Tenagnework Haile Selassie, Princess, 252
Terriba, 266–7; Map 3, 242
Tessema Abdi, *Fitawrari,* 265–7
Tessema Darge, *Dejazmach,* 91
Tessema Eshete, *Negadras,* 255, 274–5
Tessema Nadew, *Dejazmach, Ras-Bitweded,* 94, 96, 157, 224–5, 230
Tewabech Ali, Empress, 50
Tewodros II, *Aba Tatek* (r.1855–68), 4–5, 16, 18, 34, 41, 47–58, 76–7, 79, 86, 130, 156–7, 187–9, 193, 205, 223, 252, 268, 286; as *Kassa Hailu, Dejazmach,* 48–52, 156, 187, 205–6
Tewoflos (r.1708–11), 39
Thesiger, W. G., 99
Tigre, 7, 17, 29, 31, 33, 35, 37–40, 47, 51–3, 55, 61, 70, 72, 77, 79, 95, 113–14, 146, 187–8, 190–1, 205, 222–5, 231–4, 243, 253, 257, 281, 284; Map 1, 26
Tilahun, *Afe Negus,* 99
Tona, *Kao,* 17, 74, 90, 92–3, 191, 230
Toselli, Pietro, Major, 223
treasurer: *bejirond*, 93, 125–6, 135, 179, 199; *eqa bet aleqa,* 'household store commander', 179
Tsehai Work Darge, *Weyzero,* 272
Tselemt, 35

Wadera, 264; Map 3, 242
Wadla, 35
Wag, 95, 187, 190, 225
warriors, 13–15, 13 n.9, 68; challenging the state 9, 18; gender, 138–44, 248, 269, 280–3; identity, 7, 8, 19; in history, 27–31, 38, 41; leaders, 119–21, 149–50, 180–1; reputation of, 33; responsibilities of, 1, 3 16, 52, 54; rewards, 30–1; social base, 109–12, 122, 128–34; *wetader,* 'soldier', 61, 66, 121, 184, 269
weapons, 43–4, 226–8, 243–5; *ashmwatach gorade,* 'curved sword', 44; guns: *merbut, sabew, sinader,* 85; *madef,* 'mounted gun', 85; *qonchora,* 'curved knife', 91; *seyf,* 'sword', 184, 262; *tchere,* 'spear', 112
Wefla, 234
Wegera, 35, 37, 277
Welde Ashagre, *Dejazmach,* 84, 91
Welde Giyorgis, *Memher,* 86
Welde Giyorgis, *Ras, Negus,* 57, 90, 190–1, 230

Welde Maryam, 'Marami', *Abba* (a prophet), 257
Welde Mikael, *Dejazmach*, 44
Welde Selassie, *Dejazmach, Ras,* 224
Welde Tsadik, *Fitawrari*, 264
Welde Tsadik, *Wehni Azazh*, 230
Welde Tsadik Goshu, *Bitweded*, 253–5
Welde Yohannes, *Balambaras*, 248
Wele Betul, *Dejazmach (Dejach), Ras*, 104, 224–5, 229, 232, 247
Weleqa, 35
Wellega, 23, 41, 48, 57, 69, 71, 74, 76–8, 80–1, 83, 101, 169, 188, 191, 229, 249, 254, 260, 262; Map 1, 26; Map 3, 242
Wello, 40, 47, 52–4, 61, 64, 70, 79, 82, 84–6, 88–9, 91–2, 96, 98, 102–3, 105, 109, 113–14, 150, 188, 190, 205, 223–6, 232, 235, 269, 276; Map 1, 26
Welwel, 241, 241–2 n.4, 267 n.80; Map 1, 26; Map 3, 242
Wend Bewesen, *Dejazmach*, 39
Were Illu, 53, 88, 228–30
Wesen Seged, *Mer'ed Azmatch, Ras*, 41, 190
wetader, social meaning of, 61, 66, 121, 184
Weyto (Wata, *Chinesha*, Bete Isra'el), 17, 111, 113
Wube Atnafseged, *Dejazmach*, 138, 138 n.34
Wube Haile Maryam, *Dejazmach*, 47, 50, 52, 68–9, 187
Wibneh Tessema (*Amoraw*), *Ras*, 269, 276–8, 284
Wingate, Orde, Colonel, 285
WRN dynasty, 27

Yabello, 250–1 n.30
Yaregal, *Agafari*, 257
Ydlibi, Hasib, 98, 100
yegobez aleqa, 6, 9, 66
Yeha, 27
Yehabeta, 35, 38
Yeju, 38, 40, 61, 68, 77, 113, 150, 188, 224–5, 231
Yekuno Amlak (r.1270–85), 38, 42, 208
Yigeremu Gebre Tsadik, *Fitawrari*, 262–7
Yigzaw Meko, 83
Yirdaw, *Abba* (guardian of Melake Tsehai Iyasu), 272
Yirgalem, 252, 261–2, 264–5, 281; Map 1, 26
Yishaq, *Baher Negash*, 43
Yishaq I (r.1413–30), 42, 44
Yodit, Queen, 31
Yohannes I (r.1667–82), 39
Yohannes II, 39
Yohannes III, 40, 49, 51
Yohannes IV, Kassa Mercha, *Abba Bezibiz* (r. 1872–89), 18, 44–5, 53–5, 57–8, 72, 75, 78–82, 86, 88–9, 91, 113, 152, 157, 184, 188–9, 205, 222–5, 229, 233, 236, 252, 268 n.81, 286
Yohannes Iyasu, *Lij*, 270, 275–8, 285
Yohannes Jote Tulu, *Fitawrari*, 254–5
Yosef Zegelan, *Ato*, 98
Yostos (r.1711–16), 39

Zagwe dynasty, 31–2, 35, 42, 47, 53, 114, 225
Zeila, 42, 44
zemecha, 'expedition', 184, 189; *Ras* Adal's, 79–80; *Ras* Gobena's, to Embabo 78–89; Menelik, to Welayta, 89–94, 226; Menelik to Adewa, 231–2; *Ras* Mikael and *Ras* Teferi's, 94–104; rules of a march, 192–4; against second Italian invasion, 242, 245–50, 254–5, 261–2
Zemene Mesafint, 'Era of Princes' (1769–1855), 5, 34 n.34, 40, 60–1; challenge to, 47
Zera Yaqob, Qostentinos I (r.1434–68), 33, 35, 43, 60, 232
zeraf (fukera, denfata), 'declamation', 4, 7, 15, 21–3, 114–15, 184, 192, 196–21, 200–4; changes in, 102; experts: 62, 79, 84 n. 59; *aqrari*, 'motivator', 115
zeraf types: for challenging, 67, 182, *shilela*, 'challenging song', 95, 115, 156, 197, 212–15; in childhood, 149; *guma*, 'blood money', 235; during hunting, 167–8; regarding land tenure, 10–11; during mobilization, 180–1, 192, 115, *qererto*, 'motivating' song, 115, 156, 212; regarding personnal reputation, 50–1; at war 83–6, 209–15
Zeray Deress, 259
Zewde, *Dejazmach*, 212
Zewde Asfaw, *Gerazmach*, 284
Zewde Gabre-Sellassie, *Dejazmach*, 82
Zewditu Menelik, Empress (1916–30), 24 inc. n.5; changes in *chewa giber*, 220; coronation of, 101, 105, 239; crowning of two *negus*, 1, 190; marriages, 57, 89, 91; under regent, 104, 106, 133
Zewdu, *Abba Koran, Fitawrari*, 257, 273, 275, 282
Ziqwala, 257, 268
Zobel, 31, 188
Zoskales (r.131–43), 28

Eastern Africa Series

Women's Land Rights & Privatization in Eastern Africa
BIRGIT ENGLERT
& ELIZABETH DALEY (EDS)

War & the Politics of Identity in Ethiopia
KJETIL TRONVOLL

Moving People in Ethiopia
ALULA PANKHURST
& FRANÇOIS PIGUET (EDS)

Living Terraces in Ethiopia
ELIZABETH E. WATSON

Eritrea
GAIM KIBREAB

Borders & Borderlands as Resources in the Horn of Africa
DEREJE FEYISSA
& MARKUS VIRGIL HOEHNE (EDS)

After the Comprehensive Peace Agreement in Sudan
ELKE GRAWERT (ED.)

Land, Governance, Conflict & the Nuba of Sudan
GUMA KUNDA KOMEY

Ethiopia
JOHN MARKAKIS

Resurrecting Cannibals
HEIKE BEHREND

Pastoralism & Politics in Northern Kenya & Southern Ethiopia
GÜNTHER SCHLEE
& ABDULLAHI A. SHONGOLO

Islam & Ethnicity in Northern Kenya & Southern Ethiopia
GÜNTHER SCHLEE
with ABDULLAHI A. SHONGOLO

Foundations of an African Civilisation
DAVID W. PHILLIPSON

Regional Integration, Identity & Citizenship in the Greater Horn of Africa
KIDANE MENGISTEAB
& REDIE BEREKETEAB (EDS)

Dealing with Government in South Sudan
CHERRY LEONARDI

The Quest for Socialist Utopia
BAHRU ZEWDE

Disrupting Territories
JÖRG GERTEL, RICHARD ROTTENBURG
& SANDRA CALKINS (EDS)

The African Garrison State
KJETIL TRONVOLL
& DANIEL R. MEKONNEN

The State of Post-conflict Reconstruction
NASEEM BADIEY

Gender, Home & Identity
KATARZYNA GRABSKA

Women, Land & Justice in Tanzania
HELEN DANCER

Remaking Mutirikwi
JOOST FONTEIN

The Oromo & the Christian Kingdom of Ethiopia
MOHAMMED HASSEN

Lost Nationalism
ELENA VEZZADINI

Darfur
CHRIS VAUGHAN

The Eritrean National Service
GAIM KIBREAB

Ploughing New Ground
GETNET BEKELE

Hawks & Doves in Sudan's Armed Conflict
SUAD M. E. MUSA

Ethiopian Warriorhood
TSEHAI BERHANE-SELASSIE

Land, Migration & Belonging
JOSEPH MUJERE

Land Tenure Security
SVEIN EGE (ED.)

Tanzanian Development
DAVID POTTS (ED.)

Nairobi in the Making
CONSTANCE SMITH

The Mission of Apolo Kivebulaya
EMMA WILD-WOOD

The Crisis of Democratization in the Greater Horn of Africa
KIDANE MENGISTEAB (ED.)

The Struggle for Land & Justice in Kenya
AMBREENA MANJI

Imperialism & Development
NICHOLAS WESTCOTT

Kamba Proverbs from Eastern Kenya
JEREMIAH M. KITUNDA

Sports & Modernity in Late Imperial Ethiopia
KATRIN BROMBER

Contested Sustainability
STEFANO PONTE, CHRISTINE NOE & DAN BROCKINGTON (EDS)

*Decolonising State & Society in Uganda**
KATHERINE BRUCE-LOCKHART, JONATHAN L. EARLE, NAKANYIKE B. MUSISI & EDGAR CHRIS TAYLOR (EDS)

*Reimagining the Gendered Nation**
CHRISTINA KENNY

*Kenya and Zambia's Relations with China 1949–2019**
JODIE YUZHOU SUN

* forthcoming

EASTERN AFRICAN STUDIES

These titles published in the United States and Canada by Ohio University Press

Revealing Prophets
Edited by DAVID M. ANDERSON &
DOUGLAS H. JOHNSON

*East African Expressions of
Christianity*
Edited by THOMAS SPEAR
& ISARIA N. KIMAMBO

The Poor Are Not Us
Edited by DAVID M. ANDERSON &
VIGDIS BROCH-DUE

Potent Brews
JUSTIN WILLIS

Swahili Origins
JAMES DE VERE ALLEN

Being Maasai
Edited by THOMAS SPEAR
& RICHARD WALLER

Jua Kali Kenya
KENNETH KING

Control & Crisis in Colonial Kenya
BRUCE BERMAN

Unhappy Valley
Book One: State & Class
Book Two: Violence & Ethnicity
BRUCE BERMAN
& JOHN LONSDALE

Mau Mau from Below
GREET KERSHAW

The Mau Mau War in Perspective
FRANK FUREDI

*Squatters & the Roots of Mau Mau
1905-63*
TABITHA KANOGO

*Economic & Social Origins of Mau
Mau 1945-53*
DAVID W. THROUP

Multi-Party Politics in Kenya
DAVID W. THROUP
& CHARLES HORNSBY

Empire State-Building
JOANNA LEWIS

*Decolonization & Independence in
Kenya 1940-93*
Edited by B.A. OGOT
& WILLIAM R. OCHIENG'

Eroding the Commons
DAVID ANDERSON

Penetration & Protest in Tanzania
ISARIA N. KIMAMBO

Custodians of the Land
Edited by GREGORY MADDOX,
JAMES L. GIBLIN & ISARIA N.
KIMAMBO

*Education in the Development of
Tanzania 1919-1990*
LENE BUCHERT

The Second Economy in Tanzania
T.L. MALIYAMKONO
& M.S.D. BAGACHWA

*Ecology Control & Economic
Development in East African History*
HELGE KJEKSHUS

Siaya
DAVID WILLIAM COHEN
& E.S. ATIENO ODHIAMBO

*Uganda Now • Changing Uganda
Developing Uganda • From Chaos
to Order • Religion & Politics in East
Africa*
Edited by HOLGER BERNT
HANSEN & MICHAEL TWADDLE

*Kakungulu & the Creation of Uganda
1868-1928*
MICHAEL TWADDLE

Controlling Anger
SUZETTE HEALD

Kampala Women Getting By
SANDRA WALLMAN

*Political Power in Pre-Colonial
Buganda*
RICHARD J. REID

Alice Lakwena & the Holy Spirits
HEIKE BEHREND

Slaves, Spices & Ivory in Zanzibar
ABDUL SHERIFF

Zanzibar Under Colonial Rule
Edited by ABDUL SHERIFF
& ED FERGUSON

*The History & Conservation of
Zanzibar Stone Town*
Edited by ABDUL SHERIFF

Pastimes & Politics
LAURA FAIR

*Ethnicity & Conflict in the Horn of
Africa*
Edited by KATSUYOSHI FUKUI &
JOHN MARKAKIS

*Conflict, Age & Power in North East
Africa*
Edited by EISEI KURIMOTO
& SIMON SIMONSE

*Property Rights & Political
Development in Ethiopia & Eritrea*
SANDRA FULLERTON JOIREMAN

Revolution & Religion in Ethiopia
ØYVIND M. EIDE

Brothers at War
TEKESTE NEGASH & KJETIL
TRONVOLL

From Guerrillas to Government
DAVID POOL

Mau Mau & Nationhood
Edited by E.S. ATIENO
ODHIAMBO & JOHN LONSDALE

*A History of Modern Ethiopia,
1855-1991* (2nd edn)
BAHRU ZEWDE

Pioneers of Change in Ethiopia
BAHRU ZEWDE

Remapping Ethiopia
Edited by W. JAMES,
D. DONHAM, E. KURIMOTO
& A. TRIULZI

*Southern Marches of Imperial
Ethiopia*
Edited by DONALD L. DONHAM &
WENDY JAMES

A Modern History of the Somali
(4th edn)
I.M. LEWIS

*Islands of Intensive Agriculture in
East Africa*
Edited by MATS WIDGREN
& JOHN E.G. SUTTON

Leaf of Allah
EZEKIEL GEBISSA

*Dhows & the Colonial Economy of
Zanzibar 1860-1970*
ERIK GILBERT

*African Womanhood in Colonial
Kenya*
TABITHA KANOGO

African Underclass
ANDREW BURTON

In Search of a Nation
Edited by GREGORY H. MADDOX &
JAMES L. GIBLIN

A History of the Excluded
JAMES L. GIBLIN

Black Poachers, White Hunters
EDWARD I. STEINHART

Ethnic Federalism
DAVID TURTON

Crisis & Decline in Bunyoro
SHANE DOYLE

*Emancipation without Abolition in
German East Africa*
JAN-GEORG DEUTSCH

*Women, Work & Domestic
Virtue in Uganda 1900-2003*
GRACE BANTEBYA KYOMUHENDO
& MARJORIE KENISTON
McINTOSH

Cultivating Success in Uganda
GRACE CARSWELL

*War in Pre-Colonial
Eastern Africa*
RICHARD REID

*Slavery in the Great Lakes Region of
East Africa*
Edited by HENRI MÉDARD
& SHANE DOYLE

The Benefits of Famine
DAVID KEEN

www.ingramcontent.com/pod-product-compliance
Lightning Source LLC
Chambersburg PA
CBHW051558230426
43668CB00013B/1895